Mozart's Requiem

Presenting a fresh interpretation of Mozart's Requiem, Simon P. Keefe redresses a long-standing scholarly imbalance whereby narrow consideration of the text of this famously incomplete work has taken precedence over consideration of context in the widest sense. Keefe details the reception of the Requiem legend in general writings, fiction, theatre and film, as well as discussing criticism, scholarship and performance. Evaluation of Mozart's work on the Requiem turns attention to the autograph score, the document in which myths and musical realities collide. Franz Xaver Süssmayr's completion (1791–2) is also reappraised and the ideological underpinnings of modern completions assessed. Overall, the book affirms that Mozart's Requiem, fascinating for interacting musical, biographical, circumstantial and psychological reasons, cannot be fully appreciated by studying only Mozart's activities. Broad-ranging hermeneutic approaches to the work, moreover, supersede traditionally limited discursive confines.

SIMON P. KEEFE is James Rossiter Hoyle Chair and Head of Music at the University of Sheffield. He is the author of *Mozart's Piano Concertos: Dramatic Dialogue in the Age of Enlightenment* and *Mozart's Viennese Instrumental Music: A Study of Stylistic Re-Invention*, and has edited five volumes for Cambridge University Press: *The Cambridge History of Eighteenth-Century Music*, *Mozart Studies*, *The Cambridge Mozart Encyclopedia* (with Cliff Eisen), *The Cambridge Companion to Mozart* and *The Cambridge Companion to the Concerto*. He is also the author of more than forty scholarly articles and book chapters.

Mozart's Requiem: Reception, Work, Completion

SIMON P. KEEFE

CAMBRIDGE
UNIVERSITY PRESS

University Printing House, Cambridge CB2 8BS, United Kingdom

Cambridge University Press is part of the University of Cambridge.

It furthers the University's mission by disseminating knowledge in the pursuit of
education, learning and research at the highest international levels of excellence.

www.cambridge.org
Information on this title: www.cambridge.org/9781107532953

© Simon Keefe 2012

This publication is in copyright. Subject to statutory exception
and to the provisions of relevant collective licensing agreements,
no reproduction of any part may take place without the written
permission of Cambridge University Press.

First published 2012
Reprinted 2013
First paperback edition 2015

A catalogue record for this publication is available from the British Library

Library of Congress Cataloguing in Publication data
Keefe, Simon P., 1968–
Mozart's Requiem : reception, work, completion / Simon Keefe.
   p.   cm.
Includes bibliographical references and index.
ISBN 978-0-521-19837-0
1. Mozart, Wolfgang Amadeus, 1756–1791. Requiem, K. 626, D minor.   I. Title.
ML410.M9K27   2012
782.32′38–dc23

2011053269

ISBN 978-0-521-19837-0 Hardback
ISBN 978-1-107-53295-3 Paperback

Cambridge University Press has no responsibility for the persistence or accuracy of
URLs for external or third-party internet websites referred to in this publication,
and does not guarantee that any content on such websites is, or will remain, accurate
or appropriate.

For my parents, Terry and Sheila Keefe,
and in memory of
Edith Prinz (1939–2011) and Rudi Prinz (1938–2009)

Contents

List of music examples   [*page* ix]
List of tables   [xi]
Acknowledgements   [xii]

Introduction: Mozart's Requiem in context   [1]

1 The Requiem legend in the nineteenth and twentieth
   centuries   [11]
   The legend of Mozart's Requiem in the nineteenth century   [14]
   The Requiem in nineteenth-century fiction, drama and poetry   [24]
   The Requiem legend in the twentieth century   [34]
   Conclusion   [41]

2 Criticism and scholarship from 1800 to the present
   day   [44]
   Nineteenth-century critical discussion of the Requiem   [44]
   20th- and 21st-century criticism and scholarship   [65]
   Conclusion   [80]

3 The Requiem in performance   [82]
   Nineteenth-century editions   [82]
   Nineteenth-century performances   [86]
   20th- and 21st-century performances and recordings   [92]
   Conclusion   [104]

4 Mozart's work on the Requiem: sounds and
   strategies   [107]
   Sounds and strategies in the Requiem   [117]
   Requiem sounds and strategies in context   [159]
   Conclusion   [169]

5 After Mozart: the Requiem completion, 1791–1792   [172]
   The orchestration of the Sequence and the Offertory   [179]
   The Sanctus, Benedictus, Agnus Dei and Communio   [210]
   Süssmayr's completion in context   [223]
   Conclusion   [230]

6 Modern completions of the Requiem   [234]
Levin, Beyer and Maunder completions   [235]
Conclusion   [244]

Epilogue: a Requiem for the future   [247]

Appendix: original text of Franz Xaver Süssmayr's letter to Breitkopf &
Härtel (1800)   [249]
Select bibliography   [251]
Index   [258]

Music examples

4.1   Mozart, Requiem, K. 626, Domine Jesu, bars 42–6   [*page* 109]
4.2   Mozart, Requiem, K. 626, Confutatis, bars 5–8   [110]
4.3   Florian Leopold Gassmann, Requiem, Introit, bars 1–16   [119]
4.4   Mozart, Requiem, K. 626, Introit, bars 1–8   [121]
4.5   Handel, Anthem for the Funeral of Queen Caroline, HWV 264, 'The Ways of Zion Do Mourn', bars 1–17   [123]
4.6   Mozart, Requiem, K. 626, Introit, bars 19–21   [125]
4.7   Mozart, Requiem, K. 626, Introit, bars 43–8   [126]
4.8   Mozart, Requiem, K. 626, Kyrie, bars 27–33 (including Mozart's deleted bar 30)   [128]
4.9a   Mozart, Requiem, K. 626, Dies irae, bars 1–10   [131]
4.9b   Mozart, Requiem, K. 626, Dies irae, bars 19–31   [132]
4.10   Mozart, Requiem, K. 626, Dies irae, bars 40–8   [134]
4.11   Mozart, Requiem, K. 626, Dies irae, bars 66–8   [135]
4.12   Mozart, Requiem, K. 626, Tuba mirum, bars 1–18   [136]
4.13   Mozart, Requiem, K. 626, Tuba mirum, bars 44–62   [138]
4.14   Mozart, Requiem, K. 626, Rex tremendae, bars 1–7   [140]
4.15   Mozart, Requiem, K. 626, Rex tremendae, bars 17–22   [141]
4.16   Mozart, Requiem, K. 626, Recordare, bars 50–5   [144]
4.17   Mozart, Requiem, K. 626, Recordare, bars 103–12   [145]
4.18   Mozart, Requiem, K. 626, Confutatis, bars 10–12   [146]
4.19   Mozart, Requiem, K. 626, Confutatis, bars 23–30   [148]
4.20   Mozart, Requiem, K. 626, Confutatis, bars 36–40   [149]
4.21   Mozart, Requiem, K. 626, Lacrymosa, bars 1–8   [152]
4.22a   Mozart, Requiem, K. 626, Domine Jesu, bars 1–3   [155]
4.22b   Mozart, Requiem, K. 626, Domine Jesu, bars 13–18   [156]
4.22c   Mozart, Requiem, K. 626, Domine Jesu, bars 6–10   [157]
4.23   Mozart, Requiem, K. 626, Hostias, bars 44–54   [158]
4.24   Mozart, Mass in C, K. 317 ('Coronation'), Kyrie, bars 26–31   [161]
4.25   Mozart, Mass in C, K. 317 ('Coronation'), Credo, bars 56–62   [162]
4.26   Mozart, Mass in C, K. 337, Dona nobis, bars 113–19   [164]
4.27   Mozart, Mass in B flat, K. 275, Kyrie, bars 29–33   [165]

4.28   Mozart, 'Ave verum corpus', K. 618, bars 29–39   [166]

5.1   Süssmayr's completion of Mozart's Requiem, Tuba mirum, bars 51–62 [182]

5.2   Süssmayr's completion of Mozart's Requiem, Tuba mirum, bars 24–34 [186]

5.3   Süssmayr's completion of Mozart's Requiem, Rex tremendae, bars 1–7 [190]

5.4   Süssmayr's completion of Mozart's Requiem, Recordare, bars 103–12 [194]

5.5   Süssmayr's completion of Mozart's Requiem, Confutatis, bars 25–30 [196]

5.6   Süssmayr's completion of Mozart's Requiem, Confutatis, bars 5–8 [200]

5.7   Süssmayr's completion of Mozart's Requiem, Lacrymosa, bars 28–30 [203]

5.8   Süssmayr's completion of Mozart's Requiem, Lacrymosa, bars 19–23 [204]

5.9   Süssmayr's completion of Mozart's Requiem, Domine Jesu, bars 31–3 [208]

5.10   Süssmayr's completion of Mozart's Requiem, Sanctus, bars 1–5 [211]

5.11   Süssmayr's completion of Mozart's Requiem, Sanctus, bars 32–8 [214]

5.12   Süssmayr's completion of Mozart's Requiem, Benedictus, bars 18–20 [216]

5.13   Süssmayr's completion of Mozart's Requiem, Agnus Dei, bars 1–17 [219]

5.14   Süssmayr, *Missa solemnis*, SmWV 106, Agnus Dei, bars 1–7   [226]

5.15   Süssmayr, *Missa solemnis*, SmWV 106, Agnus Dei, bars 94–9 [227]

6.1   Levin's completion of Mozart's Requiem, Benedictus, bars 49–56 [238]

6.2   Maunder's completion of Mozart's Requiem, Tuba mirum, bars 1–15 [242]

Tables

4.1   Mozart's Requiem, Introit   [*page* 117]
4.2   Mozart's Requiem, Tuba mirum   [136]
4.3   Mozart's Requiem, Recordare   [143]

Acknowledgements

I am grateful to a number of scholars for their support, assistance and encouragement. Colleagues at City University London (2003–8), at the University of Sheffield (2008–) and at the Akademie für Mozart-Forschung at the Internationale Stiftung Mozarteum in Salzburg listened repeatedly to my ideas about Mozart's Requiem and offered sound advice. David Black, Neal Zaslaw and Rachel Cowgill kindly sent me unpublished materials and Anja Morgenstern alerted me to the existence of one of the more obscure nineteenth-century fictional accounts of Mozart's death discussed in Chapter 1. Holger Stüwe and Terry Keefe cast expert eyes over my German and French translations. As ever, my good friend Cliff Eisen discussed, advised and encouraged; I have much appreciated not only his Mozartian expertise, but also his ability freely to traverse musical and sports-related topics over a pint and a burger at Mabel's Tavern in London. Julian Rushton, Paul Harper-Scott and Eisen gave generously of their time in reading earlier drafts of the book; all three made numerous helpful suggestions for improvements. Parts of my article '"Die Ochsen am Berge": Franz Xaver Süssmayr and the Orchestration of Mozart's Requiem, K. 626', *Journal of the American Musicological Society*, 61 (2008), pp. 1–65 and my contribution to the subsequent 'Colloquy: Finishing Mozart's Requiem', *Journal of the American Musicological Society*, 61 (2008), pp. 602–8 are re-worked in Chapters 2, 4 and 5 with permission from the University of California Press.

My warmest thanks are extended to my family. My sister and brother-in-law Rosanna Keefe and Dominic Gregory are always on hand to chat, and to help keep the rigours of academic work in perspective. My wife Celia Hurwitz-Keefe and children Abraham and Madeleine have offered far more love and encouragement than I have had a right to expect; each has shared my passion for Mozart's Requiem and the issues it contains in different, but equally and unequivocally generous ways.

I dedicate this book to my parents, Terry and Sheila Keefe, as an all-too-small token of my gratitude for their unwavering love and support and in celebration of their fiftieth wedding anniversary in 2012, and to the memory of our life-long Austrian friends, Edith and Rudi Prinz. That my fondness for Mozart and Austria is mutually reinforcing owes much to Edith and Rudi's extraordinary generosity and hospitality during innumerable visits over three decades. They, and their small and unassuming hometown, Stadt Haag in Niederösterreich, will always have a special place in my affections.

Introduction: Mozart's Requiem in context

In 1791, the last year of his life, Mozart's compositional reputation was flourishing. His published works were widely disseminated in Vienna and beyond, his operas *Die Entführung aus dem Serail*, *Le nozze di Figaro*, *Don Giovanni* and *Così fan tutte* were staged around Europe, and his commissions were healthy in number and diverse in orientation, including the singspiel *Die Zauberflöte* for the Theater auf der Wieden in Vienna, the opera seria *La clemenza di Tito* for Emperor Leopold II's coronation in Prague, the Clarinet Concerto in A, K. 622, for the virtuoso Anton Stadler, the motet 'Ave verum corpus', K. 618, for Baden, and the cantata *Laut verkünde unsre Freude*, K. 623, for the Viennese Masonic lodge 'Zur neugekrönten Hoffnung'.

The basic facts about the commissioning, composition and completion of his final work, the Requiem in D minor, K. 626, have long been known and, on the surface at least, are a far cry from imaginative interpretations and re-interpretations of them.[1] It was commissioned anonymously by Franz, Count von Walsegg (1763–1827), an amateur musician and resident of Schloss Stuppach near Gloggnitz in Niederösterreich (Lower Austria), probably in summer 1791, in memory of his wife, who had died on 14 February 1791 aged twenty; Walsegg had earlier commissioned a memorial tomb for her, completed by the time of her internment on 27 March, from the architect Johann Henrici and the sculptor Johann Martin Fischer.[2] Walsegg's lawyer, Dr Johann Sortschan, or his business manager, Franz Anton Leitgeb, was the

---

[1] For accounts see Christoph Wolff, *Mozart's Requiem: Historical and Analytical Studies, Documents, Score*, trans. Mary Whittall (Berkeley, CA, 1994), pp. 1–4; Richard Maunder, *Mozart's Requiem: On Preparing a New Edition* (Oxford, 1988), pp. 7–24; Konrad Küster, *Mozart: A Musical Biography*, trans. Mary Whittall (Oxford, 1996), pp. 375–9. For especially succinct, sober and up-to-date discussions, see the commentary on K. 626 in Neal Zaslaw (ed.), *Der neue Köchel* (Wiesbaden, forthcoming) and the introduction to W. A. Mozart, *Requiem KV626*, ed. David Black (Frankfurt, forthcoming).

[2] Walther Brauneis reports 'Walsegg' being spelled in a number of different ways in the late eighteenth and early nineteenth centuries (including 'Wallsseck' and 'Wallsegg'); the Count signed himself 'Wallsegg' on 29 September 1819. See Walther Brauneis, '"Dies Irae, Dies Illa" – "Tag des Zornes, Tag der Klage": Auftrag, Entstehung und Vollendung von Mozarts "Requiem"', *Jahrbuch des Vereins für Geschichte der Stadt Wien*, 47–8 (1991–2), pp. 33–48, at 33. I shall retain the traditional spelling of his name.

probable intermediary between commissioner and composer, promising a payment of 50 or 60 ducats.[3] Busy with his operatic commissions *La clemenza di Tito* and *Die Zauberflöte*, Mozart almost certainly began work on the Requiem only after returning from Prague for the 6 September premiere of *Tito* and after completing *Zauberflöte* for its first performance on 30 September.[4] Work thereafter on the Requiem would have been punctuated by trips to Baden to visit Constanze, by performances of *Die Zauberflöte*, and by the composition of the Masonic cantata K. 623 (entered into Mozart's thematic catalogue, the *Verzeichnüss aller meiner Werke*, on 15 November). The decision of a Niederösterreich court in favour of Prince Karl Lichnowsky's financial claim against Mozart also dates from early November 1791.[5] It is uncertain whether Mozart worked on the Requiem after taking to his bed with his final illness on or just after 20 November. At any rate, by 5 December he had completed the Introit in full score, and had written the vocal parts, continuo and sporadic instrumental passages for the Kyrie, the Sequence (the Lacrymosa only to bar 8) and the Offertory. Following Mozart's death on 5 December, Constanze moved quickly to have the Requiem completed by his Viennese associates, enlisting the services of first Joseph Eybler (1765–1846) and then, once Eybler had given up after orchestrating most of the Sequence, Franz Xaver Süssmayr (1766–1803), who finished the work by the end of February 1792.[6] (A copy was then sent to the King of Prussia and another kept by Constanze.) The score given to Walsegg to fulfil the commission comprised the Introit and Kyrie from Mozart, with

---

[3] For further information on Walsegg, see Brauneis, 'Auftrag, Entstehung und Vollendung von Mozarts "Requiem"'. Brauneis speculates that Mozart's fellow mason Michael Puchberg may have given Walsegg the idea of commissioning a Requiem from Mozart; Puchberg lived in accommodation owned by Walsegg.

[4] According to Dexter Edge, Mozart purchased a large quantity of paper-type Tyson 62-V used for the Introit, the Kyrie (except the last page) and the Dies irae, the Tuba mirum, the Rex tremendae and the first page of the Recordare after he arrived back in Vienna on 18 September 1791. See Edge, 'Mozart's Viennese Copyists', Ph.D. thesis, University of Southern California, 2001, p. 437. H. C. Robbins Landon assigns Mozart's work on the Requiem to the precise period 8 October – 20 November 1791; on account of the awful Viennese weather between mid-October and mid-November 1791, he also confines Mozart's and Constanze's putative trip to the Prater (where Mozart supposedly suggested that he was writing the Requiem for himself) to 20 or 21 October. See Landon, *1791: Mozart's Last Year* (London, 1988), pp. 156, 167.

[5] See Walther Brauneis, '"... wegen schuldigen 1435 f 32 xr": Neuer Archivfund zur Finanzmisere Mozarts im November 1791', *Mitteilungen der Internationalen Stiftung Mozarteum*, 39 (1991), pp. 159–63.

[6] Süssmayr moved to Vienna from Kremsmünster around 1788. On his activities in late 1791, including paid work at the Burgtheater, see David Ian Black, 'Mozart and the Practice of Sacred Music, 1781–1791', Ph.D. thesis, Harvard University, 2007, pp. 364–7. For further biographical information see Henry Hausner, *Franz Xaver Süssmayr* (Vienna, 1964) and Johann Winterberger, *Franz Xaver Süssmayr: Leben, Umwelt und Gestalt* (Frankfurt, 1999).

instrumental additions to the Kyrie in an unknown hand; the Sequence and Offertory in Süssmayr's hand, incorporating Mozart's work and Süssmayr's own orchestration partly based on Eybler's; and Süssmayr's Sanctus, Benedictus and Agnus Dei followed by a partial reprise of Mozart's Introit and Kyrie for the Communio, all again in Süssmayr's hand.[7] Early performances took place at the Michaelerkirche in Vienna for Mozart's exequies (10 December 1791),[8] at Ignaz Jahn's hall in Vienna on 2 January 1793 as a benefit for Constanze and her children organized by Baron van Swieten, in Wiener Neustadt on 14 December 1793 and 14 February 1794 in memory of Walsegg's wife, at the Gewandhaus in Leipzig on 20 April 1796 under Johann Adam Hiller and at the city's Thomasschule later the same year, in Kremsmunster in 1796 and Graz in 1798, in Hamburg on 7 November 1799 under Friedrich Gottlieb Schwenke and in Dresden in December 1799.[9] Following a protracted, increasingly ill-tempered series of exchanges between Constanze and Breitkopf & Härtel, set against the backdrop of Breitkopf & Härtel's desire to publish Mozart's complete works, the first edition of the Requiem finally appeared in 1800, probably based on performance materials produced for one of the Leipzig performances in 1796.[10]

Mozart's Requiem is a liturgical work, strongly tied to traditions of sacred music; there is no evidence that its composer envisaged a concert performance. In addition to the sections set to music by Mozart and his completers, the liturgical service prescribes intoned texts between the Kyrie and Sequence (Oratio: Fidelium Deus omnium, and Lectio), the Sequence and the Offertory (Evangelium), the Offertory and the Sanctus (Praefatio defunctorum) and the Benedictus and Agnus Dei (Pater noster).[11] Mozart apparently used earlier

---

[7] For a comprehensive list of early Requiem sources (1791–1800), based on unpublished work by Ulrich Leisinger, see Zaslaw (ed.), *Der neue Köchel*.

[8] See Walther Brauneis, 'Exequien für Mozart: Archivfund über das Seelenamt für W. A. Mozart am 10. Dezember 1791 in der Wiener Michaelerkirche', *Singende Kirche*, 38/1 (1991), pp. 8–11. For a note of caution about the exact music performed at Mozart's exequies based on the inconclusiveness of documentary evidence, see Black, 'Mozart and the Practice of Sacred Music', pp. 397, 414–15.

[9] For announcements of the Leipzig, Hamburg and Dresden performances see Otto Erich Deutsch, *Mozart: A Documentary Biography*, trans. Eric Blom, Peter Branscombe and Jeremy Noble, 3rd edn (London, 1990), pp. 480–1 and *Allgemeine musikalische Zeitung*, 2 (1799–1800), cols. 176, 296–7.

[10] On the correspondence between Constanze and Breitkopf & Härtel in the run-up to the publication of the Requiem, see Ruth Halliwell, *The Mozart Family: Four Lives in a Social Context* (Oxford, 1998), pp. 590–612. Extracts from Constanze's letters are given in Wolff, *Mozart's Requiem*, pp. 139–45.

[11] A performance of Mozart's Requiem in full liturgical context under Eugen Jochum (live recording, 1955, Chorus of the Vienna Staatsoper and Vienna Symphony Orchestra, Deutsche Grammophon, 2005, 00289 477 5811) is discussed in Chapter 3.

works as models in his first two movements: Florian Gassmann's Requiem in C minor, Handel's chorus 'The Ways of Zion Do Mourn' from the Anthem for the Funeral of Queen Caroline, HWV 264, and Michael Haydn's Requiem in C minor in the Introit; and Handel's 'Dettingen' Anthem, HWV 265 (later recycled for use in the oratorio *Joseph and his Brethren*), for the fugue subjects in the Kyrie. Mozart got to know Haydn's Requiem, written to commemorate Prince-Archbishop Schrattenbach's death (16 December 1771), in Salzburg, and possibly encountered Gassmann's Requiem either at performances at the Hofkapelle in Vienna in the late 1780s, or at St Stephen's Cathedral, which owned a set of parts, once he had assumed his duties as unpaid, adjunct Kapellmeister in spring 1791.[12] He probably got to know Handel's works, the parallels with which are too close to allow for coincidental resemblance, through the civil servant and court administrator Baron Gottfried van Swieten, for whom he had previously re-orchestrated four of Handel's works, *Acis and Galatea*, K. 566 (1788), *Messiah*, K. 572 (1789), *Alexander's Feast*, K. 591 (1790), and the Ode for St Cecilia's Day, K. 592 (1790).

Beyond these specific connections, Mozart's Requiem resonates with earlier requiem settings, many of which he could have encountered in Salzburg or Vienna. He follows Michael Haydn and Johann Baptist Vanhal in the Introit, as well as four requiems by Anton Cajetan Adlgasser and Johann Ernst Eberlin that he may have heard in Salzburg, by setting the antiphon and psalm verse in one continuous movement.[13] The association between the Introit's psalm verse and Gregorian chant goes back to the seventeenth and early eighteenth centuries; like Michael Haydn, Mozart incorporates the first phrase of the *tonus peregrinus* (bars 21ff.) from the *Liber usualis*.[14] Ending the Introit on the dominant in preparation for the Kyrie follows requiems by Haydn and the Vienna-based Albrechtsberger and Gassmann; casting the Kyrie as a fugue aligns with those of Georg Reutter (known as Reutter der Junge), Gassmann, Giuseppe Bonno and Leopold Hofmann, all composers based in Vienna.[15]

---

[12] On Gassmann, see Black, 'Mozart and the Practice of Sacred Music', p. 355.

[13] Manfred Hermann Schmid, 'Introitus und Communio im Requiem: Zum Formkonzept von Mozart und Süssmayr', in Schmid (ed.), *Mozart Studien 7* (Tutzing, 1997), pp. 11–55, at p. 21. Adlgasser (1729–77) and Eberlin (1702–62) were active in Salzburg respectively as court and cathedral organist, and director of court music. A number of the requiem settings mentioned in this paragraph can be securely dated: Georg Reutter (1753); Niccolò Jommelli (1756); François-Joseph Gossec (1760); Johann Adolf Hasse (1763); Michael Haydn (1771); Florian Gassmann (1774); Peter Winter (1790).

[14] Manfred Schuler, 'Mozarts Requiem in der Tradition Gattungsgeschichtlicher Topoi', in Annegrit Laubenthal (ed.), *Studien zur Musikgeschichte: Eine Festschrift für Ludwig Finscher* (Kassel, 1995), pp. 317–27, at 319–20. See also Maunder, *Mozart's Requiem*, p. 79.

[15] See Wolff, *Mozart's Requiem*, pp. 78–80; Schuler, 'Mozarts Requiem', p. 321.

Mozart's setting of the Tuba mirum for four vocal soloists follows Reutter and Haydn among others, and is motivically similar to Adlgasser's; a first verse for solo bass and obbligato trombone featuring a falling arpeggiated melody comes close to Eberlin's.[16] Pervasive dotted rhythms in the Rex tremendae bring to mind Baroque manifestations of regal majesty and are similar to settings of the text by Niccolò Jommelli, François-Joseph Gossec, Bonno and Peter Winter; the opening three-fold 'Rex' exclamation surfaces in Johann Adolf Hasse's Requiem.[17] Like the Recordare movements of Johann Joseph Fux, Reutter and Jommelli, Mozart's is for solo voices, and like Winter's is in 3/4 with overlapping entries at the beginning.[18] Up to and including verse 15 of the Sequence, Mozart's and Gassmann's divisions of the text are the same, the two diverging only from verse 16 to the end: Gassmann sets verses 16–18 for the Confutatis and leaves the nineteenth and last verse ('Huic ergo parce, Deus') for his final movement, while Mozart opts for verses 16 and 17 for the Confutatis and verses 18 and 19 for the Lacrymosa.[19] Mozart's Lacrymosa is a choral movement in the minor mode, in line with south German and Austrian tradition, sharing its 12/8 time signature with the corresponding movement in Hasse's Requiem.[20] Mozart's solo quartet setting of 'sed signifier' in the Domine Jesu follows Eberlin, Reutter, Adlgasser, Michael Haydn and Winter, and his fugal setting of 'Quam olim Abrahae' is consonant with Requiem tradition dating back to the seventeenth century and extending through the nineteenth as well.[21]

The Requiem has always occupied a special place among Mozart's works. It entered the orbit of almost every major nineteenth-century composer: Beethoven copied out and analysed the Kyrie fugue, angrily denounced Gottfried Weber's criticisms of the work in the 1820s ('Oh, you arch ass!'), and alluded to the Recordare in the last of his Gellert songs; Schubert and Rossini drew inspiration from the Requiem in early vocal works, and Berlioz (no great lover of Mozart) in the *Grande messe des morts*; Liszt improvised memorably on it in Fribourg in 1836, published a transcription of the Confutatis and Lacrymosa, came to consider the work 'hackneyed' towards the end of his life on account of such frequent performances, and played it for the Paris-based painter Miláhy Munkácsy early in 1886 as Munkácsy contemplated his picture *The Death*

---

[16] Schuler, 'Mozarts Requiem', pp. 322–3.   [17] Ibid., p. 323.   [18] Ibid., p. 324.

[19] Ibid., pp. 321–22.

[20] Ibid., p. 325. On Lacrymosa settings both before and after Mozart's Requiem, see Andrzej Wolanski, 'Mozarts "Lacrimosa" in der Geschichtsperspektive', *Mozart-Jahrbuch 1991*, pp. 468–74.

[21] Schuler, 'Mozarts Requiem', pp. 325–6.

of Mozart in a mood of 'ecstatic reverie'; Wagner's life-long admiration included an encounter in the mid- to late 1820s that 'formed the starting point of my enthusiastic absorption in the works of that master [Mozart]' and contemplations of it late in life as well; Anton Rubinstein, Mahler, Richard Strauss, Stanford and Rimsky-Korsakov all conducted it, Rimsky-Korsakov also quoting extensively from the Introit in the final section of *Mozart and Salieri*; and Tchaikovsky wrote admiringly of the 'marvellous, poetic introduction with double fugue at the end', even though he expressed reservations about other aspects of the work.[22] Described in 1902 as one of Mozart's works that 'speaks persuadingly to every generation ... [through which] Mozart's influence still persists and must be reckoned with as a factor in the complexus of forces which is moulding the music of the new century',[23] it had similar exposure among twentieth-century composers. Bartók used examples from the Requiem in his teaching; Szymanowski wrote of its 'divine grief', the most powerful 'eruption' of the 'grim, powerful call from a world beyond ours' in Mozart's late music; Janáček conducted a highly successful performance of it in Brno in the late 1870s and another in memory of Smetana in Prague in 1916; the fifteen-year-old Walton sang a solo part in a performance at Christ Church, Oxford, in December 1917; Britten considered it an important historical precedent for the modern-day composer in writing his own War Requiem (1961–2), subsequently reacting profoundly to conducting Mozart's work (1971); and Ligeti, composer of another of the last century's

---

[22] See Bathia Churgin, 'Beethoven and Mozart's Requiem: A New Connection', *Journal of Musicology*, 5 (1987), pp. 457–77; Alexander Wheelock Thayer, *The Life of Beethoven* (London, 1960), vol. 3, p. 235; Stephen Rumph, *Beethoven after Napoleon: Political Romanticism in the Late Works* (Berkeley, CA, 2004), p. 37; Brian Newbould, *Schubert: The Music and the Man* (Berkeley, CA, 1997), pp. 130, 132; Richard Osborne, *Rossini: His Life and Works*, 2nd edn (Oxford, 2007), p. 267; Julian Rushton, *The Music of Berlioz* (Oxford, 2001), pp. 40, 193; Adrian Williams, *Portrait of Liszt by Himself and his Contemporaries* (Oxford, 1990), pp. 82–3; Derek Watson, *Liszt* (Oxford, 2000), p. 214; Adrian Williams (trans. and ed.), *Franz Liszt Selected Letters* (Oxford, 1998), p. 815; 'Munkacsy and Liszt', *The Musical Standard*, 14 (22 Dec. 1900), p. 388; Richard Wagner, *My Life*, 2 vols. (New York, 1911), vol. I, p. 36; Martin Gregor-Dellin and Dietrich Mack (eds.), *Cosima Wagner's Diaries*, vol. II: *1878–1883*, trans. Geoffrey Skelton (New York, 1977), pp. 360, 493, 571, 1116; Philip S. Taylor, *Anton Rubinstein: A Life in Music* (Bloomington, IN, 2007), p. 147; Henry-Louis de La Grange, *Mahler*, vol. I (New York, 1973), pp. 252, 317, 361, 409; Willi Schuh, *Richard Strauss: A Chronicle of the Early Years*, trans. Mary Whittall (Cambridge, 1982), pp. 95, 108; Jeremy Dibble, *Charles Villiers Stanford: Man and Musician* (Oxford, 2002), pp. 296–8; David Brown, *Tchaikovsky: The Early Years, 1840–1874* (New York, 1978), p. 278.

[23] Edward Dickinson, 'The Impress of Mozart on Musical History', *The Musical Standard*, 17 (1 Feb. 1902), p. 74.

great requiems (1965), first encountered the Sequence of the Requiem through Mozart, singing it as early as 1943.[24]

Nineteenth- and twentieth-century composers' experiences of the Requiem, while revealing its effect on great musical figures of the past, represent only a tiny fraction of the work's reception. The sheer variety and amount of reception-related activity – performances, recordings, editions, scholarship, journalistic criticism, fiction, plays, films – attest to the Requiem's profound impact on Western culture. I dedicate a substantial portion of my book to reception (Chapters 1, 2, 3), redressing a long-standing imbalance in Requiem scholarship whereby narrow consideration of the text of this famously incomplete work (in particular who wrote what, or could conceivably have written what, or *should* have written what in accordance with Mozart's perceived intentions) has taken precedence over consideration of context in the widest sense.

Above all, reception draws attention to a fundamental feature of the Requiem's ontological status, namely that our collective understandings of it derive from our imaginative (and often undifferentiated) engagement with fictional, quasi-fictional and factual circumstances of composition to a degree unrivalled perhaps by any other work in the Western canon. For running in parallel with the aforementioned facts about the Requiem's genesis are documentary accounts in which divisions between facts and fictions are hazy. As described in Chapter 1, an announcement about the circumstances surrounding the Requiem's composition was disseminated within weeks of Mozart's death, in all likelihood relying on information provided by Constanze, claiming *inter alia* that Mozart finished the work shortly before his death; Constanze then engaged in further deceptions in the account she gave to Franz Niemetschek for his biography (1798), stating that the messenger had collected the unfinished work and that she knew nothing of the commissioner's identity or of performances that may have taken place. Johann Friedrich Rochlitz adapted and intensified Niemetschek's story in his two Requiem anecdotes for the *Allgemeine musikalische Zeitung* (1798), accentuating the otherworldliness of the

---

[24] Malcolm Gillies, *Bartók Remembered* (London, 1990), p. 11; *Szymanowski on Music: Selected Writings of Karol Szymanowski*, trans. and ed Alistair Wightman (London, 1999), p. 159 (in the essay 'On Romanticism in Music' from 1928–9); John Tyrrell, *Janáček: Years of a Life*, vol. I: *(1854–1914), The Lonely Blackbird* (London, 2006), p. 113 and Tyrrell, *Janáček's Operas: A Documentary Account* (Princeton, 1992), p. 82; Malcolm Hayes (ed.), *The Selected Letters of William Walton* (London, 2002), p. 17; Mervyn Cooke, *Britten: 'War Requiem'* (Cambridge, 1996), p. 50; Richard Steinitz, *György Ligeti: Music of the Imagination* (Boston, 2003), pp. 19, 141. Britten's performance of Mozart's Requiem in Aldeburgh in 1971, and his reactions to it, are discussed in Chapter 3.

messenger and Mozart's psychological and medical frailty and frenzied composition, in the process moving further in a fictional direction. The collision of music and biography comprising the Requiem legend had by now cast a spell that would entrance the nineteenth and (to a slightly lesser extent) twentieth centuries, irrespective of implicit or explicit scholarly attempts conclusively to separate fact from fiction.

Absolute separation of fact from fiction on all matters of detail is neither possible nor (in my view) hermeneutically desirable where Mozart's Requiem is concerned. Over 200 years after the composition and completion it is impossible robustly to establish the truth-value of elements of the composite Requiem legend. Although some parts are demonstrably false, others inhabit a grey area between fact and fiction, existing in long-after-the-fact recollections of Mozart's final days from Constanze's sister Sophie Haibel – who tells of final instructions to Süssmayr and Mozart's 'last movement' of mouthing 'drum passages' – and Benedikt Schack, a friend of Mozart and the first Tamino in *Die Zauberflöte*, to whom is attributed the account of the rehearsal at Mozart's bedside hours before his death.[25] It is similarly impossible to determine the accuracy of Constanze's report that Mozart believed he was writing the Requiem for himself. Yet these elements are inextricably woven into our critical consciousness, if not always explicitly as fact then as part of an elaborate, quasi-factual hinterland that insistently reminds us why we believe the Requiem to be so special.

With a plethora of complete Mozart works on which to lavish our critical attention, why do we return time and again to a Requiem he only half finished and worked on for perhaps six or seven weeks? The Requiem project may, or may not, have held special significance for Mozart himself, beyond the fact that its commission came so soon after his appointment as adjunct Kapellmeister to Hofmann at St Stephen's Cathedral in Vienna,[26] but it has always held extraordinary significance for us, for interacting musical, biographical, circumstantial and psychological reasons. How different the

---

[25] On the Haibel account from 1825, see Emily Anderson (ed. and trans.), *The Letters of Mozart and his Family*, 3rd edn (New York and London, 1985), pp. 976–7; the Schack story, appearing in a posthumous tribute to him (1827), is given in Deutsch, *Documentary Biography*, pp. 536–7. Constanze reports singing through parts of the Requiem with Mozart and Süssmayr in a letter dated 31 May 1827; see Wolff, *Mozart's Requiem*, pp. 169–70.

[26] In his careful consideration of Mozartian myths, William Stafford swims against the critical tide: 'In truth, it may be doubted whether . . . [the Requiem] interested him very much. The correspondence of his last months bears testimony to his excitement about *Die Zauberflöte* but makes no mention of the Requiem.' See Stafford, *The Mozart Myths: A Critical Reassessment* (Stanford, CA, 1991), p. 197. On Mozart's appointment to St Stephen's and possible activities there in 1791, see Black, 'Mozart and the Practice of Sacred Music', pp. 286–301.

posthumous reception of Mozart's Requiem would have been had the remarks of Mozart's first biographer, Friedrich Schlichtegroll (1793), come to dominate the critical agenda, rather than the cocktail of Constanze's, Niemetschek's and Rochlitz's accounts. Schlichtegroll correctly reports the Requiem as incomplete at Mozart's death and uses his single reference to it to reinforce Haydn's famous assessment 'before God and as an honest man' of Mozart's supremacy over his contemporaries. But he makes nothing of the link between biography and work: 'The solemn pathos of the expression, which one finds combined there in the most effective way with the highest degree of art, moved all hearts at the performance organized to benefit the composer's widow and children [2 January 1793], and earned the admiration of all connoisseurs.'[27] Schlichtegroll's supplement to his 1790–3 obituaries, published in 1798, includes a summarized version of Rochlitz's Requiem anecdotes.[28] For so many critics before and (especially) after, the legend provided information too important to exclude. As scholars today, more critically self-conscious than our predecessors, we should embrace the often murky continuum between fact and fiction where information about the Requiem is concerned, acknowledging the role that information across this continuum has played in cultivating the intense passion we collectively feel, and have always felt, for the work and all that it conveys. The basic facts surrounding the Requiem, as always, provide our scholarly foundations; but facts and fictions together will build our elaborate hermeneutic edifices.

Recognizing the fictional and the quasi-fictional as essential to how Mozart's Requiem has been processed – and can continue to be processed – affects the organization and content of this book. Chapter 1 looks at the shaping and re-shaping of the Requiem legend, including its role as a focus for nineteenth- and twentieth-century poetry, fiction and drama. Chapter 2 traces critical and scholarly reception, including early nineteenth-century writings that demonstrate uncertainty about the genesis and completion of the work, the mid-nineteenth-century *Requiem-Streit* when its authenticity was called into question, and the ebb and flow of authorship- and aesthetics-related discussions in the late nineteenth and twentieth centuries; I also

---

[27] Friedrich Schlichtegroll, *Johannes Chrysostomus Wolfgang Gottlieb Mozart* (1793), ed. Erich Hermann Müller von Asow (Leipzig, 1942), p. 15: 'Das Feyerlich-Pathetische des Ausdruckes, das man darin mit dem höchsten Grade der Kunst auf die zweckmäßigste Art vereinigt findet, hat bey der zu dem Vortheil der Witwe und Kinder veranstalteten Aufführung alle Herzen gerührt, und sich aller Kenner Bewunderung erworben.' Haydn's assessment was originally reported to Nannerl Mozart by Leopold Mozart in a letter from Vienna on 16 February 1785; see Anderson (ed. and trans.), *Letters*, p. 886.

[28] Friedrich Schlichtegroll, *Supplement-Band des Nekrologs für die Jahre 1790, 91, 92 und 93* (Gotha, 1798), pp. 159–61.

address the legend's impact on serious criticism. Chapter 3 evaluates editions and performances, *inter alia* the mutual reinforcement of work and occasion and the intense connections felt with the Requiem, both partly attributable to engagement with the legend, and narratives conveyed in twentieth- and 21st-century recordings. Chapter 4, on Mozart's work on the Requiem, draws inspiration from the legend by focusing attention on Mozart's autograph score, the document in which myths and musical realities collide. Mysteries unresolved by an incomplete score, I argue, complement irresolvable mysteries of the Requiem legend; autograph-inspired musical interpretation and implicit and explicit legend-inspired fiction are kindred spirits.

But the Requiem legend has a basic interpretational limitation as well as stimulating interpretational virtues. The legend is, in effect, Mozart's alone, but the finished Requiem is not Mozart's alone. Especially since World War II, Süssmayr has regularly been perceived as a musical cog in Mozart's wheel; the relative absence of discussion of any of Süssmayr's works that could cast light on his contributions to the Requiem, for example, illustrates where scholarly energies have and have not been directed in studying the work, where scholarly biases traditionally lie. With a compelling narrative at the interpretative core of the Requiem, Süssmayr gets in the way for many modern-day critics, the putative mediocrity meddling with the genius. Surely pushing out of the limelight, or discrediting, or marginalizing a figure who makes a cameo appearance at a crucial stage in Mozart's life constitutes palatable collateral damage? Many might like to think this way, in an attempt to understand and appreciate the Requiem as Mozart's exclusive achievement. If biography and music perform an inspiring double act, then it stands to reason that biographical interpretation will influence musical interpretation. Even if this is a positive state of affairs in many respects, it also helps to explain why Süssmayr's musical presence has become so unwelcome to many critics. Süssmayr's completion ensured that Mozart's fragment saw the light of day as a finished, performable work and has contributed to the Requiem's critical success (as we shall see). The peaks and troughs in the reception of his work on the Requiem are therefore discussed in Chapter 2. A full re-appraisal of the completion, including Eybler's contribution, follows in Chapter 5, informed both by Mozart's contributions to the Requiem and to sacred music and by Süssmayr's own works. Finally, in Chapter 6, I turn to modern completions of the Requiem, collectively the most important body of twentieth-century editions, which adapt, revise and discard Süssmayr's contributions in different ways. I explain ideologies that shape the new completions and practical decisions taken by their editors.

1 | The Requiem legend in the nineteenth and twentieth centuries

'Mozart died finishing the requiem that was first destined to chant over its creator, and then to enchant creation', writes John Savage in an 1856 account of Irish revolutionary history.[1] In one pithy sentence he captures nineteenth-century reception of Mozart's Requiem in microcosm: adoration of it; belief in the intensely personal relationship Mozart had with it as his own death approached; and engagement with the fictional stories and myths that surround it (in this case that Mozart had completed it himself). Whether or not they believed that the Requiem was finished by Mozart – and many apparently did, even towards the end of the nineteenth century – music critics and other writers repeatedly bought into the idea that Mozart was conscious of it representing his swan song. The dominance of this metaphor is neatly demonstrated by a literal realization of it. Published in 1839, the second of 'The Remembrances of a Monthly Nurse' recounting her time with 'The Marchioness L_D and Lady Urquhart' recalls a mechanical 'magic swan . . . [measuring] not more than six inches'. Once wound up, it 'began to move like "a thing of life"', carrying out activities such as eating corn from a basket:

All were loud in their plaudits of this piece of superb mechanism; and the Marchioness and her friend were in perfect raptures, when they found the performance was not terminated. The swan at length seemed uneasy, got up from her nest, and ruffled her feathers and wings, uttered a cry of seeming agony, and then poured forth a strain of most delightful melody, sad in the extreme, whilst her frame appeared to be convulsed with the pangs of death. After about five minutes of this pathetic music, taken from Mozart's *Requiem* (of which such an astonishing tale is told), the swan appeared actually to expire; it fell down, closed its eyes, and all was silent; then there was a slight movement in the wings, then in the head; – it stood upon its feet again, rushed into the water, drank repeatedly, then proceeded back again to its nest, settled itself upon its eggs, nodded its head three times, and all was over!

---

[1] John Savage, *'98 and '48: The Modern Revolutionary History and Literature of Ireland* (New York, 1856), pp. 258–9. The remark also appears in a book on the American Civil War: George Pepper, *Personal Recollections of Sherman's Campaigns in Georgia and the Carolinas* (Zanesville, OH, 1866), p. 497.

A footnote to the 'astonishing tale' explains: 'It is reported that some supernatural being ordered this Requiem, which Mozart only finished a few hours before his death. It was sung for the first time over his remains.'[2] Even a mid-century 'monthly nurse', then, got wind of the legend of Mozart's Requiem; indeed, five years earlier in Paris, the *Revue des deux mondes* tells us that no children will have failed to have had the story of Mozart's Requiem recounted to them by their nannies.[3]

References to the Requiem in a historical work on Ireland and the memoirs of a nurse emphasize that the reception of the work cannot be viewed solely through the lens of music-related publications. It would be difficult to overstate the Requiem's impact in ostensibly non-musical cultures and contexts in addition to explicitly musical ones. In the latter category, the Requiem was described by the *Intelligenzblatt der Allgemeinen Literatur-Zeitung* (1799) as 'Mozart's last and most complete work' in advance of first publication by Breitkopf & Härtel, by E. T. A. Hoffmann (*Allgemeine musikalische Zeitung*, 1814) as 'the sublimest achievement that the modern period has contributed to the church', and by *The Musical World* (1857) as 'one of the greatest achievements of one of the greatest masters'.[4] But superlatives flow still more freely beyond the realm of the musical *cognoscenti*, often capturing intensely personal, emotional reactions. It becomes commonplace to talk of the Requiem as the 'last, and taken as a whole . . . most sublime work of Mozart' and as 'one of the highest, most serious, most vast and most expressive works that was given to the human spirit to embrace'.[5] Others seemingly outside the music profession go further still, testifying to the work's extraordinary impact. An old military man at the first Paris performance, conducted by Luigi Cherubini on 21 December 1804 – as reported by an *Allgemeine*

----

2 See John A. Heraud (ed.), 'The Remembrances of a Monthly Nurse, No. II. The Marchioness L_D and Lady Urquhart', *The Monthly Magazine*, 1 (London, 1839), pp. 171–91, at 182–3. The nurse continues: 'Should there be any scepticism respecting this magic swan, let the reader only search out for the account of the Emperor of Russia's *mechanical duck*, now in his palace at St. Petersburg, and he will not so much wonder that it has been in some degree exceeded by this swan' (p. 183).

3 As reported by A. Loeve-Veimars in *Revue des deux mondes*, series 3, 1 (Paris, 1834), p. 665.

4 *Intelligenzblatt der Allgemeinen Literatur-Zeitung*, 1 (1799), col. 1056; for the Hoffmann quotation see David Charlton (ed.), *E. T. A. Hoffmann's Musical Writings: 'Kreisleriana', 'The Poet and the Composer', Music Criticism*, trans. Martyn Clarke (Cambridge, 1989), p. 370; *The Musical World*, 35 (1857), p. 43.

5 See Louis Pujol and Rev. Daniel Cummings Van Norman, *The Complete French Class-Book* (New York, 1866), p. 452, and Richmal Mangnall, *Historical and Miscellaneous Questions for the Use of Young People* (London, 1859), p. 421; and *Revue de la Normandie*, 3 (Rouen, 1864), p. 199 ('. . . une des oeuvres les plus hautes, les plus serieuses, les plus vastes et les plus expressives qu'il ait été donné au génie humain d'embrasser . . .').

musikalische Zeitung correspondent – 'clearly lifted his chest higher and directed his bearded face upwards' as the instruments entered one by one at the beginning of the Introit; at bars 7–8 'tears streamed from his eyes, he squeezed my hand until it hurt and shouted: Almighty God!'[6] A. Schwartz, writing in *Macmillan's Magazine* (1874), explains: 'Some one has well said, that listening to Cherubini's music [his Requiem] one cannot help weeping, but that hearing "The Requiem" of Mozart one longs to die … Who that has ever heard Mozart's "Requiem" can possibly forget it?'[7] And Friedrich Nippold recalls the painter Rudolph Friedrich Watzmann's words in Dresden: 'The famous Mozart Requiem performed in a monster concert at the Neustadt Liebenfrauenkirche overpowered me to such an extent that, when I got home, I threw myself on the floor and cried and shouted nonsensically.'[8]

Nowhere does reception of Mozart's Requiem trade in hyperbole more than in the legend surrounding its composition, which is recounted innumerable times in the nineteenth and twentieth centuries. The association between Mozart's death and his composition of a Requiem is seldom ignored in the musical-critical literature (in the nineteenth century at least) and never ignored in general literature; Mozart's biography and his final work are intrinsically linked in our collective mindset.[9] Whatever its truth-value, the Requiem legend is a crucial component of the Mozart story, inspiring writers, musicians and audiences alike, not least to poetic and (explicitly) fictional ends. In order to evaluate this aspect of the Requiem's history, we turn first to the legend itself and how it emerged, was disseminated and was transformed, including its new lease of life in nineteenth-century poetry and fiction, thus addressing the work's impact on the nineteenth-century popular imagination. We then examine the continued impact of the Requiem legend in the twentieth century.

[6] *Allgemeine musikalische Zeitung*, 7 (1804–5), col. 249: '.. hob sich seine Brust sichtbar höher und das bärtige Gesicht richtete sich empor: . . . da stürtzen Thränen aus seinen Augen, er drückte meine Hand bis zum Schmerz, und rief: Allmächtiger Gott!"

[7] *Macmillan's Magazine*, 30 (1874), p. 462.

[8] Friedrich Nippold, *Welche Wege führen nach Rom? Geschichtliche Beleutung der römischen Illusionen über die Erfolge der Propaganda* (Heidelberg, 1869), p. 196: 'Das berühmte Requiem von Mozart, in einem Monstreconcert der Neustädter Liebenfrauenkirche aufgeführt, überwältigte mich dergestalt, dass, als ich heimkam, ich mich auf den Boden warf und wie unsinnig schrie und weinte.'

[9] Cliff Eisen begins critical discussion on the early propensity for reading and hearing the Requiem biographically in 'Mozart's Leap in the Dark', in Simon P. Keefe (ed.), *Mozart Studies* (Cambridge, 2006), pp. 1–24, at 21–4.

The legend of Mozart's Requiem in the nineteenth century

Just three weeks after Mozart's death and before the end of 1791, key elements of the Requiem legend had already begun to be disseminated. Announcements in the *Salzburger Intelligenzblatt* (7 January 1792) and the Graz-based *Zeitung für Damen und andere Frauenzimmer* (18 January 1792) have long been known to Mozart scholars.[10] A hitherto unknown announcement was actually published eleven days earlier, on 27 December 1791, as an 'anecdote' in *Der Baierische Landbot*:

Anecdotes.

Concerning Mozart – He received an unsigned letter some months before his death with the request to write a Requiem and to ask what he desired for it. Seeing that this work did not appeal to him at all, he thought, I want to ask for so much that the connoisseur [*Liebhaber*] will certainly let me go. The following day, a servant came to get the answer – Mozart wrote to the unknown man that he could not write it for anything less than 60 ducats and then not for two or three months. The servant returned, brought 30 ducats immediately and said he would enquire again in three months and if the mass were ready would hand over the other half of the money straight away. So Mozart had to write, which he did, often with tears in his eyes, and always said: I fear that I am writing a Requiem for myself; he finished it a few days before his death. When his death was known, the servant came again and brought the other 30 ducats, did not desire the Requiem, and since this time there has been no further enquiry. It will also be performed in his memory in fact, when copied out, at St Michael's Church.[11]

Self-evident falsities here include Mozart's completion of the work and the statement that the remaining payment was made but the score not collected; it is also unlikely that such a commission would have been unappealing to Mozart. Above all, though, the notice was good publicity, '[conferring] a special aura upon the Requiem';[12] by whom and to whom it was originally sent are difficult to determine, but it seems safe to assume that Constanze was the source of the information in it and that not all papers printing it

---

[10] For the Graz publication see Deutsch, *Documentary Biography*, p. 439 and *Mozart: Die Dokumente seines Lebens* (Kassel, 1961), p. 526; for the Salzburg publication see Cliff Eisen, *New Mozart Documents: A Supplement to O. E. Deutsch's Documentary Biography* (London and Stanford, 1991), p. 76.

[11] *Der Baierische Landbot* (27 December 1791), p. 1723 (my translation). The text is the same as for the Salzburg and Graz notices (see Deutsch, *Dokumente*, p. 526). For different translations, see Eisen, *New Mozart Documents*, p. 76 and Deutsch, *Documentary Biography*, p. 439.

[12] Stafford, *Mozart Myths*, p. 80.

would have received their own copy direct from Vienna but that some
would have picked up the story from another paper instead.[13]

The writings decisive in securing the Requiem legend's place in the
nineteenth-century consciousness were Franz Xaver Niemetschek's biography of Mozart (1798) and two of Friedrich Rochlitz's Mozart anecdotes
(5 December and 19 December 1798) in the first year of the *Allgemeine
musikalische Zeitung*'s run.[14] Constanze's fingerprints are all over
Niemetschek's account of the commissioning and composition of the
Requiem; indeed, her thoughts and actions loom large throughout the
telling of the tale.[15] The 'story of [Mozart's] last work' is said at the outset
to be 'as obscure as it is strange',[16] no doubt to heighten anticipation for
what is to come. Thereafter, the main elements of the Requiem legend are all
relayed: he received the commission in the form of a letter 'brought him by
an unknown messenger'; the messenger reappeared before the trip to
Prague to ask about the Requiem; Mozart worked on the Requiem after
Prague, but with the onset of illness became depressed, declaring to
Constanze on an outing to the Prater that he thought he was writing the
Requiem for himself and had been poisoned; Constanze took the Requiem
score away from Mozart, sensing 'he was on the verge of a serious illness,
and that the Requiem was getting on his over-sensitive nerves', and called

---

[13] With thanks to Cliff Eisen for personal communication about the normal means for distributing
announcements among late eighteenth-century European newspapers. Bruce Cooper Clarke
goes against the scholarly grain by suggesting Mozart himself rather than Constanze as the
source of the information in the announcement. But Clarke's theory that the information
reached 'a reporter associated with the Viennese establishment' through chit-chat is entirely
speculative. So too is his bold denunciation of Constanze's involvement based only on his
suggestion that Constanze 'probably had related the incident [of the ride in the Prater
conversation in which Mozart suggests he was writing the Requiem for himself] over a cup of
coffee to her mother and sisters'. Even if Clarke is right that the use of the future tense for the
10 December performance sets the writing of the announcement at 5–9 December, it rules out
neither Constanze's authorship nor her contribution to it. See Clarke, 'From Little Seeds', *The
Musical Times*, 137 (Dec. 1996), pp. 13–17.

[14] Franz Xaver Niemetschek, *Leben des K. K. Kapellmeisters Wolfgang Amadeus Mozart* (Prague,
1798), trans. Helen Mautner as *The Life of Mozart* (London, 1956), pp. 41–5; *Allgemeine
musikalische Zeitung*, 1 (1798–9), cols. 149–51, 177–80, trans. Maynard Solomon in 'The
Rochlitz Anecdotes: Issues of Authenticity in Early Mozart Biography', in Cliff Eisen (ed.),
Mozart Studies (Oxford, 1991), pp. 1–59, at 32–4. (Rochlitz was the general editor of the
Allgemeine musikalische Zeitung between 1798 and 1818.)

[15] For example: 'Mozart . . . never made the least move without his wife's knowledge . . . She advised
him to take up the offer . . . the messenger appeared like a ghost and pulled at her coat . . . One
day she was driving in the Prater with him . . . This speech fell like a load on his wife's heart. She
was unable to console him' (*Life of Mozart*, pp. 42–3). A footnote explaining that Niemetschek
relates the Requiem story 'as he has often heard it from the lips of Mozart's widow' (p. 44)
confirms Constanze as his principal source.

[16] Ibid., p. 41.

in a doctor; after an improvement in his health and general mood she returned the score to him, but the improvement turned out to be 'short-lived'; on the day he died he had the score brought to him in bed, asked rhetorically, 'Did I not say before, that I was writing this Requiem for myself?', and looked through the whole work 'with tears in his eyes'; shortly after his death the messenger came to collect the work 'in its incomplete state', Constanze learned nothing more about him or about the commissioner, and 'no performance of the piece . . . [was] traced anywhere'.[17]

Constanze's deceptions, including the messenger's receipt of the unfinished score, the continued secrecy about the commissioner's identity and the lack of performances of the work, are well known.[18] The extent to which she muddies the factual waters elsewhere in Niemetschek's story is difficult accurately to gauge; she probably would have benefited financially and emotionally from promoting a legend about Mozart's death that accentuated its 'spiritual and artistic significance', with the Requiem at the legend's core.[19]

It is beyond dispute that Rochlitz moves further towards the fictional end of the Requiem fact–fiction continuum in his anecdotes. Rochlitz's reliance on Niemetschek's account is obvious;[20] his modifications to it, however, are cleverly multi-faceted. For example, he intensifies Mozart's compositional process, lending it high-octane energy across both anecdotes: Mozart 'immediately' began work on the Requiem after the messenger left, rather than waiting until his return from Prague, writing 'day and night', his fascination with the work growing with every bar composed; he was 'ravenous' to resume work on it after Prague; and he completed it before the second four-week period granted by the messenger had elapsed. Mozart's medical and psychological fragility is also made to seem more pronounced than in Niemetschek: he was 'lost in his melancholy fantasies' even before the messenger arrived with the Requiem commission; he could not 'endure the strain' of working on the Requiem before Prague, 'several times [collapsing] in a faint from his labours'; he was 'even sicker when he returned to Vienna' than he had been in Prague; he became 'firmly convinced', presumably on account of his psychological and medical state, that the messenger 'must have been an unusual being, one who stood in close connection

---

[17] Ibid., pp. 42–5.

[18] See, for example, Stafford, *Mozart Myths*, pp. 78–9 and Gernot Gruber, *Mozart and Posterity*, trans. R. S. Furness (London, 1991), p. 19.

[19] See Stafford, *Mozart Myths*, pp. 79–80. Stafford also proposes that Requiem myth-making reflects a desire to rehabilitate Mozart following posthumous rumours about 'his alleged dissolute life': 'The aim was to depict Mozart dying in an odour of sanctity, moved to the core of his being by this work.' See ibid., p. 197.

[20] Solomon, 'The Rochlitz Anecdotes', p. 34.

with the world beyond or who had been sent to him to announce his death'. Mozart's completion of the work thus fulfils a dual function for Rochlitz: Mozart finishes the 'worthy monument to his name' (which launches the second part of the second Requiem anecdote, where the work is praised as supreme religious music); and Rochlitz finds an appropriately definitive conclusion to a story that has generated inexorable forward momentum. Maintaining a taut narrative shape over two Requiem-related anecdotes published two weeks apart probably influenced other presentational decisions as well. Moving the beginning of Mozart's work on the Requiem and the Prater conversation with Constanze to the period before the Prague trip (in the first anecdote) allows Mozart's composition of the Requiem to appear in both anecdotes and turns the post-Prague Requiem work (in the second anecdote) into a transfiguration, confirmed by the comparison with Raphael at the end of the first anecdote.[21] Both the first reference to transfiguration in the first anecdote and Mozart's 'very curious thoughts about the unusual appearance and commission of this unknown man' reported immediately afterwards whet the reader's appetite for the next *Allgemeine musikalische Zeitung* issue and the conclusion of the story; and, sure enough, Mozart's transfiguration and supernatural thoughts come to fruition in the second anecdote. Rochlitz has no need to repeat Mozart's proclamation about writing the Requiem for himself – as Niemetschek does for Mozart on the day of his death after relating it earlier at the Prater to Constanze – because the first, suitably emphatic realization ('Finally he could not deny it – he was certain that he was writing this work for his own funeral') actualizes the transfiguration. The two quoted conversations between Mozart and the messenger, one in each anecdote, fulfil a narrative function too: short, sharp exchanges propel both anecdotes into accounts of Mozart's relentlessly feverish work on the Requiem. The dialogues personalize Mozart, bringing his character to life. It is not enough for Rochlitz to relate Mozart's experience in the third person; we also need to hear Mozart himself speak, in order to come close to grasping the full significance of the momentous events that affect him.[22]

Rochlitz may have done himself harm by stretching to breaking point the 'facts' connected to the Requiem (as witnessed by the opprobrium consistently unleashed on him nowadays), but only when fact is prioritized over fiction, or indeed fact over interpretation. If we actively embrace the

[21] For more on transfiguration in Rochlitz's writings on the Requiem see Elizabeth Kramer, 'The Idea of Transfiguration in the Early German Reception of Mozart's Requiem', *Current Musicology*, 81 (2006), pp. 73–107, at 82–4.

[22] Solomon, 'The Rochlitz Anecdotes', pp. 32, 33.

fact–fiction continuum – as we do in acknowledging the not-entirely-factual status of Constanze's testimony to Niemetschek – and read Rochlitz's Requiem anecdotes as a condensed, creative re-interpretation of Niemetschek, it is easier to recognize the untold good he did for Mozart and his posthumous reputation in presenting the nineteenth century with an irresistible, tightly constructed yarn in which the protagonist is compellingly challenged by fate and circumstance. Is it significant that this is Rochlitz's interpretation, rather than a 'factual' account of events?

Rochlitz's erroneous suggestion that his anecdotes 'have the advantage of being true',[23] coupled with his desire to heighten interest in Mozart and his music in advance of Breitkopf & Härtel's publication of the complete works, should not obscure the fact that his Requiem anecdotes made very good copy, certainly for nineteenth-century readers nurtured *inter alia* on a diet of early romantic melodrama and Gothic novels.[24] It is extraordinary to note the frequency with which – and the diversity of publications in which – the Requiem legend is reproduced, paraphrased or summarized (with or without modifications) in a concise, dramatic version deriving ultimately from Rochlitz. General literary publications carry it repeatedly, as do encyclopaedias, dictionaries and anthologies.[25] It appears in religious-orientated publications, in instructional volumes and in journals and magazines addressed to specific groups, such as ladies, businessmen and boys (including in a heterogeneous issue of *The Boy's Journal* from 1868 that includes articles on mountaineers, making a screw-propeller for a small boat, the backwoods of Costa Rica, a surgeon's life and a boy trapper in the Rocky

---

[23] Ibid., p. 34.

[24] For studies of melodrama in the early nineteenth century, focusing on the French tradition, see Peter Brooks, *The Melodramatic Imagination: Balzac, Henry James, Melodrama, and the Mode of Excess* (New Haven, CT, 1976) and J. Paul Marcoux, *Guilbert de Pixerécourt: French Melodrama in the Early Nineteenth Century* (New York, 1992).

[25] For general publications, see John Timbs and Reuben Percy, *The Mirror of Literature, Amusement and Instruction* (London, 1825), p. 70; *The British Critic*, 7–8 (London, 1817), pp. 21–2; *Neues Hannoverisches Magazin*, 21 (Hanover, 1812), cols. 667–70; Wilhelm Hennings (ed.), *Deutscher Ehren-Tempel* (Gotha, 1821), vol. II, pp. 142–3; *The New Annual Register, or General Repository of History, Politics and Literature for the Year 1817* (London, 1818); William Oxberry, *The Flowers of Literature*, 4 vols. (London, 1824), vol. I, pp. 213–15; *The Kaleidoscope: or, Literary and Scientific Mirror* (Liverpool, 1821), pp. 190–1; *L'esprit des journaux, françois et étrangers*, 6 (Brussels, 1804), pp. 215–17; *Le musée des variétés littéraires*, 5 (Paris, 1824), p. 55; *Time's Telescope for 1821; or, A Complete Guide to the Almanack* (London, 1821), pp. 10–11, reprinted in *London Magazine*, 3 (London, 1821) p. 211. For encyclopaedias, dictionaries, etc., see Giuseppe Bertini, *Dizionario storico-critico scittori di musica e de'più celebri artisti di tutte le nazioni* (Palermo, 1815), vol. III, pp. 116–18; *Antologia*, vol. IV (Florence, 1821) pp. 39–40; Sholto and Reuben Percy, *The Percy Anecdotes: Original and Select*, 20 vols. (London, 1823), vol. XI, pp. 106–8 (also appearing in the same version, in *The Percy Anecdotes*. rev. edn (New York, 1838), p. 180 and *The Percy Anecdotes*. rev. edn (New York, 1847), p. 181).

Mountains).[26] It also takes its place among stories of horrific crimes and ghosts. In *The Terrific Register; or, a Record of Crimes, Judgments, Providences, and Calamities* (1825), it appears after a particularly gory story of love, murder, hanging and burning 'to the great satisfaction of justice, and all the spectators' and immediately before a sordid tale of Frederick the Great executing one of his captains in Silesia for burning a candle illegally at night as he wrote a letter to his beloved wife, '[displaying] a refinement in cruelty worthy of the most savage monster that ever disgraced human nature'.[27] And the ominous *Spectriana*, which also prints the story, begins with a picture entitled 'L'ombre de la mort' ('the shadow of death'), showing a chain-clad skeleton leading a warrior into a foreboding archway, accompanied by the caption 'Il lui ordonne de le suivre' ('he orders him to follow').[28] To be sure, Rochlitz's account was not solely responsible for the Requiem legend's attraction: Niemetschek's version, with the work remaining incomplete, is clearly the source for a number of retellings, including Thomas Busby's 'Life of Mozart: A Celebrated Musician' (December 1798), which also identified 'a catholic prince' as the commissioner, 'who perceiving himself on the verge of the grave, wished, by the execution of such a piece, to soothe his mind, and familiarize it to the idea of his approaching dissolution'. (Busby's account spawns a number of references to this unspecified patron.[29]) But Rochlitz's succinct, highly charged tale packed the biggest punch and had the biggest impact.

[26] See *Catholicon: or, The Christian Philosopher: A R. Catholic Monthly Magazine*, 5 (London, 1818), pp. 57–9; Jacques-Paul Migne et al. (eds.), *Encyclopédie théologique, ou Série de dictionnaires sur toutes les parties de la science religieuse*, vol. XLIX ('Dictionnaire des sciences occultes', vol. II) (Paris, 1848), cols. 195–6; John Pierpont, *From Modern Authors of Great Britain and America and Designed for the Use of the Highest Class in Publick and Private School* (Boston, 1825), pp. 219–20; Jonathan Barber, *The Elocutionist, Consisting of Declamations and Readings in Prose and Poetry for the Use of Colleges and Schools*, 2nd edn (New Haven, CT, 1836), pp. 174–6; Alfred G. Havet, *Havet's French Conversational Method*, 8th edn (London, 1874), pp. 195–6; Edward T. Fisher, *Easy French Reading being Selections of Historical Tales and Anecdotes Arranged with Copious Footnotes*, 6th edn (New York, 1867), pp. 39–44; *La belle assemblée, or Bell's Court and Fashionable Magazine, Addressed Particularly to the Ladies*, 2 (London, 1807), pp. 307–9; *Deutsche Reichs-und Staats-Zeitung für den Geschäfts- und Weltmann*, ed. Karl Julius Lange, 3 (1799), cols. 413–16; *The Boys' Journal: A Magazine of Literature, Science, Adventure, and Amusement for the Year 1868* (London, 1868), p. 591; *The Boy's Miscellany: An Illustrated Journal of Useful and Entertaining Literature for Youth*, 1 (London, 1863), p. 61.

[27] *The Terrific Register; or, A Record of Crimes, Judgments, Providences, and Calamities*, 1 (London, 1825), quoted material at pp. 319 and 320.

[28] *Spectriana, ou Recueil d'histoires et aventures surprenantes, merveilleuses et remarquables de spectres, revenans, esprits, fantômes, gnomes, diables et demons, etc.* (Paris, 1817), pp. 92–6.

[29] For Busby's version see *Monthly Magazine and British Register*, 6 (December 1798), pp. 445–50, at 449. References to the 'Catholic Prince' in the Requiem legend include *The Monthly Visitor, and New Family Magazine*, 12 (London, 1801), p. 245; Henry Wilson, *Wonderful Characters*

Irrespective of the specific version of events recalled, and in some instances scepticism about the veracity of aspects of the story, writers continued to regard the legend as intrinsic to understanding and appreciating the work. Mozart's biography and music, in other words, acted as mutual reinforcement. Madame de Staël is a case in point, explaining that the music of the Requiem is not beyond reproach but that the *story* is what makes the *work* so powerful:

I heard at Vienna the Requiem composed by Mozart, a few days before his death, and which was sung in the church at his funeral; it is not sufficiently solemn for the situation, and we still find in it, as in all his preceding compositions, many ingenious passages; what is there however, more affecting and impressive than the idea of a man of superior genius thus celebrating his own obsequies, inspired at the same time by the sentiment of his death and of his immortality! The recollections of life ought to decorate the tomb, the arms of a warrior are usually suspended on it, and the chefs-d'oeuvre of art cause a peculiarly solemn impression in the temple where the remains of the artist are consigned to repose.[30]

In historically self-conscious mode, writers sometimes challenge the story, but clearly need it as well. For *The Quarterly Review* (1818) the story has 'rather the appearance of romance than of real occurrences', but is told to us in any case, the author buying the idea that the Requiem 'accelerated the progress of [Mozart's] disorder'.[31] *The Repository of Arts* (1814) convinces itself that the events, while transgressing 'the common routine of human occurrences', must be right, not only because they have been verified by Constanze 'and all of [Mozart's] friends', but also because the work's status as an 'awfully sublime farewell . . . such as might be expected from the heart and the head of a Mozart' is too much to resist: 'Who can hear those heart-rending strains, borrowed, as it were, from the lamentations of angels, without forgetting all that is worldly, and elevating his thoughts into the awful regions of

(London, 1822), vol. III, p. 443; 'Mozart', in George Gleig (ed.), *Supplement to the Third Edition of the Encyclopaedia Britannica, or, a Dictionary of Arts, Sciences, and Miscellaneous Literature,* 2 vols. (Edinburgh, 1801), vol. II, pp. 279–82, at 281–2; John Mason Good, Olinthus Gregory and Newton Bosworth, *Pantologia: A New Cabinet Cyclopaedia*, vol. VIII (London, 1813) (unpaginated); *The Eccentric Biography; or, Sketches of Remarkable Characters, Ancient and Modern* (London, 1801), p. 232.

[30]   Baroness Staël-Holstein, *Germany* (trans. from the French), 3 vols. (London, 1813), vol. II, p. 408.

[31]   *The Quarterly Review* (London, 1818), p. 96. In a similar vein, see *The Illustrated Magazine of Art*, 3 (New York, 1854), p. 334, which relates a version of the Requiem legend in spite of claiming not to be able to vouch for it: 'probably there is some truth in it, embellished from the imaginations of those by whom it has been related'.

futurity?'[32] A reviewer (1821) of Vincent Novello's edition of Mozart's masses cannot accept a 'supernatural stimulus' for the Requiem, tempting though it is given the work's quality, but proposes another stimulus instead, namely 'the actual state of excessive irritability to which the nerves of Mozart were excited' and responded when receiving the commission.[33] In related fashion, the *Journal of Psychological Medicine and Mental Psychology* (1849) argues that 'The solemn figure which induced Mozart to write the "requiem," which was first, indeed, chaunted [*sic*] over his own grave, was doubtless but a phantom of his own creation.'[34] *Tait's Edinburgh Magazine* (1859), citing 'absurd tales . . . circulated about the requiem', also turns the story eloquently around to illuminate Mozart's psychological state:

The circumstances of that stranger's visit were mysterious, certainly, but not supernatural. Mozart's sand had nearly run; the stranger came at a time when the composer was in an excited state . . . His life, and mind – the light of life – were tottering. His thoughts, depressed by long anxieties and disappointments, had taken a morbid tone. When physical weakness came, the mental – so strangely incorporated with the physical – gave way. He imagined gloomy things; his speech was of death; he impressed on his wife the certainty he felt of his own speedy dissolution. She combated the notion; he adhered to it. The work under his hands related to death; he had entered into the service of the dead. What wonder, then, that his mind, thus tuned, should ring in union with that which sprung from his genius – the stranger's requiem. It was the most natural conclusion for his distempered brain to draw, that the death chaunt he created would be used at the ceremony which he felt would take place at its termination, that his funeral would be the time of its production.[35]

The story of the supernatural messenger is downplayed, but having a story to relate is crucial nonetheless. For so many in the nineteenth century, the Requiem *had* to be heard biographically: 'it makes us feel the melancholy of the composer, which remains so fully in it';[36] it is 'a work overflowing with beauty of melody, displaying the profoundest learning, and conceived in such a spirit of solemn grandeur as might have been expected from one who felt that he was standing on the verge of eternity';[37] it is 'the history of

---

[32] *The Repository of Arts, Literature, Commerce, Manufactures, Fashions, and Politics, for January 1814*, 11 (1814), pp. 132–3.

[33] *The Quarterly Musical Magazine and Review*, 3 (1821), p. 100.

[34] *Journal of Psychological Medicine and Mental Pathology*, 2 (London, 1849), p. 275.

[35] *Tait's Edinburgh Magazine*, 26 (Edinburgh, 1859), p. 210.

[36] Frederick August Rauch, *Psychology; or a View of the Human Soul; or, A View of the Human Soul: Including Anthropology* (New York, 1840), p. 214.

[37] *Authorized Report of the Church Congress held at Dublin, on September 29th, 30th, October 1st, 2nd, 3rd 1868* (Dublin, 1868), p. 418.

Mozart's life – a reproach to mankind for their neglect of the mightiest genius that ever dwelt upon the earth'.[38]

Perhaps the deep-seated desire to bring biography and music into perfect harmony explains why the patently incorrect Rochlitz-inspired story of Mozart completing the work before his death is so frequently retold long after the high-profile *Requiem-Streit* (Requiem Conflict) of the late 1820s and 1830s had blown the lid off the completion theory. (The *Requiem-Streit* is discussed in Chapter 2.) It is difficult to determine, of course, whether writers were inadvertently perpetrating a fiction here or found the fiction just too convenient and compelling to dismiss, even in the face of incontrovertible evidence to the contrary. Whatever the case may be, numerous publications between 1830 and 1875, from cities and towns across Europe and America, continue to give voice to the myth that Mozart finished his Requiem before he died.[39]

Bizarrely, even Constanze may have participated in such myth-making eight months or so before her own death. An American travelling in central Europe who visited her in Salzburg in summer 1841 wrote back at length to a friend in Boston in a letter published in *The Monthly Chronicle, or Events, Discoveries, Improvements and Opinions*:

Only a few days since I saw the widow of *Mozart*, and had frequent conversations with her upon her husband. She is now nearly 80 years old, but lively, spirited, and full of enthusiasm for every thing relating to Mozart. She was actually ill in bed on the morning of the day that I first saw her, but the conversation about her

---

[38] See *The Musical Examiner*, 1 (1843), pp. 254–5, at 255.

[39] See, *inter alia*, Eliakim Littell and W. Keenan, *Lives of Remarkable Youth of Both Sexes* (Philadelphia, 1830), pp. 111–13; John Pierpont, *The American First Class Book* (Boston, 1835), pp. 218–20; Samuel Griswold Goodrich, *Curiosities of Human Nature* (Boston, 1852), pp. 105–7; James Hogg, *Hogg's Weekly Instructor*, 1 (Edinburgh, 1845), p. 159; *The Monthly Repository and Library of Entertaining Knowledge* (New York, 1834), pp. 367–9; Edward Colby Sharpin (ed.), *Death Scenes* (Yarmouth, 1842), pp. 61–2; *Youth's Magazine; A Monthly Miscellany, 1840–1841* (New York, 1841), pp. 210–12; *Musical Review and Record of Musical Science, Literature and Intelligence*, 1 (1838–9), pp. 388–9; Raphael, *The Familiar Astrologer: An Easy Guide to Fate, Destiny and Foreknowledge* (London, 1841), pp. 192–3; *Le cabinet de lecture et le cercle réunis*, 3 (1842), p. 177; William Thomas Parke, *Musical Memoirs* (London, 1831), pp. 168–70; J. Collin de Plancy, *Dictionnaire infernal*, 4th edn (Brussels, 1845), p. 374; *The American Phrenological Journal and Life Illustrated*, 47–8 (New York, 1868), p. 175; *The Norwich Spectator*, 2 (Norwich, 1863), pp. 258–60; John W. Moore, *Complete Encyclopaedia of Music, Elementary, Technical, Historical, Biographical, Vocal, and Instrumental* (Boston, 1852), p. 627 (although the article on Süssmayr, p. 905, says that Mozart left the work 'unfinished'); Mary Mapes Dodge (ed.), *St. Nicholas: Schribner's Illustrated Magazine for Girls and Boys*, 2 (New York, 1875), pp. 129–30; Robert Chambers (ed.), *The Book of Days: A Miscellany of Popular Antiquities Including Anecdote, Biography and History Curiosities of Literature and Oddities of Human Life and Character*, 2 vols. (London, 1864), vol. II, pp. 658–9; Kazlitt Arvine, *The Cyclopaedia of Anecdotes of Literature and the Fine Arts*, 3rd edn (Boston, 1856), p. 389.

distinguished husband seemed to inspire her, and drive far away all malady . . . You know the mysterious story of the *Requiem*. She spoke of that. *What you have read is nearly all true.* The requiem was ordered by a stranger, paid for in advance, called for once, but being unfinished was left for a future day – three days later – the time came – Mozart finished the requiem, and died the next day; but it was never called for; and, notwithstanding efforts to discover who had given the order, *neither she nor her friends are aware, even to this day!*[40]

Either the author, who was well informed about performances of Mozart's works in America, reported exactly what he wanted to report (and not what Constanze said), participating consciously in the myth-making process that kept the completion legend on the boil for so long, or else Constanze – even after everything that had happened in the previous fifty years – figured that a travelling American ought to be treated to the dramatized version of events.[41] And the latter is not quite as outrageous a supposition as it may seem when we remember that Constanze astonishingly allowed the Niemetschek version of events to appear in Nissen's biography of 1828 – complete with messenger collecting the unfinished work and unknown patron disappearing without trace – in spite of knowing that many details were false.[42]

Another nineteenth-century traveller, based in Austria and going by the initials R. H. B., demonstrates deep-rooted commitment to the legend of Mozart's Requiem.[43] Arriving in Salzburg Cathedral and hearing the 'exquisite tones of the organ brought back to mind the story that had often charmed me in childhood, of Mozart's Requiem – his last work – performed there for himself'.[44] Our traveller first gives a version of the Requiem 'legend' (identified as such), embellished with Mozart's and Constanze's

[40] Nathan Hale (ed.), *The Monthly Chronicle, or Events, Discoveries, Improvements and Opinions*, 2 (Boston, 1841), pp. 361–2 (italics as in original).

[41] Around this time Constanze appears to have given another visitor a more straightforward account of the genesis and completion of the Requiem, making reference to Süssmayr's role in the completion; see *The Manchester Guardian* (7 September 1842), p. 4 (reproducing material from Mainzer's *Athenaeum*).

[42] Stafford, *Mozart Myths*, p. 22. Constanze admits to knowing the identity of the commissioner in a letter to Breitkopf & Härtel (30 Jan. 1800), having sent to the publishers the draft of an appeal for the commissioner 'kindly to acquaint her of his intentions [for the Requiem] within three months' (18 Oct. 1799). See Deutsch, *Documentary Biography*, p. 488. Frederick Samuel Silverstolpe, present at the evaluation of Requiem manuscripts at Sortschan's office in 1800 attended by Nissen and Stadler on behalf of Constanze, identifies the commissioner as 'Count Waldsek' in a letter to his father on 22 April 1801. The letter is given in Wolff, *Mozart's Requiem*, p. 149.

[43] R. H. B., 'Traditions of Tirol', in *The Monthly Packet of Evening Readings for Members of the English Church*, new series, 10 (London, 1870), pp. 499–502.

[44] The writer mixes up here the probable posthumous performance of Mozart's Requiem (what existed of the work at that stage at least) at St Michael's Church in Vienna on 10 December 1791 with a performance at Salzburg Cathedral.

quoted reactions to the visit of the mysterious man. From Mozart: 'the thrill of mingled terror and joy which had risen in my breast when he [the messenger] said: "Remember, it will be the last time!" convince me that this time when he comes I shall not see him in the flesh, for it is my soul that he came to call'.[45] The legend is similarly dramatized with references to Mozart's 'short paroxysm of feverish excitement' working on the Requiem on his final day, and with Constanze anxiously awaiting the arrival of the mysterious messenger to break the curse on her husband 'amid the crowds who came hour by hour to inquire after … [his] health'.[46] But there then follows a *volte face*, a 'prose account of the origin of the Requiem', with well-informed references to the Walsegg commission, the work's incomplete status at Mozart's death, Walsegg's attempt to pass off the work as his own and Gottfried Weber's claim that much of the Requiem was by Süssmayr, as well as footnotes to Otto Jahn's biography and Ignaz von Mosel's essay on the original score.[47] The juxtaposition of 'legend' and 'prose account' tells us that the Requiem legend must be retained, even if it is known to be incorrect; it is too important a part of history (in this case the writer's personal history) to be discarded.

Whether nineteenth-century writers related events associated with the Requiem in self-conscious fashion or deliberately continued to perpetrate myths long revealed conclusively to be false, they remained collectively entranced by the Requiem legend. With such compelling events to contemplate, a number of writers set them to poetry, or – apparently intending to up the ante – used them as a stimulus for unambiguous, unadulterated fiction.

The Requiem in nineteenth-century fiction, drama and poetry

The Requiem legend was perfectly suited to nineteenth-century poetry – poignant, powerful and (at least to the romantically inclined imagination) inspiring. A number of verses are devoted exclusively to the Requiem, including widely disseminated poems from the late 1820s by Rufus Dawes and Felicia Hemans.[48] Both focus, predictably, on Mozart's emotions (anxiety, fear, resignation) as he comes to realize he is writing the Requiem for

---

[45] R. H. B., 'Traditions of Tirol', p. 501.   [46] Ibid., p. 502.   [47] Ibid.

[48] For Rufus Dawes's poem 'Mozart's Requiem', see John Frost, *The Class Book of American Literature* (Boston, 1826), pp. 188–9. It is also printed in George Barrell Cheever, *The American Common-Place Book of Poetry* (Boston, 1831), pp. 275–6; Cheever, *The Poets of America* (New York, 1857), pp. 275–6; A. Cunningham (ed.), *The Standard Elocutionist; and Gem-Book of British*

himself, his life seeping away. Hemans's poem is prefaced by a short version of the Requiem legend telling us that the 'sensitive imagination of the composer immediately seized upon the circumstances as an omen of his own fate' and that the work was completed a few days before Mozart's death; a poem by Nicholas Mitchell also refers in an editorial insertion to Mozart's belief about writing the Requiem for himself (and to the last-gasp indications for the timpani, from Sophie Haibel's account), as does an introduction to a re-publication of Dawes's poem.[49] The legend, then, is the catalyst for poetry. It is unsurprising that Henry Innes selected Dawes's poem among those used to instruct students in the art of elocution, since the 'turns and shades of passion and expression' necessary for mastering this art are so noticeable in the poem (and duly annotated by Innes in the left-hand margin).[50] Hemans, it would seem, behaved like the quintessential romantic artist, dangerously absorbed by her own poem. As the *Southern Literary Messenger* (1835–6) explains: 'So perilously ... was she excited by the composition of Mozart's Requiem, that she was prohibited by her physician from any further exercise of her art, for some weeks after it was written.'[51]

References to Mozart's Requiem in nineteenth-century poems on other topics also attest to the work's cultural impact and influence. Catherine Grace Garnett's 'On the Sister of Körner, the German Poet', addressing the sister's reactions to her beloved brother's death, contains a footnote to the Mozart Requiem legend when observing that Körner worked on his own 'death-dirge'.[52] Two poems refer specifically to a real and a desired performance of the Requiem at commemorations for dead individuals (an archbishop and an admiral), and another to a performance of the work required

---

Authors (London, 1850), pp. 181–2. For Felicia Hemans's 'Mozart's Requiem' see *The New Monthly Magazine*, 22 (London, 1828), pp. 325–6. It is also published in Dorothy Hazard (ed.), *The Poetical Works of Mrs Felicia Hemans, Complete in One Volume* (Philadelphia, 1836), pp. 317–18; Frederic Rowton, *The Female Poets of Great Britain* (Philadelphia, 1849), pp. 398–400; Felicia Dorothea Brown Hemans, *The Works of Mrs. Hemans, with a Memoir by her Sister*, ed. Harriet Mary Browne Owen, 7 vols. (Philadelphia, 1840), vol. V, pp. 313–15; George Croly, *The Beauties of the British Poets* (London, 1828), pp. 362–4; Hemans, *Records of Woman, and Other Poems* (Edinburgh and London, 1850), pp. 165–7; Frederic Rowton, *The Female Poets of Great Britain* (Philadelphia, 1854), pp. 398–400.

[49] See 'The Last Work of Mozart', in William Francis Ainsworth (ed.), *New Monthly Magazine*, new series, 6 (London, 1874), pp. 239–40; and Dawes, 'Mozart's Requiem', in Henry Innes (ed.), *The Rhetorical Class Book; or The Principles and Practice of Elocution* (London, 1834), pp. 303–5.

[50] For the quotation see Innes (ed.), *Rhetorical Class Book*, p. viii; the poem appears on pp. 303–5.

[51] *Southern Literary Messenger*, 2 (Richmond, 1835–6), p. 612. The poem is identified in 1836 as 'perhaps the finest of her lyrics', with a description of 'the manner in which she herself felt [the Requiem's] thrilling influences'. See Rose Lawrence (ed.), *The Last Autumn at a Favourite Residence, with Other Poems and Recollections of Mrs Hemans* (Liverpool, 1836), p. 339.

[52] See Catherine Grace Garnett, *A Spanish Tale. Sappho, A Dramatic Sketch, and Other Poems* (London, 1824), pp. 198–200 (poem) and 219–20 (footnote).

to accompany a reading of a poem entitled 'Requiem'.[53] All three attest to the Requiem's status as work of choice at nineteenth-century funerals and commemorations (see Chapter 3).

The most famous nineteenth-century fictional account of Mozart's death, with the Requiem at its core, is Alexander Pushkin's play *Mozart and Salieri* (1830), one of his so-called 'little tragedies'.[54] At the end of Scene 1, Mozart and Salieri arrange to eat together at the Golden Lion Inn, Salieri informing us in his soliloquy that he intends to kill Mozart, his 'mortal foe', with the poison he has possessed for the last eighteen years but not yet used.[55] In Scene 2, Mozart professes to being in a sombre mood ('I must confess, my Requiem is on my mind'), relating the story of the 'man, all dressed in black', who commissioned the Requiem and then disappeared, not yet to return.[56] After Mozart consumes the drink that Salieri has laced with poison, he goes to the fortepiano and plays his Requiem. Salieri weeps with 'pain and joy' as Mozart performs, his soul '[filled] once more with magic sound'; before he dies, Mozart praises 'the power of music' and the ability to recognize beauty.[57]

In having Mozart play his Requiem in the face of now-inevitable death, Pushkin dramatizes the swan song – the final musical utterance that Salieri finds so overwhelming – like the mechanical swan reported at the beginning of the chapter. Pushkin also dramatizes the story of the messenger, not only by giving it to Mozart to relate to us himself, foregrounding his disturbed reaction ('my caller dressed in black looms heavy in my mind and haunts my peace'[58]), but also by linking the ominous actions of the messenger in Mozart's mind with the murderous actions of Salieri on stage. Mozart dies a victim of both the mysterious psychological torment wrought by the messenger and the villainous act of a fellow composer; we are thus invited to experience his death as a personal, artistic, fatalistic tragedy.

An earlier German play about Mozart's death by Adolph von Schaden (1825) also dramatizes the Requiem as a swan song.[59] An unknown man (*Unbekannte*), first encountered by Konstanze in a scarlet coat and black plumed hat bearing a gift of champagne for the manic-depressive Mozart, commissions a Requiem from him. Mozart immediately recognizes the significance of the commission in his soliloquy at the end of Act 2:

---

[53] See, respectively, *The British Friend; A Monthly Journal*, 12/1 (1846), p. 7; *Dublin University Magazine: A Literary and Political Journal*, 56 (1860), p. 366; and Thomas Aird (ed.), *The Poetical Works of David Macbeth Moir* (Edinburgh and London, 1852), vol. II, pp. 297–8.

[54] Alexander Pushkin, *Mozart and Salieri* (1830), trans. James E. Falen, in Svetlana Evdokimova (ed.), *Alexander Pushkin's Little Tragedies: The Poetics of Brevity* (Madison, WI, 2005), pp. 321–9.

[55] Ibid., pp. 325–6.   [56] Ibid., p. 327.   [57] Ibid., p. 329.   [58] Ibid., p. 327.

[59] Adolph von Schaden, *Mozarts Tod: Ein Original-Trauerspiel in drei Akten* (Augsburg and Leipzig, 1825).

'The gloomy last tune of the Mass for the Dead is Amadeo's swan song!'[60] These are his last words in the play, in fact, for his death is announced at the beginning of Act 3. The swan song is invoked again at the end of the play, as the Dies irae is heard and Konstanze envisages Mozart's spirit taken off by angels.[61]

Salieri and the mysterious messenger are not alone in nineteenth-century fiction in being implicated in Mozart's death; Emanuel Schikaneder and Hofer (cousin of the singer Franz de Paula Hofer who (perhaps) sang parts of the Requiem with Mozart, Schack and Franz Xaver Gerl at Mozart's bedside) suffer a similar fate in 'The Story of "The Requiem"' (c.1850).[62] An Englishman by the name of Vaughan, after a chance encounter with Hofer's daughter, who faints at a performance of 'Sento o Dio' from *Così fan tutte*, befriends Hofer over a period of time. When Hofer falls ill (with what Vaughan supposes is a fatal illness), he decides to relate a story to Vaughan that he has previously kept secret about his and Schikaneder's involvement in Mozart's death. The story begins with Hofer drinking one day with Schikaneder and Stadler in 1791, learning that Schikaneder and Mozart had been at a masquerade a couple of years earlier at which Mozart had been cursed with ominous news about his future fate. Mozart had then had a dream in which an unearthly messenger appeared before him, breathing the words 'Requiem aeternam', which reminded Mozart of the curse. Stadler is sceptical about Schikaneder's story and the two have a bet, Schikaneder wagering that he can 'half kill Mozart with fright by a trick, which would convince all Vienna of his foolish belief in supernatural agency'. Schikaneder asks Hofer to act as the intermediary who, clad in dark, mourning attire, will commission a requiem from Mozart. Hofer and Schikaneder rehearse, with Schikaneder taking the Mozart role, and Hofer goes to visit Mozart for the first time on 11 August. Hofer delivers his lines perfectly, explaining that the commissioner wishes to remain anonymous, that he (the messenger) will give no details about himself and will pick up the work when finished, and that Mozart can name his date of completion. Schikaneder laughs heartily at Mozart's scared reaction as relayed to him by Hofer and tells Hofer to go back on 3 September, just before Mozart leaves for Prague. (Schikaneder intends evilly to profit from the Requiem by selling it in London, where his treachery would be likely to go

---

[60] Ibid., p. 76 ('Des Todenamtes dumpfer letzter Klang, / Sei Amadeo's Schwanensang!').

[61] Ibid., pp. 95–6.

[62] 'The Story of "The Requiem"', in E. Littell (compiler), *Littell's Living Age*, 26 (Boston, 1850), pp. 37–44; see also *Fraser's Magazine for Town and Country*, 41 (London, 1850), pp. 539–50.

undetected.) On 3 September Mozart tells Hofer it is unfinished; Hofer says he will return on 3 October, after Mozart's Prague trip, but he does not ultimately do so, as by then Mozart has learned of Schikaneder's trick, and, Hofer surmises, may have been prepared to take legal action against Schikaneder. Mozart was taken ill on 21 November: 'he had finished the Requiem and the fact of no one coming to claim it persuaded him more firmly that it was for himself'. Hofer guesses that Schikaneder has poisoned Mozart, fearing 'heavy punishment' for his actions, and fearing that had Mozart written three operas under commission at that time, his own possession of *Die Zauberflöte* would have had considerably less significance (that is, no longer representing Mozart's *last* opera). Hofer cannot tell Vaughan how Schikaneder poisoned Mozart, but claims: 'I will believe anything rather than that *I* frightened him to death.'[63]

This story therefore attempts – in a fictional context – to account for Mozart's mysterious Requiem commission and death, imagined scenarios flowing freely from knowledge of the Requiem legend and, in the case of Schikaneder and Stadler, of characters in Mozart's orbit in the final months of his life. Like Pushkin, the author intensifies the experience of Mozart's death by personalizing it, in this case through the protagonists Vaughan and Hofer. Vaughan's reverence for Mozart's music is woven into the fabric of the story and stimulates his fascination for Mozart's life and personality; quite by chance he, a lucky, besotted admirer, learns a truth about Mozart's Requiem known only to Hofer. (Perhaps readers are encouraged to think that they too can learn unknown truths about the master if, like Vaughan, they remain ceaselessly devoted to him?) In turn, Hofer's situation, with death looming, parallels Mozart own: Hofer's narrative is less a swan song than a final confession, of course, but still represents a last (productive) outpouring before his own death. And his desperate attempt to absolve himself of responsibility in Mozart's death, palming it off on to Schikaneder, represents an anxiety-ridden death rattle that highlights the horror that Mozart himself would have felt as he approached death. Thus, the death of the genius penetrates the realm of the death of the ordinary man.

Other mid-century stories also personalize the experience of Mozart's death in relation to his Requiem by processing it through the reactions of individuals who were touched by him at the time, and/or by giving a voice to Mozart himself. 'Le Requiem de Mozart' focuses on George Rutler, who worked in a Viennese boutique frequented regularly by a man well known to

---

[63] For quoted material in this paragraph see 'The Story of "The Requiem"', pp. 42, 44.

Rutler (but not by name).[64] On discovering that Rutler's wife was expecting their twelfth child, the man (Mozart) says that he would like to help him out by paying the 100 florins for the baptism and requests that the baby is called Gabrielle. He then asks to sit for a few moments at a piano in Rutler's boutique; he says that an idea has come to him for completing one of his works and that he must play and notate it before it slips away. Passers-by congregate in front of the door of the boutique as he plays, listening in silence to the 'celestial harmony' (*harmonie céleste*) and figuring that the music must indeed be by Mozart. A while later Rutler goes to the address Mozart gave him and is horrified to learn that Mozart has died. Returning to his boutique, the tearful Rutler looks at the piano where Mozart's final chords had come to him for the famous Requiem.

In the 'Last Moments of Mozart', it is Mozart's (imaginary) daughter, Emilie, who experiences her father's death, the Requiem serving as the story's springboard.[65] His countenance is pale, but he has a 'strange fire in his eye'; he has finished the Requiem that had occupied him for weeks, telling Emilie that it is a Requiem for himself. She protests ('The idea of death broke so suddenly on her mind, that it checked every mode of utterance, and she gazed upon his countenance as in a dream'), but is asked by Mozart to sing a hymn tune beloved of her mother that includes the words

Spirit! Thy labor is o'er,
Thy term of probation is run
Thy steps are now bound for the untrodden shore,
And the race of immortals begun.

When she goes over to her father after finishing the hymn, she realizes he is dead.[66]

---

[64] See 'Le Requiem de Mozart', in Henri La Fayette Vilaume Ducoudray Holstein, *Le glaneur français* (Geneva, 1833), pp. 22–4. A story about 'Ruttler' entitled 'Mozart's Violin' and differing in some details – including Mozart as a violinist not a pianist – was published in Britain and America in the mid-nineteenth century. See *The British Minstrel and Musical and Literary Miscellany*, 1 (Glasgow, 1843), p. 138; *The London Saturday Journal* (1841), pp. 107–8; William Strickland (ed.), *Odd Fellows' Literary Casket*, 1 (Cincinnati, 1854), pp. 50–2. The 'Mozart's Requiem' version is also published in *The Metropolitan: A Monthly Magazine Devoted to Religion, Education, Literature and General Information*, 4 (London, 1856), p. 372.

[65] See *Supplement to the Connecticut Courant for the Years 1840 and 1841* (Hartford, 1840–41), p. 237, and *The Musical Magazine*, 27 (Boston, 1840), pp. 268–70. The story is also published in Joseph Foulkes Winks, *The Baptist Reporter and Missionary Intelligencer* (London and Leicester, 1847), pp. 105–6; *The American Vocalist* (Boston, 1849), p. 300 (shortened version); J. K. (ed.), *The Dew Drop: A Magazine for the Young*, 1/1 (1848), pp. 11–12 (shortened version); Charles W. Sanders, *Sanders' Rhetorical, or Union Sixth Reader* (New York, 1862), pp. 246–8.

[66] *Supplement to the Connecticut Courant* (1840–1), p. 237.

'Mozart and Schach: An Imaginary Dialogue' is no doubt inspired by Benedikt Schack's purported association with the Requiem as well as *Die Zauberflöte*.[67] Mozart is preoccupied with the idea of writing the Requiem for himself ('How could I fill it with such sobbing tones for a stranger's death? I have only to finish it – this swan song – and then – all is over with Mozart').[68] He confesses: 'its music has an unearthly spell that I cannot resist any more than the quivering bird can shun the glare of the serpent's eye. Think you it is in my power to shake off this conviction? God knows how gladly I would be rid of its baleful, blasting presence; for the fear of death is strong upon me, and a horrible dread overwhelms me.'[69] Thereafter he muses on his artistic place in the world and his legacy, and on musical stars of the future, before Constanze enters, bringing the conversation with Schach to a close.

Even the 'spirit from the other world' who commissions the Requiem is personalized in the first part of one German story, 'Mozart's Requiem: A Sketch by Ortleff'.[70] Mozart is, in effect, a high-living, devil-may-care Don Giovanni-type character, brave in the face of the 'strange apparition' confronting him ('in his heart he felt no trepidation') and irreverent in conversation, injecting expressions in different languages. He insists on the spirit sitting down to drink with him, whereupon the said spirit, who does not like Mozart's champagne, produces bottles of his own, to Mozart's delight: 'In that night, both drank a great quantity of genuine champagne together, toasting and talking of music, men, and spirits of all kinds.'[71] (Mozart acknowledges that the encounter could have been a dream.) Events take a more sinister turn in the second part of the story, an ailing Mozart working feverishly on the Requiem, imagining return visits from the 'dark stranger', who tells him ominously, 'You know you will compose yourself to death ... I help you to write your own death mass!'; in the final part of the story Mozart goes for a walk on a beautifully clear and transparent autumn afternoon (the day of his death), but is profoundly melancholic, is shocked by his own 'ghastly features' and ultimately takes his feelings from that afternoon 'to the silent grave'.[72]

In all of these stories, either Mozart himself or characters close to him fully realize, and actively embrace, the momentous biographical and

---

[67] William and Robert Chambers (eds.), *Chambers's Edinburgh Journal*, new series, 15 (Edinburgh, 1851), pp. 167–9.

[68] Ibid., p. 167.   [69] Ibid., p. 168.

[70] See *The Musical World*, 24 (1849), pp. 771–2, 787 quotation at p. 772. The titles of the three parts are 'The Contract', 'II. Progress of the Work' and 'III. The Last Promenade'.

[71] *The Musical World*, 24 (1849), pp. 771, 772.   [72] Ibid., p. 787.

musical link between Mozart's composition of a requiem and his impending death – about which the known medical information may be conveniently forgotten. Historicizing and monumentalizing Mozart's position in the musical world develops from this link: Rutler's contemplation of the piano on which Mozart completed his last, great work; references to immortality in the Emilie story; and Mozart's opinions about Haydn, Beethoven and the future international successes of his own works in the Schach dialogue. Explicitly fictional accounts of the Requiem, then, encourage the nineteenth-century reader to bring together intimate and personal experiences of, and wider historical resonances associated with, Mozart's death; mutually reinforcing, the personal and historical – alongside transfiguration (Emilie and Ortleff stories) – project Mozart's Requiem and his death into a mythical realm. The message is that we *must* understand both personal and historical dimensions in order properly to process the momentous conflation of musician, Requiem and biography, if not through Mozart directly then through fictionalized individuals who are close to him and can immediately comprehend and convey (in ideally cognizant fashion) the full impact of his Requiem and of his death. For Mozart, death had to be the way it was, and not only for writers of fiction. As A. W. Ambros explains:

Mozart did live *in* music and *for* music; music was his all, until he drew his last breath – he died with a passage of his requiem on his lips. It would have been impossible for him to promenade in his old days, idly about the boulevards of Paris, picking his teeth, and playing the wit, or to turn fish-vendor – he would never have been able to do that.[73]

Mozart died, then, in the right way and at the right time, as if subliminally aware of a pre-ordained biographical imperative; for this reason, his Requiem and his death possessed the profoundest of meanings.

The final two chapters of Heribert Rau's *Mozart: A Biographical Romance* (1858) capture in microcosm mid-nineteenth-century fictional trends associated with the Requiem and, above all, the murky continuum between fact and fiction.[74] Events and emotions are characteristically intense, including: a 'thickly veiled' woman outside Mozart's house who listens to the Requiem ('music that breathed an awed, unspeakable grief . . . woven of love and sorrow and sacred tears') and sees in front of her a coffin next to which hundreds kneel tearfully singing, 'Requiem aeternam dona eis Domine';[75] a Requiem

[73] A. W. Ambros, 'Rossini and the Principle of Sensual Enjoyment in Music', trans. W. F. Muller, *The Musical Review and Musical World*, 12 (New York, 1861), p. 268.

[74] Heribert Rau, *Mozart: A Biographical Romance* (1858), trans. E. R. Still (Boston, 1870).

[75] Ibid., pp. 314–15.

rehearsal at which Constanze 'heard far-off angel choirs imploring at the throne of God for her darling, her dying beloved';[76] and final moments for Mozart, after Dr Closset has applied the cold compressions, during which his 'meaning look' to Süssmayr leads Süssmayr to leaf slowly through the score for him until he imitates the drums in the Sanctus, and to place the Requiem score on his heart, the 'muffled drum-beats' of which grew 'slower and fainter'.[77] Mozart gets due historical recognition too, Constanze extolling his 'true music – coming out of the heart and penetrating the heart . . . the true path of music . . . giving the death-blow to the cling-clang of the false Italian school', Süssmayr acknowledging 'what the world was soon to lose' and Seyfried bringing in letters from Vienna, Amsterdam and Pressburg (now Bratislava) that attest to the high esteem in which his music is held.[78] The genre of Rau's book seems unproblematic in that his preface distinguishes Oulibicheff's and Jahn's books for well-informed musicians, with a purpose lying 'purely in the sphere of art and science', from his own, which 'by means of the familiar and confidential style of a romance, [aims] to bring closer to the heart of the German people one of its noblest sons'.[79] But at least two contemporary reviewers are seduced into believing that Rau's text is to all intents and purposes factual, and that Requiem-related events are not embellished:

Truth is said to be stranger than fiction; it is certainly more interesting. In reading *Mozart*, a novel, by Heribert Rau . . . we are constantly and forcibly reminded of this fact by the footnotes with which the author conscientiously garnishes his pages. The most striking incidents, the most interesting details, are all matters of history; the "novel", in fact, is nothing more than highly-colored biography . . . It is the old tale of the nightingale that "sings darkling, with her breast against a thorn," and the strange episode of the Requiem formed a fitting close to such a life. Of this incident, strange to say, the novelist makes nothing [. . .].[80]

The other reviewer is similarly convinced that the reader 'while enjoying the romantic story, has also the consolation of knowing that he is perusing not a mere fiction, but the tale of an actual human life' providing in events such as 'the great composer [dying] swan-like to the music of his own requiem . . . not only a faithful portraiture of Mozart, but also a vivid and truthful mirror of his age and his contemporaries'.[81] A notice of 1901 about an English translation of Rau's book also relates Rau's account of the Requiem without concern for how the 'alleged facts' may have been embellished.[82]

---

[76] Ibid., p. 322.   [77] Ibid., p. 323.   [78] Ibid., pp. 317, 319, 321.   [79] Ibid., pp. 3, 4.
[80] *Putnam's Magazine*, new series, 1 (New York, 1868), p. 771.
[81] *The Michigan University Magazine*, 2 (Ann Arbor, 1868), p. 320.
[82] *The Musical Standard*, 16 (5 October 1901), pp. 215–16.

Just as Rau's fiction is read as fact, so the Emilie story migrates from a fictional arena into an ostensibly factual one. The Rev. Thomas De Witt Talmage's sermon 'The Anthem of Heaven' reports Mozart's Requiem as an example of a work in which 'every note . . . is a spark dropped from the forge of [the author's] own burning emotions . . . Mozart composed his own requiem, and said to his daughter Emily, "Play that;" and while Emily was playing the requiem, Mozart's soul went up on the wave of his own music into glory.'[83] Other publications from the 1850s and 1860s (and even as late as 1909) present this well-disseminated story as fact, in spite of its easy identification as fiction, not least because Mozart had no living daughter in 1791.[84] It is also the inspiration for a poem, 'Mozart's Last Request', by H. M. Parsons.[85]

The Requiem's nineteenth-century fact–fiction continuum, then, is not only murky, but also temporally and generically complex. Niemetschek's account, at least partially a product of Constanze's fictions, inspires Rochlitz's further move in a fictional direction. In turn, Rochlitz becomes spiritual ancestor to the popularly orientated nineteenth-century versions of the Requiem legend, including the explicitly fictional ones. And further on, elements of these explicitly fictional tales feed back into, or are read as, 'fact'. This is not in any way a negative state of affairs, for it lies at the heart of the Requiem's nineteenth-century identity – its ability to hold audiences spellbound, in some cases exclusively (it would seem) on account of the stories and legends that had accrued to it.

With the century drawing to a close, Rimsky-Korsakov wrote his self-described 'two operatic scenes in recitative-arioso style' *Mozart and Salieri* (1897), based on Pushkin's play.[86] From the perspective of reception, the Requiem quotation at the end adeptly summarizes key activities from the preceding 100 years: Salieri swoons at the first sixteen bars of the Introit

[83] Rev. Thomas De Witt Talmage, *Fifty Sermons* (London, 1874), pp. 82–3.

[84] See S. B. Brittan, *Man and his Relations: Illustrating the Influence of the Mind on the Body* (New York, 1864), pp. 501–2; 'The Dying Mozart', *The National Magazine: Devoted to Literature, Art and Religion*, 13 (New York, 1858), p. 285; Matthew Baxter, *The Missionary's Legacy to his Friends, or Glimpses of the Land of the Blessed* (London, 1868), pp. 118–20; 'Face to Face with Death: The Last Words of Famous Men', *The London Journal*, 8 (4 Dec. 1909), p. 132 (modified so that the daughter sings the Requiem itself to Mozart rather than a favourite hymn).

[85] See *The Ladies' Companion*, 19 (New York, 1843), p. 61; Alexander Campbell (compiler), *The Millenial Harbinger*, third series, 1 (Bethany, VA, 1844), p. 96. Both printings of this two-stanza poem are prefaced by the following text: 'It is somewhere stated that Mozart having completed his Requiem, desired his daughter to sing a favorite melancholy song; and while she was singing his spirit took its flight to the world of the spirits.'

[86] Nikolay Andreyevich Rimsky-Korsakov, *My Musical Life*, trans. Judah A. Joffe (New York, 1972), p. 367.

performed on stage on the piano, and off stage fully orchestrated (as he imagines it), representing the perfectly behaved nineteenth-century Requiem worshipper (albeit a murderous one) who can marvel at Mozart's genius and can immediately understand the full musical potential of the incomplete work; the slow, portentous performance ($\downarrow = 40$) epitomizes the work's acquired momentousness; the simultaneous presentation of original and piano reduction captures in microcosm the copious variations to which the Requiem was subjected musically as well as narratologically (see Chapter 3); and the swan song, a nineteenth-century constant, is dramatized in the clearest possible way, Mozart performing his Requiem between taking Salieri's poison and succumbing to its effects. V. V. Yastrebtsev did not especially enjoy the first performance of *Mozart and Salieri* on 10 March 1899, but considered the Requiem one of the few moments that 'produced a profound impression'; for V. V. Stasov two years later, the recitative preceding the Requiem 'is the finest … created by Rimsky-Korsakov thus far' – not coincidentally, we can assume, because 'its poetic spirit and mood … is strikingly close to the spirit of the music which opens the *Requiem*'.[87] Mozart's Requiem was, indeed, a work to which the nineteenth century aspired.

The Requiem legend in the twentieth century

The Requiem legend, comprising the confluence of music and biography with fictional and quasi-fictional additions, has continued to exert an influence since 1900, especially in popularly orientated publications and media. In 1903, romanticism lingering in the air, magazines report Mozart '[dropping] still singing into the sudden grave … his "Requiem" [floating] out to us through its closing doors', writing 'not an art-work for Life-purposes, but a personal expression involuntarily uttered as the Valley of the Shadow of Death loomed into view', and witnessing a messenger 'who seemed to bring his commission from another world'; the claim about the messenger reappears in 1911 and 1912 to reveal Mozart's purported eccentricity and his supposed realization that 'the hand of death [was] upon him'.[88] In 1925, narrative licence is re-invoked in a dramatized account of

---

[87] V. V. Yastrebtsev, *Reminiscences of Rimsky-Korsakov*, ed. and trans. Florence Jonas (New York, 1985), pp. 226–7, 517.

[88] See 'The Young Mozart', *Academy and Literature*, 1607 (21 Feb. 1903), p. 181; Rutland Boughton, 'Meditation in the Study', *The Musical Standard*, 19 (14 March 1903), p. 161; 'A Lecture on Mozart', *The Musical Standard*, 20 (24 Oct. 1903), p. 259; Henry F. Gosling, 'Music

the final-day rehearsal: 'the effort [of singing] was too great: the manuscript slipped from his nerveless hand and he fell back speechless with emotion'.[89] And in 1936, in an article on phobias, illusions and delusions, a 'tormented' Mozart is said to have experienced 'one of the most horrible obsessions suffered by man . . . a "dreadful fixed idea, a truly insane hallucination," as a friend described it', namely being required to write his own requiem.[90]

Marcia Davenport and Annette Kolb, two writers from the 1930s who freely traverse the fact–fiction continuum in their accounts of Mozart's life, also foreground and dramatize the Requiem legend. For Davenport, Mozart 'stood looking after him [the messenger who came to commission the work], trembling with surprise and with a vague sense of terror – a strange sort of fright, almost premonitory'. He then reacted feverishly to learning that a requiem mass was desired:

Suddenly there seemed no breath in Wolfgang's body. A cold wind, on this hot afternoon, seemed to stab him, coming from – nowhere [. . .] He looked out of the window, whistled at the canary, settled his hair before the window. But the thing was there. It wasn't a thing really. Nonsense. It wasn't a man either. Damn it . . . it was *something*. You couldn't shrug off a thing like this. It was in the room. Finally he gave up. He might as well stop trying to control his poor tired mind. *The thing was a message from the other world. A call from Death.*[91]

The straightforward account of Walsegg's involvement was not known to Mozart, Davenport explains, but would not have been accepted by Mozart had it been told to him in any case: 'For him the experience was unearthly and otherworldly.'[92] Understanding the intense psychological web ensnaring Mozart is, for Davenport, fundamental to appreciating the music of the Requiem:

Of all the motives that provided fuel to create this burning thing [the Requiem], his feeling for death was the clearest. He was about to die and he was writing a requiem for himself. That is simple. The rest is a matter of hearing the terrific beat of life moving by [the 'Quam olim Abrahae' fugue] . . . knowing the meaning of the strings

and Eccentricity', *Cremona: The Magazine of Music*, 5 (Nov. 1911), pp. 118–23, at 120; Gustav Kobbé, *The Loves of Great Composers* (London, 1912), p. 27. For more early twentieth-century manifestations of the Requiem legend in popularly orientated publications see 'Premonitions of Death', *London Journal*, 9 (1910), p. 544; S. K. Ludovic, 'Artists and Musicians', *The Strand Magazine*, 27 (April 1904), pp. 424–32, at p. 428; Louie Gray-Heald, 'The Musician's Mecca [Vienna]', *The English Illustrated Magazine* (Feb. 1911), pp. 439–49, at 439–40.

[89] Harriette Brower, *Story-Lives of Master Musicians* (London, 1925), p. 85.

[90] William Wolf, 'Are you Sane? Mental Quirks Produce Strange Behavior', *Popular Science Monthly* (Dec. 1936), pp. 25, 123–4, at p. 123.

[91] Marcia Davenport, *Mozart* (New York, 1932), pp. 358–9 (italics in original).   [92] Ibid., p. 360.

snarling upward [Dies irae] . . . [realizing] that those who do not know tears do not know anything [Lacrymosa].[93]

In Kolb's account too the legend's psychological dimension crucially affects our understanding of the music. Mozart was 'haunted by the thought of the man who had commissioned the *Requiem*', who 'became in his imagination a messenger from another world'. Obsessed by the Requiem, he nevertheless has a transcendental experience: 'His farewell from life was that of a martyr; but his death was that of a conqueror. The *Requiem* affords proof of this: that graceful elegy is pervaded with the security, the confidence, the indestructible peace of his spirit, far removed from the terrors that pervade the *Qui Tollis* of his Mass in C minor.'[94]

As in the nineteenth century, the Requiem legend asserts itself in explicitly fictional works as well as in critically orientated books and magazines. In 1923, Hans Duhan (1890–1971), the Austrian baritone, conductor and composer, premiered his comic opera *Mozart* at the Vienna Volksoper, setting Mozart's death in Act 3 to the music of the Requiem.[95] Five years later, the US playwright and novelist Thornton Wilder (1897–1975) dramatized the Requiem's commissioning in a short, three-person playlet, *Mozart and the Gray Steward*. Mozart is asked by the ominous steward, who is dressed like 'an elegant undertaker', to write anonymously, and thereby guesses that Count Walsegg is the man behind the commission. Believing desperately that he is writing the Requiem for himself nonetheless, Mozart falls asleep and dreams of the steward's return. This time the steward informs him: 'It is Death itself that commands you this Requiem. You are to give voice to all those millions sleeping, who have no one but you to speak for them. There lie the captains and the thieves, the queens and the drudges, while the evening of their earthly remembrance shuts in, and from that great field rises an eternal *miserere nobis*.'[96] Thus the Requiem, as well as representing a psychologically charged symbol of Mozart's own impending death, comprises a musical symbol of death in general, just as it did in the nineteenth century.

The Requiem has also featured prominently in Mozart-related films, beginning with the short silent film *La mort de Mozart* (1909) from Louis

---

[93] Ibid., p. 373.

[94] Annette Kolb, *Mozart*, trans. Phyllis and Trevor Hewitt (London, 1939). See the edition from Prion Books (London, 1998), pp. 302, 319–20.

[95] For a review of the premiere, see Paul Bechert, 'Vienna', *Musical Times*, 64 (Sept. 1923), p. 651.

[96] See A. Tappan Wilder (ed.), *The Collected Short Plays of Thornton Wilder* (New York, 1998), vol. II, pp. 57–62, at 62, and R. E. R., 'Thornton Wilder's Plays', *Bookman*, 75 (Dec. 1928), pp. 187–8.

Feuillade. Interrupted by the messenger when playing music with a friend, Mozart imagines writing the Requiem for himself and collapses in horror. After a doctor attends to him and he wakes, he acquires manuscript paper and composes swiftly. With friends present, Mozart conducts the Requiem but breaks down in exhaustion and dies; as in the nineteenth century, the Requiem is dramatized as his swan song.

The psychological torment wrought by the Requiem is further explored in Karl Hartl's *Wen die Götter lieben* (Austria, 1942).[97] Back in Vienna following *Don Giovanni* in Prague (where Mozart finally realizes he was wrong to retain his love for Aloysia), Mozart returns home to Constanze to find a visitor waiting dressed in black, with ghostly white hair and a bleached appearance; the visitor is mysterious, vacant and resigned. Mozart asks hopefully if he wishes to commission a quartet from him, or a piece for a wedding; no, the visitor replies, a requiem. Meanwhile, at a rehearsal of *Die Zauberflöte*, Schikaneder is frustrated that parts of the work are still incomplete and goes to visit Mozart. Seeing the Requiem at Mozart's piano, Schikaneder tries to replace it with a score of *Die Zauberflöte*, provoking one of the mild-mannered Mozart's only angry reactions in the film. Schikaneder tries to cheer up Mozart, but to no avail – Mozart is preoccupied with his Requiem. Mozart then tries to compose *Die Zauberflöte*, but quickly turns to the Recordare from his Requiem instead. As the Recordare plays he recollects scenes from his youth (playing games outside, bidding an emotional farewell to his mother, performing at famous courts as a child accompanied by his father), with images representing these recollections projected in the dark, silhouetted space occupied by his head. After a visit from a young and troubled Beethoven – the musical torch passed from the mighty figure of one generation, who admits to being old and tired (albeit at only thirty-five), to the mighty figure of the next – Mozart is seen composing in bed, with Süssmayr helping at his side.[98] Friends come to visit, including Sophie Weber and Aloysia, and musicians congregate, whereupon Süssmayr gives Mozart the score of the Requiem. After imagining the performance of *Die Zauberflöte* taking place elsewhere in Vienna at that time, Mozart feebly conducts two singers and four instrumentalists in a performance of the 'Confutatis maledictis' portions

---

[97] *Wen die Götter lieben* was re-issued on DVD in 2006, together with a film, *Unsterblicher Mozart* (directed by Alfred Stöger in 1954), comprising scenes from several Mozart's operas: see *Unsterblicher Mozart: Jubiläumsedition zum 250. Geburtstag*, Arthaus, 501242. (No English subtitles are available on this DVD.)

[98] Beethoven was not in Vienna in 1791, moving there from Bonn in November 1792. He may have played for Mozart during an earlier visit to Vienna in spring 1787.

of the Confutatis. (The other portions occur in Mozart's imagination.) At the second 'Voca me' Mozart puts his hands down on the score and dies; the 'Oro supplex' sequence is then heard as Constanze rests her head on her dead husband's body.

Mozart dies not only in action, his swan song on his lips in a dramatized account of the purported final-day Requiem rehearsal, but also greatly revered by the musicians and friends in attendance (as well as by Beethoven in the previous scene); they mark his passing by remaining completely motionless, one eventually telling Constanze that Mozart will live on in his 'immortal works' ('unsterbliche Werke'). The frozen figures are representatives of us all, paying homage to Mozart, just as Mozart has in effect paid homage to himself through the 'worthy monument to his name' (Rochlitz). Here, as in the ponderous and dejected two-minute performance by the dark-clad messenger (seen ominously from behind, then from a distance and finally close up) and in the psychological linkage of life and death in the Recordare scene, we are offered compelling celluloid interpretations of key components of the Requiem legend, even if key components are only in our collective imagination.

Peter Shaffer and Milos Forman's *Amadeus* (1984) contains the best-known appearance of the Requiem in film, blending Mozart the man and Mozart the myth, and Mozart's musical activity and the reception of his music even more adventurously than *Wen die Götter lieben*. The concurrent composition of the Requiem and *Die Zauberflöte* shown in the film, though certainly incorrect, nonetheless provides close musical juxtapositions that dramatize Mozart's knack of composing strongly contrasting works near-simultaneously. (The piano concertos in D minor, K. 466, and C major, K. 467, the string quintets in C, K. 515, and G minor, K. 516, and the symphonies No. 40 in G minor, K. 550, and No. 41 in C, K. 551 are famous examples.) But by the time we reach the dictated composition of the Confutatis, a scene that replaces the final-day rehearsal dramatized in both *La mort de Mozart* and *Wen die Götter lieben*, the Requiem is Mozart's exclusive concern.[99] So much here is fictional: Mozart did not dictate this movement to anyone, let alone Salieri, and the hand of Salieri is not evident anywhere on a Requiem manuscript; Mozart was not himself responsible for

---

[99] The dictation scene – original to the film, having not featured in Peter Shaffer's play – is the scene most often praised by scholars. See Melanie Lowe, 'Claiming Amadeus: Classical Feedback in American Media', *American Music*, 20/1 (2002), pp. 102–19, at 108; Jon C. Tibbetts, 'Faces and Masks: Peter Shaffer's *Amadeus* from Stage to Screen', *Literature-Film Quarterly*, 32/3 (2004), pp. 166–75; Paul Corneilson, 'Mozart as a Vocal Composer', in Simon P. Keefe (ed.), *The Cambridge Companion to Mozart* (Cambridge, 2003), pp. 118–30, at 127.

writing a number of the parts dictated to Salieri in the opening bars (the bassoons, trombones, trumpets and timpani);[100] and he did not even complete all the parts in a particular passage at one time in his orchestral and vocal works as the film sequence suggests, preferring instead first to write down on the appropriate staves of the eventual full score a continuous draft comprising the most significant instruments and voices (for the Confutatis, the vocal parts and bass line throughout, the first violins in bars 7–12 and 17–48, the second violins from bar 38, beat 4, to bar 40 and the bassethorns and bassoons in bars 26–9), and then to return to the score to complete it. In the case of the Confutatis, as well as the Kyrie fugue, Dies irae, Tuba mirum, Rex tremendae, Recordare, Domine Jesu Christe, Hostias and first eight bars of the Lacrymosa, Mozart died before being able to do so. Yet the film sequence offers genuine insight not only into how a Mozart score is layered, how parts fit together, interact, and complement one another, but also into the urgency with which Mozart was so often required to work in order to meet a tight deadline.[101] Shaffer and Forman's Salieri, like the static figures in Mozart's room acknowledging his death in *Wen die Götter lieben*, is a representative of us all – in his case in awe at the creative mind at work, with which he struggles to keep up. Some people will also want to see him as a kind of stand-in for Süssmayr on account of his bewilderment ('No, no … I don't understand!'), or will interpret his role as deliberately rubbing out Süssmayr's involvement. Nearly forty years after Mozart's death, in 1827, Constanze reported her husband 'often' saying to Süssmayr 'Oy – there you are again at a complete loss [*die Ochsen wieder am Berge*]; you are far from understanding that.'[102]

As a comment on how our collective constructions of the Requiem legend have fundamentally shaped understandings of Mozart's life and works after his death, it is highly pertinent that the Lacrymosa is the soundtrack's centrepiece at the end of Salieri's narrative. From the moment when Constanze and Salieri realize that Mozart is dead up to the final image of the wrapped body in the pauper's grave, we hear the entire movement.[103]

---

[100] The material Mozart dictates to Salieri for the strings in unison actually appears only in the organ and bass line in his hand in the autograph.

[101] A good illustration of Mozart rushing to complete a work – with speedier notation in the finale, for the most part, than in the first movement – appears in the autograph score of the Piano Concerto No. 23 in A, K. 488; see the high-quality facsimile Wolfgang Amadeus Mozart, *Klavierkonzert A-dur KV488: Faksimile nach dem Autograph MS. 226 im Besitz der Musikabteilung der Bibliothèque Nationale de France, Paris* (Munich, 2005).

[102] Wilhelm A. Bauer and Otto Erich Deutsch (eds.), *Mozart: Briefe und Aufzeichnungen, Gesamtausgabe*, vol. IV: *1787–1857* (Kassel and New York, 1963), p. 491. On the translation of this sentence, see Chapter 5.

[103] Bizarrely, in his highly charged attack on *Amadeus* ('Mozart as Midcult: Mass Snob Appeal', *The Musical Quarterly*, 76 (1992), pp. 1–16, at 12), Joseph Horowitz claims that 'Other than five

Like the priest reacting to the end of Salieri's confession, desolate and with head bowed, how can we fail to be moved by the tale told, music and biography in perfect harmony as Mozart writes his own epitaph (a Lacrymosa, 'day of weeping', after all)? All is not so simple, though, as we know he did not write it himself, not beyond bar 8 at least, where Süssmayr took over. The combined weight of image and music at the end – Mozart's body in the ground accompanied by the emphatic 'Amen' plagal cadence – underscores a decisive first act in posthumous Mozart reception (Süssmayr's completion), a decisive first act by 'us' collectively in shaping Mozart's posthumous image. The transition in the film from Mozart alive to the reception of Mozart dead is seamless.[104]

We would be wrong, then, to regard all twentieth-century manifestations of the Requiem legend as unhelpfully arcane perpetrations of romantic legend (accepting that the legend itself has varied connotations and expressions in the nineteenth century), or as evidence of lazy preference for fictional aspects of the story over hard-and-fast 'facts'. For the Requiem legend can brightly illuminate the fact–fiction continuum that is intrinsic to our collective understandings of the work; divisions between traditional 'scholarly' and 'popular' points of focus can be transcended by an interpretation (as in *Amadeus*) that is simultaneously relevant to both.

The Requiem's status as locus of inspiration for cultural activities beyond music's exclusive remit can also be partially attributed to the Requiem legend's ability to stimulate and consolidate artistic creativity. Although the Requiem is acknowledged as un-conducive to dance,[105] it has still featured repeatedly in dances of the last twenty-five years or so, an indication that choreographers choose it more for its potent musical signification of death in general (ultimately attributable to the Requiem legend) than for its explicitly musical qualities. In the process, Requiem legend and music inspire and support – and enhance spectators' appreciation of – the dance spectacle. Examples include Twyla Tharp's musings on death in her ballet with David Van Tiegham from the early 1980s,

minutes from the slow movement of the D minor piano concerto, which accompanies the closing credits, only one musical extract [from the *Don Giovanni* Act 2 finale] is heard at any length during the . . . film.' In actual fact, both the Confutatis and the Lacrymosa from the Requiem are heard complete.

[104] For more on *Amadeus*, see Simon P. Keefe, 'Beyond Fact and Fiction, Scholarly and Popular: Peter Shaffer and Milos Forman's *Amadeus* at 25', *The Musical Times*, 150 (spring 2009), pp. 45–53. (The two paragraphs above are adapted from pp. 51–2.)

[105] See, for example, the *New York Magazine* (25 March 1991), p. 64 (on the dancer Edward Stierle's 'Lacrymosa') and the choreographer Jean-Paul Comelin from the Ballet du Nord in Roubaix, France, as reported in Mary Clarke, 'Flirting with Failure', *The Guardian* (8 Feb. 1992), p. 21.

Jean-Paul Comelin's integration of contemporary dance and ballet techniques, Stewart Trotter's dance-drama on tribal war and peace, the Brazilian Grupo Corpo's *Orphanage Mass*, Vicente Saez's eight dancers inspired by Andalusian Catholicism, Birgit Scherzer's abstract dance for the Mozart bicentennial and most recently Emanuel Gat's *K. 626*, all of which are set primarily or exclusively to the Requiem.[106] The lure of the Requiem's music-biography synergy, transferred from composer to choreographer, has also resurfaced in dance. Edward Stierle's *Lacrymosa* (1988), as he explains himself, features 'a lot about what I was going through at the time'. He was diagnosed with HIV in 1988, while coming to terms with the long illness and death from AIDS of the Joffrey Ballet founder Robert Joffrey in the same year; Stierle died of AIDS in 1991 aged twenty-three.[107] The Requiem has also been used in non-Mozart-related plays and films such as Peter Nichols's *Passion*, Jean-Luc Godard's *Passion*, Jean Genet's posthumously discovered play *Splendid's* and Pier Paolo Pasolini's film *Teorema*,[108] testifying to its status as a prime musical marker of despair and sadness as well as death.

Conclusion

The Requiem legend can be understood to have a negative impact on the reception of the work only if the establishment of absolute 'facts' is rigidly privileged over broad-based enthusiasm for the mythical and the fictional. Tracing Requiem reception exclusively or primarily through scholarly developments would be misleading, not only because it represents just one portion of reception-related activity, but also because the fact–fiction

---

[106] For reports of these dances, see Dale Harris, 'How Tharp Stays Sharp', *The Guardian* (9 Dec. 1983), p. 15; Mary Clarke, 'Flirting with Failure', *The Guardian* (8 Feb. 1992), p. 21 and Jann Parry, 'Heartily Sick of the Cyclical', *The Observer* (9 Feb. 1992), p. 60 (on Comelin); Desmond Christy, 'Requiem for Future Imperfect', *The Guardian* (22 July 1993), p. A9 (on Stewart Trotter); Judith Mackrell, 'Grupe Corpo, Sadler's Wells', *The Guardian* (13 Oct. 1994), p. A14; Mackrell, 'Dance', *The Guardian* (1 June 1996), p. B11 (on Vicente Saez); and Stephanie Ferguson, 'Dance: Requiem, Grand Theatre Leeds', *The Guardian* (17 Feb. 2003), p. 20 (on Birgit Scherzer); www.nytimes.com/2008/03/27/arts/dance/27joyc.html (accessed 12 April 2011) (on Emanuel Gat).

[107] See the obituary in the *New York Times*, www.nytimes.com/1991/03/09/obituaries/edward-stierle-23-a-leading-dancer-with-joffrey-ballet.html (accessed 12 April 2011). In addition: 'His ballet apparently springs from the [Joffrey] company's suffering over Joffrey's prolonged illness and death'. See *New York Magazine* (25 March 1991), p. 64.

[108] See Michael Billington, 'Passion Play', *The Guardian* (14 Jan. 1981), p. 10 (on Nichols); Richard Roud, 'Shooting the Wind with Godard', *The Guardian* (1 April 1982), p. 13 (on Godard); *The Guardian* (22 June 1995), p. 2 (on Genet).

continuum, so warmly (if often unknowingly) welcomed, is a *sine qua non* where the Requiem is concerned. (We will never know for certain what verbal instructions, if any, Mozart issued to Süssmayr for the completion of the work, whether there was really a rehearsal at Mozart's bedside shortly before his death, whether Mozart thought he was writing the work for himself, etc.) Accepting that mysteries will remain involves accepting that mysteries can be positively embraced; they become part – even a major part – of the meaning of the work, a stimulus for writing fiction, for perpetrating myth, for processing performances. The fact–fiction continuum is energized in the nineteenth century by Requiem-inspired fictional accounts, by the promotion far and wide of the old Rochlitz-inspired story, and by a fixation with biographical-musical links; it is further animated in the twentieth century by popularly orientated criticism, plays, films and dance. Indeed, the extraordinary reputation accruing to the Requiem, notably from near-mythical nineteenth-century performances (repeatedly described as the best ever, as we shall see in Chapter 3), has depended precisely on musicians, audiences and critics processing their experiences in a manner unencumbered by hard-and-fast 'facts'.

First published in 1800, the Requiem became, in effect, a nineteenth-century work, which few encountered before 1800. It has resonated so vividly in our collective imagination that even in 1866 it seemed more a present than a historical work: 'the "Requiem" mass of Mozart belongs by right of its gracious melody, elaboration of harmony, and orchestral effect, to the present rather than to past time'.[109] In a similar vein, it was adjudged in 1902 to be one of Mozart's most influential works, 'reckoned with as a factor in the complexus of forces which is moulding the music of the new century'.[110] Its innumerable performances at funerals (see Chapter 3), where death is processed in the present, have lent the Requiem a present-ness of its own – the death of the musical genius blends with the death of the memorialized figure. Shrouded in myth that valorizes the inseparability of biography and music, the sublime individual artist fighting against his fate and the divinely inspired composition that ultimately transcends death, the Requiem hits a raw nerve. As if to encapsulate intense commitment to the work, a fund was established in Senftenberg, Bohemia, in 1857 to ensure that a yearly mass was said for Mozart in perpetuity, accompanied on every occasion by a performance of the Requiem, 'the loftiest

[109] *The Observer* (9 Dec. 1866), p. 3.
[110] Edward Dickinson, 'The Impress of Mozart on Musical History', *The Musical Standard*, 17 (1 Feb. 1902), p. 74.

composition we possess . . . of sacred music':[111] the Requiem Mozart wrote
for himself (so the legend goes) performed for him, without fail, every
year. It was one small community's gift to Mozart's Requiem and to the
musical future, symbolizing an adoration by so many that has continued
through to the present day.

[111] As reported in *The Musical World*, 35 (1857), p. 715.

The colourful reception of Mozart's Requiem in the nineteenth and twentieth centuries includes opinionated and passionate criticism and scholarship as well as the manifestations of the legend discussed in Chapter 1. For the most part, the critical issues considered most significant have remained the same since 1800. The work's aesthetic attributes and authorship have always been centre stage, the latter focusing on the extent of Mozart's involvement in the final movements and on the quality of Süssmayr's contributions. (Late twentieth-century completions of the Requiem, which are evaluated in Chapter 6, bring a new dimension to authorship debates.) Mozart's work on the Requiem has met with great acclaim, but Süssmayr's with both criticism and praise up to 1950, the criticism intensifying from the mid-twentieth century onwards. The Requiem legend, a less explicit influence on serious criticism than on popularly orientated work, nonetheless continues to make its presence felt.

Nineteenth-century critical discussion of the Requiem

Early criticism, to 1824

As with the fictions that accrue to Mozart's Requiem, all nineteenth-century critical roads relating to aesthetics and authorship lead back to Rochlitz, in this case not to his anecdotes, but to his review of the Breitkopf & Härtel edition in the *Allgemeine musikalische Zeitung* (1801).[1] His praise for the aesthetic qualities of the work carried out by Mozart is unstinting. The opening of the Introit achieves an 'extraordinary power, vigour and firmness'; the Dies irae is 'a strong, powerful, terrifying, frenziedly and fearsomely exciting chorus'; the Tuba mirum excels in its 'simply beautiful, natural melodies and modulations'; the Rex tremendae is an 'excellently worked, astonishingly reverent, exciting chorus full of dignity and power'; the Recordare is 'full of the loveliest and most charming' melodies, thoughts

---

[1] *Allgemeine musikalische Zeitung*, 4 (1801–2), cols. 1–11, 23–31 (the issue is dated 1 Oct. 1801).

and varied dissonances; the Confutatis is a 'shuddering, anxiously and horrifyingly exciting chorus'; the Domine Jesu is 'a great, intensely worked chorus' somewhat similar to the Introit; and the Hostias is full of 'beauty, gracefulness and gentle dignity'.[2]

Rochlitz also tackles Süssmayr's involvement in the completion of the Requiem, quoting at length Süssmayr's letter on the topic to Härtel (discussed in Chapter 5) and treating it with suspicion. He is happy to accept Süssmayr's role in the instrumentation of the work, given the errors he detects, but cannot countenance a larger compositional role, on account of the perceived qualitative discrepancy between Süssmayr's extant works and Mozart's Requiem. Rubbing salt in the wound, he thanks Süssmayr for even such a 'small and insignificant contribution to the completion'.[3] The Sanctus, Benedictus and Agnus Dei then receive as high praise as the earlier movements. The Lacrymosa contains 'a very pretty, picturesque, expressive modulation to F major [bars 15–19], completely devout in passion'. The 'true' Sanctus embodies 'perfectly elevated simplicity, splendour and dignity. What mortal has announced more powerfully the peace of infinity and its untold richness as it occurs here through the unison strengthened C [bar 6]?' The Benedictus is 'without doubt in the Requiem as well as in general . . . one of the most simple, most enjoyable, and completely enticing pieces, on account of the consistently prevailing light, comprehensible and natural melodies and harmonies'. The Agnus Dei, featuring more 'strange, distinguishing beauties', particularly pleased the reviewer for the 'noble, peaceful and wistfully expressive' material first heard at bar 10, representing a 'repeatedly heartfelt plea for eternal peace'.[4] E. T. A. Hoffmann's famous description a few years later of Mozart's Requiem as 'the sublimest achievement that the modern period has

[2] Ibid., col. 6 ('ausserordentliche Kraft, Nachdruck und Festigkeit'); col. 9 ('ein starker, kraftvoller, Schrecken, Wuth und Schauder erregender Chor'); col. 10 ('Einfach schöne natürliche Melodien und Modulationen'); cols. 10–11 ('vortrefflich gearbeiteter, staunende Ehrfurcht erregender Chor . . . voll Würde und Kraft'); col. 23 ('Voll der lieblichsten und anmuthigsten'); col. 24 ('Ein Schauder, Angst und Entsetzen erregender Chor'); col. 26 ('Ein grosser, stark gearbeiteter Chor'); col. 27 ('Schönheit, Anmuth und sanfter Würde').

[3] Ibid., col. 4 ('so kleinen und undeutenden Antheil an der Vollendung').

[4] Ibid., col. 25 ('eine sehr schöne, mahlerische, ganz die fromme Empfindung ausdrückende Modulation nach f dur'); col. 28 ('ein wirkliches Heilig, voll hoher Einfalt, Pracht und Würde. Welcher Sterbliche hat die Ruhe des Unendlichen und seine unermessliche Fülle kräftiger verkündet, als es hier durch das im Einklange verstärkte C . . . geschieht?'); col. 28 ('ohnstreitig sowohl im Requiem als überhaupt eins, wegen der durchaus darin herrschenden leichten, fasslichen und natürlichen Melodien und Harmonien, der einfachsten, gefälligsten und allgemein einschmeichelnden Tonstücke'); col. 29 ('eigenthümlich . . . auszeichnende Schönheiten', 'edle, rührende und sehnsuchtsvolle Ausdruck', 'wiederholten innigen Bitte um ewige Ruhe').

contributed to the church' is similar to Rochlitz in emphasizing the powerful, true, dignified and devotional qualities of the work.[5]

Clearly indebted to Rochlitz's review, an extended, little-known commentary on Mozart's Requiem was published over several issues of the *Correspondance des amateurs musiciens* in 1804 to coincide with the first French performance of the work by members of the Paris Conservatoire at the Église St Germain l'Auxerrois.[6] (The performance was originally scheduled for 30 November, as explained in a letter to the journal from Cherubini, Méhul and Gossec, but ultimately delayed until 21 December.)[7] It follows Rochlitz's plan, beginning with general information that includes scepticism about Süssmayr's claim to have played a major role in the completion, then progressing diachronically through the work and ending with a list of misprints in the Breitkopf & Härtel edition (the same as Rochlitz's list). Much of the admiring commentary is similar to Rochlitz: 'the astonishing force and vehemence' of the Dies irae; the expressiveness of the Rex tremendae, which is 'full of dignity' and 'inspires respect and veneration'; the Confutatis chorus that 'inspires anxiety and terror' until we are 'reassured and in a way consoled' by the 'Voca me'; the 'intensely worked' Domine Jesu; the 'noble and touching vocal phrases where the voices ask for eternal rest' in the Agnus Dei.[8] But at other times the review is discernibly original. At 'Oro supplex' in the Confutatis, for example: 'Never has music known better how to dispose our souls towards pious contemplation and express with more truth the sentiments of profound devotion and

---

[5] On Hoffmann's references to Mozart's Requiem, situated in the context of the emergence of the new religious music, see Kramer, 'Early German Reception of Mozart's Requiem', pp. 86–7. For the quotation, see Charlton (ed.), *E. T. A. Hoffmann's Musical Writings*, p. 370. Ignaz Arnold remarks similarly in 1803 that Mozart's Requiem is the best example of 'elevated church style' ('erhabenen Kirchenstils') in *Mozarts Geist: Seine kurze Biographie und ästetische Darstellung seiner Werke* (Erfurt, 1803), p. 422.

[6] See *Correspondance des amateurs musiciens rédigée par le citoyen Cocatrix suivie de la Correspondance des professeurs et amateurs de musique* (1802–5) (reprint Geneva, 1972), cols. 708–11 (5 Nov. 1804), 724–5 (10 Nov. 1804), 734–5 (17 Nov. 1804), 742–3 (24 Nov. 1804), 750–2 (1 Dec. 1804), 757–8 (8 Dec. 1804), 766–7 (15 Dec. 1804), 773–5 (22 Dec. 1804), 783–4 (29 Dec. 1804).

[7] Ibid., cols. 743–4.

[8] Ibid., col. 734 ('un choeur en re mineur d'une force et d'une véhémence étonnante'); col. 742 ('pleine de dignité', 'inspire le respect et la vénération'); col. 750 ('inspire l'inquiétude et l'effroi', 'tranquillisé et en quelque sorte consolé'); col. 758 ('fort travail'); col. 774 ('l'expression noble et touchante des phrases de chant où les voix demandent le repos éternel'). The review of the Paris Conservatoire performance in the 29 December 1804 issue of the same journal notes that all movements conveyed the appropriate sentiments and variety of expressions, and that the performance demonstrated a level of perfection that the audience perhaps did not have a right to expect. See ibid., col. 782.

complete resignation.'[9] The reviewer counters suggestions that the harmonically complex 'Oro supplex' is impossible to perform properly by singers and orchestral musicians by citing the excellent rendition at the first general rehearsal for the Paris performance.[10] The Benedictus also shows Mozart's rare talent for rendering all four vocal parts musically significant, rather than just two or three as is all too often the case in vocal music: 'everything there is equally animated, and each one of the voices always a following melody, which, far from hindering the ensemble, only adds there a higher degree of interest'.[11]

Rochlitz's and the *Correspondance* reviewer's laudatory comments on the concluding movements of the Requiem (those now known to be Süssmayr's) are the first but by no means the last to record their popularity in the early years of the nineteenth century. The *Allgemeine musikalische Zeitung's* report on the 1804 Paris Conservatoire performance notes the Lacrymosa (Süssmayr's movement from bar 9), Sanctus and Agnus Dei as three of the eight movements that had the 'greatest effect' on the public; the Lacrymosa, Benedictus and Agnus Dei are three among four that make the 'deepest impression' at the Leipzig performance in memory of General Macon in 1806.[12] The Benedictus was the only portion of the Requiem performed at London concerts in the first decade of the nineteenth century, after the London premiere of the entire work at the Theatre Royal, Covent Garden, in 1801; much later, it continued to receive high praise from the likes of Samuel Wesley and Ignaz Ritter von Seyfried.[13] It is difficult to determine how widespread knowledge of Süssmayr's involvement was in musical and critical circles at this stage. On the one hand, Otto Jahn and Hermann Abert tell us retrospectively that Mozart's and Süssmayr's different contributions were fairly well known at the performance of the Requiem in the Jahnscher Saal in Vienna on 2 January 1793, and that news travelled quickly to Munich and Prague, 'where at the first performance . . . no secret

---

[9] Ibid., cols. 750–1: 'Jamais la musique n'a mieux su disposer nos âmes à un pieux recueillement, et exprimer avec plus de verité les sentimens d'un profonde dévotion et d'une entière résignation.'

[10] Ibid., col. 751.

[11] Ibid., col. 774: 'tout y est également animé, et chacune des voix constamment un chant suivi, qui bien loin de contrarier l'ensemble, ne fait qu'y ajouter un plus haut degré d'intérêt'.

[12] *Allgemeine musikalische Zeitung*, 7 (1804–5), col. 249, and 9 (1806–7), col. 76.

[13] See Rachel Cowgill, '"Hence Base Intruder Hence": Rejection and Assimilation in the Early English Reception of Mozart's Requiem', in Cowgill and Julian Rushton (eds.), *Europe, Empire and Spectacle in Nineteenth-Century British Music* (Aldershot, 2006), p. 20, and Cowgill, 'Redeeming the Requiem: Themes in the Early English Reception of Mozart's Last Work', unpublished paper given at the Institute of Musical Research, London, 17 May 2007.

was made of the fact that the Sanctus was composed by Süssmayr';[14] contemporary writers across Europe also recognized Süssmayr's participation – especially his orchestration work – by including references to his letter printed in the *Allgemeine musikalische Zeitung*.[15] On the other hand, misinformation was rife. John Ashley's publication of the text of the Requiem, with accompanying biographical information (1801), claimed that Mozart 'finished it on the day of his death'; Jean-Baptiste-Antoine Suard reported (1804) that Mozart completed the work before the four weeks assigned to him by the stranger who commissioned it had elapsed; the first Paris edition of the Requiem (1805) prints translated extracts from Niemetschek's biography acknowledging an incomplete work but making no mention of Süssmayr's involvement; and Placidus Scharl reported received wisdom that Joseph Haydn completed it (1808).[16]

Where admiration for Mozart's orchestration of the Requiem is concerned, Rochlitz's review again leads the way, beginning with the observation that Mozart is the unsurpassed master in this domain. Examples in the Requiem include the trombones' three-note entry in bar 7 of the Introit, the bassethorns' reinforcement of the voices at the unison at 'Exaudi' in the Introit, the skilful transference of the cello's accompanimental figure to the melodic writing in the violins at the opening of the Recordare and (thanks at least in part to Süssmayr, although this was not recognized by Rochlitz) the distribution of wind, brass and string instruments in the 'Confutatis maledictis' and 'Voca me' statements at the opening of the Confutatis.[17] Other critics also commend the orchestration of the Requiem in the initial decades of the nineteenth century, including positive assessments of Süssmayr's work (even if not acknowledging it as such). While praise is often expressed in general terms – a product (in all likelihood) of listeners and critics

---

[14] Otto Jahn, *Life of Mozart* (1856), trans. Pauline Townsend, 3 vols. (London, 1891), vol. III, p. 366; Hermann Abert, *W. A. Mozart* (1919), trans. Stewart Spencer, ed. Cliff Eisen (New Haven, CT, 2007), p. 1315. See also *Allgemeine musikalische Zeitung*, 29 (1827), col. 520.

[15] Ernst Ludwig Gerber, *Neues historisch-biographisches Lexicon der Tonkünstler*, 4 vols. (Leipzig, 1812–14), vol. III, col. 481; *Harmonicon*, 1 (1823), p. 60; César Gardeton, *Bibliographie musicale de la France et de l'étranger* (Paris, 1822), pp. 377–8; Leopold Chimani, *Vaterländische Merkwürdigkeiten*, vol. V (Vienna, 1819), pp. 145–6; Carl Nicolai (ed.), *Magazin der Biographien denkwürdiger Personen der neuern und neuesten Zeit*, vol. III (Leipzig, 1817), p. 450.

[16] John Ashley, *The Requiem, or, Grand Funeral Anthem Composed by W. A. Mozart … as Performed under the Direction of Mr. John Ashley at the Theatre Royal, Covent Garden, during Lent 1801* (London, 1801), p. 5; Jean-Baptiste-Antoine Suard, 'Anecdotes sur Mozart' (Paris, 1804), given in Deutsch, *Documentary Biography*, p. 501; *Messe de Requiem par Mozart, executée pour la première fois à Paris par le Conservatoire de Musique* (Paris, 1805); Placidus Scharl, *Meine eines Mönches merkwürdige Lebensumstände* (Andechs, 1808), given in Deutsch, *Documentary Biography*, p. 512.

[17] *Allgemeine musikalische Zeitung*, 4 (1801), cols. 4, 5, 7, 23, 24.

articulating aural impressions rather than of critics analysing the score – it remains striking historical testimony. A report on an early Berlin performance (1805) praises the 'grandiose effect' ('pompösen Effekt') of the trombones in the 'marvellous' Benedictus (which follows the 'splendid' [*prächtige*] Sanctus), continuing that 'the complete winds stood out most praiseworthily through gentle treatment'.[18] To be sure the specific performers get credit here, but praise is also implied for Süssmayr. Peter Lichtenthal (1807) identifies the powerful support of the orchestra on the thrice-stated 'Rex' at the opening of the Rex tremendae as one of the moments that made his hair stand on end; he is equally impressed by the thunder of the timpani in the Sanctus.[19] For Ignaz Arnold (1803), nothing matches the devotional 'sublimity' ('Erhabenheit') of the Sanctus, which is achieved through 'the thunder of the timpani' and 'the trombones that sing with the vocal parts' as well as the prominent chorus.[20] He also praises orchestration carried out throughout the Requiem (including Süssmayr's involvement), such as the 'melancholy tone' of the bassethorns and bassoons and the 'wise economy' with which the trumpets and timpani are used, which accentuate their 'awe-inspiring grandeur'.[21] And a reporter at the music festival in Edinburgh (1819) finds that the 'grand and beautiful [instrumental] effects ... added an inexpressible charm to the music'.[22]

The years of the *Requiem-Streit*, 1825–1842

Collective uncertainty about who had written what in the Requiem, coupled with investment in the Requiem as Mozart's supreme masterpiece and swan song, led to heated controversy in the critical arena. Jacob Gottfried Weber, a professional lawyer well trained in musical matters, lit the touch paper in an article entitled 'Über die Echtheit des Mozartschen Requiem' (On the Authenticity of Mozart's Requiem) in the journal *Cäcilia* (1825). He began with the most provocative statement possible:

Of all the works of our marvellous Mozart, there is hardly one other that enjoys such general and idolized adoration as his *Requiem*.

---

[18] *Allgemeine musikalische Zeitung*, 7 (1804–5), col. 431 ('sämmtliche Blasinstrumente zeichneten sich durch sanfte Behandlung rühmlichst aus').

[19] Peter Lichtenthal, *Der musikalische Arzt* (Vienna, 1807), p. 192.

[20] Arnold, *Mozarts Geist*, p. 419 '(der Donner der Pauke', 'die mit den Vokalstimmen singenden Possaunen').

[21] Ibid., pp. 420–1 ('schwermüthige Ton', 'weise Oekonomie', 'schauerlichen Grossen').

[22] *The Edinburgh Magazine, and Literary Miscellany; A New Series of the Scots Magazine*, 5 (Edinburgh, 1819), p. 472.

But this is actually very striking, and we might almost say strange, as this work among all of them is without hesitation his most imperfect, his least complete – indeed, it can hardly really be called a work of Mozart.[23]

Weber was motivated above all by a desire to sort out fundamental discrepancies in accounts of authorship. He argues that Mozart left only sketches for the Requiem, that Süssmayr cobbled the Requiem together from these sketches – the final version thus representing largely his work rather than Mozart's – and that contradictions are consequently resolved between the reports of Rochlitz (in his anecdotes), Süssmayr (in his letter to Härtel) and Gerber (in his *Neues historisch-biographisches Lexicon der Tonkünstler*).[24] Confident in his belief that the Requiem is not authentic Mozart, Weber criticizes the music, including the 'gurglings' ('Gurgeleien') of the voices in the Kyrie and 'Cum sanctis' fugue, the inappropriately 'sweetened echoes' ('versüsslichende Anklänge') among first violin and wind instruments in the Tuba mirum, the 'unctuous' ('schmeichlerisch') expression in parts of the Confutatis and the movement's overly strong affective contrasts, the undesirably long reprise of the 'Quam olim Abrahae' fugue at the end of the Hostias and the 'insignificant' ('bedeutungslose') oscillation of high and low registers midway through the Hostias.[25]

If Weber's article is a product of uncertainty about authorship, it also reinforces a critical posture set by Rochlitz in his *Allgemeine musikalische Zeitung* review, namely speculative 'fact' and value-laden interpretation treated as mutually reinforcing features of a Requiem-related argument. (In a later contribution to the *Streit*, Weber accuses his opponents, in reaching conclusions about authenticity, of allowing laudatory aesthetic judgments about the Requiem to override historical – that is factual – judgments, without apparently recognizing that he does the same himself, but negatively.[26]) Rochlitz and Weber reach diametrically opposed positions about Mozart's and Süssmayr's involvement in the Requiem – both turning out to be wrong – on the basis of their respective views about the aesthetic strengths and weaknesses of the end product; absolute confidence in their aesthetic judgments enables Rochlitz to cast doubt on Süssmayr's

---

[23] Jacob Gottfried Weber, 'Über die Echtheit des Mozartschen Requiem', *Cäcilia*, 3 (1825), pp. 205–29: 'Von allen Werken unsers herrlichen Mozart, genieset kaum irgend Eines so allgemeines, so vergötternde Anbetung, als sein *Requiem*. Dies is aber eigentlich sehr auffallend, und beinah wunderlich zu nennen, indem grade dieses Werk ohne Anstand sein unvollkommenstes, sein wenigst vollendetes, – ja kaum wirklich ein Werk von Mozart zu nennen ist.'

[24] Ibid., pp. 211–14. [25] Ibid., pp. 216–17, 219, 221, 223–4, 224.

[26] Jacob Gottfried Weber, 'Weitere Nachrichten über die Echtheit des Mozartschen Requiem', *Cäcilia*, 4 (1826), pp. 257–352, at 320.

testimony in his letter and to attribute only an insignificant role to him in the completion of the work, and enables Weber to propose Süssmayr as the work's principal composer. In a similar vein, John R. Parker (1825) lauds the Requiem up to and including the Recordare, citing the 'terrour [*sic*] and dismay' of the Dies irae, the 'magnificent display of regal grandeur' in the Rex tremendae and the 'beautiful' Recordare 'which supplicates in the softest infexions [*sic*]', but then implies in his statement '[it] is too evident where the pen of our author was arrested' that nothing from the Confutatis onwards is by Mozart.[27]

It is right to suggest that '[nothing] less . . . than the integrity of Mozart's genius was at stake' for many participants in the *Requiem-Streit*.[28] Maximilian Stadler provides the decisive riposte to Weber in 'Vertheidigung der Echtheit des Mozart'schen Requiem' (Defence of the Authenticity of Mozart's Requiem) (1826), his text astutely shaped to achieve maximum rhetorical impact. He first establishes his credentials for evaluating Mozart's work in the Requiem, credentials designed to add gravitas to his ensuing arguments and pointedly *not* possessed by Weber: his friendship with Mozart; his assistance to Constanze and Nissen in compiling a catalogue of the manuscripts Mozart left at his death; his discoveries made from looking at Mozart's manuscripts, including 'the most exact knowledge possible of Mozart's handwriting'.[29] He then provides the meat of his response, endorsing the veracity of Süssmayr's letter to Härtel, identifying passages where Mozart added instrumental indications in the Domine Jesu and Hostias, explaining how copies of the work came into existence and offering information on the original manuscripts. Several of Weber's views are reiterated – reminding the reader why the reply is necessary – but quickly countered; Stadler also strengthens his position as a reliable witness by referring to his examinations of the original Requiem manuscripts.[30] Debate between Weber and Stadler rumbled on for a while, but their basic positions in regard to the ontological status of the work remained the same.[31]

---

27 John R. Parker, *Sketches of the Lives and Writings of Eminent Musical Characters* (Boston, 1825), pp. 57–85, at 82–3.

28 Wolff, *Mozart's Requiem*, p. 11.

29 As given in translation in ibid., section III ('Contemporary Documents'), pp. 149–50 (quotation at 150).

30 See ibid., pp. 150–2.

31 For additional articles by Weber, see *Cäcilia*, 4 (1826), pp. 257–352; *Cäcilia*, 6 (1827), pp. 133–53. For writings by Stadler, see *Nachtrag zur Vertheidigung der Echtheit des Mozart'schen Requiem* (Vienna, 1827) and *Zweyter und letzter Nachtrag zur Vertheidigung der Echtheit des Mozart'schen Requiem* (Vienna, 1827).

While in the short term the *Streit* put the authenticity of Mozart's Requiem under the microscope, in the long term it enshrined a belief remaining with Requiem scholarship to the present day (as we shall see below): that definitive information about who composed, completed or generally participated in what is attainable for the *entire* Requiem and that a precise ontological status for the work can consequently set an unshakeable foundation for critical activity and judgment. Given that some fundamental uncertainties will always remain part of our interpretative landscape where the Requiem is concerned, including the nature of instructions and materials (if any) that Mozart conveyed to Süssmayr for finishing it, this overly confident perspective solidifies the quixotic link between value-laden interpretation and 'fact'-based information mentioned above. To be fair to Stadler, he admits uncertainty about whether Süssmayr used any Mozart sketches in carrying out his work on the concluding movements. ('The widow told me that a few scraps of paper with music on them were found on Mozart's desk after his death, which she had given to Herr Süssmayr. What they contained, and what use Süssmayr made of them, she did not know.'[32]) But, arguing against Weber, he still describes the Requiem as Mozart's 'most perfect, his most finished [work], as far as he was able to execute it before his death, a work genuinely and purely Mozart's',[33] without exploring how a quality such as perfection can ultimately be achieved in an incomplete work, or how aesthetic evaluation only of Mozart's 'finished' work can be separated from aesthetic evaluation of the completed whole.

Johann Anton André, in his Requiem edition (1827), is similarly confident about appropriating 'fact' as a catalyst for interpretation. André identifies Mozart's and Süssmayr's contributions respectively with the letters 'M' and 'S' marked on the score – in rough and ready fashion, as explained in Chapter 3 – presumably so that the user can separate the work of the genius from the work of the mediocre completer. (He has little interest in Süssmayr, who is described merely as 'a friend of the household', and doubts Süssmayr's account of the completion process in the Härtel letter.[34]) Aesthetic judgment also supports an erroneous theory that Mozart began the Requiem in 1783:

For it is only … from the entry of the tenor solo 'Mors stupebit' [in the Tuba mirum] that I believe I hear those magical sounds that give Mozart's later

---

[32] Wolff, *Mozart's Requiem*, p. 152.   [33] Ibid., p. 150.

[34] See André's lengthy preface to his edition both for an explanation of the 'M' and 'S' indications and for his doubts about Süssmayr's letter, given in ibid., pp. 158–64 (quote at p. 162).

compositions their uniquely individual character, and which I fail to hear, on the whole, in everything before that point, except for the glorious introduction of No. 1, whereas they continue to resound unmistakably not only throughout the rest of the number (No. 3) but also in the following movements, up to and including bar 8 of the 'Lacrymosa' (No. 7).[35]

A number of writers found unpalatable the basic message coming out of the *Streit* – that Mozart was not responsible for substantial portions of the completed work – allowing perception of 'facts' associated with the Requiem's composition to be influenced by aesthetic judgments (following Weber, André and Rochlitz). Thus, William Ayrton comments in the *Harmonicon* (1824) that

[it] has always been understood, and never before denied, that the whole of the *requiem*, except the latter portion of the final movement, was the work of one vast genius whose name it bears, and it carries in every part of it, internal evidence of that fact. Had another written the *Recordare* or the *Benedictus*, the *Confutatis*, or the *Hosanna*, he would have burst out of obscurity, and put in his claim to immortality.[36]

Vincent Novello (1829) explains: 'The "Sanctus," "Benedictus," "Agnus Dei" and "Dona eis requiem" bear such internal proofs of their having been written by Mozart that I never for a moment believed they could have been produced by another composer, especially such an obscure writer as Süssmayr of whom nothing whatever can be shewn as having the least resemblance to the style of Mozart's Requiem.'[37] The *Harmonicon* still attributed the Sanctus to Mozart in 1826: 'The Sanctus is magnificent beyond expression; we only lament that Mozart was in such a hurry to conclude what he could have made so much more of.'[38] Joseph Warren comments in *The Musical World* (1839) that 'If Süssmayr composed this movement [the Benedictus] he must be as great a composer as Mozart; there is not a note in the *Benedictus* but what every one will say is Mozart's.'[39] J. S. from Trinity College, Cambridge, follows suit in *The Musical World* (1839): 'how any man has the face to claim it [the Benedictus], I can scarcely imagine. Is it believed among his own people that Sussmayer wrote it? If so, is he not looked up to as an equal to Mozart … ? Lastly, could any musician, after playing, hearing, or reading over the score of the *Benedictus*,

---

[35] Ibid., pp. 162–3.   [36] *Harmonicon*, 2 (1824), p. 42.

[37] Nerina Medici and Rosemary Hughes (eds.), *A Mozart Pilgrimage: Being the Travel Diaries of Mary and Vincent Novello in the Year 1829* (London, 1955), p. 129.

[38] *Harmonicon*, 4 (1826), p. 103.

[39] Joseph Warren, 'Mozart's Requiem', *The Musical World*, 12 (London, 1839), pp. 462–8, at 468.

withstand the conviction that no other than Mozart could have written it[?]'[40] And A. B. Marx (1825) is unable to countenance a compositional role for Süssmayr in the Agnus Dei: 'Who wants to attribute to him [Süssmayr] the violin figure, the three phrases "dona eis requiem"? If Mozart didn't write them, well now he who wrote them is Mozart.'[41]

Reactions to the *Streit* spread far and wide in the years after Weber's initial article, focusing on the key contributions of Weber, Stadler and André. François-Joseph Fétis, for example, brings the French up to speed in 1827.[42] He begins with information on the first publication of the work in 1800, translating an extended extract from Süssmayr's letter, warmly commends Süssmayr for his faithful adherence to Mozart's style throughout, his effective realizations of the accompaniment indications left by Mozart and his ability to be inspired by Mozart's genius even in the later movements of the work, and recognizes the widespread negative reaction to Weber's article in Germany (with which he is in agreement).[43] K. Ebers reflects on the explosive nature of Weber's article in A. B. Marx's *Berliner Allgemeine musikalische Zeitung* in 1825; Marx provides his own lengthy, broadranging responses to Weber later that year and the following year, countering individual criticisms voiced by Weber as well as addressing issues in new church music, the interlinking of a composer's music and spirit, and expressive individuality.[44] Carl Friedrich Zelter (with André's score to hand) writes disparagingly about 'jackass' Weber's article in a letter to Goethe (1827), explaining that the Benedictus – certainly by Süssmayr in his opinion – is an example of an accomplished man inspired to produce a work of greatness.[45] The *Harmonicon* (1828) notes the attention given to authenticity in the German press and the publication of the André edition, reproducing André's preface in translation; the preface is also published in

<hr>

[40] J. S., 'Mozart's Requiem: To the Editor of the Musical World', *The Musical World*, 12 (1839), p. 391.

[41] Adolph Bernhard Marx, 'Ueber Mozarts Requiem', *Berliner Allgemeine musikalische Zeitung*, 2 (1825), pp. 378–82, at 379: 'Wer mag jenem die Violinfigur, die drei Sätze "dona eis requiem" zuzuschreiben? Hat das Mozart nicht geschrieben, nun wohlan! so ist der, der es geschrieben, Mozart.'

[42] François-Joseph Fétis, 'Sur l'authenticité du Requiem de Mozart', *Revue musicale*, 1 (Feb. 1827), pp. 25–30.

[43] Ibid., pp. 26–9.

[44] *Berliner Allgemeine musikalische Zeitung*, 2 (1825), pp. 370–1, 378–82; 3 (1826), pp. 269–73. For a succinct assessment of Marx's contributions to the *Requiem-Streit*, focusing on ideas of transfiguration, see Kramer, 'Early Reception of Mozart's Requiem', pp. 90–1, 93–6.

[45] For a translation of the Requiem-related passage from Zelter's letter see *The Musical Standard*, 16 (28 Sept. 1901), p. 199. See also Lorraine Byrne Bodley (trans. and ed.), *Goethe and Zelter: Musical Dialogues* (Aldershot, 2009), pp. 378–80.

The Quarterly Musical Magazine and Review (1827) and *The Musical World* (1839).[46] And Carl Ferdinand Becker's articles on Gottfried Weber and Maximilian Stadler in a historical assessment of literature on music (1836) focuses nearly exclusively on their contributions to the *Requiem-Streit*, demonstrating that the two men's careers in musical scholarship were in effect defined by this exchange.[47] Georg Sievers provides a rich endorsement of Süssmayr's work on the Requiem in *Mozart und Süssmayr* (1829), also acknowledging the composer's opera *Der Spiegel von Arkadien* as a masterwork.[48] Either the Requiem is wholly by Mozart, Sievers argues, and Süssmayr only completed the instrumentation where it was missing, or Mozart's spirit descended from the heavenly realm in order to inspire Süssmayr as he finished the work; if the latter, Sievers continues, 'the whole world should kneel down in front of Süssmayr and worship if not him, then Mozart in him'.[49] No-one is magnanimous enough to mention Süssmayr's name admiringly, Sievers points out, in spite of his important work on the Requiem.[50] Joseph Mainzer in 1838 is similarly positive, explaining that Süssmayr finished the Requiem so well that it is difficult to tell 'where the work of the great master ended and where that of his friend started. The Benedictus from the Requiem is entirely by Süssmayr, and this number alone proves the loftiness of his conception and the nobility of his style.'[51] Nissen's biography (1828) makes no reference to the *Streit*, and only an oblique reference to Süssmayr's completion, via the anecdote from Sophie Haibel about Mozart's final-day Requiem-related instructions to Süssmayr.[52] Superlatives, though, appear throughout the volume: the Requiem is described *inter alia* as 'terrifyingly sublime', 'unsurpassable', 'everlasting', 'heavenly' and his 'swan song'.[53]

---

[46] *Harmonicon*, 6 (1828), pp. 101–3; *The Musical World*, 12 (1839), pp. 463–6; *The Quarterly Musical Magazine and Review*, 9 (1827), pp. 406–12.

[47] Carl Ferdinand Becker, *Systematisch-chronologische Darstellung der musikalischen Literatur von der frühesten bis auf die neueste Zeit* (Leipzig, 1836), cols. 137–8 and 524.

[48] Georg Sievers, *Mozart und Süssmayr* (Mainz, 1829), pp. 11–12.

[49] Ibid., p. 9: 'In letzterem Falle aber sollte die ganze Welt vor Süssmayr niederknien und, wenn auch nicht ihn, sondern Mozarten in ihm, anbeten.'

[50] Ibid., p. 10.

[51] Joseph Mainzer, *Esquisses musicales et souvenirs de voyage*, vol. I (Paris, 1838), p. 151: '. . . où le travail du grand maitre a cessé et où celui de son ami a commencé. Le *Benedictus* du Requiem est entièrement de Suessmayr, et ce numéro seul prouve et la hauteur de sa conception et la noblesse de son style.'

[52] Georg Nikolaus von Nissen, *Biographie W. A. Mozarts* (1828) (Hildesheim, 1991), p. 574.

[53] Ibid., pp. 547 ('furchtbar erhaben'); 595 ('unübertrefflich'); and Nissen, *Anhang zu Wolfgang Amadeus Mozart's Biographie* (1828) (Hildesheim, 1991), pp. 58 ('ewig'), 162 ('himmlisch'), 10 ('Schwanengesang').

As well as by reactions to Weber, Stadler and André, the years of the *Streit* are marked by the public re-emergence of the original Requiem manuscripts. Stadler sold the autograph of the first five movements of the Sequence to the Court Library in Vienna around 1829, having acquired it from a 'friend' in 1826; Joseph Eybler, the composer first entrusted with the completion of the Requiem, gave the Lacrymosa, Domine Jesu and Hostias to the same library in 1833, following a stroke he suffered when conducting the work. Finally, the score presented to Walsegg in early 1792 to fulfil the Requiem commission surfaced in 1838 among music he had owned at his death (1827); again it was sold to the Court Library.[54]

With the original manuscripts to hand, Ignaz von Mosel, curator of the music collections at the Court Library, immediately examined them in consultation with a panel of Viennese experts, with attention focused on the manuscript submitted to Walsegg. His resulting report, *Über die Original-Partitur des Requiem von W. A. Mozart* (1839), is historic in that it made all of the principal Requiem sources available together for the first time for consultation, evaluation and comparison.[55] Faced with incontrovertible evidence of Süssmayr's involvement in the Requiem completion – both hands were identified in the Walsegg score through comparison with other Mozart and Süssmayr autographs – Mosel had an ideal opportunity to assess Süssmayr's contribution in a fair, level-headed fashion. Instead, he takes every opportunity to undermine Süssmayr, steadfast in his belief that the autograph materials offer more rather than less evidence that Mozart came extremely close to completing the work. Mosel is baffled that a man of Stadler's repute could have validated the contents of Süssmayr's letter to Härtel, the credibility of which is 'destroyed' by its supposedly faulty assertion that Mozart wrote only the four vocal parts and occasional instrumental indications in the Sequence and Offertory.[56] Neither Stadler nor Constanze was fully aware of the work carried out by Süssmayr, Mosel explains, for example the use to which he put the 'small leaves of music' given to him by Constanze after Mozart's death. Like Rochlitz in his review in the *Allgemeine musikalische Zeitung* (1801), Mosel cannot countenance a substantive compositional role for Süssmayr. Thus, the Court Library in Vienna possesses '*All* in fact *that exists of the dying strain of Mozart in his handwriting*; what remains [that is, the Sanctus, Benedictus, Agnus Dei], if not from his *pen*, came, surely, by every principle of art, from his *brain*.'[57]

---

[54] For more see Wolff, *Mozart's Requiem*, pp. 12–13.

[55] Ignaz von Mosel, *Über die Original-Partitur des Requiem von W. A. Mozart* (Vienna, 1839); trans. in *The Musical World*, 34 (1856), pp. 292, 309–10, 324–5, 339–40, 356, 389–90.

[56] *The Musical World*, 34 (1856), pp. 389, 339.   [57] Ibid., p. 390 (italics in original).

Curiously, even the consecutive fifths in bar 4 of the Sanctus are considered too good for Süssmayr, 'the effect of which is softened, and almost annulled by the contrary motion of the first and second violins'. Mosel explains that they 'may have escaped the composer's attention in the ardour of writing, or may intentionally have been written by him as an exception that may well be permitted to such a master'.[58]

On the surface, then, Süssmayr is the fall guy in the *Requiem-Streit*. His words are criticized (by André, Mosel and others such as George Hogarth)[59] and his contributions marginalized (André, Mosel). Aesthetic, biographical and pragmatic agendas – a desire to hear the Requiem as Mozart's perfect swan song and (in André's case) to promote the historical significance of a commercial edition – dictate that it must be, in essence, Mozart's alone (or, in Weber's case, not really Mozart's at all); Süssmayr is consequently an unwelcome guest at the party. But when evaluation of the music *per se* is taken into consideration, Süssmayr can be seen to come out of the *Requiem-Streit* rather well, following on from the positive coverage he received prior to the *Streit*. For passages to which he is known to have contributed compositionally as well as in orchestration elicit explicit praise from the likes of Fétis, Sievers, Mainzer and Zelter. Those who refuse to believe he participated actively in the completion of the Requiem may allow aesthetic judgments to cloud 'facts', but the judgments themselves – paying Süssmayr the ultimate compliment of mistakenly attributing his work to Mozart – testify to the extraordinary aesthetic qualities that the Requiem in its entirety was seen to possess in the mid-nineteenth century. Ironically, even Weber, whose article kicked off the *Streit*, greatly admired the Sanctus and the Benedictus, the former for its 'very highest, completely dignified opening' and its 'indescribably effective C♮ at "Pleni"' and the latter for its 'wonderfully glorious, childishly devout and still so nobly elevated' qualities.[60]

1842–1900

The deaths of Constanze (1842) and Eybler (1846), following the deaths of Walsegg (1827) and Stadler (1833), brought the era of first-hand accounts of Mozart's Requiem to a close; the work entered a new phase in its reception

---

[58] Ibid., p. 324.

[59] See George Hogarth, *Memoirs of the Musical Drama*, 2 vols. (London, 1838), vol. II, p. 265.

[60] Weber, 'Über die Echtheit', p. 226 ('Allerhöchsten ganz würdigen Anfang', 'unbeschreiblich wirkenden C♮ bei "Pleni"', 'wunderherrliche, kindlich fromme und doch so edel erhabene Benedictus!').

history, marked by the end of the *Streit* and by the emergence of the original manuscripts into the public arena. On the whole, though, critical writings on the Requiem from 1842 to 1900 are characterized more by continuities with than by fundamental departures from preceding discourse, the *Streit* casting a long shadow.

Links between work and biography – evidence of the Requiem legend's influence – continue long after the *Streit* to assume prominence in nineteenth-century hermeneutic contexts. Edward Holmes's biography of Mozart (1845), for example, offers no new information about the work, focusing on well-known aspects of the Requiem legend.[61] When writing his biography Holmes was no doubt influenced by the experience of looking at the original Mozart manuscript in the late 1820s, when it was still in Stadler's possession. Holmes's assessment of compositional process and perception of biographical circumstance are directly aligned: 'In some of the passages, I thought I could discern a tremulousness in the marks, which seemed as if he apprehended life would be gone before he could make his thoughts eternal.' Furthermore, he was struck by 'the thin, sickly fingers that had pressed that paper, the pale anxious face that had been bending over it – how must Mozart have looked, and how felt, when penning the *Lachrymosa* [*sic*] and the *Rex tremendae*'.[62] G. A. Macfarren (1857) emphasizes the connection between biography and work in the preface to his account of the Requiem for the Sacred Harmonic Society, explaining at the end of his piece: 'In conclusion, there is but to revert to the circumstances under which Mozart's *Requiem* was produced, to ensure that every hearer will feel that in witnessing its performance he pays an act of peculiar homage to the genius of its author, – an act that cannot be paid irreverently.'[63] The *Authorized Report of the Church Congress Held at Dublin* (1868) describes the Requiem as 'conceived in such a spirit of solemn grandeur as might have been expected from one who felt that he was standing on the verge of eternity'.[64] And Filson Young (1898) interprets the Requiem as a duel between Mozart and the grim reaper:

---

[61] Edward Holmes, *The Life of Mozart, Including his Correspondence* (1845), ed. Christopher Hogwood (London, 1991), pp. 284–92. The same can also be said for Ludwig Nohl, *The Life of Mozart* (1863), trans. Lady Grace Wallace, 2 vols. (London, 1877), vol. II, pp. 276–308.

[62] Edward Holmes, *A Ramble among the Musicians of Germany* (London, 1828), pp. 132, 131–2.

[63] See G. A. Macfarren, *Requiem; Service for the Dead, the Music Composed in the Year 1791, by Wolfgang Amadeus Mozart, with an Analysis of the Work Written Expressly for the Sacred Harmonic Society* (London, 1857), pp. iii–v, 17, 24.

[64] *Authorized Report of the Church Congress Held at Dublin, on September 29th, 30th, October 1st, 2nd, 3rd 1868* (Dublin, 1868), p. 418.

We may regard it as a priceless jewel wrung from the very hands of Death, a monument of his [Death's] impotence utterly to destroy the better part of his victims . . . [Not] Death himself could bend that stout spirit, nor still the echoes of that solemn, kindly voice whose notes were lost to our ear only when they mingled with the jar of the closing gates.[65]

Writers in the second half of the nineteenth century also attest to the intense, personally felt impact of the work; the drastic action taken by the painter Rudolph Friedrich Watzmann after a performance in Dresden (see Chapter 1) is a case in point. And they often link it to Mozart's biographical situation. Thus the Requiem 'expresses the religious awe and mystery of his soul, his singular presentiment of death, his constant feeling of the Infinite', and 'is a symphonic and choral picture of the Last Judgment, dealing with its varied scenes, its hopes, its fears, with mighty power, and yet in a manner so human and impassioned as at times . . . to suspend the hearer between earth and heaven'.[66] Alexandre Oulibicheff (1843) is overcome by the Rex tremendae, the opening choral and orchestral exclamations depicting 'the glorious King who descends slowly from the skies, carried on the wing of the seraphim'.[67] For the *Observer* (1866), 'Nothing is more awful in its beauty than the opening movement, "Requiem aeternam" . . . How overwhelming in its majesty is the "Rex tremenda!" [*sic*] how plaintive the "Lacrymosa!"'[68] Macfarren's and Albert Hahn's surveys of the work (1857 and 1867) testify to the forceful impact of almost every movement.[69] For Young (1898), the 'flood of sound' in the Introit and Kyrie 'carries me clean away from the contemplation of finality; I recognise plainly and without dismay that fact which sometimes shocks me so much, namely: that the round world will roll merrily on even after I, who to myself am the centre of it, have gone; and never be a penny the worse'.[70] And for A. M., writing in the *Musical Standard* (in 1901, just into the new century), 'the tears never

---

[65] Filson Young, 'Mozart's Requiem', *The Musical Standard*, 10 (20 Aug. 1898), pp. 119–20, at 120.

[66] See *Graham's Magazine*, 40 (Philadelphia, 1852), p. 159; *Fraser's Magazine for Town and Country*, 47 (London, 1853), p. 579.

[67] Alexandre Oulibicheff, *Nouvelle biographie de Mozart*, 3 vols. (Moscow, 1843), vol. III, p. 443 ('. . . le Roi de gloire qui descend lentement des cieux, porté sur l'aile des séraphins').

[68] *The Observer* (9 Dec. 1866), p. 3.

[69] See Macfarren, *Requiem*, pp. 7–24 and Albert Hahn, *Mozart's Requiem. Zum besseren Verständniss bei Aufführungen mit einer neuen Uebersetzung nebst einem Nachtrage und den Resultaten eines Vergleiches der Breitkopf und Härtelschen Partitur mit den Original-Manuscripten der K. K. Hofbibliothek zu Wien* (Bielefeld, 1867), pp. 12–36.

[70] Young, 'Mozart's Requiem', p. 120.

fail to drop, even from men's eyes' when the Lacrymosa, 'a heart-piercing strain of mingled grief and pious resignation', is performed.[71]

The treatment of Süssmayr after the *Streit* is similar to his treatment during it, being characterized explicitly by marginalization and negativism but implicitly (and sometimes explicitly) by praise. Music journalists in Britain and America project an air of self-satisfaction in heralding resolution of authorship issues. *The Musical World* (1857) hails Süssmayr's claims to the Sanctus, Benedictus and Agnus Dei as 'now so triumphantly refuted', having three years earlier criticized Constanze for '[allowing] a pretender, called Sussmayer, to assume almost a partnership in what the world regarded as [Mozart's] greatest work';[72] the *Musical Examiner* (1843), garbling Mosel, reports cursorily that the 'true, original score' of the Requiem is in the Court Library in Vienna, and that '[in] this copy, every note is in Mozart's handwriting';[73] and *The United States Catholic Magazine and Monthly Review* (1846) identifies Süssmayr as a 'dishonest … plagiarist', whose case for composing the Sanctus, Benedictus and Agnus Dei was dismissed 'when a full score of the "Requiem" in Mozart's handwriting was discovered, and set at rest the question of authorship'.[74] A later article in *The Musical World* (1870) accuses Süssmayr of 'contradictions and untruths' in his letter to Härtel, claims his work up to the Sanctus as 'merely something almost entirely insignificant, as the first nine numbers were already entirely completed by Mozart', and attributes the 'grandiose commencement' of the Sanctus to Mozart, but considers the movement 'decidedly weaker' after that, featuring a 'very defectively carried out' fugue.[75] And Filson Young explains straightforwardly: 'It matters little to me whether it was Mozart's or Süssmayer's hand that actually wrote down the latter portion of this mass; I am convinced that the essence is all Mozart.'[76] Among serious critics, too, complacency occasionally rears its head: Macfarren dismisses Süssmayr's 'indecorous effrontery' in claiming the Sanctus, Benedictus and Agnus Dei ('three of the most beautiful movements') as his own, after it had been 'pretended that Mozart lived not to conclude this work'.[77] Macfarren

---

[71] A. M., 'Mozart's "Requiem" Mass', *The Musical Standard*, 16 (5 Oct. 1901), pp. 215–16, at 216.

[72] See *The Musical World*, 35 (1857), p. 43; *The Musical World*, 32 (1854), p. 233.

[73] *The Musical Examiner*, 1 (1843), p. 329.

[74] Charles White and M. J. Spalding (eds.), *The United States Catholic Magazine and Monthly Review*, 5 (Baltimore, 1846), p. 182.

[75] *The Musical World*, 48 (1870), p. 717. The editor tells us that this account is taken from 'another paper', and goes on to refute elements of it (pp. 717–18).

[76] Young, 'Mozart's Requiem', p. 120.   [77] Macfarren, *Requiem*, p. iv.

thereby circumvents authorship issues in his analysis and considers the Requiem, in effect, as a finished work by Mozart.

Criticism of the Sanctus, Benedictus and Agnus Dei as voiced by *The Musical World* (1870) is rare from 1842 to 1900, whereas evidence of their perceived esteem (associated with Süssmayr or not) is commonplace.[78] Oulibicheff (1843) regards them as inferior in small ways to the preceding movements – the 'Osanna' fugue is too short, for example – but not in important style-, idea- and colour-related respects.[79] Convinced that Süssmayr did not write these movements by himself, and that he used Mozart's written and/or unwritten instructions, Oulibicheff cannot in any case accept Süssmayr's involvement in the first part of the Sanctus: 'What grandeur! What solemnity! We get ready to listen with our whole soul, all ears, and everything is already finished. Who would have the generosity to gift these ten bars to Süssmayr? No-one has done so, not even Mr. Weber.'[80] The Benedictus, 'a prayer of soft and touching solemnity, a work of the most rare elegance and an admirable masterpiece of the polyphonic style', is also 'a lot for Süssmayr, in truth', and the Agnus Dei reveals Mozart's indelible compositional imprint.[81] Macfarren lavishes praise on all three movements, citing the C♮ at 'Pleni sunt' in the Sanctus, 'which amazes us with its unexpected introduction, and exalts us with its wondrous grandeur', the 'singularly exquisite' Benedictus, whose 'true eulogy is the ecstacy [*sic*] with which it fills everyone who hears it', and the 'intense pathos' of the Agnus Dei, which 'embodies the subtlest feelings of the soul'.[82] Other writers continue to claim that the Benedictus is simply too good to have been written by Süssmayr (although the 'Osanna' fugue 'might be written by any scholar, standing upon one leg'), or represents 'one of Mozart's most divine inspirations'; a 'Grand Musical Performance' at the Free Trade Hall in Manchester on 2 September 1846, featuring a huge programme of Haydn, Schubert, Bellini, Donizetti, Rossini, Mendelssohn and Handel, as well as Mozart, identifies as the 'sublimest piece of the evening … the selection

---

[78] The Lacrymosa (from bar 9) receives a lukewarm reception from Albert Hahn; he ostentatiously records (in bold font) the moment that Mozart's work ended. The Sanctus, Benedictus and Agnus Dei, in contrast, are positively received. See Hahn, *Mozarts Requiem*, pp. 28, 34–5.

[79] Oulibicheff, *Nouvelle biographie*, vol. I, p. 247.

[80] Ibid., vol. I, pp. 247 and 248: 'Quelle grandeur! Quelle solennité! On s'apprête à écouter de toute son âme, de toutes ses oreilles, et déjà tout est fini. Qui aurait la générosité de faire cadeau de ces dix measures à Süssmeyer? Personne ne l'a eue, pas même Mr. Weber.'

[81] Ibid. vol. III, pp. 450–1: 'Au total, le *Benedictus* est une prière d'une solennité douce et touchante, un travail de la plus rare élégance, et un admirable chef-d'oeuvre du style polyphonique. C'est beaucoup pour Süssmeyer, en vérité.'

[82] Macfarren, *Requiem*, pp. 21, 22.

from Mozart's Requiem, consisting of the "Sanctus" (chorus), the "Benedictus" (quartet) and the "Hosanna" chorus … The solemn pealing shouts of multitudes, as if scattered over a vast plain, sending their mingled praises up to the Lord God of Sabaoth, realised in massive grandeur what the composer appears to have aimed at.'[83] Richard Wagner, a great admirer of the Requiem, was particularly fond of the Benedictus as well as the Recordare.[84]

Otto Jahn's magisterial Mozart biography (1856) and an incisive book by William Pole (1879) are the two highpoints of Requiem scholarship in the mid to late nineteenth century.[85] Jahn is sympathetic towards Süssmayr and circumspect in speculating about the composition of the final movements: 'It must be allowed … that Süssmayr's share in the work [up to the end of the Offertory] has been on the whole successfully performed; it is quite in keeping with the rest, and he has plainly refrained from making any alterations or surreptitious interpolations.'[86] The Sanctus, while 'not on the whole equal to the best of the preceding movements', features an 'animated, vigorous, and faultlessly concise' fugue that offers 'nothing against the supposition that Mozart might have written it'; the Benedictus, following Zelter, is beautiful and excellent, but is not by Mozart (although Jahn believes that Mozart sketches were used for both the Sanctus and the Benedictus); and the Agnus Dei 'displays the perfect mastery of the musician', thus betraying Mozart's involvement.[87] He is mildly critical of Süssmayr on occasion, citing orchestration at the end of the Tuba mirum and heavy instrumentation in the Lacrymosa, and also of Mozart in the Tuba mirum, a movement that 'fails to rouse in us a sense of the grandeur and elevation which belong to the subject'.[88] Overall, though, Jahn testifies eloquently to the Requiem's nineteenth-century status as a compelling masterpiece, drawing attention to the 'overpowering' effect of the opening of the Rex tremendae, the 'union of loveliest grace with chaste severity and earnest depth of thought' in the Recordare, where 'we despair of reproducing in words anything but a mere skeleton of the beauty of this wonderful

---

[83] 'Mozart's Requiem: How Much His?', *Orchestra*, 12 (1869), pp. 394–5, at 395; *The Manchester Guardian* (9 Dec. 1866), p. 3; *The Manchester Guardian* (5 Sept. 1846), p. 9.

[84] See Martin Gregor-Dellin and Dietrich Mack (eds.), *Cosima Wagner's Diaries*, vol. II: *1878–1883*, trans. Geoffrey Skelton (New York, 1977), p. 360. On 9 Dec. 1880 Cosima records Wagner playing through the Benedictus for friends (ibid., p. 493).

[85] Pole carried out his Requiem work at least a decade before it was published in book form as *The Story of Mozart's Requiem* (London, 1879). Its contents are serialized in *The Musical Times*, 14 (1869), pp. 39–41 (April), 71–4 (May), 103–7 (June), 137–9 (July), 167–70 (Aug.).

[86] Jahn, *Life of Mozart*, vol. III, p. 386.   [87] Ibid., vol. III, pp. 388, 389, 390.

[88] Ibid., vol. III, pp. 365, 380.

quartet', and the 'succession of harmonies such as no mortal ear had ever heard' in the 'Oro supplex' (Confutatis), where 'we feel a breath of the immortality which had already touched the brow of the master as he wrote'.[89]

Jahn's conclusion is an interpretative *tour de force*:

that full, unfettered devotion which is the indispensable condition of genuine artistic production is never disturbed, but human emotion, religious belief, and artistic conception go hand in hand in fullest harmony. On this unity rests the significance of the Requiem, for on this ground alone could Mozart's individuality arrive at full expression, and – working freely and boldly, yet never without consciousness of the limits within which it moved – produce the masterpiece which reveals at every point the innermost spirit of its author. In this sense we may endorse his own expression, that he wrote the Requiem for himself; it is the truest and most genuine expression of his nature as an artist; and is his imperishable monument.[90]

The Requiem, then, is Mozart's complete musical statement (though an incomplete work), Jahn succinctly reconciling troublesome ontology with transcendent status. Mozart wrote it for himself not only in sensing impending death but also in promoting his 'innermost' artistic spirit through the work's emotional, religious and artistic unity: biography and music are perfectly aligned. Indeed, for Jahn, appreciating Mozart's biographical situation is essential to recognizing the work's remarkable qualities (the 'expression of his nature as an artist ... his imperishable monument'). By highlighting the transcendental status of the work and the inseparability of biography and music in an interpretative context, Jahn captures in microcosm much of the spirit of nineteenth-century popular and scholarly Requiem reception.

Like Jahn's commentary, Pole's *The Story of Mozart's Requiem* is detailed and thoughtful, providing a more fluent and coherent account of the work than Albert Hahn's book published a few years earlier.[91] Apart from its value as a musical composition, Pole informs us, the Requiem is significant for its extraordinary history, which is 'like a novel, the interest of which hangs on a mystery only revealed in the last chapter'.[92] Pole proceeds to tell this story, covering separately the work's publication and circulation prior

---

[89] Ibid., vol. III, pp. 380–1, 382–3, 383–4.   [90] Ibid., vol. III, pp, 391–2.

[91] See Hahn, *Mozart's Requiem*. Hahn moves abruptly from topic to topic, dividing his short volume into thirty-one numbered sections that combine rudimentary contextual information with brief analyses. The appendix ('Nachtrag') comprises more than half of the book.

[92] Pole, *Story of Mozart's Requiem*, pp. 2–3.

to the *Requiem-Streit*, the *Streit* itself, the appearance of the Walsegg score, the genesis of the Requiem and issues of authorship. He is aware that guesswork has played a big role in Requiem scholarship – André, in the preface to his 1826 edition 'like everybody else, thought it his duty to aid the discussion then going on by some speculations of his own'[93] – and firmly lays the blame at Constanze's door for fundamental confusions. He describes it as 'past comprehension' that information about the mysterious messenger picking up the unfinished Requiem soon after Mozart's death and then vanishing could have made it into Nissen's biography, explains that Constanze's on-going obfuscations cannot be excused by her financial plight because 'long before her misdoings ceased, she had taken leave ... of her poverty and of Mozart's name' and states baldly that her dealings with André were 'disgraceful'.[94] Süssmayr, on the other hand, is well received, Pole explaining that 'fortunately for Mozart and for the world, [the incomplete Requiem score] ... got into the right hands'.[95] Pole points out errors in Süssmayr's letter to Härtel, but excuses them on account of the composer's modesty and the time elapsing between the completion of the Requiem and the penning of the text; he also highlights the ambiguity of the German verb that Süssmayr chooses to describe his participation in the Sanctus, Benedictus and Agnus Dei, 'verfertigen', which can designate either composition from scratch or construction from existing materials.[96] He is sceptical that Süssmayr's relative obscurity counts against his significant involvement in the Requiem completion; we are told that many continental composers of merit were scarcely known in England at this time. Citing respect for Süssmayr's music from the likes of Gerber, Fétis, Seyfried, Sievers and Jahn, he deduces: 'although we must not attribute to Süssmayr powers capable of producing original works stamped with a genius like Mozart's, he was unquestionably a musician of much talent, thoroughly imbued with Mozart's spirit and style of composition, and who, moreover, in this particular case, was working under the rare advantage of having received Mozart's special instructions'.[97]

Pole's final chapter, 'Conclusions in Respect to the Authorship of the Requiem', is intended as the dénouement to his 'story'. Ultimately, after surveying the scene in detail, he concludes: 'although no historical proof exists of Mozart having had any part in these portions of the Requiem ... the fact of the scraps of music being given to Süssmayr, and his communications with Mozart, render it possible that the ideas of the great master may

---

[93] Ibid., p. 33.   [94] Ibid., pp. 38, 58, 61.   [95] Ibid., p. 59.   [96] Ibid., pp. 75–6.
[97] Ibid., pp. 78–81 (quotation at p. 81).

have been used therein; a supposition which the testimony of the music itself, as interpreted by the best critics, renders more than probable, if not absolutely certain'.[98] By resisting a knockout blow, Pole does not resolve the 'mystery' of his 'story', but in effect embraces the mystery as part of the message of the story; he is happy, it would seem, to accept speculative 'facts', such as Mozart's 'special instructions' to Süssmayr and the 'scraps of music' left for him to use. Indeed, Pole freely acknowledges that the desire for a well-shaped narrative affects the ordering of material in his book: 'it is necessary to keep back some of the earliest incidents, the knowledge of which did not transpire till the end'.[99] One early reviewer notes Pole's plan as 'the great charm of the work, for the thread of the narrative is so skilfully presented throughout that the reader cannot lay down the book when once fairly carried on by the events which seem constantly arising to lure him forward'; another explains that 'the whole narrative is so extraordinary as to read more like a romance than history . . . yet Dr. Pole has stated nothing which cannot be clearly established'.[100] Thus, even one of the nineteenth century's most important scholarly interpretations of the Requiem implicitly foregrounds the fact–fiction continuum, the work of the story-teller influencing the work of the serious critic.

20th- and 21st-century criticism and scholarship

1900–1950

The Requiem legend, as in the nineteenth century, influences critical-related activities in the first half of the twentieth century. A writer comparing Mozart and Wagner at the Proms in 1927 follows a standard historical distinction between music of the eighteenth century and music of the nineteenth in finding 'Mozart's sensuousness . . . impersonal, whereas that of Wagner . . . [is] always egotistic and, one might say, self-indulgent', but sees Mozart 'tending at the end of his life towards the later attitude of mind' especially in the Requiem. We feel 'the same almost physical heart-ache' in the Requiem as in *Tristan*, a pain that 'is sharpened when we are aware of the circumstances in which the two works were composed; and although this knowledge is external to the music and makes it neither better nor worse as music, the very fact that it enlarges our understanding of their meaning proves that they belong to the same

---

[98] Ibid., p. 91.   [99] Ibid., p. 2.
[100] *The Musical Times*, 20 (June 1879), pp. 323–4, at 324; *The Academy*, 366 (1879), p. 423.

category of self-expressionism'.[101] The Requiem *legend* and our reactions to it, then, rather than the music *per se*, confirm the Requiem's status as a proto-nineteenth-century work. The legend also assumes a prominent position in Sacheverell Sitwell's Mozart biography (1932), the psychological disintegration witnessed in Davenport and Kolb (see Chapter 1) again finding a home: 'it is necessary to lay stress upon the appalling nerve-strain under which Mozart must have been labouring at the time [of the Requiem commission], from money worries, from family troubles, and from an absolutely incessant production. He was in an exaggerated, hysterical state ... he was at breaking point, and just this additional commission, on top of the two operas already in hand, brought on the crisis from which he was never to recover.'[102] The supposed second visit by the messenger just before the trip to Prague for *Tito* tipped Mozart over the edge: 'he became obsessed by the idea that the stranger was from the next world and that the Requiem was to celebrate his own death. It would seem, almost, as if his mental balance was upset. The idea was for ever in his mind, and he felt that his days were doomed.'[103] Henri Ghéon (1932) strikes much the same psychological tone – the 'mystery' of the commission 'struck Mozart forcibly in his already worried state' and seemed to him 'a message from another world' – extending it to Mozart's compositional engagement with the work. Art and life thus interact actively and productively to the bitter end: 'He struggled and accepted his trials. Till his last breath he clung to art. The *Dies Irae* and the *Agnus Dei* shook him profoundly, calmed him and inspired him ... When they thought he was resting he was composing ... When they thought he was complaining he was constructing ... and between his crises he dictated or wrote.'[104] Dyneley Hussey (1928), also toeing a psychological line by identifying Mozart's 'already overwrought' mental and physical state at the time of the commission and his 'obsession' about composing the work for himself, projects his perception of the legend into his perception of the music:

there entered another factor – the delusions under which Mozart laboured concerned the work on which he was engaged. For once, a note of hysterical passion sounded in his music, ordinarily so disciplined and so detached from any morbid reference to his own personal feelings. It is this note of hysteria which makes the *Requiem* one of the most painful works to contemplate, painful in the way that the

---

[101] 'Music. At the "Proms": Mozart and Wagner', *The Saturday Review of Politics, Literature, Science and Art*, 144 (20 Aug. 1927), p. 249.

[102] Sacheverell Sitwell, *Mozart* (Edinburgh, 1932), pp. 134–5.   [103] Ibid., pp. 135–6.

[104] Henri Ghéon, *In Search of Mozart* (1932), trans. Alexander Pru (London, 1934), pp. 324, 334 (all ellipses are given in Ghéon's text).

cry of an animal caught in a snare … [is] painful … The *Requiem* shows a falling-off, if not always from the musical standard, at least from the untroubled confidence of *Die Zauberflöte*, which is not unnatural in a man wasted by disease and face to face with the inevitable foe whom in better days he had been able to regard with an unflinching eye.[105]

Hussey's equivocal note is echoed (and sometimes magnified) in other early twentieth-century British criticism. The Requiem appears not to have been performed often in Britain between 1900 and the onset of World War II, as reported in the *Manchester Guardian* (1902, 1905, 1934).[106] P. A. S. in *The Observer* noted in 1921: 'When Mozart's Requiem was last done in London nobody seemed to remember. Some said ten or twelve years ago, and others had never in their lives heard it. … Here is one of the most famous works in the whole range of music, and yet it came to many of us as a complete novelty.'[107] Perhaps writers felt free to criticize the work as it was rarely performed, and/or because of lingering anti-Catholic sentiment that had shaped its earlier reception in Britain.[108] At any rate, P. A. S.'s first impressions in 1921 were of disappointment: Mozart's 'instrumental inter-ludes are often charming' but charm has no place in a Requiem; the music of both the Tuba mirum and the Dies irae is inadequate 'to express the tremendous import of the words'; and the Requiem as a whole pales in comparison with Bach's B minor Mass and Beethoven's *Missa solemnis*.[109] Harold E. Watts (1922) explained: 'As a piece of characteristic expression of most beautiful and solemn words, it is a travesty and nothing else.'[110] For Feste (1926), legends associated with the work have exaggerated its impor-tance. Moreover,

I can never hear it without chafing at its almost complete failure to rise to the height of its tremendous text. Think of that complacent trombone solo in the 'Tuba mirum', for example … [A] composer who, in a setting of this passage, makes a

[105] Dyneley Hussey, *Wolfgang Amade Mozart* (New York, 1928), as given in 'The Requiem', in Louis Biancolli (ed.), *The Mozart Handbook* (New York, 1954), pp. 541, 545–6.

[106] *The Manchester Guardian* (24 Oct. 1902), p. 7; (12 Oct. 1905), p. 3; (13 June 1934), p. 20; (6 Sept. 1934), p. 16.

[107] P. A. S., 'Music of the Week: Mozart's Requiem and "The Fountains of Rome"', *The Observer* (30 Jan. 1921), p. 8. The Requiem was actually performed at the Royal Albert Hall by the Royal Choral Society on 1 March 1919, but on that occasion for the first time by the society in twenty years. See *The Musical Times*, 60 (April 1919), p. 179.

[108] For an anti-Catholic perspective, see 'Requiems and Protestants', *The Musical Times*, 57 (March 1916), p. 146. On early nineteenth-century British reception, see Cowgill, 'Early English Reception of Mozart's Requiem'.

[109] P. A. S., 'Mozart's Requiem', p. 8.

[110] Harold E. Watts, 'Our Decadence', *The Musical Times*, 63 (Sept. 1922), pp. 649–50.

brass solo a prominent feature is taking a risk. Mozart took it, and (I venture to say) came down heavily … [The Requiem] contains some excellent music, and some that is lame (not only in the Süssmayer portion, that is). Being good only in parts, it is not good enough. For a Requiem we want a standard higher than that of a curate's egg.[111]

G. A. H. (1934), in contrast to Feste, found the legend's presence beneficial, but like Feste did not have a high opinion of the work:

The experience of hearing that music which the composer in his poverty and wretchedness hastened, but without success, to finish before death overtook him is bound to be a most poignant one, yet though we listen reverently we cannot delude ourselves that this is Mozart at his best or even at his second best … Perhaps the weakest number is that one – 'Tuba Mirum' – which has sometimes been named as showing Mozart's fine treatment of the trombone.[112]

Discussion of the thorny topic of authorship in the first half of the twentieth century is similar to discussion in the second half of the nineteenth. Aside from occasional expressions of weariness and desire to move beyond the issue,[113] critics happily speculate about Mozart's involvement in the concluding movements and pass positive or negative judgment on Süssmayr's work. Hussey (1928), for example, attributes the Sanctus and Benedictus to Süssmayr, finding them 'competent and mediocre' and explaining that they 'might pass for authentic Mozart in an uninspired moment', but suggests that the first part of the Agnus Dei is by Mozart and the continuation by Süssmayr. He concludes: 'even when we deny to Süssmayr the credit for all those things which impress us most deeply in the *Requiem*, we must acknowledge our admiration for the way in which he carried out his task'.[114] 'H.' (1927) likewise speculates that the beginning of the Agnus Dei comes from Mozart but that the 'weaker and decidedly sentimental setting of the words "dona eis requiem"' is by Süssmayr.[115] On the other hand, Rutland Boughton (1922) claims that 'it is only a very prejudiced person who will declare any movement of it to be seriously below

[111]   Feste, 'Ad Libitum', *The Musical Times*, 67 (April 1926), pp. 312–15, at 315.

[112]   G. A. H., 'The Three Choirs Festival', *The Manchester Guardian* (6 Sept. 1934), p. 16. For another early twentieth-century jibe at the Tuba mirum and its 'dreadful' trombone solo, see Cecil Forsyth, *Orchestration* (London, 1914), p. 149.

[113]   See Rev. J. T. Lawrence, 'The Requiem', *Musical Opinion and Music Trade Review*, 28 (Sept. 1905), pp. 869–70; 'Leeds Musical Festival', *Musical Standard*, 28 (19 Oct. 1907), pp. 240–3, at 242.

[114]   As given in Biancolli (ed.), *Mozart Handbook*, pp. 543, 544.

[115]   'H.', 'Mozart's Requiem Mass', *Saturday Review of Politics, Literature, Science and Art*, 143 (8 Jan. 1927), pp. 47–8.

the standard of the rest of the work'.[116] John F. Runciman (1905) takes up a nineteenth-century thread in claiming that 'If the Sanctus was not written by Mozart it was written by a composer as great as Mozart.'[117] Robert Handke attributes parts of the Benedictus to Mozart, including the vocal lines at the beginning and the figured bass, and the remainder to Süssmayr, above all the middle segment and the end.[118] And Ghéon suggests that 'Mozart alone could have thought of the orchestral and choral design of the *Lacrymosa*; it is one of those luminous complaints where he shows us his inward contradiction, divided between joy and suffering, the emotional and the spiritual. If Süssmayr put the last touches to it then we must admit his skill.'[119]

Accounts of the Requiem from the eminent early twentieth-century Mozart scholars Hermann Abert (1919), Eric Blom (1935), Alfred Einstein (1945) and Georges de Saint-Foix (1946) address legend-, authorship- and music-related issues in greater depth than the critics discussed above. For Abert, the sacred attributes and emotional intensity of the work come to the fore: the Introit is 'concerned less with a subjective outpouring of emotion than with an expression of the work's strictly liturgical character'; the Kyrie fugue '[reflects] the state of guilt-laden humanity at the imminence of Divine Judgement … [and] as a whole is truly demonic in its emotional expression'; the Tuba mirum 'pictures the Lord not as a strict and implacable judge but as a lenient, albeit just and serious, God'; the Rex tremendae reveals the Lord 'in all of his sombre majesty', invoking 'a mood of supreme emotion'; the Recordare is 'a wonderful combination of Mozartian interiority and sacred rigour' in which 'comfort and trust [have] entered the supplicants' hearts'; and the 'searing' Confutatis includes the 'shattering' 'Oro supplex' sequence, in which '[all] that we have heard so far … confined to the world of the warm-blooded human emotion, including the emotions of terror, horror and impassioned, childlike entreaty' gives way to 'the spirit of eternity … a world free from desires and anxieties … with an unconscious awareness of the divine mystery'.[120] Abert believes steadfastly in the unity of the work, Mozart individualizing liturgical and contrapuntal elements throughout and allowing 'the music always [to serve]

---

[116] Rutland Boughton, 'Our Decadence', *The Musical Times*, 63 (July 1922), pp. 474–7, at p. 475.

[117] John F. Runciman, 'Verdi's Requiem', *Saturday Review of Politics, Literature, Science and Art*, 100 (9 Dec. 1905), p. 746.

[118] Robert Handke, 'Zur Lösung der Benedictusfrage in Mozarts Requiem', *Zeitschrift für Musikwissenschaft*, 1 (1918), pp. 108–30.

[119] Ghéon, *In Search of Mozart*, p. 336.

[120] Abert, *W. A. Mozart*, pp. 1318, 1321, 1324, 1324, 1325, 1326–7.

the text without ever indulging in purely musical pleasures'.[121] The through-compositional effect witnessed from the Kyrie fugue to the Dies irae and from the Rex tremendae to the Recordare (the latter '[picking] up the mood of the final request' from the former albeit in a less intense context) further promotes coherence.[122]

Abert is optimistic that 'stylistic examination' of the Requiem will shed light on authorship, while acknowledging that 'the absence of evidence will never allow us to be absolutely clear'.[123] He holds a very high opinion of the Lacrymosa, excepting the 'elaborate use of trombones', deeming the climactic 'dona eis requiem' statement so good that Süssmayr's involvement is in doubt. The Sanctus, on the other hand, fails to realize Mozart's intentions: 'The listener has the clear impression that ... [the material preceding the fugue] is a makeshift solution and that the arranger was unclear what Mozart himself intended'; and the fugue is 'elaborated along increasingly feeble and superficial lines before coming to a particularly trivial conclusion'. He sides with Handke in regarding the Benedictus as a composite of Mozart's and Süssmayr's work, and criticizes the 'impersonal, mechanical deployment' of instruments. And, for the Agnus Dei, he takes a leaf out of the nineteenth century's book (particularly applied to the Sanctus and Benedictus) in claiming that '[belief] in miracles' is the only way of countenancing Süssmayr's involvement: 'The whole of the Agnus Dei is sustained by such a high level of inspiration that Süssmayr's authorship is virtually ruled out, no matter how much respect we may have for his abilities.'[124]

Eric Blom, who relates the familiar narrative of Mozart's dread at receiving the commission and carrying out his work, assesses authorship differently from Abert: 'Without any manuscript evidence one would swear that this is [all] Mozart, not Süssmayr or any one else. For the rest, it is not always easy to decide merely from what the ear receives where Mozart leaves off and Süssmayr begins.'[125] The slight unevenness of some of Mozart's as well as Süssmayr's work – including the Kyrie fugue, the Tuba mirum and the 'suspiciously short' Osanna fugue – raises 'the ghost of a doubt' as to whether the Requiem is, ultimately, 'a work of the highest inspiration'.[126] Alfred Einstein also strikes an impartial pose towards Mozart as well as Süssmayr. While the Recordare 'is one of the purest, most skilful and most enrapturing [movements] Mozart ever wrote', Mozart's trombone solo in

---

[121] Ibid., p. 1336.   [122] Ibid., pp. 1321, 1325.   [123] Ibid., p. 1314.

[124] Ibid., pp. 1328, 1332, 1332, 1334, 1335.

[125] Eric Blom, *Mozart* (1935) (New York, 1966), pp. 161–2. On Mozart's terror, see pp. 146, 149–50.

[126] Ibid., pp. 162–4.

the Tuba mirum does not 'shake off the impression that the heavenly player is exhibiting his prowess instead of announcing terribly the terrible moment of the Last Judgment'; the 'Quam olim Abrahae' is 'a rather neutral chromatic fugue … not without an archaistic flavor'; and the short Osanna fugue 'completely [upsets] the proportions of the work'.[127] Einstein continues: 'And yet, by the return of the *Requiem* to the words "Lux aeternae" the work is rescued once more for Mozart, the self-contradiction of the whole is somewhat – not entirely – overcome. The total impression is contradictory, but Mozart's intention is clear. Death is not a terrible vision but a friend.'[128]

Georges de Saint-Foix, unlike Blom and Einstein, is completely convinced about the quality of Mozart's work in the Requiem. The Introit is profound and solemn; the Rex tremendae contains 'imposing majesty' at the beginning and 'irresistible contrast' at 'Salve me'; the Recordare is a masterpiece for its instrumental and vocal writing; the Confutatis alternates 'desperate combat' and 'ineffable simplicity' ('Voca me') and provides, in the 'Oro supplex', 'two pages that we will not hesitate to describe as the high point in all his art'; and the Offertory contains brilliantly multifarious and forceful text setting.[129] Saint-Foix criticizes only the Tuba mirum in Mozart's work, citing its first page as the weakest in the entire Requiem score.[130]

Süssmayr receives a more mixed report from Saint-Foix. While Süssmayr is thanked for his original compositional contributions to the work, which are integrated in ways that do not negatively affect the whole, his orchestration is criticized, especially the 'often heavy and clumsy' trombones, which Saint-Foix claims 'could be revised and amended'.[131] (He wistfully considers such revision insignificant in relation to what a more original and independent mind – namely Mozart's – would have dared to attempt had he lived to complete the Requiem.) Saint-Foix suggests that Süssmayr's compositional role may have been limited to parts of the Benedictus, the Sanctus and the Osanna fugue, bequeathed to him in a fragmentary state by Mozart.[132]

---

[127] Alfred Einstein, *Mozart: His Character, his Work*, trans. Arthur Mendel and Nathan Broder (Oxford, 1945), p. 354.

[128] Ibid.

[129] Georges de Saint-Foix, *W.-A. Mozart: Sa vie musicale et son oeuvre*, vol. V: *Les dernières années (1789–1791)* (Paris, 1946), pp. 283–4, 287 ('imposante majesté'), 288 ('contraste irrésistible'), 290 ('combat désespéré', 'ineffable simplicité'), 290 ('deux pages que nous n'hésiterons pas à qualifier de culminantes dans tout son art'), 294.

[130] Ibid., p. 286.

[131] Ibid., p. 281 ('souvent lourd et maladroit', 'pourrait être révisé et amendé').   [132] Ibid., p. 281.

From 1950 onwards

If a collective note of uncertainty about the musical quality of the Requiem echoes through the first half of the twentieth century – for Mozart's work as well as Süssmayr's – it more or less disappears in the second half of the century, at least where Mozart is concerned. *Ad hoc* remarks from newspaper critics are occasionally critical: 'Sentiment makes us indulgent to this work, which remains a favourite although not among Mozart's greatest' (1961); and 'There is magic in the name, and in the story, of Mozart's Requiem, but it is a flawed masterpiece' (1975).[133] But such comments very rarely appear in scholarly writings. John Rosselli's downbeat assessment of the Requiem in his Mozart biography (1998) is an exception, following the likes of Jahn, Blom, Einstein and Saint-Foix in singling out the Tuba mirum: 'We had best not see Mozart out of life with this hybrid work . . . Parts of the Requiem are merely decorous – and they are not all Süssmayr's: the trombone solo at the Tuba mirum (the annunciation of the last trump), with its upward sequence that strains after majesty and fails, is Mozart's.'[134]

The Requiem legend retains its cache in late twentieth-century criticism, continuing to direct interpretations of the music. At a performance to celebrate the bicentennial of Mozart's birth (1956), one critic calls the Requiem

an intensely personal affirmation made under the shadow cast by the conviction of approaching death . . . The music compels by its sheer genius, which is contained in spite of prophetic inflections, within the framework of the period style; yet, over and above that, it harrows and disturbs as few later manifestations of feeling even when made in the full panoply of romantic technique have succeeded in doing.[135]

For Brigid Brophy (1964), Mozart's premonition of death captures the Requiem, *Don Giovanni* and Mozart's relationship with his father in the same biographical web, foreshadowing a similar narrative conflation in the film *Amadeus*: 'The visitor bearing an invitation is merged [for

---

[133] Colin Mason, 'Last Night's Prom', *The Guardian* (11 Aug. 1961), p. 7; John Reed, 'Liverpool: The RLPO', *The Guardian* (29 Oct. 1975), p. 10.

[134] John Rosselli, *The Life of Mozart* (Cambridge, 1998), p. 160. Daniel Heartz is also critical of the Tuba mirum: 'Ghosts of Mozart's secular music were to be expected in the Requiem, but the concentration on them in the "Tuba mirum" is disconcerting. The composer himself perhaps realized that he had taken a wrong or inappropriate turn, for he discontinued writing the trombone's solo at this juncture, where the tenor voice enters, although the instrument's tenor clef continued on in the score, unoccupied, giving indication that he intended to reintroduce it.' See Heartz, *Mozart, Haydn and Early Beethoven, 1781–1802* (New York and London, 2009), p. 267.

[135] 'Students in the "Requiem"', *The Manchester Guardian* (28 Jan. 1956), p. 5.

Mozart] with the visitor who comes in answer to Don Giovanni's invitation – the revenant father, come to seek vengeance and carry off his quasison.'[136] The psychological dimension to the legend, repeatedly aired earlier in the twentieth century, affects Brophy's interpretation of the Requiem's stylistic and aesthetic qualities: 'the coalescence between his opposite points of view', namely 'to retreat from the rococo of his own ecclesiastical manner to the baroque assurance of Handel's', dangerously implying a move from Catholicism to Protestantism, is 'agonizingly forced on Mozart. That Mozart died before he could finish the Requiem almost suggests that the coalescence could not be made – almost that Mozart died rather than finish the Requiem.'[137] Michael Levey (1973) adopts a similar position in claiming the unfinished work as evidence of 'emotional, and perhaps also artistic, doubt', and in mapping the Requiem on to Mozart's difficult relationship with his father,[138] but also moves in a new direction. As for Karl Hartl's Mozart in *Wen die Götter lieben*, who composes the Recordare as memories of his early life flood back (see Chapter 1), the Requiem for Levey's Mozart 'is more likely to have prompted thoughts of life [than of death]: much earlier life at Salzburg, as a boy in church again, hearing the services, as a boy at home practicing the clavier to his father's satisfaction'.[139] The Requiem legend's emphasis may have changed here, but the fundamental need to relate a story that links biography and work is still apparent, just as it was in nineteenth-century re-interpretations of the familiar narrative.

The most significant development in late twentieth-century reception of the Requiem is the treatment of Süssmayr and his contributions to the completed work. While negativism and marginalization characterize much Süssmayr reception in the last three quarters of the nineteenth century, it is offset by implicit praise from Süssmayr's critics and by explicit praise from his admirers (see above). The early twentieth century also brings both criticism and commendation. But from 1950 onwards, admiration – even ambivalence – plays a meek second fiddle to critical condemnation. The supposed clumsiness, awkwardness and technically imperfect qualities of his orchestration have assumed near-axiomatic status in the secondary literature; the putative superiority of Eybler's orchestration of the

---

[136] Brigid Brophy, *Mozart the Dramatist* (London and New York, 1964), p. 265. On the linking of Leopold's death, *Don Giovanni* and the Requiem commissioning in *Amadeus* see Keefe, '*Amadeus* at 25', pp. 47–8.

[137] Ibid., p. 264. It is unclear whether Brophy is aware of Mozart's use of Handel as a model in the Requiem.

[138] Michael Levey, *The Life and Death of Mozart* (London, 1973), p. 258.   [139] Ibid., p. 258.

Sequence over Süssmayr's has been cited with increasing frequency too.[140] Fuelled by Constanze's statement that Süssmayr received 'a few scraps of paper with music on them … found on Mozart's desk after his death'[141] in addition to the Requiem score, scholars have speculated tirelessly about which music and musical procedures in the Sanctus, Benedictus and Agnus Dei might be attributed to Mozart, inclining to the belief that Süssmayr had at his disposal sketches or other additional materials in Mozart's hand when he came to complete the work, even though hard evidence that he did is lacking.[142] In general, they are content to put Süssmayr in a no-win position: when the quality of the final movements of the Requiem is deemed high, they suggest that material by Mozart must have been involved; when the quality is deemed low, they register their disapproval of Süssmayr.[143] Criticism of Süssmayr grows to a climax in the prefaces and materials accompanying the new Requiem completions of the 1970s, 1980s and 1990s, which find fault with Süssmayr's work; his orchestration, harmonic procedures, improper and inopportune use of instruments, and part-writing are all reprimanded.[144] Flippant attacks also become commonplace,

[140] On the former, see Friedrich Blume, 'Requiem, but no Peace', in Paul Henry Lang (ed.), *The Creative World of Mozart* (New York, 1963), pp. 103–26, at 116–20; Arthur Hutchings, *Mozart: The Man, the Musician* (London, 1976), p. 118; Gruber, *Mozart and Posterity*, p. 244; Wolff, *Mozart's Requiem*, pp. 38, 40, 87–8, 90; Jane Glover, *Mozart's Women: His Family, his Friends, his Music* (London, 2005), p. 317; Julian Rushton, *Mozart* (Oxford and New York, 2006), p. 228. On the latter, see Paul Moseley, 'Mozart's Requiem: A Re-Evaluation of the Evidence', *Journal of the Royal Musical Association*, 114 (1989), pp. 203–37, at p. 219 (citing 'common consent'); Wolff, *Mozart's Requiem*, p. 22; *Neue Mozart-Ausgabe*, I:1/2/2, ed. Leopold Nowak, pp. xii–xiv; Mattias Korten, *Mozarts Requiem KV626: Ein Fragment wird ergänzt* (Frankfurt, 2000), p. 38.

[141] As reported in 1826 by Maximilian Stadler, Constanze's friend and ally in musical matters; see Wolff, *Mozart's Requiem*, p. 152.

[142] A sketch for an 'Amen' fugue at the end of the Lacrymosa was discovered by Wolfgang Plath in the early 1960s; see Plath, 'Über Skizzen zu Mozarts Requiem', in Georg Reichert and Martin Just (eds.), *Bericht über den internationalen musikwissenschaftlichen Kongress Kassel 1962* (Kassel, 1963), pp. 184–7. It is possible that Mozart would have rejected the sketch had he completed the Lacrymosa (or even that he had done so at the time of his death); see Thomas Bauman, 'Requiem, but no Piece', *19th Century Music*, 25 (1991), pp. 151–61, at 160, and Moseley, 'Mozart's Requiem', p. 215. In any case, it is not known whether Süssmayr was aware of the sketch, or, if he was, whether he preferred not to use it.

[143] Karl Geiringer, 'The Church Music', in H. C. Robbins Landon and Donald Mitchell (eds.), *The Mozart Companion* (London, 1956), pp. 361–76, at 373–4; Maunder, *Mozart's Requiem, passim*; Wolff, *Mozart's Requiem*, pp. 41, 42, 103, 111–12. Wolff adds a twist to this critical stance, suggesting that Süssmayr may have 'misinterpreted' Mozart's indications; see *Mozart's Requiem*, pp. 38–40.

[144] See Mozart, *Requiem KV 626, Instrumentation Franz Beyer* (Zürich, 1971); Maunder, *Mozart's Requiem*; and Mozart, *Requiem, K. 626*, ed. and completed Richard Maunder (Oxford, 1988); Mozart, *Requiem für Soli, Chor, Orchester und Orgel d-moll KV 626*, ed. and completed H. C. Robbins Landon (Wiesbaden, 1991); Mozart, *Requiem, for Soprano, Alto, Tenor and Bass Soli, SATB and Orchestra K. 626*, ed. and completed Duncan Druce (London, 1993); Mozart,

as if intending to damn merely by nasty insult: Blume (1963) talks of Süssmayr's instrumentation 'today [covering] the whole work like a thick, gray crust, comparable to the layer of whitewash that was plastered over the naves of Gothic churches in the period of restoration'; Levey identifies 'a mixture of barrenness and Mozartean pastiche' after the Offertory; and the composer Stephen Oliver, believing himself to be better than Süssmayr since 'A glow-worm would be a better composer than Süssmayr', says the Requiem 'has the feel of a massive ancient cathedral held together with bits of plastic'.[145] Stephen Walsh, writing in 1983, states that Süssmayr is 'nowadays universally despised'.[146]

To be sure, there are pre-1950 precedents for the types of criticism listed above: the purported awkwardness of Süssmayr's orchestration appears in Abert and Saint-Foix; and the no-win scenario, whereby 'good' material in the concluding movements of the work is assigned to Mozart and 'bad' material to Süssmayr, surfaces in Blom, Saint-Foix and Hussey, as well as in nineteenth-century writings.[147] But the confident zeal with which Süssmayr's technical and stylistic errors are identified, addressed and deemed significant is new to the post-war period. Franz Beyer (1971), the first of the modern-day Requiem completers, finds Süssmayr's orchestration work particularly problematic, since it 'suffers most from Süssmayr's lack of accomplishment . . . This discipline has been considered the test of musical intelligence, and if one subjects Süssmayr's orchestration to a severe scrutiny it becomes evident that this young musician had very little feeling for the supreme mastery of his teacher.'[148] Beyer harnesses Mozart's intentions in matters of orchestration – or what are construed as Mozart's intentions, since no-one can be sure about them, certainly not 200 years later – to generalized understandings of good practice, in order to construct a stick with which to beat Süssmayr. Perceived ineptitude in matters of harmony and of part-writing and lack of imagination in matters of instrumentation

---

 Requiem d-moll/D minor KV 626, ed. and completed Robert D. Levin (1994) (Stuttgart, 2004 (study score)).

[145] Blume, 'Requiem, but no Peace', p. 116; Levey, *Life and Death of Mozart*, p. 279; Tom Sutcliffe, 'Why Oliver Asks for More', *The Guardian* (16 May 1991), p. 27. Oliver had just composed new *secco* recitatives for *La clemenza di Tito* to replace those thought to be by Süssmayr.

[146] Walsh, 'Mostly – but Hardly Pure – Mozart', *The Observer* (10 April 1983), p. 29.

[147] On the former see Abert, *W. A. Mozart*, p. 1331 and Saint-Foix, *W.-A. Mozart*, vol. V, p. 281. On the latter see Blom, *Mozart*, pp. 164–5, Saint-Foix, *W.-A. Mozart*, vol. V, pp. 296–8, Hussey, 'The Requiem', p. 544. Nineteenth-century critics foreshadowing their twentieth-century counterparts in putting Süssmayr in a no-win position include Frederik Samuel Silverstolpe (in his memoirs dated 1800–1 but unpublished until 1838), given in Wolff, *Mozart's Requiem*, p. 147; Anton Herzog (1839), given in Wolff, *Mozart's Requiem*, p. 135; and Oulibicheff, *Nouvelle biographie*, vol. I, p. 248, and vol. III, pp. 450–1.

[148] Mozart, *Requiem*, ed. Beyer, p. v.

are laced with spicy rhetoric – the 'histrionic blare' of the Dies irae, the 'bathos' of trumpets and timpani in the Confutatis, the 'grotesque syncopation' of the 'de poeni inferno' in the Domine Jesu, the 'garrulousness' of the trombone in the Tuba mirum – in an attempt to demonstrate thoughtless, shoddy workmanship.[149]

Richard Maunder's book (1988), serving as an extended introduction to his own Requiem completion, goes considerably further than Beyer. Even before presenting his detailed comments on Süssmayr's work on the Requiem, Maunder seeks to undermine him: Süssmayr is a 'rather obscure musician who would otherwise long since have been forgotten'; he would not have been Mozart's choice to complete the Requiem and was not held in high regard by Mozart; and he combined 'a certain talent for superficial imitation of Mozart with a lack of technical expertise'.[150] Maunder then turns to the 'basic grammar of counterpoint' to separate Mozart's contributions from Süssmayr's and to judge Süssmayr's work.[151] But the 'rules' by which Mozart lived (according to Maunder) are unconvincing, in that Maunder's details do not match his rhetoric. For example, he identifies Mozart's 'horror of outright consecutives', explains that 'Mozart really did stick to his rule' and thus surmises that 'a passage containing breaches of the rules is almost certainly not genuine Mozart'.[152] But Maunder himself qualifies the 'rule' by finding four examples of consecutives in the Introit, Kyrie and Dies irae, by suggesting that Mozart's 'horror' does not extend to operatic arias, where consecutives occur more often than in his sacred music, and by claiming that Mozart would have consented to including hidden octaves and fifths when they were deemed 'occasionally unavoidable'.[153] Thus Mozart's 'horror', even according to the information Maunder provides, is generically specific, has exceptions and allows for judgment as to unavoidability, which make it a much fuzzier 'rule' than he implies, and unable to provide certainty in establishing authorship.

More important, it is unclear from Maunder how Süssmayr's micro-level technical transgressions by themselves affect – or should affect – listeners' perceptions and understandings of the Requiem. The relationship between an individual musical event in the Requiem and its wider aesthetic resonance will determine whether a part-writing 'error', say, is distracting or blends easily into the musical fabric, and in the latter case whether it is, in fact, an 'error' at all. For Maunder, the Lacrymosa completion from bar 9 is so strewn with errors that Mozart cannot have had any involvement with it.

---

[149] Ibid., pp. v–viii.   [150] Maunder, *Mozart's Requiem*, pp. 1–6 (quotations at pp. 1, 3).
[151] Ibid., p. 5.   [152] Ibid., pp. 28, 30.   [153] Ibid., p. 30.

But Maunder is uninterested in the aesthetic dimension and function of the completion. As Thomas Bauman remarks, by not undertaking a scholarly transition from 'breaking down suspicious compounds' to 'trying to make sense of a passage' or from 'analytic exercise into . . . inductive, hermeneutic encounter' Maunder misses the hermeneutic wood for the authorial trees.[154] In any case, 'rules' slip into high-octane criticism grounded in a combination of general stylistic rights and wrongs and narrow focus on Mozart's working practices in his late works. Thus, in a *tour de force*, the Benedictus for Maunder contains an 'obviously garbled version of bars 43–4 of the "Requiem aeternam" . . . totally out of place' (bars 18–27), 'aimless meandering in no particular key . . . followed by five bars of utter banality' (bars 21–7), two bars that are 'just as empty as bars 10–11' (bars 33–4) and another two that are 'frankly boring' (bars 46–7), and an 'absurd' modulation to the 'wrong key' of F major (bar 38). Ending in a spirit of pithy hauteur, judge and jury at his own court, Maunder wonders why anyone confronted with 'such an unrelieved display of technical incompetence' in the Sanctus and Osanna fugue as well as the Benedictus 'should want to convince himself that Mozart had any part in such poor music'.[155] For another modern-day completer, Robert D. Levin, the rhetoric is similar: 'That a composer of such total mastery as Mozart should have endured the fate of having such rampant quantifiable faults running through the entirety of Süssmayr's completion is one of the cruelest ironies in music history.'[156]

It is intrinsically questionable, as Levin has recently suggested in a line of argument consonant with Maunder, that we are in a better position to judge the quality of Süssmayr's contribution now than were musicians in the nineteenth century, or that our 'objective' views are more relevant than those of earlier writers on the Requiem, in essence because we study the score and the style in more detail than they did.[157] The principal danger here is that the same kind of assumptions about technique that come from Maunder – Levin tells us to 'eschew subjective utterance and make points with which any well-trained musician would agree'[158] – will obliterate historical-aesthetic contexts and the ramifications and resonances they may contain. (And again Levin's position assumes that the kind of technical

---

[154] Thomas Bauman, 'On Completing the Requiem', *Mozart-Jahrbuch 1991*, pp. 494–8, at p. 496.

[155] Maunder, *Mozart's Requiem*, pp. 56, 57.

[156] Robert D. Levin, Richard Maunder, Duncan Druce, David Black, Christoph Wolff and Simon P. Keefe, 'Colloquy: Finishing Mozart's Requiem. On "'Die Ochsen am Berge': Franz Xaver Süssmayr and the Orchestration of Mozart's Requiem, K. 626" by Simon P. Keefe, Spring 2008', *Journal of the American Musicological Society*, 61 (2008), pp. 583–608, at 585.

[157] Ibid., pp. 583–8.　　[158] Ibid., p. 584.

errors on which he and others call Süssmayr to account – voice-leading, grammatical details, etc. – will, or should, affect our perception of the relevant moments in performance.) Extending Levin's argument, we would need to suggest that Mozart's views on the technical attributes of J. S. Bach's counterpoint are qualitatively less significant than those of distinguished scholars today, as Mozart had fewer pieces at his disposal in 1780s Vienna and in Leipzig (which he visited in spring 1789), did not benefit from centuries of discussion of Bach's technical skill and knew less about Bach in general. Levin might consider that critical consensus about Bach's contrapuntal brilliance obviates the need to answer this question; he would be brave (indeed wrong-headed) to claim that Mozart's views on technique are inherently less significant than those of recent writers. Critical agreement is the key for Levin, then, as well as the (perceived) status of the person or people concerned, rather than the passing of time and the increase in scholarly sophistication as a harbinger for more refined value judgment.

It is well to remember that commentaries on stylistic issues relating to the Requiem, whenever and however carried out and whether intent on determining authorship and/or technical 'errors', remain interpretative speculations, not historical truths. They cannot establish with certainty the degree of Mozart's involvement (if any) in the Sanctus, Benedictus and Agnus Dei; philological evidence (the movements in Süssmayr's hand) cannot be superseded or negated, in short, by stylistic 'evidence'. Stylistic studies inevitably bear the strong ideological imprint of the era in which they are written, an imprint characterized as much by what is omitted from discussion as by what is included. Those who seek out 'errors' in Süssmayr's work – or use 'errors' to determine Süssmayr's contributions – privilege technical attributes (as they construe them, at least) over aesthetic attributes, buying into a modernist aesthetic of improvement and progress in which value judgments inevitably assume general acceptance of musical rights and wrongs, good practices and bad practices, even when historical criteria are also invoked. Ultimately Süssmayr's completion stands or falls on its aesthetic strengths or weaknesses, since it is only through an evaluation of them that we are able to reconcile the historical, cultural and stylistic aspects of his work in totality.

The rhetoric of late twentieth-century criticism, like earlier criticism, puts Süssmayr on the back foot. But the latest rhetoric has a new dimension, servicing a disconnection between positive aesthetic experiences of the work as a whole for the musical public – witness the Requiem's continued popularity in performance in Süssmayr's completion – and scholarly disapproval of Süssmayr's technique. (In earlier eras, in contrast, anti-Süssmayr rhetoric – with notable exceptions such as Gottfried Weber's contributions to the *Requiem-Streit* – sought primarily to *align* positive aesthetic experience with positive critical experience, often by attempting to show that the glories of the work *in toto* are Mozart's glories alone.)[159] Thus Blume, re-invoking the age-old distrust of Süssmayr by disputing Einstein's claim that the authorship controversy could have been avoided had 'people … wanted to believe the explanation that Süssmayr had delivered to Breitkopf & Härtel' in 1800,[160] challenges Süssmayr (through his music) to prove he is good enough to have composed the concluding movements:

The assumption operative up to now, according to which Süssmayr is to be considered the composer of the missing portions as nothing can be proved to the contrary, seems today less justified than the assumption that the independent composition of the closing portions cannot be ascribed to Süssmayr so long as the doubts concerning his talent … are not resolved by demonstrating a corresponding accomplishment of his own from his pen.[161]

While not an intrinsically unreasonable viewpoint, it gives undue weight to the possible existence of sketches by Mozart for the final movements and insufficient weight to the fact (as Blume himself knew) that only Süssmayr's hand is evident in the autograph materials for the Sanctus, Benedictus and Agnus Dei. Maunder provides a subtler variation on the same theme after a survey of well-known contemporary, if ultimately inconclusive, comments on authorship: 'There appears to be no more documentary evidence that throws any light on the extent of Süssmayr's contributions. The only way to make further progress is to examine the music itself, to see how far its craftsmanship measures up to Mozart's rigorous standards.'[162] Put another way, documentary evidence, in the form of philological evidence, suggests that Süssmayr *was* the composer of the Sanctus, Benedictus and Agnus Dei. Maunder does indeed conclude that these movements are by Süssmayr except for parts of the Agnus Dei. But it is hard to see how he or anyone else can make discernible 'progress' on authorship by enshrining an ideology – for Maunder the association of 'craftsmanship' and 'Mozart's rigorous

<hr>

[159] Along similar lines in the late twentieth century, see Geiringer, 'The Church Music', pp. 373–4. Geiringer claims that 'all the movements of the score have the characteristic Mozartean touch' and that, in consequence, Süssmayr 'should not be considered as the composer of large sections of the Requiem'.

[160] Given in Blume, 'Requiem, but no Peace', p. 107.

[161] Ibid., p. 112. Blume's scepticism acts as a catalyst for harsh criticism of Süssmayr's orchestration; see ibid., pp. 117–20.

[162] Maunder, *Mozart's Requiem*, pp. 23–4.

standards' with a narrow determination of technical competence – that is unsupported, even contradicted, by philological evidence.

I do not intend naively to imply that the absence of evidence of Mozart's involvement in the later movements is definitive evidence of his complete compositional absence – that philological materials solve all authorship problems where the Requiem is concerned – but rather to suggest that authorship discussions as narrowly conceived for so long (is this bit by Mozart, or by Süssmayr?) have well and truly run their course. If authorship issues are to stimulate interpretational insights, they will need to be more broadly and more imaginatively conceived than hitherto.

Conclusion

The prevailing wind in English-language Mozart scholarship from the last twenty to thirty years towards contextually, aesthetically and historically driven interpretations of his works has more or less bypassed the Requiem.[163] Bogged down in narrowly conceived authorship debates, Mozart scholars have collectively failed to recognize that the enormous amount at stake in the Requiem – for the biographer coming to terms with stories surrounding the composer and his death, for the historian studying reception, for the musicologist working on style or compositional method, for the philologist evaluating sources – translates into enormous hermeneutic potential. Discussions of authorship thus far have been motivated, ultimately, by a desire to negate the impact of the purportedly romantic exigencies of the composite Requiem legend, which are considered unhelpful because unscholarly and untrue; attempts are made to de-mythologize the Requiem by trying *exactly* to distinguish Mozart's contributions to the completion from the contributions of others. But this is an unrealizable task, as the endless (and endlessly different) interpretations and re-interpretations of documentary, stylistic and philological evidence concerning authorship have shown. They provide often insightful hypothesis and conjecture supported by evidence of various kinds, thus acquiring scholarly credibility, but can offer no incontrovertible proof; as one critic recently explained, we must now 'accept that the frontiers between what was composed by Mozart, what was done by Süssmayr on the basis of Mozartian

---

[163] A notable exception is Cliff Eisen, 'Mozart's Leap in the Dark', which approaches Mozart's Requiem in the light of eighteenth-century ideas of death. Reception studies include Bauman, 'Requiem, but no Piece' and Cowgill, 'Early English Reception of Mozart's Requiem'.

material, and what was written new by Süssmayr are fluid'.[164] In any case, the Requiem legend, it seems, still fascinates us. It is not an outdated romantic story, then, but one that continues – just as it always has – to condition our collective perceptions and understandings of the work.

Authorship issues more broadly and empirically conceived than hitherto are not, I would suggest, an impediment to greater hermeneutic sophistication where the Requiem is concerned, but an inspiration, encouraging rather than discouraging critical insight. We need to embrace, far more systematically than hitherto, the musical and aesthetic resonances of the Requiem as a multi-authored work, in the process evaluating Süssmayr's and also Eybler's contributions in a new light informed by historical and aesthetic contexts. The Requiem legend has provided a locus of inspiration for so many people for so long, apparently including two highlights of twentieth-century reception, Peter Shaffer and Milos Forman's Requiem scenes in *Amadeus* and Benjamin Britten's performance at Aldeburgh in 1971 (discussed in Chapters 1 and 3 respectively). Thus, the legend can also surely inspire and inform our scholarly interpretations of Mozart's contributions, inviting the replacement of narrow, ideologically drawn style-analytical criteria with richer and freer perception and reception criteria. At any rate, detaching our knowledge of the composite Requiem narrative from our scholarly appreciation of the work – trying to show that the former does not influence the latter – would be impossible, not least because we are continually reminded that Mozart worked on the Requiem as he himself approached death and that he died before completing it. So many other details of the legend sit on the slippery slope between fact and fiction; we debate their likely truth-value without acknowledging that these details also provide an elaborate psychological backdrop to our understandings of the work. If the Requiem legend was told by all Parisian nannies to their children as early as 1834 (see Chapter 1), we will not be able entirely to resist its influence, in ways large and small, over 175 years later, even if we actively resist individual elements of it. Like Mozart's music, the Requiem legend is all around us.

---

[164] Küster, *Mozart: A Musical Biography*, p. 390.

3 | The Requiem in performance

Performances and editions of the Requiem bring together popular and critical trends in reception. Editions, aiming for accurate and reliable musical texts, naturally feed off and feed into scholarly developments, facilitating performances of the work; performances, in turn, not only inspire critical writings but also add to the Requiem's mystique and impact. Following an examination of the most important nineteenth-century editions, I turn to nineteenth-century performances, assessing *inter alia* the mutual reinforcement of work and occasion and the intense connections felt with the Requiem. By the late twentieth century, the availability of innumerable recordings adds immeasurably to our appreciation of the work in performance; I therefore include a survey of representative recordings made since 1940, drawing attention to the Requiem's apparently endless potential for re-interpretation and renewal in the contexts of momentous gravity and intense drama.

Nineteenth-century editions

With primary source materials unavailable, the first published edition of the Requiem from Breitkopf & Härtel (1800) was probably based on a copy of the score used in Leipzig in 1796.[1] According to Rochlitz, the edition's most striking error, an obbligato bassoon rather than trombone in the Tuba mirum (bars 5–18), was attributable to the unavailability of a sufficiently adept trombonist in Leipzig; the bassoon line was written into the score in pencil (maybe by Hiller himself), inadvertently making its way from there into the first edition.[2] (As late as 1878, a well-informed 'German amateur'

---

[1] For discussion of an early copy of the Requiem, probably dating from the first decade of the nineteenth century and discovered in Graz, see Ingrid Schubert, 'Eine frühe Abschrift von Mozarts "Requiem" aus dem Besitz des Aloys Weiß – Umfeld und Folgerungen', in Joachim Brügge (ed.), *Musikgeschichte als Verstehensgeschichte: Festschrift für Gernot Gruber zum 65. Geburtstag* (Tutzing, 2004), pp. 331–46.

[2] As reported by Mosel in *The Musical World*, 34 (1856), pp. 309–10. Rochlitz, while not mentioning the link to the Leipzig performance, refers to this instrumentation issue in his review of the Breitkopf & Härtel edition (*Allgemeine musikalische Zeitung*, 4 (1801–2), col. 10), accepting that a bassoon can be used if an adequate trombonist is unavailable.

countered the disappointment of a Requiem listener who had regretted the absence of the bassoon in a Hallé Orchestra performance, illustrating that the erroneous bassoon line had its own nineteenth-century performance tradition.)[3] The transition from Leipzig score to Breitkopf edition might account for differences in tempo markings between the first edition and the Requiem autograph materials, but performers' and/or editors' interpretations may also have contributed. Tempo markings in the first edition for the Rex tremendae, Lacrymosa and Agnus Dei ('Grave', 'Larghetto' and 'Larghetto' respectively) do not appear in either Mozart's or Süssmayr's hand in the autograph. Two tempos are also changed: the Offertory movements, Domine Jesu and Hostias, are 'Andante' and 'Larghetto' in the edition rather than 'Andante con moto' and 'Andante' in the Walsegg score.[4] By altering the Hostias from 'Andante' to 'Larghetto' the Breitkopf editors – and/or Leipzig performers – bring the end of the Offertory into line with the end of the Sequence (the Lacrymosa featuring an interpolated 'Larghetto' marking). Tempo contrasts are accentuated in three movements situated close together: the 'Grave' of the Rex tremendae is distinguished from 'Andante' in the Tuba mirum and Confutatis. Elsewhere, tempo adjustments do not result in especially marked contrasts: the Lacrymosa 'Larghetto' and the Confutatis 'Andante'; the 'Andante' – 'Larghetto' for the Domine Jesu and Hostias; and the Agnus Dei 'Larghetto' after the Benedictus 'Andante'.[5]

The two most important full-orchestra editions later in the nineteenth century come from Johann André (1827) and Johannes Brahms (1877, for *Wolfgang Amadeus Mozarts Werke*). Both editors distinguish Mozart's and Süssmayr's contributions with the letters 'M' and 'S', considering it essential to communicate directly to performers the authorship distinctions vigorously debated in nineteenth-century critical circles. André's technique in particular is rough and ready. In the Dies irae, for example, a bracket designated 'Süssmayr' is correctly applied to the three wind-instrument lines (*corni di bassetto, fagotti, clarini* in D) plus timpani. Other indications in this movement, however, are unclear and misleading: 'Mozart' is marked

---

[3] See *The Manchester Guardian* (18 Jan. 1878), p. 7. Grove's *Dictionary of Music* regretfully reports in the 1880s that bassoonists still regularly performed the trombone solo on account of insufficiently reliable trombonists. See Trevor Herbert, *The Trombone* (New Haven, CT, and London, 2006), p. 159.

[4] Mozart's autograph of the Domine Jesu and Hostias does not contain tempo markings, but Süssmayr's does (for the Walsegg score). There is no tempo marking for the Recordare from Mozart, Süssmayr or Breitkopf & Härtel.

[5] On 'Larghetto' in relation to 'Andante' in the late eighteenth century see Clive Brown, *Classical and Romantic Performing Practice, 1750–1900* (Oxford, 1999), pp. 349–50.

for the string parts (as well as for the voices and the organ) at the opening
and 'S' at bar 15, when in fact only bars 1–9 in the first violins and bars 1–4
in the second violins and viola were notated by Mozart; the 'M' attached to
the first violin line at bar 19 and 'S' at bar 31 are correct only if we assume –
and it is unclear whether we are right to do so – that André's 'M' refers only
to the first violin and not all of the string parts;[6] and an 'M' is given to the
first violin at bar 48, beat 3, and an 'S' at bar 57, when in fact Mozart's
contribution begins at bar 40, beat 3. Brahms is more punctilious in his
markings than André, demonstrating his 'editor's instinct'.[7] He acknowledges that editing the Requiem was a 'difficult job' and that he 'did not cease
looking alternately at the two [original] manuscripts'; the 'M' and 'S'
designations, he tells us in his critical report, are vital to providing 'a true
and reliable picture of how Mozart left the work, and how immediately after
his death his pupil completed it'.[8]

While scholarly perspectives inform André's and Brahms's editions,
popular orientations inform other nineteenth-century editions. Both the
Requiem text published by John Ashley for the first London performance
(1801) and the score produced for the first Paris performance at the
Conservatoire (1805) include biographical materials, from which we infer
that knowledge of Mozart's life and death is vital for understanding the
Requiem.[9] Ashley, 'induced by a sense of duty' to relate Mozart's biography
given the lack of information about it in England, claims that Mozart
finished the Requiem 'on the day of his death'; the Conservatoire edition
provides Niemetschek's account (duly acknowledged) in which the work is
recognized as incomplete.[10] While the stories differ, attaching a story of
some kind is paramount for compilers of early editions, just as it is for
nineteenth-century writers (see Chapter 1).

Nineteenth-century arrangements of the Requiem attest to the popularity
and marketability of the work, fuelling further popularity. André brought
out a vocal score in 1801 (voices plus piano reduction), based on the
Breitkopf & Härtel edition. (It reproduces the earlier edition's editorial

---

[6] At the opening of the Rex tremendae, for example, André (correctly) marks an 'M' for the first
violin, and an 'S' for the second violin and viola, which suggests that the single 'M' at bar 19 of the
Dies irae applies to all string parts.

[7] Michael Musgrave, *A Brahms Reader* (New Haven, CT, 2000), p. 160.

[8] As quoted in Imogen Fellinger, 'Brahms's View of Mozart', in Robert Pascall (ed.), *Brahms:
Biographical, Documentary and Analytical Studies* (Cambridge, 1983), pp. 41–57, at 49.

[9] Eisen, 'Mozart's Leap in the Dark', p. 23.

[10] Ashley, *Grand Funeral Anthem Composed by W. A. Mozart*, pp. 1–5; *Messe de Requiem par
Mozart*, p. v.

tempo markings.)[11] Somewhat cluttered, especially in the underlay of both Latin and German texts, it also contains musical oddities such as a complete minor triad, rather than an open fifth, in the final chord of the Kyrie and 'Cum sanctis' fugue. Vocal scores and piano arrangements then appear regularly, including numerous vocal scores of the Benedictus alone (beginning in 1805) that collectively attest to the movement's great popularity in England.[12] Carl Czerny was responsible for a number of piano arrangements, including a rich, resonant version for piano four hands.[13] Friedrich Ferdinand Brissler's vocal score for C. F. Peters circulated widely in the late nineteenth century and includes instrumental indications in the piano part, as if to remind listeners of the textural and sonic delights they were missing.[14] Another popular piano arrangement by K. Klindworth (1871) features innumerable expressive and dynamic markings that produce heightened musical effects.[15] This foregrounds not only the common nineteenth-century predilection for editorial intervention and interpolation but also the nineteenth-century belief in the Requiem's extraordinary dramatic potential. Liszt's transcription of the Confutatis and Lacrymosa (1865) conveys similar expressive intensity: the Confutatis includes 'marcatissimo' markings for the 'Confutatis maledictis' (bars 1, 10), 'dolcissimo' at 'Voca me' (bars 7, 17) and several 'perdendo' markings in the 'Oro supplex', including one from *pp* to *ppp* for the final bar; the Lacrymosa features tremolandos in bars 10–14 – the big Neapolitan sixth at 'Qua resurget' acting as the catalyst – and ostentatious flourishes and heavy left-hand chords in the concluding 'dona eis requiem'.[16] 1865 also witnessed the

---

[11] *W. A. Mozarti [sic], Missa pro Defunctis Requiem. W. A. Mozarts Seelenmesse im Klavierauszuge, mit lateinisch und deutschem Texte*, ed. Johann André (Offenbach, 1801). The Recordare is designated 'Andante', even though no marking is given in the Breitkopf edition.

[12] See *Benedictus. Verse for 4 Voice Voices [sic]* (London, 1805). See also *Benedictus qui venit in nomine Domini, the Celebrated Quartetto* (London, c.1820); *Benedictus, or Blessed is he that Cometh in the Name of the Lord* (London, 1825); *Benedictus for Four Voices* (London, 1830); *The Benedictus, No. 1 of a Selection of Anthems Adapted to English Words by E. F. Rimbault* (London, 1846). There is also an arrangement for solo harp: *Benedictus, Mozart's Celebrated Requiem, Arranged for the Harp by N. C. Bochsa* (London, 1846).

[13] See *Mozart's Requiem, Arranged by Czerny* (London, 1853); *The Requiem, Arranged for the Pianoforte by Carl Czerny* (London, 1855 and 1860); *W. A. Mozarts Requiem für das Pianoforte allein von Carl Czerny* (Vienna, 1827); *W. A. Mozarts Requiem für das Pianoforte zu 4 Händen von Carl Czerny* (Vienna, 1828).

[14] See *Mozart Requiem, Klavier-Auszug von F. Brissler* (Leipzig, 1870), and the re-engraved edition (Moscow, c.1895).

[15] *Requiem de W. A. Mozart, arrangé pour piano seul par K. Klindworth* (Leipzig and Moscow, 1871). Editorial additions are especially dramatic in the Dies irae, with crescendos from *ff* and numerous accents, and the Confutatis, which includes a 'marcatissimo' indication at the opening.

[16] Franz Liszt, *Zwei Transcriptionen über Themen aus Mozart's Requiem für Piano* (Leipzig, 1865).

premiere of Liszt's concerto *Totentanz, Paraphrase über 'Dies irae'*, which treats an eight-note theme derived from the Introit as a subject for several variations. Liszt's work is rooted in his association between Pisa's Campo Santo – where the thirteenth-century fresco *Trionfo della morte* that inspired *Totentanz* is located – and Mozart's Requiem.[17]

Nineteenth-century performances

Following first publication in 1800, performances of the Requiem gain a head of steam. It was the work of choice across Europe at funerals and memorial services for the great and the good, explicitly recorded as such by Joseph Mainzer in 1838 and implicitly by mid-century poets:[18] for musicians, such as Carl Fasch (1800; the first Berlin performance), Giovanni Punto (1803), Joseph Haydn (1809), Jan Ladislav Dussek (1812), Giovanni Paisiello (1816), Andreas Romberg (1821), Johann Gottfried Schicht (1823), Carl Maria von Weber (1826), Beethoven (1827), Schubert (1828), Alexandre-Étienne Choron (1834), Mme Blasis (1838), Ludwig Berger (1839), Chopin (1849), Luigi Lablache (1858), Rossini (1868), Berlioz (1869), Sir Charles Hallé (1895); for literary and cultural figures including Schiller (1805), the dramatist Heinrich Joseph von Collin (1811), the actor Johann Franz Hieronymous Brockmann (1812), Goethe (1832), the painter Peter von Cornelius (1867); for royalty, nobility, statesmen, politicians and religious and military figures such as the Mayor of Leipzig Karl Wilhelm Müller (1801), France's Duc de Montebello (1810), Britain's Princess Charlotte Augusta (1817), Portugal's Princess Isabella (1819), Halle's Chancellor August Hermann Niemeyer (1828), Rome's Cardinal Weld (1837), Napoleon (1840), Baltimore's Bishop England (1842), Lord Westmoreland, patron of the Royal Academy of Music (1860), and Westminster's Cardinal Wiseman (1865).

Work and occasion are mutually reinforcing at nineteenth-century performances of the Requiem, the two together fuelling extraordinary experiences for listeners. Thus the Requiem at Carl Maria von Weber's funeral in

---

[17] See Anna Celenza, 'Liszt's Piano Concerti: A Lost Tradition', in Kenneth Hamilton (ed.), *The Cambridge Companion to Liszt* (Cambridge, 2005), pp. 152–70, at 163, 169.

[18] Joseph Mainzer, *Esquisses musicales et souvenirs de voyage* (Paris, 1838), vol. I, pp. 89–90. For poems making it apparent that Mozart's Requiem is the quintessential musical signifier of death, see Thomas Aird (ed.), *The Poetical Works of David Macbeth Noir* (Edinburgh and London, 1852), pp. 297–8; John Poyer, *Harp Echoes: Songs in the Night* (London, 1868), pp. 141–6; *Dublin University Magazine: A Literary and Political Journal*, 56 (1860), pp. 364–7 (with the reference to Mozart's Requiem on p. 366).

London 'had an effect, aided especially by the powerful contingencies of the awfully melancholy occasion, the place, the imposing ceremony of the high mass ... to thrill every nerve, and to enwrap the soul in the sublimest extasies [*sic*] of devotional feeling'.[19] Gerhard von Breuning gives a similarly exalted account of the performance at Vienna's Augustinian Court Chapel on 3 April 1827 in honour of Beethoven:

The church could hardly contain the crowds who came. My father and I stood next to Canova's memorial to Christina, said to be the spot with the best acoustics in the church. No one will ever hear the Dies irae sung again as it was that day; never will there be a more inspired performance of the Requiem. Lablache's voice to the trumpet accompaniment [*sic*; presumably the trombone in the Tuba mirum], the feelings aroused by the occasion – everything had a shattering effect.[20]

And it was not only formal funereal occasions that elicited lofty reactions. In St Petersburg, mourning huge losses sustained at the Siege of Sevastopol in the Crimean War (1855), a group of black-clad aristocrats at an open house were joined by the pianist M. Eckhart. While 'no one stirred' as he played preludes and mazurkas, the situation changed when he turned to the Requiem:

At last, M. Eckhart, impressed himself by the sadness of the scene, or lured on by one of those sudden caprices which sometimes overmaster an artist's will, began, in a subdued and almost muffled manner, to play the first bars of the commencement of Mozart's requiem! Nothing can describe ... the effect gradually produced. At first, the solemn and plaintive strains were not recognized; but little by little, all that the awful music recalled struck every individual imagination, and in a few minutes, that brightly lighted saloon, with its sable clad hosts and visitors ... was filled with silent weeping and smothered wail.[21]

Mozart's situation composing the work was often compared to the situation of the individual honoured in a particular performance: Karl Wilhelm Müller had put on a performance of Mozart's Requiem three weeks before his death, without knowing that the work would commemorate his own death, as it had for Mozart; and Theodor Körner, reflecting in poetry on Brockmann's memorial service, hears a 'swan song ... life reconciled with

---

[19] *The Examiner, a Sunday Paper on Politics, Domestic Economy, and Theatricals for the Year 1826* (London, 1826), p. 410.

[20] Gerhard von Breuning, *Memories of Beethoven*, ed. Maynard Solomon, trans. Solomon and Henry Mins (Cambridge, 1992), pp. 112–13.

[21] As reported by the French correspondent in *The Manchester Guardian* (27 Nov. 1855), p. 2, relating the contents of a letter from St Petersburg.

death', Mozart's position resonating with the homage to Brockmann.[22] In short, performance and occasion were mutually reinforcing at least in part because stories attached to the work were so memorable, rendering it such an apposite musical representation of death.

Where circumstance reinforced musical experience and vice versa, the definitive nineteenth-century performance of Mozart's Requiem was at Les Invalides in Paris on 15 December 1840 for Napoleon's re-interment. The so-called 'retour des cendres' was a momentous event, eagerly anticipated in the second half of 1840 after the decision of the *Chambre des députés* to bring back the remains from St Helena and the journeys to and from the South Atlantic island. Huge crowds watched the procession through Paris, including 500,000 on the Avenue de Neuilly alone and a 'vast multitude' elsewhere.[23] Once the remains reached Les Invalides, the mass at which Mozart's Requiem was performed began:

I will not try to convey to you the tremendous impression produced by Mozart's Requiem, performed under the direction of M. Habeneck, by a band of 300 musicians, 150 singers and 150 instrumentalists, the elite of our lyric theatres. How could I express in words the effect of Duprez's voice or of Lablache's? . . . But I will tell you on the other hand how this band produced such a full, harmonious, powerful effect; how these harmonized sounds of all the instruments and all the voices filled up the church and vibrated in a more harmonious ensemble than was ever heard elsewhere. The reason is that the organizers had been skilled enough to position the orchestra admirably in order to obtain the most magnificent, most imposing effect; the orchestra, almost entirely out of contact with the masonry, and borne by wooden pillars themselves formed of fir planks, vibrated completely as a single instrument, and since each one of the sounds, as a consequence of this common vibration, lost any slight dissonance that it might have had, the result was a harmonious ensemble of unprecedented appropriateness, amplitude and precision comparable only to the harmony of the spheres on which the ancient philosophers wrote such beautiful things, without anyone ever hearing it, I am sure.[24]

---

[22] *Blicke auf Karl Wilhelm Müller's Leben, Charakter und Verdienste um Leipzig* (Leipzig, 1801), p. 19; Theodor Körner, *Sämmtliche Werke*, 2 vols. (Reutlingen, 1837), vol. I, p. 105 ('Ein Schwanenlied . . . das Leben mit dem Tode zu versöhnen').

[23] See *The Observer* (20 Dec. 1840), p. 4.

[24] *L'artiste: journal de la littérature et des beaux-arts*, 6 (Paris, 1841), pp. 396–7: 'Je n'essayerai pas de vous rendre compte de la terrible impression produite par le *Requiem* de Mozart, exécuté sous la direction de M. Habeneck, par un orchestre de trois cents musiciens, cent cinquante chanteurs et cent cinquante instrumentalistes, l'élite de nos théâtres lyriques. Comment exprimer avec des paroles l'effet de la voix de Duprez ou de Lablanche? . . . Mais je vous dirai en revanche comment cet orchestre a produit un effet si plein, si harmonieux, si puissant; comment ces sons harmoniés

The occasion, music and assiduous attention to the placement of the instrumentalists for greatest effect produced a more perfect performance – for this reviewer at least – than could ever have been previously possible.

Others commenting on the Napoleon ceremony are hardly less awe-struck. For Henri Panofka, occasion, hero and musical work are symbiotically linked:

There was only the immortal Requiem of Mozart that could convey all that we felt at that moment. This sublime music, performed in a wonderful way by the admirable orchestra of Habeneck and by the voices [of the soloists] . . . produced an effect that it is impossible to describe. Never have we heard more pure, more angelic singing; the orchestra has never accompanied with more marvellous discretion or nuances. In short, everything was dominated and inspired by the monumental genius of this man who, alas, did not reawaken, who was lying under that lid of lead and who could see only from the heavens his old military colleagues on their knees, tears in their eyes, his people sighing with pain, and who was listening from up there to this divine music that the angels might have envied.[25]

General Count Montholon reported that the Requiem 'produced an effect difficult to describe; the sanctity of the spot alone prevented the expressions of transport from bursting forth'. And *The Observer*, five days after the event, explained that the singers 'combined in rendering it so extremely sublime and beautiful that it may fairly be said never to have [been] better or more ably given'.[26] The association between the Requiem and Napoleon's funeral continued in 1841, well after the event itself. A 'repeat' performance of the work was given at the Opéra, for a specially chosen audience of elite Parisians. Once more, music and occasion were

de tous les instruments et de toutes les voix remplissaient l'église, et vibraient dans un ensemble plus harmonieux qu'on ne l'entendit jamais ailleurs. C'est que les architectes avaient su disposer l'orchestre admirablement pour obtenir l'effet le plus magnifique, le plus imposant; c'est que l'orchestre, presque entièrement isolé de la maçonnerie, porté sur des piliers de bois et formé lui-même de planches de sapin, vibrait tout entier comme un seul instrument, et que chacun des sons perdant par l'effet de cette vibration commune ce qu'il pouvait avoir de légèrement dissonant, il en résultait un ensemble d'harmonie d'une justesse, d'une ampleur, d'une précision inouïes, comparable seulement à l'harmonie des asters sur laquelle les philosophes de l'antiquité ont écrit de si belles choses, sans que jamais personne l'ait entendre, je m'assure.'

[25] *Revue et gazette musicale de Paris*, 7 (1840), p. 617: 'Il n'y avait que l'immortel *Requiem* de Mozart qui pût traduire tout ce qu'on éprouvait en ce moment. Cette sublime musique exécutée d'une manière prodigieuse par l'admirable orchestre Habeneck et par les voix . . . a produit un effet impossible à décrire. Jamais on n'a entendu un chant plus pur, plus angélique; l'orchestre n'a jamais accompagné avec une discrétion, avec des nuances plus merveilleux, enfin tout était dominé et inspiré par le génie monumental de cet homme qui, helas! ne se réveillait point, qui était couché sous ce couvercle en plomb, et ne voyait que du ciel ses vieux militaires à genoux, les larmes aux yeux, son peuple soupirant de douleur, et qui écoutait de là-haut cette musique divine que les anges auraient pu envier.'

[26] General Count Montholon, *History of the Captivity of Napoleon at St. Helena* (London, 1847), p. 390; *The Observer* (20 Dec. 1840), p. 4.

mutually reinforcing in a performance yet again described as the best ever: 'Never had the sorrowful testament of the great Mozart been performed with such admirable perfection, for such a brilliant gathering.'[27] At St James's Bazaar in London, too, an exhibition of paintings of Napoleon's funeral was accompanied by a performance of Mozart's Requiem that was 'very cleverly managed', being 'executed during the time of the exhibition by concealed musicians'.[28]

Intensely felt connections between the Requiem and individuals or groups of individuals capture in microcosm its grip on the nineteenth-century cultural consciousness. Chopin and his circle were a case in point. The composer, present at Les Invalides for the Napoleon ceremony in 1840, at which his friends Pauline Viardot, Alexis Dupont and Luigi Lablache were among the performers, requested the Requiem (to which he was particularly devoted) for his own funeral at the Madeleine in 1849.[29] The funeral had to be delayed until permission was granted for women to participate, including Viardot again,[30] or, according to a more romantically inclined Liszt, 'so that the performance of this great work would be worthy of master and disciple'.[31] Lablache, another singer at both the Napoleon and Chopin performances, had a special affinity for the work. His participation in it at Paisiello's memorial service (1816) contributed to the launch of his illustrious career: 'Lablache, who had hitherto remained unknown to fame, took a part in the celebration, and in the *Tuba mirum* his magnificent voice obtained the most complete success – a success that decided his prosperity for life.'[32] As noted above, he had also sung it at Beethoven's memorial service in Vienna on 3 April 1827 (for which it is said he willingly paid a fine of 200 gulden to his impresario Barbaja for breaking a contractual commit-ment to perform only in the theatre).[33] Needless to say, it was performed at Lablache's own funeral in 1858, a request, we are told, that related directly to his 'feeling of grateful reminiscence'.[34] Nostalgia, personal history and myth (whether Lablache really was 'engaged by a judicious impresario' the

---

[27] *L'artiste*, 6 (Paris, 1841), p. 401: 'Jamais le douloureux testament du grand Mozart n'avait été exécuté avec cette admirable perfection, devant une assemblée aussi brillante.'

[28] *The Times* (5 April 1841), p. 5.

[29] See Frederick Niecks, *Frederick Chopin as a Man and Musician*, 2 vols. (London, 1888), vol. II, p. 322; Jim Samson, *Chopin, The Master Musicians* (New York, 1996), p. 282.

[30] See Benita Eisler, *Chopin's Funeral* (New York, 2003), pp. 6–7; Samson, *Chopin*, p. 282.

[31] Franz Liszt, *Frederic Chopin* (1851), trans. Edward N. Waters (New York, 1963), p. 181.

[32] 'Musical Chit Chat', *Dwight's Journal of Music* (1858), p. 407.

[33] Breuning, *Memories of Beethoven*, p. 112.

[34] 'Musical Chit Chat', p. 407. Lablache's son, Frederick Lablache, sang the Requiem on at least one occasion in England, at the Free Trade Hall in Manchester in 1846; see *The Manchester Guardian* (5 Sept. 1846), p. 4.

moment he left the church after the Paisiello performance is difficult to determine) merge into one.[35]

The desire for Mozart's Requiem to fulfil its correct funereal function informed Sigismund Neukomm's additions to the work for early New World performances. Neukomm (1778–1858), a Salzburg native and aficionado of Mozart's works from an early age, directed a performance in Rio de Janeiro in 1819. On 24 January 1821 he completed the autograph of '*Libera me Domine* (to follow Mozart's *Requiem*) … The *Requiem Mass* always ends with the absolutes [prayers for the dead, prior to burial], during which the *Libera* is sung. Mozart had not been able to complete his immortal masterpiece; the *Libera* is missing. I tried to supply it by recalling many parts of Mozart's mass, indicated by the lyrics of the *Libera*.'[36] Indeed, the last fifteen bars of Mozart's Introit and the beginning of the Dies irae are brought back by Neukomm towards the end of his 'Libera me', the Dies irae somewhat modified and quickly concluded. His additions in all segments are stylistically conservative: the 'Libera me' (D minor) at the beginning and end of his short sequence of movements is harmonically straightforward, featuring occasional purple patches such as the flat supertonic followed by diminished seventh harmonies (bars 19–22, 25–8), and is entirely homophonic; the solemn, march-like 'Tremens factus sum ego' moves from G minor to the dominant of D minor; and the 'Quando coeli', entirely homophonic again, returns to the bII – dim.7 progression (bars 59–62) showcased in the 'Libera me'. On a manuscript now in Paris, Neukomm noted that his additions were performed at the Church of the Congregation of St Cecilia in Rio de Janeiro.[37]

Little is known about the performance forces employed by Neukomm in Brazil, or, for that matter, about the exact forces employed for most nineteenth-century performances. But, clearly, large numbers of performers were often used, the momentousness of the work – its accompanying story, its power to commemorate, its music – matched, in the choral movements at least, by a momentousness of sound. Hamburg (1818) and Dresden (1843) performances featured 500 and 400 participants respectively; the

---

[35] 'Musical Chit Chat', p. 407.

[36] Translation slightly adapted from Sigismund Neukomm, *Libera me, Domine* (1821), ed. Luciane Beduschi and Vincent Boyer (Lyons, 2006), p. v. For a preliminary discussion of Neukomm's 'Libera me', expressing uncertainty as to whether Mozart would have included this section had he lived to complete the work, see Ulrich Konrad, 'Sigismund von Neukomm: *Libera me, Domine* D-moll NV 186: Ein Beitrag zur Liturgischen Komplettierung von Wolfgang Amadé Mozarts *Requiem* D-moll KV626', in Paul Mai (ed.), *Im Dienst der Quellen zur Musik: Festschrift Getraut Haberkamp zum 65. Geburtstag* (Tutzing, 2002), pp. 425–34.

[37] Neukomm, *Libera me, Domine*, p. v.

Napoleon performance (1840) included at least 300 musicians, one source recording 350; and the celebratory performance at the unveiling of the Mozart statue in Salzburg on 5 September 1842 must have been huge, given the 2,600-strong orchestra (with representatives from conservatoires across Europe) playing Mozart's works the previous day.[38] And a large number was sometimes expressly desired when not actually present, or when not accommodated by Mozart. A review of the Paris Conservatoire performance (1804) requested that a repeat rendition include more sopranos, altos and tenors, as they were insufficiently clearly heard in *forte* passages.[39] And Berlioz (1834) bemoaned the presence of only a single trombone in the Tuba mirum: 'Why just one trombone to sound the terrible blast that should echo round the world and raise the dead from the grave? Why keep the other two trombones silent when not three, not thirty, not three hundred would be enough?'[40]

20th- and 21st-century performances and recordings

The Requiem legend, crucial to the special status the work enjoyed in nineteenth-century performances in powerfully fusing biographical and musical parallels for Mozart with mourning for specific individuals, has continued to have an impact on twentieth- and 21st-century performance. The work has featured frequently at memorial services for mass (or multiple) fatalities, continuing as death's musical standard-bearer at least partially by virtue of its association with a compelling narrative: at a 'Requiem for Europe' (1915) during World War I, eliciting biting, satirical criticism from the poet Karl Kraus in 'Beim Anblick eines sonderbaren Plakats' (On Seeing a Remarkable Poster) as an unconscionable appropriation of Mozart's 'divine music' for propaganda purposes; at a commemoration of Armistice Day at St Michael's Church in Cornhill, London (12 November 1928); at the Salzburg Festival in memory of Nazis killed during

---

[38] On the Hamburg and Dresden numbers see *The Times* (3 Sept. 1818), p. 3, and Allan Cunningham, *The Life of Sir David Wilkie with his Journals, Tours and Critical Remarks*, 3 vols. (London, 1843), vol. II, p. 330. Numbers in the Paris performance for Napoleon are given at 300 in *L'artiste*, 6 (Paris, 1841), pp. 396–7 and at 350 in *Universalist Union*, 7 (New York, 1842), p. 503. On the performance in Salzburg for the unveiling of the Mozart statue, see *The Gentleman's Magazine*, new series 18 (1842), p. 518.

[39] *Correspondance des amateurs musiciens*, col. 782 (29 Dec. 1804).

[40] As given in Hugh Macdonald (ed.), *Berlioz's Orchestration Treatise: A Translation and Commentary* (Cambridge, 2002), p. 220. Berlioz airs this criticism in *Le rénovateur* (30 March 1834), ten years before the first publication of the *Traité*.

disturbances in Austria (July 1938); at a hastily arranged memorial to the victims of the Kent State Massacre given by Oberlin students at the Washington Cathedral (1970); at services for Lithuanians killed during an uprising against the Soviet Union (January 1991), Bosnians killed during the 1990s war (June 1994) and Dresden residents who fell victim to the Allies' bombing in World War II (January 1995); and at an internet-based, day-long choral tribute to the victims of the 9/11 attacks in the United States ('The Rolling Requiem', featuring at least 125 choirs worldwide, September 2002).[41] As in the nineteenth century, distinguished dead individuals are honoured with performances, including the singer Maria Cebotari (1949), Cardinal Faulhaber, Archbishop of Munich (1952), John Christie, the founder of Glyndebourne Opera House (1962), President John F. Kennedy (1964), the last Bavarian 'King', Franz Josef Strauss (1988), Empress Zita of Austria, Queen of Hungary (1989), Federico Fellini (1993) and the Greek Prime Minister Andreas Papandreou (1996), as well as Mozart himself, of course, in a slew of performances to commemorate the bicentennial of his death in 1991.[42]

References to the Requiem legend also continue for specific performances. An early broadcast of the Requiem on the 'London Regional' radio pro-gramme in 1930 is accompanied by an extended account of the commission and the feelings of foreboding it elicited in Mozart, but nothing on the music itself, thus in effect re-affirming that biographical knowledge is the true conduit for understanding the work.[43] Edward Greenfield (1972) compli-ments a Daniel Barenboim Requiem recording for 'to an exceptional degree

---

[41] See Gruber, *Mozart and Posterity*, pp. 208–9; *The Musical Times*, 69 (Dec. 1928), p. 1118; *The British Musician and Musical News*, 15/9 (Sept. 1938), p. 193; *The New York Magazine* (29 June 1970), p. 5; *The Observer* (20 Jan. 1991), pp. 21–2; *The Guardian* (20 June 1994), p. 8; *The Observer* (15 Jan. 1995), p. 22; *The Guardian* (5 Sept. 2002), p. B6.

[42] 'Vienna's Last Tribute to Opera Star', *The Manchester Guardian* (14 June 1949), p. 6; 'Last Homage', *The Manchester Guardian* (18 June 1952), p. 10; *The Guardian* (4 Sept. 1962), p. 10; *The Guardian* (22 Nov. 1964), p. 40; Anna Tomforde, 'Munich Stops to Mourn the Passing of Latterday Bavarian King', *The Guardian* (8 Oct. 1988), p. 7; Ian Traynor, 'Austria's Last Empress is Buried with Pomp', *The Guardian* (3 April 1989), p. 9; Ed Vulliamy, 'Social Satire and Spectacle Mark Fellini's Final Scene', *The Guardian* (4 Nov. 1993), p. 24; Helena Smith, 'Greece Laments its Champion of Democracy', *The Guardian* (27 June 1996), p. 15.

[43] *The Manchester Guardian* (29 April 1930), p. 12. Introductions to the musical qualities of recordings and performances through abbreviated accounts of the legend are common in twentieth-century popularly orientated publications. For example: 'Mozart. *Requiem*. The Vienna Hofmusikkapelle, Josef Krips. Richmond B 19077. Biographers tell how a "mysterious stranger" commissioned this mass, and Mozart, struggling unsuccessfully to complete it in his last unhappy hours, spoke of it being for himself. The ethereal qualities of this lovely and affecting work are enhanced in this performance by the luminous singing of the Vienna boy soloists.' See *Changing Times: The Kiplinger Magazine*, 15/4 (April 1961), pp. 19–20.

[making] one share Mozart's personal tragedy ... Barenboim's Mozart is above all personally involved'.[44] And, relating his memories of Benjamin Britten's performance of the Requiem at Aldeburgh in 1971, Donald Mitchell (2003) equates Britten's situation at the time of the performance with Mozart's at the time of composition. After an extraordinary performance 'so overwhelming – chilling, even unnerving in its intensity', Mitchell encountered Britten backstage: 'I had never before seen a post-performance Britten so pallid, so silent, so drained of life. It was a shock – as if his immersion in the Requiem, and his knowledge of the circumstances surrounding Mozart's inability to complete the work, lent a particular vehemence to his interpretation of it.' Britten's lengthy programme note for the concert makes reference to the 'grey stranger' who allegedly commissioned the work, and in so doing instilled in Mozart the fearful anticipation of death; for Mitchell, the Requiem 'perhaps initiated in [Britten] a comparably powerful awareness of his own mortality'. The period of ill health that culminated in Britten's death in 1976 had not yet begun. But Mitchell, close friend and associate of Britten and a respected scholar, believes that 'what we heard, unforgettably, on Sunday 20 June 1971 may have had its source in Britten's self-identification with Mozart at the end of his life'.[45]

Mitchell's assessment of Britten's performance (the recording of which is discussed below) highlights an apparent *sine qua non*: Requiem performances must convey intensity, urgency or drama, irrespective of the instrumental and vocal forces employed. Uncommitted performances of Mozart's music are rarely appealing, but are especially unpalatable for the Requiem, on account (it would seem) of our collective perceptions of the work's co-existent musical qualities and extramusical connotations. Time and again, late twentieth-century critics draw attention to the virtues of intense, dramatic engagement in specific performances, or bemoan its absence: a Manchester Cathedral performance (1962) lacks the requisite 'burning intensity and torment of spirit'; the Barenboim recording (1972) foregrounds an 'urgency of communication' that is 'irresistible'; a Rafael Frühbeck de Burgos rendition of the Confutatis (1980) 'had one almost seeing before one's eyes the contrasted demons and angels of male and female voices'; a Christoph Eschenbach performance (1983) 'intensifies and darkens colours so as almost to romanticize the music'; a John Eliot Gardiner recording (1987) is 'frequently thrilling and powerful' in its choral

---

[44] Edward Greenfield, 'Choral Records', *The Guardian* (22 May 1972), p. 10.

[45] See Donald Mitchell, 'The Consciousness of Mortality', CD liner notes to Mozart, Requiem: Benjamin Britten, Aldeburgh Festival Chorus and English Chamber Orchestra, BBC Legends, 2003, BBCL 4119-2, pp. 6–7, at 6.

sound.[46] Performances and recordings are sometimes considered to over-emphasize or to undersell drama and intensity, or to negotiate a balance with other ostensibly contrasting musical qualities such as intimacy and poignancy.[47] Judgment calls of these kinds situate drama and intensity at the centre of the listening experience, irrespective of where we draw our own lines between too much, too little and the right amount.

To be sure, we want to witness engaged, intense recordings and live performances of the Requiem, but we also need to remain open-minded about potentially contradictory features of individual interpretations: a romanticized rendition need not in itself be compromised by the use of period instruments or a modern-day Requiem completion; a 'time-travelling', nineteenth-century approach can still deliver a convincing rapport between audience and performers in the modern era; and a 'traditional' approach and sound are not necessarily incommensurate with using period instruments.[48] For the work itself, at least as we have collectively construed it, radiates contradictions: it is regarded as a fragment but as a completed work in performance, as a multi-authored work but a Mozart masterpiece, as a product of the late eighteenth century but one known to only a tiny number of people before the nineteenth. Perhaps performers can even try to use such contradictions as a spur, rather than an impediment, to interpretative crea-tivity? At any rate performers are obliged to tell us stories in their renditions of the Requiem, even if only general stories that involve highlighting partic-ular features and qualities of the work. We may want musical narratives to emerge in performances of all of Mozart's instrumental and vocal works, of course, but especially of the Requiem, where performers can be reasonably expected to offer an interpretative perspective on multi-authorship and its musical ramifications, and to respond to our collective penchant for marrying a highly charged story of extramusical events with perceptions of musical events. Needless to say, we do not want to prescribe specific perspectives and narratives and we no doubt welcome interpretative diversity in surveying a

[46] J. H. Elliot, 'Mozart's Requiem in Manchester Cathedral', *The Guardian* (14 March 1962), p. 7; Greenfield, 'Choral Records', p. 10; Edward Greenfield, 'RFH: Philharmonie/Burgos', *The Guardian* (16 June 1980), p. 13; Hugo Cole, 'Festival Hall: LPO', *The Guardian* (9 May 1983), p. 11; Nicholas Kenyon, 'Record of the Week', *The Observer* (18 Oct. 1987), p. 25.

[47] For representative criticism see Gerald Larner, 'Edinburgh: Giulini/NPO', *The Guardian* (25 August 1977), p. 10; Meirion Bowen, 'St John's Orchestra', *The Guardian* (25 May 1978), p. 10; Nicholas Kenyon, 'Lightweight', *The Observer* (29 November 1987), p. 25 (on Giulini's Requiem); Tom Service, 'Philharmonia/Dohnanyi, RFH, London', *The Guardian* (27 March 2001), p. 16.

[48] See Cole, 'Festival Hall: LPO', p. 11; Neil Mackay, 'Leningrad Philharmonic', *The Guardian* (23 Aug. 1991), p. 38; Kenyon, 'Record of the Week', p. 25.

number of different recordings. My study of Requiem recordings cannot do justice to all of the hundreds available; I therefore examine a representative cross-section, including recordings from the early 1940s onwards, performances on period instruments and modern instruments with large or small forces, live performances as well as studio recordings, and performances that use three modern-day completions (by Franz Beyer, Richard Maunder and Robert Levin) as well as those that use Süssmayr.[49]

Four Requiem recordings from the 1940s and 1950s, from Bruno Kittel (1941), Victor De Sabata (1941), Eugen Jochum (1955) and Bruno Walter (1958), all foreground momentous and intense gravity and grandeur, but in different ways. Chillingly, Kittel's recording incorporates alterations to the text to accommodate Nazi requirements: 'Deus in Zion' (God in Zion) becomes 'Deus in coelis' (God in Heaven); 'in Jerusalem' becomes 'hic in terra' (in the world); and 'Quam olim Abrahae' (as promised to Abraham) becomes 'Quam olim homini promisisti' (as promised to man). Self-evidently revolting though such textual adjustments are, the musical interpretation is carefully considered and executed. Kittel highlights gravity and grandeur of effect through slow, emphatic renditions of choral movements such as the Rex tremendae, Confutatis and Domine Jesu (respectively at ♪ = 66; ♩ = 46; ♩ = 63),[50] particularly noticeably in the first six bars of the Rex tremendae and throughout the Confutatis and Domine Jesu. But gravity and

---

[49] The recordings I examine are as follows: Bruno Kittel (1941), Bruno-Kittel Choir and Berlin Philharmonic, Deutsche Grammophon, 459 004-2; Victor De Sabata (1941), Rome and Turin Orchestra and Choirs of the Italian Broadcasting Authority, Naxos, 2006, 8.111064; Eugen Jochum (live recording 1955), Chorus of the Vienna Staatsoper and Vienna Symphony Orchestra, Deutsche Grammophon, 2005, 00289 477 5811; Bruno Walter (live recording 1958), Chicago Symphony Orchestra and Chicago Symphony Chorus, IDIS, 6533; István Kertész (1966), Vienna State Opera Choir and Vienna Philharmonic, Universal Classics, B0001225-02; Benjamin Britten (live recording 1971), Aldeburgh Festival Chorus and English Chamber Orchestra, BBC Legends, BBC Music, BBCL 4119-2; Carlo Maria Giulini (1979), Philharmonia Chorus and Orchestra, Seraphim Classics, 7243 5 73702 2 6; Helmut Rilling (1979), Gächinger Kantorei Stuttgart, CBS, MBK 42614; Peter Schreier (1982), Rundfunkchor Leipzig and Staatskapelle Dresden, Phillips, 464 878-2; Christopher Hogwood (1984), Academy of Ancient Music, Decca, 1990, 4117122; George Guest (1987), Choir of St John's College, Cambridge, and English Chamber Orchestra, Chandos Classics, 10208X; Leonard Bernstein (live recording 1989), Bavarian Radio Symphony Orchestra and Chorus, Deutsche Grammophon, 427 353-2; John Eliot Gardiner (1986), English Baroque Soloists and Monteverdi Choir, Deutsche Grammophon, B000ASAEKI; Martin Pearlman (1995), Boston Baroque, Telarc, TLC 80410; Helmuth Rilling (2000), Stuttgart Bach Collegium and Gächinger Kantorei Stuttgart, Hänssler Classic, 2004, HAN 98146; Sir Charles Mackerras (2002), Scottish Chamber Orchestra and SCO Chorus, Linn Records, 2003, CKD 211; Christophe Spering (2002), New Berlin Chamber Orchestra and Chorus Musicus Cologne, Naïve, V5108; Andreas Delfs (2005), St Paul Chamber Orchestra and St Olaf Choir, Avie Records, AV 0047.

[50] Tempos cited here and below are approximations. Fluctuations are common within movements and become conventional in certain contexts (such as bars 1–6 of the Rex tremendae, taken

grandeur co-exist with clean, clear and crisp vocal and instrumental articulation, thus conveying precise weightiness, not heavy sludge.

De Sabata takes a different approach. Rather than providing a slow Rex tremendae and Confutatis like Kittel, he offers up sluggish solo movements (Tuba mirum: ♩ = 56; Recordare: ♩ = 52), perhaps attempting to impart gravity where it is not immediately apparent in the music, and a lugubrious Lacrymosa (♩. = 26), surpassed in slowness among my surveyed recordings only by Leonard Bernstein. A ponderous Hostias (♩ = 48), followed by an astonishingly quick Sanctus (♪= 132), suggests that De Sabata wants us to hear the Requiem as a sequence of grand and dramatic emotional and musical extremes. But the blunt use of inter-movement tempo changes to put this into effect lends an air of disconnectedness to the performance as a whole. If De Sabata intended to draw attention to the Requiem as a series of individualized, unconnected movements, it is unclear why he also then minimizes differences in pulse between the affectively contrasting Benedictus and Agnus Dei (♪= 96; ♪= 100).

The apparent driver for Jochum's sonic gravity and grandeur, in contrast to De Sabata's, is momentous unity. The first five movements of the Sequence, both movements of the Offertory, and the Sanctus and Benedictus adopt very similar pulses (Dies irae: ♩ = 74; Tuba mirum: ♩ = 72; Rex tremendae: ♪= 76; Recordare: ♩ = 72; Confutatis: ♩ = 69; Domine Jesu: ♩ = 76; Hostias: ♩ = 69; Sanctus: ♪= 72; Benedictus: ♪= 74). Similarities are all the more striking because Jochum's Requiem forms part of a complete mass for the dead recorded live at St Stephen's Cathedral in Vienna; intoned texts between Kyrie and Sequence, Sequence and Offertory, Offertory and Sanctus, and Benedictus and Agnus Dei and an organ improvisation between Sanctus and Benedictus would have hindered rather than facilitated consistent pulses and tempos across the performance. While the Lacrymosa is considerably slower than the preceding movements in the Sequence (♩.= 42), it is envisaged as a sonic climax to the first half of the Requiem, strongly accentuating the crescendo to bar 8, the 'dona eis requiem' statement (bar 22) and the final 'Amen' plagal cadence. For Jochum, movement-to-movement homogeneity supersedes heterogeneity and even localized, intra-movement contrasts that inevitably isolate and promote individual timbres and textures.[51] Jochum thus tries hard to show that the Requiem, though left incomplete by Mozart, is in fact a tautly unified work.

---

slower than the contrapuntal continuation in bar 7, and the 'Confutatis maledictis' sections of the Confutatis, taken faster than the 'Voca me' and 'Oro supplex' sections).

[51] The extent to which contrasting individual timbres and textures are downplayed is difficult to determine precisely given the technically imperfect quality of the recording.

Bruno Walter's outstanding live recording with the Chicago Symphony Orchestra and Chorus is no less grand and momentous than Kittel's, De Sabata's and Jochum's, but foregrounds greater intimacy and poignancy as well. The impression of the Requiem as a momentous drama of stark contrasts is evident right at the outset: the entry of the trombone and trumpets in bars 7–8 and the emphatic thumps at 'et lux perpetua' (bars 43–4) of the Introit are set against the quietly intense *piani* at 'luceat eis' (bar 18), at the orchestral transition to 'Requiem aeternam' and 'Dona eis Domine' (bars 32–4) and at the final iteration of 'et lux perpetua' (bars 46–8). Contrasts continue impressively in the Rex tremendae (mighty grandeur at the opening, refined intimacy at 'Salva me'), the Confutatis (assertive at 'Confutatis maledictis', hushed at 'Voca me' and 'Oro supplex'), the Hostias (meditative at the opening, forceful at the exclamations from bar 23 onwards) and the Agnus Dei (momentous at the opening and as soft as possible at 'dona eis requiem'). The Sanctus superbly captures the grandeur highlighted in nineteenth-century criticism, representing a climactic moment in this performance. Similarly, the Lacrymosa is an apotheosis of both grandeur and intimacy, the gentle swelling of the opening vocal lines co-existing with the momentous crescendo to bar 8, the grand 'dona eis requiem' statement and the huge 'Amen'. Walter's slow tempos and frequent *ritardandi* will disturb some modern-day listeners. But Walter lulls us compellingly into his story of oscillating grandeur and intimacy, qualities vividly and often delicately balanced in his recording.

The variation in interpretations of the Requiem from the 1940s and 1950s continue into the 1960s, 1970s and early 1980s. Like Jochum, István Kertész (1966) foregrounds homogeneity in his consistent pulses for the first five movements of the Sequence and near-identical tempos for the Domine Jesu and Hostias ($\,=76;\,=76$), and the Sanctus and Benedictus ($\,=84;\,=88$). Kertész, similar again to Jochum, encourages listeners to look beyond the divisions between Mozart's and Süssmayr's work in order to appreciate the coherence and completeness of the Requiem as a whole. The initial Sanctus statement, as for Walter, projects magnificent grandeur through triumphant sound; we are invited to process it as a climactic outcome to all that precedes it. Equally, the *fortissimi* of the boldly realized, full-wind tutti chords in bars 18–20 and 50–2 of the Benedictus – both marked in Süssmayr's autograph – come across as the winds' most emphatic contributions to the work. Kertész is more attuned than Jochum to intra-movement contrasts and changes of colour. The Offertory movements are notable for effectively conveying *piano* and *forte* contrasts, and the Tuba mirum is particularly rich in colourful dynamic and affective variety, the trombone alone projecting a full, emphatic opening arpeggio, a muted continuation of the obbligato line and a rare adherence to Süssmayr's *forte* marking in bar 28 in the link to the new phrase beginning in bar 29. In short, Jochum's story of grand homogeneity and Walter's of grand drama and intimacy becomes Kertész's story of grand homogeneity *and* drama.

Benjamin Britten's live recording from Aldeburgh (1971) is an essay in all-consuming dramatic intensity and commitment, as Donald Mitchell claims. In the Dies irae, for example, both the overall sound from the large assembled forces – 'Quando judex est venturus' (bars 53ff.) is particularly memorable – and the *attacca* continuation from the end of the Kyrie fugue, amply convey these qualities. In effect, the *attacca* projects the rhythmic and sonic energy from the fugue directly into the Sequence, a process accentuated by closely aligned pulses from movement to movement ($\lrcorner$ = 90; $\lrcorner$ = 84). Other highlights (which are numerous) include the sighing accompaniments from the opening of the Lacrymosa that are transformed into sighing one-bar 'Lacrymosa' and 'dies illa' vocal figures; the momentous sound at the end of the Domine Jesu (in both the 'Quam olim Abrahae' fugue and the concluding 'et semini ejus'); the subdued falling-away (and slowing-down) of the Hostias followed by the dramatic onset of the reprised fugue; the huge, imposing sound of the Sanctus; and the tautly intense 'Agnus Dei qui tollis' statement at bar 34 of the eponymous movement. Britten goes too far in his pursuit of rhythmic and contrapuntal energy and intensity in the Rex tremendae, which is taken at such a fast speed ($\lrcorner$ = 80, far and away the fastest among my surveyed recordings[52]) that details are inevitably lost. But, as Hugo Cole wrote on the day of the performance, it is churlish to criticize individual moments when the impact of the whole is so powerful. Britten's own minor adjustments to the score pale similarly into insignificance, 'swamped by the splendour of Britten's ideas about the work'.[53]

Three recordings from the late 1970s and early 1980s, from Carlo Maria Giulini (1979), Helmuth Rilling (1979) and Peter Schreier (1982), offer expansive but varied interpretations of the Requiem. Giulini, in the spirit of Jochum, prioritizes a large-scale canvas over individual detail, as demonstrated in his broadly conceived Introit. The first six bars open out gradually and effectively – continuing to do so in bars 8–14 – but are followed by a damp squib of a trombone entry in bars 7–8 (marked *forte*

---

[52] The next quickest performances of the Rex tremendae are Christophe Spering at $\flat$= 120 and Martin Pearlman at $\flat$= 108; several recordings (Victor De Sabata, Christopher Hogwood, Charles Mackerras) take the movement at $\flat$= 100.

[53] Hugo Cole, 'Aldeburgh Festival', *The Guardian* (21 June 1971), p. 8.

by Mozart) overpowered by the strings. At the end of the Introit, a grand sweep is again preferred to colouristic detail: after a big climax at 'luceat eis' (bars 45–6), the final three bars slow down ostentatiously and fade away almost to nothing, as if projecting a momentous ending to a momentous musical experience. The choral movements have a greater overall impact than the solo movements – the Tuba mirum, Recordare and Benedictus are unremarkable – and eventually offer up memorable individual effects to complement Giulini's emphasis on the big picture: a warm, consolatory F major chord at the end of the affect-laden Confutatis; an intense explosion at bar 23 of the Hostias after a subdued and understated opening; and (as in Britten) a dramatic transition to the reprised 'Quam olim Abrahae' fugue in the Hostias. Giulini's recording does not quite create the impression of his later performance of the work with the Philharmonia Chorus in 1987, 'which existed on some distant plateau, in a different time-world, where every lively feature and rhythmic angularity had been softened out to create an icon which we could only barely glimpse from afar'.[54] But it does lack the direct, urgent performer-to-listener communication evident in earlier and later Requiem recordings.

Peter Schreier's recording with the Staatskapelle Dresden (1982) is similar to Giulini's in tempo choices and attention to large-scale shape, but ultimately demonstrates a clearer vision for the work as a whole. Singing and orchestral playing are well blended through to the Rex tremendae, but the sound is perhaps too monochrome; the recording picks up from the Recordare onwards, Schreier more effectively conveying his vision of dramatic contrast interacting with sonic climax. At 'Ingemisco, tamquam reus: Culpa rubet vultus meus; Supplicanti parce, Deus' (Recordare, bars 72–83), the desperate cries of the initial segments are followed by intensely hushed, fragile responses. In the Confutatis, strongly contrasted 'Confutatis maledictis' and 'Voca me' segments are fused by exquisitely graded, one-bar links in the bassethorns (bars 6–7, 16–17), which start assertively and then die away in preparation for the entry of sopranos and altos. Smoothly blended wind chords at 'Oro supplex' in the Confutatis are also memorably distinguished from the crisp articulation of the simultaneously singing voices. Local musical contrasts and sonic climaxes complement large-scale ones: Schreier's dynamic and affective contrasts in the Offertory – in the 'Quam olim Abrahae' fugue, between the beginning of the Hostias and the 'Hostias', 'tibi' and 'laudis' exclamations (bars 23–32) and at the onset of the 'Quam olim Abrahae' reprise – are supported by a striking difference

---

[54] Kenyon, 'Lightweight'.

between the Domine Jesu and Hostias tempos ($\downarrow$ = 86; $\downarrow$ = 60), where tempos are usually closely aligned. Schreier's extraordinary initial Sanctus statement, with forceful impact at the opening, a strong presence of basses, bass trombone and bassoons presence at 'pleni sunt' (bar 6) and a yearning g′ in the tenor (bars 9–10), is a genuinely climactic moment, as (more subtly) is his wind colouring in the Benedictus, where the full, rich tutti chords in bars 18–20 and 50–2, the bassethorns' fading-away in bars 21–2 and the *forti* in bars 46–9 are conveyed with particular clarity.

Helmuth Rilling's Requiem (1979) is a more ponderous drama than Schreier's, but no less effective. Like Giulini, Rilling envisages a grand shape for the work, individual effects feeding into a larger narrative, with beginnings and ends of movements repeatedly emphasized: the Introit spreads its wings impressively in the first seven bars, introducing the expansive drama that is to follow; the Lacrymosa articulates a big crescendo to bar 8 and ends with an ostentatious *rit.* in the penultimate bar (the first chord of the 'Amen' plagal cadence) followed by a big decrescendo in the final bar; the Agnus Dei provides a big crescendo at the opening (to bar 9) and a *ritardando* at the end; and the Kyrie, Rex tremendae, Recordare, Confutatis, Domine Jesu and Hostias all contain discernible *ritardandi* at the close. Rilling goes too far in the Confutatis, the 'Oro supplex' slowing down considerably only for a further *ritardando* at the end of the movement to bring the music practically to a standstill: the F major chord and the dominant seventh of D minor of the final bar are heard so far apart that the function of this bar as both an end to the Confutatis and a transition to the Lacrymosa is lost. But Rilling's repeated articulation of beginnings and ends, and his consistent pulses for both Mozart's and Süssmayr's movements (Domine Jesu, Hostias, Sanctus, Benedictus and Agnus Dei), give us a coherent, grandly dramatic Requiem, not dissimilar to those of Jochum and Kertész.

Period-instrument recordings from Christopher Hogwood (1984), John Eliot Gardiner (1986) and Martin Pearlman (1995) ably transfer taut dramatic conceptions of the Requiem to a new performing context. Hogwood's Requiem, to my knowledge one of only two commercially available recordings of Maunder's completion,[55] features tight, clean playing and singing, and a large, powerful sound when required (Dies irae, Rex tremendae, Confutatis) in spite of the small forces employed. At times we may wish

---

[55] The other recording of Maunder's completion features Cantoria Plagensis and the Erstes Barockorchester Heiligenberg, conducted by Rupert Gottfried Frieberger (Convert, 1991, B0000262YR).

for a more subdued sound, for instance at 'Salva me' in the Rex tremendae, and at 'Voca me' and 'Oro supplex' in the Confutatis. (Hogwood's 'Voca me' and 'Oro supplex' are pure, emotionless pleas, unlike his emotion-laden 'Confutatis maledictis' statements.) But elsewhere Hogwood's contrasts are more effective, particularly in the unsettling juxtaposition of tense, rigid string playing and more relaxed vocal articulation in the 'Quam olim Abrahae' fugue. His control and clarity of sound make us wonder wistfully how he would have interpreted the Sanctus and Benedictus – with their climactic raw sound and increased wind participation respectively – had Maunder's edition not encouraged their omission.[56]

No such uncertainty besets Gardiner's Requiem, which returns to Süssmayr's completion. According to one reviewer, Gardiner's 'darkly dramatic' rendition conveys a marked 'threat of death'.[57] Indeed, the prominent trombones and rasping trumpets are ominously intense in the Kyrie, Dies irae, Rex tremendae and Confutatis, and are balanced in an effectively precarious fashion with the fragility of 'Voca me' in the Confutatis. The Sanctus ($\flat$= 100) if taken at a slightly slower tempo would better convey the movement's sonically climactic qualities, but the brass instruments are still triumphant in the initial statement.

Pearlman's Requiem on period instruments with Boston Baroque, using Levin's completion, is just as dramatic as Hogwood's and Gardiner's from moment to moment, and no less meticulous. An exciting sound is created in the Introit, in the Dies irae and at the beginning of the Confutatis, enhanced in part by quick tempos. Yet the quick tempos do not always work in Pearlman's favour, especially in movements that would have benefited from some breathing space. The Tuba mirum and Recordare are the fastest among my surveyed recordings ($\downarrow$ = 92 and $\downarrow$ = 104); colours and details are lost and the movements seem perfunctory. Equally, the fast 'Voca me' and 'Oro supplex' of the Confutatis ($\downarrow$ = 90), the orchestra's rigorous playing from the opening resurfacing in the string accompaniment, foreground mechanical performance more than affective contrast. If Pearlman is trying to make a point about the musical roles of the Tuba mirum, Recordare and Confutatis in the work as a whole, it is unclear what this point is.

---

[56] Maunder's edition, published four years after the original release of Hogwood's recording, includes the Sanctus and Benedictus in an appendix. His half-hearted justification for including the Sanctus and Benedictus in the appendix but not the main text – 'for all their shortcomings, they are pieces by a late eighteenth-century composer written specifically for inclusion in Mozart's Requiem' – and his belief in their 'dubious craftsmanship and commonplace invention' do not encourage performance. See Mozart, *Requiem*, ed. Maunder, p. vi.

[57] Edward Greenfield, 'Voices Raised to Epic Heights', *The Guardian* (11 Dec. 1987), p. 16.

Two recent recordings, on modern instruments and using modern-day completions, capture in microcosm the Requiem's apparently endless potential for re-interpretation and narrative renewal, even in the context of well-established performing traditions. Leonard Bernstein's and Charles Mackerras's Requiems (1989, 2003) are worlds apart in execution, ambience and mood but equally convincing on their own terms. Bernstein's is musical drama on an epic scale worthy of Bruno Walter, heavy and emphatic at times (Lacrymosa, Agnus Dei), but also intimate (Recordare) and powerful and frenetic (Dies irae, Confutatis). It is a journey through coherently articulated emotional extremes: a Dies irae that begins *attacca*, thus drawing strength (as did Britten's) from the preceding Kyrie;[58] a fast and furious Confutatis that initially invokes the Dies irae and later ('Voca me' and 'Oro supplex') the fragility of the Rex tremendae's 'Salva me'; a grandly articulated Sanctus in tune with Bernstein's vision for the work as a whole; and remarkably slow, deeply felt Lacrymosa and Agnus Dei movements that bring the Sequence and the Sanctus–Benedictus–Agnus complex to a close in similarly momentous ways. On occasion, Beyer's adjustments to Süssmayr's completion resonate with Bernstein's vision: at the beginnings of the Lacrymosa and Agnus, Beyer's graded crescendos (in the Agnus, p in bar 2, crescendo to mf in bar 6, crescendo to f in bar 8) complement Bernstein's gradually unfolding dramas. More often than not, though, Beyer's edition hinders Bernstein: the added melodic fragment for violin in the penultimate bar of the Rex tremendae draws attention away from Bernstein's otherwise effective and poignant fade; the links between 'Confutatis maledictis' and 'Voca me' (bars 6–7, 16–17), bassethorns and bassoons doubling each other in octaves, lack the warmth of the contrary motion from e' and g' to c', e' and c'' in Süssmayr's completion (bars 6–7) that would have been better suited to the nuances of Bernstein's emotional, contrast-driven interpretation; and the tenor's yearning g' in bars 9–10 of the Sanctus is lost amid trumpet elaborations. But Bernstein's Requiem still comes across as the passion-fuelled 'cry to grant rest to the souls of the dead' that he intended.[59] He often talked of 're-composing' a work in performance;[60] in this Requiem he perhaps comes closer than any other conductor in the late twentieth century to 're-composing' the drama of the biographically inspired Requiem legend, whereby the music's emotional

---

[58] Admittedly, this is possible only in a concert performance of the Requiem; in a liturgical performance, Oratio and Lectio texts are intoned between the Kyrie and Dies irae.

[59] As reported by the solo tenor in the recording, Jerry Hadley, in William Westbrook Burton (ed.), *Conversations about Bernstein* (Oxford, 1995), p. 128.

[60] Ibid., p. 130.

extremes are understood to equate with Mozart's emotional extremes in composing the work.

Mackerras, in contrast, appropriates the taut, meticulous playing of the period-instrument tradition to a dramatic rendition on modern instruments. Precise, powerful articulation is the order of the day in the Introit, Kyrie, Dies irae and Rex tremendae; an urgent, almost angry pleading features at 'Ingemisco' in the Recordare (bars 72ff.); rasping strings at 'Confutatis maledictis' are set against fragile, tentative strings and voices at 'Voca me' in the Confutatis; the 'Quam olim Abrahae' fugal reprise explodes into action after a *ritardando* and a dying-away almost to nothing at the end of the Hostias; and a robust, triumphant sound characterizes the initial Sanctus statement. Mackerras's use of Levin's edition is less distracting to his interpretation of the work than Bernstein's use of Beyer's edition is to Bernstein's interpretation, in part because Levin's rationale for many adjustments is clearer than Beyer's (see Chapter 6). But Levin's changes to the initial Sanctus statement and the Benedictus do not help Mackerras. The embellishments to the violin lines in the Sanctus (bars 1–11) detract attention from the monumentality that Mackerras apparently intends. In addition, the lighter wind parts in the Benedictus – trumpets and trombones are omitted entirely before the return of the Osanna fugue, rendering material such as the wind chords in bars 18–20 and 50–2 less rounded and resonant than in Süssmayr's completion – create uncertainty as to what role the Benedictus plays (or what it is intended to convey) in Mackerras's interpretation of the work as a whole. Süssmayr's fuller, more forceful wind writing would have better suited Mackerras's assertive, strong-willed drama.

Conclusion

It is perhaps unsurprising that intense experience of Mozart's Requiem in the nineteenth century and dramatic renditions of the work in the twentieth and early twenty-first centuries both feature prominently in our evaluation of the Requiem in performance. The emotional fluctuations of the music, both between and within movements, point to the general association of drama with heightened intensity; the ebb and flow of these emotions, encouraging us to monitor affective similarities, dissimilarities and developments across the work, also brings to mind the process-orientated drama that renders Mozart's piano concertos and symphonies (for example) metaphorically, if not literally, dramatic.[61] In including strikingly dramatic moments and developments over time, Mozart's Requiem demands of its interpreters active negotiation of the local and the global, in terms of effects, sounds and affects. And where conductors seem neither to respond to the task nor to tell us a story about the negotiation – as in George Guest's, Christophe Spering's and Andreas Delfs's recordings (1987, 2002, 2005) – a disappointing blandness ensues. Mozart's Requiem is not a work, ultimately, for the disengaged.[62]

Collectively, Requiem recordings from the last seventy years or so demonstrate remarkable interpretative diversity – in sounds and effects delivered, energy and vitality conveyed, and in overall visions communicated. It would be wrong to imply that some of the later recordings I have discussed are simply redolent of old-fashioned approaches to the work, or that period-instrument recordings depart radically from earlier interpretations. Rilling (1979) and Bernstein (1989) favour the large-scale, expansive approach prominent in earlier times, resonating with Jochum, Kertész and Walter, but make their own unique interpretational marks on the work as well, whereas Hogwood, Gardiner and Pearlman, showcasing a new vitality and tautness of performance, continue to foreground the Requiem's drama, like so many of their predecessors on modern instruments.

It is difficult to judge whether nineteenth-century performances of the Requiem, which can be evaluated only through written criticism, are as interpretatively diverse in total as their late 20th- and early 21st-century counterparts. But a common theme emerges across the 220-year performance history of the work: the legend of the Requiem has had a consistent, pervasive influence. The death of the venerated individual at a memorial performance acquires special emotional momentousness because the music representing the death emanates from its creator's own experience of approaching death; the mysteries surrounding the work inspire

---

[61] On the concertos, see Simon P. Keefe, *Mozart's Piano Concertos: Dramatic Dialogue in the Age of Enlightenment* (Woodbridge and Rochester, NY, 2001); on the symphonies, focusing on the 'Jupiter', see Keefe, 'The "Jupiter" Symphony in C, K. 551: New Perspectives on the Dramatic Finale and its Stylistic Significance in Mozart's Orchestral Oeuvre', *Acta musicologica*, 75 (2003), pp. 17–43 and Keefe, *Mozart's Viennese Instrumental Music: A Study of Stylistic Re-Invention* (Woodbridge and Rochester, NY, 2007), pp. 137–64.

[62] Helmuth Rilling's recording from 2000 is a disappointment on account of its lack of engagement with the score. Since Rilling uses the Levin completion rather than the Süssmayr employed in his 1979 recording, we would expect interpretative changes; few, however, are forthcoming. (Ironically, the Introit tempos are most different in Rilling's two recordings; as Mozart's movement alone, the musical text does not change from Süssmayr's version to Levin's.) Rilling's continued interpretation of the Requiem as a ponderous drama is not well served, ultimately, by Levin's edition.

performances and reactions to performances; narratives projected and perceived depend on musicians, audiences and critics processing fictions and quasi-fictions associated with the work, as well as facts. We need Requiem performances to tell us stories, because stories associated with the Requiem are intrinsic to our understandings of the work. Profound musical emotion, public or private veneration and the extraordinary biographical circumstances associated with the creation of the work come together to produce momentous gravity and intense drama in performance, feeding our collective appetite for compelling accompanying narratives.

4 | Mozart's work on the Requiem: sounds and strategies

The Requiem legend and the music of the Requiem intersect most poignantly and most powerfully in the autograph materials. Myth and reality collide brutally, beautifully, bizarrely: at the abrupt end to the Lacrymosa in Mozart's hand and two-bar aborted continuation from Eybler; at the fading-away of the Hostias, complete with 'quam olim Da capo' indications, and subsequent empty pages; in Mozart's and Eybler's combined contributions to the Sequence manuscript; in the sudden disappearance of Mozart's hand between the Kyrie fugue and the Dies irae in the score prepared for Walsegg. The collective audience also makes its presence felt: in the pencil markings that distinguish Mozart's from Eybler's handwriting in the Sequence, written in at the office of Walsegg's lawyer Dr Johann Nepomuk Sortschan (1800);[1] and in the corner of the final page of the Hostias ripped away during the World Fair in Brussels (1958) by an unknown admirer who no doubt believed, rightly or wrongly, that 'quam Olim d: C:' at the bottom right was Mozart's final contribution to a musical work of any kind before his death. (The tear is a neat one, affecting no material at all on any stave, not even a bar-line, as if demonstrating deep respect for Mozart's score even in the act of mutilating it.) The manuscript materials in their entirety comprise the Introit and Kyrie in Mozart's hand (excepting the instrumental parts for the Kyrie contributed by an unknown person) followed by the remainder of the work in Süssmayr's hand; the Sequence movements in Mozart's hand with Eybler's partial completion; the Domine Jesu and Hostias from Mozart without further additions; and sketches for the Rex tremendae from bar 7 and for the beginning of an 'Amen' fugue assumed to be for the Lacrymosa.[2] Perusing these materials, in light of all that has been

---

[1] Wolff, *Mozart's Requiem*, pp. 21, 164–5.

[2] The autograph materials are held at the Österreichische Nationalbibliothek, Vienna. They are collected together (except for the sketches) in *Wolfgang Amadeus Mozart, Requiem, KV626: Vollständige Faksimile-Ausgabe im Originalformat der Originalhandschrift in zwei Teilen nach Mus. Hs. 17.561 der Musiksammlung der Österreichischen Nationalbibliothek*, ed. Günter Brosche (Kassel, 1990). For further discussion of autograph materials see Wolff, *Mozart's Requiem*, pp. 17–24 (Wolff transcribes the sketches on pp. 30, 33). Leopold Nowak proposed Jacob Freystädler as the writer of the instrumental parts in the Kyrie autograph ('Wer hat die Instrumentalstimmen in der Kyrie-Fuge des Requiems von W. A. Mozart geschrieben?',

written about the Requiem, factual, fictional and quasi-factual alike, is an intense, often overwhelming experience.

The beauty of the Requiem autograph is, in part, the beauty of Tintern, Fountains, Furness: visiting these ruined abbeys, we marvel at what is there and imagine what is not.[3] Some of the inner beauties of both are revealed through close contemplation; many remain (perhaps frustratingly, perhaps beguilingly) hidden, even to the best-informed scholar. But the Requiem autograph left by Mozart offers us something that a Cistercian ruin cannot, perhaps even enhanced rather than hindered by its fragmentary status; interrupted by death, rather than disturbed by human intervention and neglect (and inclement weather), the autograph provides intimate insight into the world of its creator at an incomplete stage of the work's existence, into his thought-processes, priorities and strategies. With vocal parts and bass-line completed by Mozart for the Kyrie, Sequence (only to bar 8 of the Lacrymosa) and Offertory, it is his fragmentary instrumental indications for upper strings and wind in the Sequence and Offertory that are most revealing in this respect. (As we shall see, the different ink colours in the Introit also allow us to distinguish what Mozart wrote at the first stage of the Introit's genesis from what he wrote on returning to complete it.) The impact of such indications can be both visually and aurally striking, as in the Domine Jesu. After seven pages of only vocal parts and an instrumental bass-line, where we gaze at the bottom third of Mozart's score, a two-and-a-half-bar first violin line, marked *forte* after a protracted *piano* passage, appears at the top of the page as a bolt of lightning, four inches (10 cm) and a sound-world away from the preceding material (see Example 4.1).[4] The abrupt leaps and angularity of the violin contribution first

---

Mozart-Jahrbuch 1973–4, pp. 191–201), although this theory has now been discounted; see Maunder, *Mozart's Requiem*, pp. 125–9, Moseley, 'Mozart's Requiem', p. 209, Michael Lorenz, 'Freystädtler's Supposed Copying in the Autograph of K. 626: A Case of Mistaken Identity', paper presented at the conference 'Mozart's Choral Music: Composition, Contexts, Performance', Bloomington, IN, 12 February 2006. Freystädtler's involvement with Mozart is also discussed in Lorenz, 'Franz Jacob Freystädtler: Neue Forschungsergebnisse zu seinen Spuren im Werk Mozarts', *Acta mozartiana*, 44 (1997), pp. 85–108.

[3] A similar point is made by A. H. Fox Strangways in 'Music of the Week: Three Choirs Festival', *The Observer* (9 Sept. 1934), p. 12. On 'ruins' in nineteenth-century musical aesthetics, see John Daverio, *Nineteenth-Century Music and the German Romantic Ideology* (New York, 1993), pp. 19–47.

[4] Musical examples from the Requiem are compiled from the autograph materials for both Mozart's and Süssmayr's work. Editorial intervention is kept to a minimum (including, for example, the placement of the text, the addition of instrument names, and the use of standard SATB clefs for vocal parts, rather than C-clefs). No editorial standardizations are applied to articulation and dynamics; in addition, the score layout and the placement of dynamics are as they appear in the autograph. For reasons of space empty staves are excluded, with the exception of Example 4.1. The examples from Gassmann's Requiem, Handel's anthem and Mozart's masses K. 275, 317 and 337 (Chapter 4) and from Süssmayr's *Missa solemnis* (Chapter 5) are adapted from the following editions: Florian Leopold Gassmann, *Kirchenwerke: Missa in C, Introitus und*

Example 4.1   Mozart, Requiem, K. 626, Domine Jesu, bars 42–6

act as a link from the end of the 'in lucem sanctam' to the beginning of the
'Quam olim Abrahae' fugue (bars 43–4) and immediately set the tone for the
fugal accompaniment. The contribution ends on bar 46, beat 1, as quickly as it
begins in bar 43, Mozart presumably having notated enough of the line to
remember how to continue it when he returned to the score to complete the
movement. Even that most 'objectively' orientated Mozart scholar – Thomas
Bauman is right to identify us as a fundamentally conservative bunch[5] –
cannot fail to be moved, surely, by the combination of sound and image. It
is not necessarily that Mozart 'undermines faith and confronts fear' here, or
that the violin line represents the first thing 'that absolutely *had* to be said in
the orchestra' in this movement.[6] But he provides us with an irresistibly
urgent, explosive sound. Bar 6 of the Confutatis is no less remarkable sonically
(albeit visually obfuscated by Eybler's additions to the autograph and the

Kyrie aus dem Requiem-Fragment [etc.], ed. Franz Kosch (Vienna, 1938); George Frideric Handel,
Anthem for the Funeral of Queen Caroline: HWV264, ed. Annette Landgraf (Kassel, 2004); *Neue
Mozart-Ausgabe*, I:1/1/4; Franz Xaver Süssmayr, *Missa solemnis in D*, ed. Walter Wlcek and Erich
Duda (Graz, 2010). The example from 'Ave verum corpus' is compiled from the autograph. See
Wolfgang Amadeus Mozart, *Ave verum corpus: Faksimile nach dem in der Österreichischen
Nationalbibliothek in Wien aufbewahrten Autograph* (Vienna, 1956).

[5]   Bauman, 'Requiem, but no Piece', p. 152.   [6]   Eisen, 'Mozart's Leap in the Dark', p. 21.

Example 4.2 Mozart, Requiem, K. 626, Confutatis, bars 5–8

page-turn after bar 6), especially as it is located at the nexus of starkly
contrasted 'Confutatis maledictis' and 'Voca me' passages (Example 4.2).
While tenor and bass voices continue loudly to the end of their phrase on
bar 6, beat 2, finishing on a bare unison E, the cellos and double basses begin
their four-note link to 'Voca me' *piano* on the same beat and the same pitch;
understated and forthright sounds (on the same note) are therefore directly
juxtaposed.[7] It is not unusual, of course, for entering and exiting *piano* and *forte*
entries to overlap for a beat or so in a Mozart vocal or instrumental work. But
here, more unusually, the overlap is between the exiting tenors and basses and
the beginning of the lead-in, rather than the beginning of the next phrase. We
cannot know whether Mozart intended to add any instruments above the E in
the low voices and instruments; but he must have considered the instrumental
piano sufficiently audible against the loud voices. Thus the bare lead-in to 'Voca
me' possibly intended by Mozart – accepted by Eybler, but contradicted

---

[7] The onset of Mozart's *piano* dynamic in the bass instruments is absolutely precise; *pia:* (cello and bass)
is notated directly under the second beat of the bar here and in the lead-in to the second 'Voca me'
(bar 16, beat 2). A *pia:* notation can sometimes indicate a decrescendo either before the marking,
moving down to the dynamic at the moment that it is notated, or after it to reach the dynamic shortly
after it is notated. It is not impossible, then, that Mozart wanted the basses and organ gradually to
adjust their dynamic to *piano* over the course of bars 6 and 16. Since Mozart generally extends his *pia:*
indication over several notes when wanting a decrescendo, and does not do so here, a decrescendo is
unlikely to be desired by Mozart in this particular case. On realizations of diminuendos (and
crescendos) for *pia:* and *for:* notations see Wolfgang Amadeus Mozart, *Violin Sonatas*, ed. Cliff Eisen
(London, 2003), p. iv and Mozart, *Konzert für Klavier und Orchester ('Jeunehomme') Es-dur KV 271*,
ed. Cliff Eisen and Robert D. Levin (Wiesbaden, 2001), 'Preface'.

by Süssmayr, as we shall see in Chapter 5 – begins with a bare juxtaposition of *f* and *p* on beat 2. The mystery of the effect – what Mozart intended by it and whether he would have added to it – is part of its allure; the very fact that Mozart wanted to create an effect at this juncture, irrespective of how the final sound would have been realized by him upon completion, is significant.

We know both from late eighteenth-century documentary testimony and from adjustments to the autograph scores of his Viennese works that Mozart was meticulously sensitive to individual sounds, sound effects and sound-related environments, even in ostensibly innocuous contexts. Nannerl, Mozart's sister, claims that as a child he noticed 'the slightest mistake even in fully orchestrated music' and was 'incensed by the slightest noise during a piece of music'; Niemetschek explains that 'His hearing was so sensitive, he understood the differences in sounds so certainly and correctly, that he noticed the slightest mistake or discord even in the largest orchestra and could indicate exactly which character or instrument made it. Nothing incensed him more than restlessness, a racket or chattering during music.'[8] Changes to his piano concerto autographs, even tiny changes to orchestral parts in the brilliant build-up to a piano cadential trill (for example), and re-scorings, small-scale deletions and adjustments to thematic presentations catch Mozart in the act of creating and manipulating sounds and effects.[9]

Late eighteenth- and early nineteenth-century critics quickly identified the important aesthetic attributes of Mozart's sounds, sound effects, orchestration and orchestral effects, of which the Domine Jesu and Confutatis examples discussed above comprise just two. Niemetschek explains (1798): Mozart 'judges with the finest senses the nature and range of the instruments' and is unparalleled in his ability to pick apposite moments for wind instruments to make their effect.[10] Admiring how Mozart's wind instruments participate in the presentations of themes, how they blend with voices and how they provoke contrast, he continues: 'Never is an instrument wasted or misused and thus superfluous. But only he understood the economy of conjuring up his greatest effect with the least effort, often through the single note of an

---

[8] Deutsch, *Dokumente*, p. 404; translation (slightly amended) from Deutsch, *Documentary Biography*, p. 462. Niemetschek, *Leben*, p. 58 (my translation); also *Life of Mozart*, p. 65. See Simon P. Keefe, '"We hardly knew what we should pay attention to first": Mozart the Performer-Composer at Work on the Viennese Piano Concertos', *Journal of the Royal Musical Association*, 134 (2009), pp. 185–242, at 189.

[9] See Keefe, 'Mozart the Performer-Composer at Work on the Viennese Piano Concertos', especially pp. 195–242.

[10] *Life of Mozart*, pp. 58, 59 (translation adapted).

instrument, through a chord, a trumpet blast, a drum roll.'[11] Ignaz Arnold (1803) builds directly on Niemetschek's argument, quoting (unacknowledged) Niemetschek's passage about appropriately placed effects and the magic of the single-note effect (and paraphrasing other comments too).[12] The resultant 'instrumental economy', to which Arnold dedicates an entire chapter, thus becomes one of the fundamental indicators of Mozart's style.[13] Mozart, he explains, was the unparalleled (and first) master of the art of instrumentation, who should be studied by one and all; each note in the music for the three boys in *Die Zauberflöte*, for example, 'demonstrates wise ordering [*weise Anordnung*] and correct calculation [*richtige Berechnung*]'.[14] Details on Mozart's use of individual instruments follow. For the trumpets and timpani: 'We find no places where he ought not to have brought them in, but we find periods where they perhaps would have been brought in by some others, and only Mozart leaves them out in the interest of wise economy.'[15] Oboes are according to Arnold particularly prone to misuse, where a few misplaced notes could ruin a whole piece. Mozart's effects are very successful, though, on account of 'an appropriate, wisely economical solo' here and there.[16] For example: 'how touchingly he depicts the pain of the dying Commendatore in the solo [oboe] c–b–b♭–a–a♭–g–f (in the Introduction of *Don Giovanni*). Each note is a new stab to the heart.'[17] The economical orchestration in the Requiem is duly commended: 'How sparsely [trumpets and timpani] ... are brought into his Requiem and what a terrifyingly beautiful effect they make here in combination with the trombones, superbly so in the *Dies irae* (No. 2), and how spine-chillingly they are immediately heralded at the beginning [that is, in the

---

[11] Niemetschek, *Leben*, p. 49 (my translation). 'Nie ist ein Instrument verschwendet oder missbraucht, und daher überflüssig. Aber nur er Verstand die Oekonomie mit dem geringsten Aufwande, oft durch einzigen Zug eines Instruments, durch einen Akkord, einen Trompetenstoss, einen Paukenwirbel die grösste Wirkung hervorzuzaubern!' Mautner's translation is given in Niemetschek, *Life of Mozart*, pp. 57–8. For an article taking Niemetschek's remark as a point of departure for considering the piano concertos, see Simon P. Keefe, '"Greatest Effects with the Least Effort": Strategies of Wind Writing in Mozart's Viennese Piano Concertos', in Keefe (ed.), *Mozart Studies* (Cambridge, 2006), pp. 25–46.

[12] See Arnold, *Mozarts Geist*, pp. 209–10; and Niemetschek, *Life of Mozart*, pp. 57–8 and *Leben*, pp. 49–50.

[13] Arnold, *Mozarts Geist*, 'Oekonomie der Instrumente', pp. 208–31.

[14] Ibid., pp. 208, 208–9, 211.

[15] Ibid., p. 214: 'Man findet keine Stelle, wo er sie nicht hätte anbringen sollen, aber es finden sich Perioden, wo sie vielleicht jeder andre angebracht hätte und nur Mozart aus weiser Oekonomie wegliess.'

[16] Ibid., p. 226: 'ein mit weiser Sparsamkeit angebrachtes Solo'.

[17] Ibid., p. 227: 'wie herzangreifend mahlt er den Schmerz des sterbenden Komthuers in dem Solo: c h b, a as g f (im Eingange zum Don Juan). Jede Note ist ein neuer Stich ans Herz.' See *Don Giovanni*, Act 1, scene 1, bars 190–1.

Introit] after the first six bars rest.'[18] The reviewer of the Breitkopf Requiem edition, Friedrich Rochlitz, also draws attention in laudatory tones to the 'exceedingly sparse' use of trumpets and timpani, again referring to the powerful effect of their three notes in bars 7–8 of the Introit.[19]

Elsewhere in his book, Arnold develops ideas allied to his concept of economical orchestration, especially in his chapter on Mozart's accompanimental writing.[20] Echoing Niemetschek, he explains that a single accompanimental trumpet blast in one of Mozart's orchestrated recitatives could have a remarkable effect, citing bars 3–4 and 15–16 of Donna Anna's 'Don Ottavio, son morta!' from Act 1 of *Don Giovanni* (where he praises Mozart's use of horns as well as trumpets).[21] For all the variety of his accompanimental writing in a single piece, Mozart never compromises the 'unity of the whole', exchanging accompanimental figures so inconspicuously that a new one always seems a natural consequence of the preceding one. An instrumental accompaniment by Mozart 'breathes every time the spirit of feeling that dominates the whole'.[22]

Arnold's appropriation of Niemetschek's commentary is only the most obvious of a number of links between his writing on Mozart's orchestration and instrumental effects, and the remarks of his predecessors. Intentionally or not, Arnold extends positive arguments of the past – explicitly so in the case of Niemetschek – and counters existing disapproval. A number of Mozart's operas, including *Idomeneo*, *Die Entführung aus dem Serail* and *Don Giovanni*, were initially criticized for their 'overloaded' instrumental parts; Arnold's view is that Mozart never overloads his orchestra, because instruments are employed only where their employment is absolutely necessary.[23] While for Knigge's 'Dramaturgische Blätter' (1788) Mozart's wind instruments in *Die Entführung* obfuscate melody and harmony, 'a fault into which the best Italian composers never fall', for Arnold melody and accompaniment 'are so exactly interwoven that one cannot happily be imagined without the other', the full power ('Vollkräftigkeit') of the *Don Giovanni* and *La clemenza*

---

[18] Ibid., pp. 214–15: 'Wie sparsam sind diese Instrumente in seinem Requiem angebracht, und welchen fürchterlich schönen Effekt machen sie hier in Verbindung mit den Posaunen, vorzüglich im: *Dies irae* (No. II) und wie schauerlich kündigen sie sich gleich im Anfange nach den ersten 6 Takten Pause an.' The trumpet, trombone and timpani parts in the Dies irae were actually written by Süssmayr.

[19] *Allgemeine musikalische Zeitung*, 4 (1801–2), cols. 4–5 ('äusserst sparsam').

[20] See Arnold, *Mozarts Geist*, pp. 185–99.   [21] Ibid., pp. 197–8.

[22] Ibid., p. 191: 'die Einheit des ganzen'; 'Sie athmet jedesmal den Geist der Empfindung, der über das Ganze herrscht.'

[23] Ibid., pp. 185–6. For the early criticism see Deutsch, *Documentary Biography*, p. 270 (on *Idomeneo* in 1786), p. 328 (on *Die Entführung* in 1788), pp. 380 and 381 (on *Don Giovanni* in 1790 and 1791).

di Tito scores being patently superior to the 'thinness' ('Magerheit') of scores from the best of the rest in Germany and Italy.[24] The *Theater Zeitung für Deutschland* (1789) claims that *Die Entführung* 'is so individual and varied that on first hearing it is not entirely understandable even to a trained ear', but 'as a result ... [it] produces new fascination with each repeated hearing'.[25] Arnold goes further, strongly advising young composers to purchase and study Mozart's scores: 'Above all, one must see, hear, feel Mozart oneself; also it is not done all at once. The immense richness is not spotted with one glance and the practised eye misses beauties at the beginning that are evident only through repeated study. One can comment on his accompaniment only through diligent reading of his scores';[26] Arnold's attention to orchestration detail is a practical realization of this conceptual premise. Writing ambivalently about the first Berlin performance of *Don Giovanni* in early 1791, the 'Chronik von Berlin' reports that in theatre music 'Not the overloading of instruments, but the heart, the feelings and the passions must be allowed to speak by the composer', going on to say that Mozart does not meet these criteria; the critic concludes (prophetically) that he would be better suited to writing grand church music.[27] For Arnold, in contrast, Mozart employs instruments not only judiciously and creatively at all times, but also as a direct conduit to the expression of passions (and to his audience's appreciation of the expression): the oboe line at the Commendatore's death causes the listener an 'involuntary contracting of the chest', and the dead Commendatore's contribution to the graveyard scene sends a 'cold shudder through the listener', who 'imagines hearing a voice from the other world and believes in ghosts'.[28]

On account of its protracted consideration of instrumentation issues, close attention to musical detail and engagement with earlier, less formalized discussion, Arnold's *Mozarts Geist* represents a summative point in the early reception of Mozart's orchestration; as such it highlights the value of, and provides an interpretative framework for, a historically

---

[24] Deutsch, *Documentary Biography*, p. 328. Arnold, *Mozarts Geist*, p. 188 ('Er machte Melodie und Begleitung . . . zu einer so genauen Verwebung, dass sich eines ohne andere nicht wohl denken lässt'), p. 190.

[25] In Eisen, *New Mozart Documents*, p. 58.

[26] Arnold, *Mozarts Geist*, pp. 196–7: 'Überhaupt muss man bei Mozart selbst sehen, selbst hören, selbst empfinden; auch ist es mit einem Male nicht gethan; der ungeheure Reichthum lässt sich nicht mit einem Blick erspähen, und die geübsten Auge entgehen im Anfange Schönheiten, die sich nur bei widerholtem Studium entfalten. Sein Akkompagnement kann man blos durch's fleissige Lesen seiner Partituren abmerken.'

[27] Deutsch, *Documentary Biography*, p. 380.

[28] Arnold, *Mozarts Geist*, p. 323: 'ein unwillkührliches Zusammenziehen in der Brust'; 'Kalte Schauer überfahren den Zuhörer, er wähnt eine Stimme aus der andern Welt zu hören, und glaubt an Gespenster'.

based re-appraisal of sound effects in Mozart's portions of the Requiem.[29] Arnold clarifies that instrumental effects are successful when heard in combination with surrounding and supporting musical materials and events, rather than in isolation from them: a 'single note of an instrument' can be one of Mozart's 'greatest effects' only when location, time and context are right. An instrumental effect in the Requiem is best evaluated, then, as part of a sequence of effects, as part of an orchestration process that features mutually dependent effects.[30] Thus, the historical, theoretical and aesthetic foundation laid by Arnold encourages us to understand an instrumental effect in the Requiem as an 'economical' moment or passage of orchestration distinctive in itself and in the context of surrounding materials and events; by virtue of their infrequency and 'economy', Mozart's instrumental indications in the Sequence and Offertory provide particularly appropriate material for studying such effects.

That Mozart intends sounds and effects to be deployed strategically in his vocal music is demonstrated by works in which orchestration (and re-orchestration) is his principal task, namely the arrangements for Baron van Swieten of Handel's *Acis and Galatea* (K. 566, 1788), *Messiah* (K. 572, 1789), *Alexander's Feast* (K. 591, 1790) and the Ode for St Cecilia's Day (K. 592, 1790). In *Acis and Galatea*, for example, Mozart's updating of Handel's orchestration involves accommodating a larger complement of wind instruments than Handel had done and, as a result, a much wider array of instrumental colours: the duet No. 7 ('Wohl uns') and choruses Nos. 8 ('Wohl uns') and 9 ('Arme Hirten') are cases in point, as are numbers such as 'Every Valley' and 'O Thou that Telleth Good Tidings to Zion' from *Messiah*. Musical strategies also underscore Mozart's instrumental decisions; he builds directly on Handel as well as on procedures he initiates himself. Thus, Poliphemus's aria No. 11 ('Fleh' nicht mehr zur stolzen Schönheit') follows Handel's scoring of two oboes and strings (with violas added) but deploys the oboes more strategically, that is as semi-independent lines in transitions between vocal statements rather than as instruments doubling

---

[29] Arnold's study of Mozart's instrumentation in general, and his notion of instrumental economy in particular, quickly gained recognition. A reviewer of *Mozarts Geist*, for example, approves of the latter, considering it indicative of Arnold's very careful study of Mozart's scores; see *Allgemeine musikalische Zeitung*, 5 (1802–3), col. 691. A. Choron and F. Fayolle are particularly impressed by Arnold's observations about Mozart's 'profound knowledge of the effect and the use of wind instruments'. See Choron and Fayolle, *Dictionnaire historique des musiciens*, 2 vols. (Paris, 1810–11), vol. II, p. 75.

[30] For recent discussion of orchestral effects across broad temporal and generic spectrums, see John Spitzer and Neal Zaslaw, *The Birth of the Orchestra: History of an Institution, 1650–1815* (New York, 2004), pp. 436–501.

the violins at all times, thereby focusing colouristic use of the oboes on isolated segments of the aria. In contrast, Acis's larghetto aria No. 3 ('Wo, such' ich sie, die Holde Nymph?'), expanding Handel's wind contingent from a single oboe to two oboes, two clarinets and two bassoons, introduces a new octave sustained-note figure for all winds (bars 1–3, 5–7 and 13–15), and re-introduces it for the bassoon a few bars before the da capo (bars 61–2) both to fill a textural gap and to foreshadow the re-appearance of the material at the onset of the da capo; and Damon's Andante aria No. 4 ('Schäfer, was suchst du so ängstlich') adds semi-obbligato bassoon parts that include links and new points of imitation throughout, lending new fluidity to the aria and providing dialogue with Handel's string lines. The long instrumental introduction to 'What Passion Cannot Music Raise and Quell' from the Ode for St Cecilia's Day captures in a nutshell Mozart's combined strategy of adhering to Handel's original material and exploiting the potential of his own, new material, with constant ebb and flow between them. Handel's introduction includes an obbligato cello part to which Mozart makes additions: sustained upper strings at the opening (bars 1–12); a bassoon line that is interweaved with the cello line in the Andante (bars 13–25); and pizzicato upper strings that accompany the cello (bars 26–30). Mozart's pizzicato figure is then passed to his entering flute (bars 31–4) while the bassoon is again given its own material, interleaved solo lines (Handel and Mozart) co-existing with a dialogued accompaniment (Mozart only). The sustained note heard concurrently in Handel's bass (bars 31–4) then migrates to Mozart's bassoon after the pause (bars 36–9); Mozart lends the sustained notes of Handel's *bassi* greater audibility at the opening, reinforcing them with upper strings, just as he now makes a musical feature of exchanging the sustained notes between the *bassi* and the bassoons. In sum, Mozart integrates his own sounds and strategies with Handel's sounds and strategies.

Since Mozart's decisions about instrumental sounds and effects in his own music were not taken in isolation, of course, and intersect with decisions about harmonies, melodies, rhythms, dynamics, formal shaping and text-setting, my discussion of his portions of the Requiem will neces-sarily involve considering these other elements of the work as well. But a focus on sounds, effects, timbres and orchestration is ultimately appropriate in a study drawing hermeneutic inspiration from the Requiem's incom-pleteness and, in consequence, its legend. If the incomplete Mozart auto-graph gives insight into Mozart in the act of creating, it is insight predominantly into his world of sound, since the sounds that he fore-grounds, and by extension those that he does not, leap out from almost every page. After proceeding diachronically through Mozart's score, I look at those of Mozart's own earlier sacred works that were probably fresh in his mind in late 1791, by virtue of either their recent composition or their presence (and possible performance) at St Stephen's Cathedral, demonstrating that organized sounds and effects were fundamental features of his stylistic vocabulary for sacred music long before he turned his attention to the Requiem.

Sounds and strategies in the Requiem

Introit

Requiem aeternam dona eis, Domine:	Grant them eternal rest, O Lord,
et lux perpetua luceat eis.	and let perpetual light shine upon them.
Te decet hymnus, Deus, in Sion,	A hymn becomes you, O God, in Zion,
et tibi reddetur votum in Jerusalem.	and to you a vow shall be repaid in Jerusalem.
Exaudi orationem meam;	Hear my prayer;
ad te omnis caro veniet.	to you all flesh shall come.
Requiem aeternam dona eis, Domine:	Grant them eternal rest, O Lord,
et lux perpetua luceat eis.	and let perpetual light shine upon them.

Mozart's setting of the Introit follows an ABA′ formal pattern that matches the liturgical text. It is preceded by a seven-bar orchestral introduction. The A section sets the antiphon text 'Requiem aeternam dona eis, Domine: et lux perpetua luceat eis', with a varied musical reprise of the antiphon at the end (bars 34ff.). The B section comprises a psalm verse that begins 'Te decet hymnus, Deus, in Sion'. Discernible musical blocks supporting changes of text interlink with the ABA′ pattern as shown in Table 4.1.

Table 4.1 Mozart's Requiem, Introit

Formal section	Text/music block	Bars	Tonality
A	Introduction, 'Requiem aeternam dona eis, Domine'	1–14	d – V/d (with inflection to a in bars 6–7)
	'et lux perpetua luceat eis'	15–19	F – B flat
B	'Te decet hymnus, Deus, in Sion, et tibi reddetur votum in Jerusalem'	19–26	B flat – g
	'Exaudi orationem meam; ad te omnis caro veniet'	26–33	g – B flat – g
A′	'Requiem aeternam . . .'	34–43	d – B flat
	'et lux perpetua . . .'	43–8	B flat – d – V/d

As is well known, the main theme of the Introit heard first in the orchestra and then in the voices is similar to that of Gassmann's (incomplete) Requiem in C minor and to that of the first chorus from Handel's Anthem for the Funeral of Queen Caroline (HWV 264), 'The Ways of Zion Do Mourn'.[31] Mozart had a number of opportunities to hear Gassmann's Requiem at the Hofkapelle in Vienna, including performances in memory of Joseph II (25 February 1790 and 2 March 1790) and to mark the anniversaries of Maria Theresia's death (29 November 1788, 1789, 1790, 1791). He could also have encountered the set of parts owned by St Stephen's Cathedral once installed there as adjunct Kapellmeister in spring 1791.[32] While the thematic and presentational similarities are beyond dispute, the musical differences are striking (given the existence of such similarities), especially in the respective orchestral introductions. Gassmann's introduction is fourteen bars long (see Example 4.3), features entries on the same beats of the bar (the second beats of bars 1, 2, 4 and 6) and reaches a melodic peak on the final entry (bars 6–7) whereupon a descending sequence begins that lasts until the establishment of the dominant of C minor in bar 12. A prolonged dominant (bars 12–14) precedes the confirmation of C minor and the entry of the voices. Gassmann uses the brass instruments selectively and quietly for effect: the trumpets are given single-crotchet and two-crotchet figures in bars 5–12 inclusive, and the two trombones get minim–crotchet figures that coincide with the falling melodic sequence.

Mozart's seven-bar opening (Example 4.4) follows a similar pattern, but is more concise, economical and powerful, serving as a discourse in its own right on understatement and assertion. The four entries of the Requiem theme are irregularly placed (bar 1, beat 2, bar 2, beat 2, bar 3, beat 4, bar 4, beat 2). The first two are pre-empted at pitch by the immediately preceding string quavers (in an offbeat accompaniment figure not heard in Gassmann); the third and fourth entries have attention drawn away from them by rhythmic distinctiveness elsewhere, namely the first appearance of consecutive quavers in a single part and in two parts together (bars 3–4, second bassethorn and first bassoon). It dawns on us only gradually, in short, that an individual instrument has entered with the theme. The modest climactic point of the initial entries (bar 5, beats 1–2) is registrally and rhythmically co-ordinated; the first bassethorn's peak at the beginning of bar 5 coincides with the first semiquavers of the movement, the phrase subsequently subsiding to the cadence in bars 6–7, in an analogous fashion

---

[31] On parallels – in the Introit and elsewhere – between Mozart's Requiem and both Gassmann's Requiem and Michael Haydn's C minor Requiem see Maunder, *Mozart's Requiem*, pp. 74–88.

[32] Black, 'Mozart and the Practice of Sacred Music', pp. 133–6, 351, 354, 355.

Example 4.3　Florian Leopold Gassmann, Requiem, Introit, bars 1–16

Example 4.3   (cont.)

to Gassmann's opening. Mozart's bars 7–8, in contrast, are a moment of unambiguous authority, utilizing brass and timpani with a concision – Niemetschek's and Arnold's 'economy of conjuring up ... [the] greatest effect with the least effort' – foreign to Gassmann: they re-confirm D minor, following the relatively strong inflection to A minor, and are marked *forte*; they progress emphatically from a weak to a strong beat (bar 7, beat 2 – bar 8, beat 1), unlike the main Requiem theme in the preceding bars; and they complete, in emphatic mood, the stepwise melodic descent from the end of the previous phrase. It is as if trombones, trumpets and timpani deliberately bring the orchestra into line after the events of bars 1–7, preparing for the regularly spaced, assertive choral entries of the Requiem theme in bars 8–9.

While Mozart's opening goes far beyond Gassmann's in sound and effect, its parallels with Handel's 'The Ways of Zion Do Mourn', to which Mozart was probably introduced by Baron van Swieten, are more profound (Example 4.5). Handel's instrumental introduction and vocal entries overlap, unlike Mozart's, but resonate deeply with Mozart nonetheless. Handel downplays his orchestral theme at the opening, just as Mozart understates

Example 4.4 Mozart, Requiem, K. 626, Introit, bars 1–8

his, in effect assembling it over the initial few bars: it is first heard in crotchets in the strings, then in minims in the oboes and violins, where the melodic motion G–F♯–G–A halts before B♭ is reached and melodic descents are initiated first to bar 13 and then to bar 17. The altos enter with the main theme during the initial descent rather than after it, Handel thus underplaying the entry of the voices, in contrast to Mozart, who treats it as a moment of arrival. But Mozart, borrowing Handel's theme and matching his understated instrumental opening, draws inspiration from Handel in other ways. Handel promotes his wind instruments, as does Mozart, both projecting their themes to a modest registral climax (the violin and oboe a″ in bar 7, beat 3 for Handel) before they fall to the close of the phrase; Handel, like Mozart, demonstrates sensitivity to individual instrumental sounds and effects, first introducing sustained notes to coincide with the entering violin and oboe (bar 4, beat 3) and then avoiding a B♭ in the

Example 4.4 (cont.)

violin and oboe in bar 8 to lend the note greater emphasis in the first vocal entry (semibreve, bar 13). Mozart engages creatively with Handel, his forefather's model acting as his inspiration, continuing an imaginative process begun in the earlier Handel arrangements for van Swieten.

Mozart's opening focuses attention on orchestral instruments as introducers of vocal material, a role that continues to promote instrumental effects throughout the movement and that was evident at the first writing stage in the Introit's genesis.[33] Bars 1–7 invoke the subtle, rhetorically inspired *insinuatio* type of exordium from Baroque ricercars, whereby 'the voices creep in

---

[33] Mozart's first- and second-stage notation of the Introit can be distinguished in the autograph and facsimile by the dark, clear ink colour of the former – for voices, basses and other instruments from time to time – and the lighter, faded ink colour of the latter.

Example 4.5   Handel, Anthem for the Funeral of Queen Caroline, HWV 264, 'The Ways of Zion Do Mourn', bars 1–17

quietly one by one, gradually and almost imperceptibly increasing the numbers of parts from one, to two, three, four, with unobtrusive subjects avoiding large leaps or faster rhythms',[34] while bars 7–8 comprise a forceful lead-in to the entry of the voices. The violins' piercing figures from bar 8 onwards aggregate to a kind of assertive unsettledness in response to both, growing from their own offbeat, *forte* answers to the trombone thuds and continuing their offbeat playing from the opening; Mozart's early-stage notation of the first violins at bars 8–10 and 14–19 demonstrates his desire from the start to retain the violin offbeats through to bar 15 and to create an emphatic instrumental effect on the downbeat of bar 15 (immediately before 'et lux perpetua'), despite the necessary withdrawal of trumpets and timpani, by giving the first and second violins triple- and double-stopped chords. Every other instrumental link between vocal material (except one) was written at the first notational stage, indicating that such effects were an early priority for Mozart: the bassethorns, bassoons, violins and violas (bar 17) that bridge the gap to 'luceat eis' both allude to the opening (*p*, offbeats, semitone falls) and echo the first two beats of bar 17 (given at the first notational stage in the first violins); the first violins' dotted semiquavers that precede 'Exaudi' on the first beat of bar 26; and the bassethorns and bassoons and first violins' transition (bars 32–4) to the 'Requiem aeternam' reprise.

Instrumental decisions and effects in Mozart's later notational phase complement his early-stage decisions and effects. The one instrumental link not apparently written at the Introit's early stage, the transition in the bassethorns, bassoons and strings (bars 19–20; see Example 4.6) to 'Te decet hymnus', constitutes the first appearance (chronologically in the completed movement) of a line set to 'dona eis, Domine' in bars 34–5. It is impossible to know whether Mozart intended the theme as an instrumental transition at this point right from the start but felt no need to notate it at the early notation stage; the fact that the 'dona eis, Domine' theme appears at the early notation stage in the violins in bars 33–4 and takes shape in truncated, inverted and incomplete forms in the strings in bars 21–5 makes it unlikely that he did. Since the theme is introduced for the first time unambiguously in the bassoon and first violin in bars 19–20 at the late notational stage, it is possible that Mozart decided to enhance at the late stage the prominent orchestral role envisaged at the early stage. Indeed, the impact of the orchestra

---

[34] Warren Kirkendale, 'Ciceronians versus Aristotelians on the Ricercar as Exordium, from Bembo to Bach', *Journal of the American Musicological Society*, 32 (1979), p. 27.

Example 4.6　Mozart, Requiem, K. 626, Introit, bars 19–21

is also intensified in the late notation stage through the new, big effect at the 'et lux perpetua' reprise (bassethorns, bassoons, trumpets and timpani operating together for the first time at bar 43) and the new, subdued role for trumpet and timpani in the last bar of the movement (Example 4.7)

Mozart's Introit, then, is a discourse in sound and effect, ultimately conveying an unsettled quality that will resonate through later movements as well. The orchestra's quickly acquired assertiveness (bars 7–8) is unsettling not only at the first appearance of the violins' piercing figures but also at their reappearance in inverted form (bar 34) before the dialogue between the violins and bassoons and the voices is realized for the 'dona eis, Domine' theme; we are unsure whether priority resides with the collaborative dialogue or with the re-establishment of bar 8's assertive unsettledness. And the *piano* trumpets and timpani in bar 48 are not reassuring in their uncharacteristic cautiousness. Mozart cultivates uneasiness.

Example 4.7   Mozart, Requiem, K. 626, Introit, bars 43–8

Example 4.7 (cont.)

Kyrie

Kyrie, eleison.	Lord, have mercy upon us.
Christe, eleison.	Christ, have mercy upon us.
Kyrie, eleison.	Lord, have mercy upon us.

Mozart borrows from Handel again in the Kyrie, on this occasion the fugue and countersubject from the 'Dettingen' Anthem, HWV265, later recycled for use in *Joseph*. Just as Mozart's autograph materials for the Introit offer insight into instrumental roles, sounds and effects, so those for the Kyrie shed light on harmonic, structural and thematic strategies.

The Kyrie contains the only whole bar – just three beats of a bar to be precise – that Mozart crossed out in his Requiem score, namely the original version of bar 30 (Example 4.8). When he arrived at the projected A on beat 3 of the basses – it

Example 4.8 Mozart, Requiem, K. 626, Kyrie, bars 27–33 (including Mozart's deleted bar 30)

remains un-notated in the original bar – he will have realized that a (presumably undesired) 6–4 had been created. Also, as originally conceived, bar 30 does not provide an opportunity for a further 'Christe' entry, and would have brought to an end Mozart's alternate 'Kyrie' and 'Christe' entries at one-bar intervals (bars 27, 28, 29). So, in changing the D minor 6–4 to F major 6–3, Mozart adapted the alto part, shortened the tenor 'Christe' entry that began in bar 28 by adding rests and introduced a further tenor 'Christe' entry on the third beat.

Thus far, Mozart's fugal entries are all complete – three-and-a-half bars for the 'Kyrie' theme and two-and-a-half for the 'Christe'. They are also balanced through alternation. As a result of the revision, the tenor 'Christe' in bars 28–30 is the first shortened entry, and a watershed moment in the movement. While alternation is preserved with the 'Christe' entry in bar 30, the musical urgency wrought by the shortened entry, followed immediately by another entry, sets the scene for the 'Christe' theme's dominance over the 'Kyrie'. The renewed tenor entry in bar 30 projects towards the F minor 'Kyrie' entry (bar 32), but the 'Kyrie' theme is then subdued by the 'Christe', which is the dominant idea from bar 33 onwards with five and four consecutive entries in bars 33–7 and 44–7 respectively that drive towards the climactic interrupted cadence in bar 50. By shortening the 'Christe' in bars 28–30 and immediately including another entry a fifth higher than the previous one, Mozart gives a first indication of its potential to ratchet up the intensity level. The subsequent sets of ascending 'Christe' entries – chromatically enhanced by raising the fifth and thirteenth notes in each bar – culminate in the cadence in bar 50 and fully activate this potential. Thus, Mozart's revision to the autograph in bar 30 catches him in the act of negotiating harmonic, thematic and structural issues pertinent to the Kyrie as a whole. Indeed, his revision represents the opening gambit in establishing the 'Christe' as the dominant sound of the final twenty bars or so, propelling us towards the end of the movement.

The Sequence: Dies irae

Dies irae, dies illa,	Day of wrath! O day of mourning,
Solvet saeclum in favilla:	See fulfilled the prophets' warning;
Teste David cum Sibylla.	Heaven and earth in ashes burning.
Quantus tremor est futurus,	Oh, what fear man's bosom rendeth
Quando judex est venturus	When from heaven the Judge descendeth,
Cuncta stricte discussurus!	On whose sentence all dependeth![35]

[35] Unless otherwise indicated, translations of the Sequence text are taken from the well-known nineteenth-century English translation by William Josiah Irons, published in the English Missal (London, 1912), in which the Latin rhyming and metrical schemes are retained.

Thomas of Celano's thirteenth-century Latin hymn 'Dies irae', in nineteen verses, comprises the Sequence of the Requiem Mass, which Mozart divides into six separate movements. Mozart draws on the first two verses for his Dies irae movement, concerning the day of wrath and the fear of judgment for all eternity, the poetic form dictating the musical form (as in the Introit). It divides into three sections: a setting of the full, two-verse text (d: F – a, bars 1–19); a second setting of the full text (a: c – V/d, bars 22–40) preceded by a three-bar instrumental transition between first and second verses (bars 19–21); and a two-fold exchange of 'Quantus tremor est futurus' and 'Dies irae, dies illa', mainly on the dominant, cadencing into D minor for the completion of the second verse from bar 53.

In addition to the vocal parts and instrumental bass, Mozart composed the first-violin line for forty-three of the movement's sixty-eight bars. At first glance it may be surprising that he writes so much of an orchestral part at this early notational phase and that shorter cues would not have provided him with a sufficient *aide-mémoire* for the later (unrealized) notational phase. On closer examination, though, the quantity of violin material can be explained by Mozart's meticulous attention to nuances of sound, even small changes to accompaniments in this fast, loud, frenetic movement. A comparison of the violin accompaniments to the same text at the beginnings of the first and second sections offers a case in point (Example 4.9a and 4.9b). The second setting includes more frequent and larger registral leaps (bars 22–5 and 28 in particular), and three-note chords across a tenth and an eleventh that lend weight to the downbeats of bars 26 and 31 and exemplify the violins' increased athleticism. The violin part in the second setting is also more independent from the vocal lines: the first four bars (22–5 compared with bars 1–4), though still rising through a minor third, no longer track the contours of the soprano line; and bars 26–7 provide a slightly more virtuosic flourish than bars 5–6, spread out over more than two octaves (including the d′) and peaking on an e‴. These new features of the second setting are foreshadowed in the preceding instrumental transition (bars 19–21): the opening leap of a tenth is the biggest instrumental leap so far (the violins begin on the sopranos' and altos' precise exiting note (a′) but then immediately propel themselves away from it); and the spirit of the original instrumental transition (bars 8–10) is retained, but with more jagged lines for violins and basses. Thus, Mozart's new instrumental sounds contribute to an intensification of instrumental participation in the second setting of the Dies irae text.

Developments in accompaniment style are taken significantly further in the third section of the movement, where a dialogue between the bass voices

Example 4.9a Mozart, Requiem, K. 626, Dies irae, bars 1–10

Example 4.9b Mozart, Requiem, K. 626, Dies irae, bars 19–31

('Quantus tremor est futurus') and the sopranos, altos and tenors ('Dies irae, dies illa') juxtaposes unharmonized voices and violins at the unison, with harmonized voices and unshackled, angular violin figurations (see bars 40–8, Example 4.10). Contrast between segments is also foregrounded by big violin leaps at the switch between segments (a twelfth in bar 44, beats 2–3 and two octaves in bar 48, beats 2–3) and by a verbatim repeat of the first 'Quantus tremor' in bars 44–6 that comes across as obstinate unresponsiveness to the preceding 'Dies irae' statement. The dialogue is not explicitly confrontational: contrasting segments are thematically similar, and orchestral parts (at least as represented by the violin annotations) are not explicitly aligned with one segment or the other.[36] There is no sense, then, that the music underscores a textual conflict between 'fear' ('Quantus tremor est futurus') and the 'day of judgment' ('Dies irae, dies illa'). An uneasy rapprochement follows in bars 50–2, the 'Quantus tremor' prevailing texturally and thematically in the multi-voice, harmonized presentation previously reserved for the 'Dies irae'. Unambiguously collaborative dialogue follows at the end of the movement at 'Cuncta stricte discussurus' (bars 57–66), the violins returning again to the independent semiquaver writing from the beginning of section 2 and from the 'Dies irae' segment earlier in the final section.

It is unclear, then, how we are to understand Mozart's evolving instrumental roles in the Dies irae. Close alignment between the violins and the voices at the beginning of the first full statement of the text in section 1 gives way to greater instrumental independence in the second full statement in section 2, to juxtaposed alignment and independence at the beginning of section 3 and finally to a return to agitated independence in the last twelve bars or so of the movement. We are bombarded with forceful instrumental sounds – precipitous leaps, piercing syncopation, chords, contrasts between low growling and vivacious angularity – and receive no clear lead from Mozart on how to process them collectively. But as in the Introit, unsettledness is surely the key. Setting a text that conveys the fear of judgment for all eternity, Mozart cultivates musical unease. And after all of the frantic, frenetic (perhaps frightening) semiquavers we end with a duplication of the movement's most precipitous instrumental leap (two octaves d$'''$–d$'$) and an explosive, unaccompanied crotchet in the violins, played on two strings (Example 4.11). The wrath, terror, bluster and unremitting energy culminate in a single note resonating unsettlingly into the musical void.

---

[36] On the musical characteristics of confrontational dialogue in Mozart's music see Keefe, *Mozart's Piano Concertos* and Keefe, *Mozart's Viennese Instrumental Music*, pp. 19–42.

Example 4.10   Mozart, Requiem, K. 626, Dies irae, bars 40–8

Example 4.11   Mozart, Requiem, K. 626, Dies irae, bars 66–8

The Sequence: Tuba mirum

Tuba mirum spargens sonum	Wondrous sound the trumpet flingeth,
Per sepulcra regionum,	Through earth's sepulchres it ringeth,
Coget omnes ante thronum	All before the throne it bringeth.
Mors stupebit et natura,	Death is struck and nature quaking,
Cum resurget creatura,	All creation is awaking,
Judicanti responsura.	To its Judge an answer making.
Liber scriptus proferetur,	Lo! the book exactly worded,
In quo totum continetur,	Wherein all hath been recorded;
Unde mundus judicetur.	Thence shall judgment be awarded.
Judex ergo cum sedebit,	When the Judge His seat attaineth,
Quidquid latet, apparebit:	And each hidden deed arraigneth,
Nil inultum remanebit.	Nothing unavenged remaineth.
Quid sum miser tunc dicturus,	What shall I, frail man, be pleading,
Quem patronum rogaturus,	Who for me be interceding,
Cum vix justus sit securus?	When the just are mercy needing?

The Tuba mirum describes the process of judgment initiated by a trumpet that calls 'all before the throne'. It comprises a dialogue between trombone and bass soloist, successive solos for tenor, alto and soprano, and a final section for all four soloists, as shown in Table 4.2.

Just as a single note ends the wrath and fear described in the Dies irae, so a very different single note (trombone b♭) initiates the judgment process explained in the Tuba mirum. The trombone sound, so strident in bars 1 and 2, quickly interlinks with the sound of the voice (Example 4.12). Vocal imitation of the trombone at the opening precipitates a mellifluous exchange in which melodic lines grow organically within and between the two: the descending arpeggio becomes the trombone's upward arpeggiated continuation (bars 4–6); the trombone's conjunct ending to the phrase (f′–e♭′–d′, bars 6–7) is continued by the voice (d–c–B♭, bar 7). The trombone line in bars 11–13 and the vocal line in bars 10–13 seem both self-generating and mutually dependent, and the ascending trombone scale in bar 15 grows

Table 4.2 Mozart's Requiem, Tuba mirum

Soloists	Text	Bars	Tonality
Trombone, bass	Bass: 'Tuba mirum'	1–18	B flat – F[a]
Tenor, alto, soprano	Tenor: 'Mors stupebit'	18–34	F/f – d
	Alto: 'Judex ergo'	34–40	d – B flat
	Soprano: 'Quid sum miser'	40–4	B flat – V/B flat
Soprano, solo quartet	'Cum vix justus sit securus?'	45–62	B flat

[a] Harmonically, Eybler and Süssmayr treat beats 1–2 of bar 18 differently in the absence of unambiguous evidence from Mozart as to whether a major or a minor chord is desired: Eybler gives an F major chord, switching to F minor on beats 3–4, as dictated by Mozart's A♭ for the tenor on beat 3; Süssmayr gives F minor harmony throughout the bar.

Example 4.12   Mozart, Requiem, K. 626, Tuba mirum, bars 1–18

from the voice's conjunct end to the previous phrase (bars 14–15). Voice and trombone are cut from the same cloth; seamless interweaving sublimates inter- and intra-phrase links. As dialogue, it is similar to the fluid, self-perpetuating exchanges among voices and instruments in the letter duet from *Le nozze di Figaro*.[37] In Mozart's sacred oeuvre the closest equivalent is the free-flowing dialogue among the soprano and wind soloists in the 'Et incarnatus est' (also unfinished) from the C minor Mass, K. 427.

While no instrumental annotations appear in the middle section of the Tuba mirum (bars 18–44), links between vocal phrases – deriving from immediately preceding vocal material – appear in Mozart's instrumental bass line (bars 23, 28, 36); the sinuous exchange between instrument and voice from the movement's opening has gone (or not yet been composed), but the bass remains an activator of smooth transition between vocal statements, as in the Introit. The violins' lead-in to 'Cum vix justus' (bars 44–5, Example 4.13) fulfils the same function, but also apparently initiates a new role for the strings, namely leading rather than simply receiving the melody. Each of the three statements of 'Cum vix justus' has a different, distinctive emphasis. The first, preceded by the two violin parts, features a repeated one-note exchange between the violins and the soprano (bar 45); the second includes the first simultaneous entry of all four soloists (bar 51), a *sotto voce* indication and an increasingly elaborate violin line a few bars later (bars 52–4); and the third features a triple-stopped *forte* violin at the outset, followed by an oscillation between *forte* and *piano* (bars 57–8). The understated climax to the movement (bars 59–60) includes one of only two crescendos marked by Mozart into his Requiem score.

As in the Dies irae and Introit, it is unclear how to process the totality of Mozart's instrumental sounds and effects in the Tuba mirum. They evolve judiciously, flowering modestly for the strings at 'Cum vix justus', where each of the three statements offers new sounds and effects. The Tuba mirum's final verse ('Quid sum miser') is the only one in which the text turns from abstract description to personal reaction. The strings' close engagement with the voices when the just indicate that mercy is needed ('Cum vix justus sit securus?') could therefore be interpreted as orchestral consolation in the face of fear and doubt. But the same cannot be said so clearly for the trombone's interweaving with the voice at the opening of the movement, where the text straightforwardly describes the trumpet's sound. If in fact consolation and sympathy are intended here by Mozart then they do not reinforce textual implications. With another tantalizingly incomplete

---

[37] On the Countess and Susanna's letter duet see Keefe, *Mozart's Piano Concertos*, pp. 135–6.

Example 4.13 Mozart, Requiem, K. 626, Tuba mirum, bars 44–62

array of sounds and effects, we are left to wonder whether mild sonic disorientation is intended to support the nervous uncertainty of the text.

The Sequence: Rex tremendae

Rex tremendae majestatis,	King of majesty tremendous,
Qui salvandos salvas gratis,	Who dost free salvation send us,
Salva me, fons pietatis.	Fount of pity, then befriend us.

The Rex tremendae sets the eighth verse of the Sequence and, like the Dies irae and Tuba mirum, divides into three clearly delineated sections: the homophonic first line, 'Rex tremendae majestatis', with two-bar orchestral introduction (g – V/g, bars 1–7); the contrapuntal setting of the first two lines, with a homophonic statement in the middle (g – F: d – V/d, bars 7–17); and the homophonic 'Salva me, fons pietatis' (V/d – d, bars 17–22).

Mozart writes a first violin line for the entire movement.[38] The evolving relationship between the violin and instrumental bass is central to the articulation of structure, perhaps explaining why Mozart notated the violin throughout. The violin and bass are aligned in the first section, with octaves in bars 1–4, and come together again in the final section. At the midpoint of the middle section their imitative counterpoint is suspended for three beats (bar 11) to coincide with the vocal homophony.

Procedural parallels between instrumental involvement in the opening and closing sections are matched by harmonic and sonic relationships. The plea to be saved ('Salva me') invokes the earlier epithet for its recipient; the King of Majesty becomes the fountain of mercy when the 'Salva me, fons pietatis' replays the opening in reverse by disintegrating rather than building to a climax, and by mirroring the forceful, detached 'Rex' statements in the understated, equally detached 'Salva me' statements (Examples 4.14 and 4.15). Mozart downplays the onset, at which violin and bass parts are realigned (bar 17, beat 2): marking it *piano* and *tasto solo* (i.e. no organ chord), he leaves out dotted rhythms in the bass descent. The continuation brings further subdued material (with no dotted rhythms in the bass) and a fade-away to nothing in the final bar. All four voices come together homophonically in bars 20–2, as in the 'Rex' and (especially) 'Rex tremendae majestatis' exclamations in bars 3–5 and 6–7 respectively, but the impact is minimized through a *piano* dynamic. The harmonic progressions outlined in bars 1–3 and bars 18–22 are similar (bars 1–3: i – iv – ii6 – i6-4 – V – i; bars 18–22: i – VI – ♭II6

---

[38] There are two gaps in the first violin line without rests: bar 6, beats 2–4 and bar 20, beat 2 – bar 21, beat 4. Eybler and Süssmayr add string material to the second, but not to the first.

Example 4.14   Mozart, Requiem, K. 626, Rex tremendae, bars 1–7

(Neapolitan) – Dim.7 – i6 – V – i); the E♭ Neapolitan in bar 20, though new to the movement as a functional harmony, also revisits the E♭ as the submediant of G minor from bar 4, in submissive rather than emphatic mode.

Irrespective of internal correspondences and complementation, the end of the Rex tremendae has an affinity with the end of the Dies irae. The uneasy Dies irae text and the plea in the Rex tremendae text may partially explain the

Example 4.15 Mozart, Requiem, K. 626, Rex tremendae, bars 17–22

explosive first-violin d′ resonating in the musical ether of the former and the dying-away in the final bar of the latter, but connections run deeper. Both short movements offer a panoply of memorably forceful effects – tutti exclamations and emphatic uniform statements in the Rex tremendae – only to end in unsettling violence (Dies irae) and subjugation (Rex tremendae) in final bars conveyed by the orchestra alone. Mozart's annotation of the last three notes for the first violins in the Rex tremendae, after the longer of the two segments in which they receive no material, indicates his desire to create a precise effect at this moment: an outwardly innocuous D minor arpeggio, off the beat until the third beat, is sufficiently important to be annotated at the early notational phase. In addition to marking a subdued conclusion, is it, perhaps, a tonal, rhythmic and gestural reference to the opening of the Introit, demonstrating the economy of means praised by Niemetschek and Arnold, and/or a setting of the scene for the calm instrumental opening to the Recordare? Such interpretations, of course, are in the eyes and ears of the beholder; Mozart's incomplete score, half revealing compositional strategies and priorities, renders contemplation of his sonic environment and sonic intentions a particularly imaginative interpretative act.

The Sequence: Recordare

Recordare, Jesu pie,	Think, good Jesu, my salvation
Quod sum causa tuae viae:	Caused thy wondrous incarnation.
Ne me perdas illa die.	Leave me not to reprobation.
Quaerens me, sedisti lassus:	Faint and weary, thou hast sought me,
Redemisti Crucem passus:	On the cross of suffering bought me.
Tantus labor non sit cassus.	Shall such grace be vainly brought me?
Juste judex ultionis,	Righteous Judge! for sin's pollution
Donum fac remissionis	Grant thy gift of absolution,
Ante diem rationis.	Ere the day of retribution.
Ingemisco, tamquam reus:	Guilty, now I pour my moaning,
Culpa rubet vultus meus;	All my shame with anguish owning;
Supplicanti parce, Deus.	Spare, O God, thy suppliant groaning.
Qui Mariam absolvisti	Thou the sinful woman savedst;
Et latronem exaudisti,	Thou the dying thief forgavest;
Mihi quoque spem dedisti.	And to me a hope vouchsafest.
Preces meae non sunt dignae:	Worthless are my prayers and sighing;
Sed tu bonus fac benigne,	Yet, good Lord, in grace complying,
Ne perenni cremer igne.	Rescue me from fires undying!
Inter oves locum praesta,	With thy favoured sheep O place me,
Et ab haedis me sequestra,	Nor among the goats abase me,
Statuens in parte dextra.	But to thy right hand upraise me.

Setting seven verses of the Sequence for the supplicant's prayer for salvation, the Recordare is by a considerable margin the longest of Mozart's six Sequence movements. Perhaps to accommodate its length, Mozart's

Table 4.3 Mozart's Requiem, Recordare

Section	Bars	Tonality	Thematic material
Instrumental introduction	1–13	F	MT + RT – RT
Verse 1, 'Recordare'	14–37	F – C	MT + RT – CT – RT (transition)
Verse 2, 'Quaerens me'	38–52	c – d	RT – CT (re-ordered) + RT – RT (transition) (V/B flat, bar 53)
Verse 3, 'Juste judex'	54–71	B flat	MT (derivation) – CT – RT (transition)
Verse 4, 'Ingemisco'	72–83	B flat – c – d	CT (derivation)
Verse 5, 'Qui Mariam'	83–92	d – a – g – C	FT
Verse 6, 'Preces meae'	93–109	F – C – V/f	MT + RT – RT/CT (as 'Ne perenni')
Verse 7, 'Inter oves'	110–26	V/f – F	CT – FT
Instrumental coda	126–30	F	RT

movement is tightly knit thematically (see Table 4.3). He bases it on the main theme (MT, bassethorns and cellos, bars 1–7); a ritornello on a motif from the cello accompaniment to the main theme (RT, strings, bars 7–13); a falling theme (FT, voice, bars 83–8), also derived from the main-theme accompaniment; and a continuation theme (CT, voice, bars 26–34). Each verse is characterized by a different configuration of materials; an instrumental introduction and coda precede and follow verses 1 and 7 respectively. Short instrumental transitions also appear after verses 1, 2 and 3.

Mozart produces instrumental links between verses by passing the ritornello motif freely between melody and bass lines and by manipulating other materials as well. The ritornello motif migrates from the upper strings to the bass line between the Introduction and verse 1, between verses 1 and 2 and between verses 2 and 3, and connects with the conjunct, descending semiquavers in the soprano at the end of verse 3 (see bars 67–70); the derived falling motif (bar 83–5) moves from voices to upper strings (as the ritornello) at the end of the movement. In the transition to verse 3 (bars 52–3), Mozart also notates only three notes in the first violin (Example 4.16). Beginning on the note on which the soprano has completed its phrase (d″) and ending on an a′ that leads to the soprano b♭′ for initiating verse 3, Mozart adds a further instrumental layer to this particular link, over ascending and descending versions of the ritornello motif. The result is a retrograde of the material that immediately follows in the soprano (d″–e♭″–a′–b♭′; b♭′–a′–e♭″–d″).

Mozart's *pièce de résistance* among Recordare transitions and instrumental and vocal interactions comes at the end of verse 6. At 'ne perenni cremer igne', a reference to the eternal fire featured in the upcoming Confutatis, Mozart opposes contrasting instrumental arpeggios and harmonized voices

Example 4.16   Mozart, Requiem, K. 626, Recordare, bars 50–5

(Example 4.17). It represents clear confrontation according to late eighteenth- and early nineteenth-century musical and aesthetic criteria, contrasting materials and textures alternating in equal-length units.[39] The immediate preparation for and exit from the confrontation is poised and precise: Mozart prepares for the instrumental bass ♫ rhythm by gently increasing the frequency with which the rhythm is heard in the bars before the confrontation (especially bar 104); and the forceful, *f* instrumental bass (adding double basses to cellos) becomes a delicate, *p* fragment for first and second violins, the repeated c'' and c''' quavers and crotchet in turn taken up as repeated quavers and crotchets in the *bassi* and bass voices (bars 109–11). We are given both a seamless connection to the next verse and an immediate re-integration of the agent of confrontation into a smooth musical fabric.

While Mozart's setting of 'ne perenni cremer igne' can reasonably be interpreted as a musical response to the text, his transitions to and from it are less clear in intent. The 'ne perenni' disrupts the mood of the Recordare, arriving and departing suddenly as dictated by the text, but is also tightly integrated into the surrounding music in the spirit of earlier verse transitions. Mozart prioritized at his early notational phase both harsh confrontation and immediate, subtle re-integration; his economy of effect thus

---

[39]   See, for example, Antoine Reicha, *Traité de mélodie* (Paris, 1814), p. 91. Reicha's writings on dialogue and confrontation are an outgrowth of eighteenth-century views; see Keefe, *Mozart's Piano Concertos*, pp. 24–41.

Example 4.17 Mozart, Requiem, K. 626, Recordare, bars 103–12

extends to the succinct manipulation of effects. As in the Introit, it is not obvious how to process the assimilation of recalcitrant music, the immediate re-integration of the storm into the calm prayer. Inevitably, as we contemplate text and sound of the 'ne perenni' confrontation, we will hear them as a portent of things to come.

The Sequence: Confutatis

Confutatis maledictis,   While the wicked are confounded,
Flammis acribus addictis,   Doomed to flames of woe unbounded,
Voca me cum benedictis.   Call me with thy saints surrounded.

Oro supplex et acclinis,   Low, I kneel, with heart-submission;
Cor contritum quasi cinis: See, like ashes, my contrition;
Gere curam mei finis.   Help me in my last condition.

Mozart sets the sixteenth and seventeenth verses of the Sequence as his Confutatis. The text and its resonance again shape Mozart's musical setting: the rebuking of those consigned to eternal flames ('Confutatis maledictis, Flammis acribus addictis': a – V/a, bars 1–6; c – V/a, bars 10–16) twice alternates with the plea to be placed among the blessed ('Voca me cum benedictis': C, bars 7–10; a, bars 17–25). The contrite prayer for salvation occupies the remainder of the movement ('Oro supplex et acclinis'), the three lines cadencing in A flat minor, G minor and F (bars 26–39) and the dominant seventh of D minor in bar 40 linking to the Lacrymosa.

The aforementioned juxtaposition of a loud and soft e in the second beat of bar 6 – the link between 'Confutatis maledictis' and 'Voca me' – is representative of Mozart's sensitivity to individual sounds and their implications in the movement as a whole. Mozart's markings bring to life his desire for sharp contrast between 'Confutatis' and 'Voca me' segments: the strokes in the instrumental bass and violin for 'Confutatis', perhaps denoting accentuation,[40] are set against the *sotto voce* markings and slurs in 'Voca me'; and the instrumental basses return *f* for the second 'Confutatis' after one of their longest absences in Mozart's score thus far (three-and-a-half bars for 'Voca me'). The violin line at the opening of the second 'Confutatis' (bars 10–12, Example 4.18), having not

Example 4.18   Mozart, Requiem, K. 626, Confutatis, bars 10–12

---

[40] On strokes in late eighteenth-century music, see Brown, *Classical and Romantic Performing Practice* pp. 98–103 and 208–12.

appeared during the first 'Confutatis', is surely a register-related *aide-mémoire*, Mozart wanting to distinguish where the violins are to play in octaves with the cellos from where they are to play in unison. Instead of having the violins track the basses at the octave in the first half of bar 11 and bar 12 as the implied continuation to the second half of bar 10, Mozart has them snarl in their lowest register, *f* and still with stroke articulation markings, further accentuating the contrast with flowing, lyrical writing in the preceding and ensuing 'Voca me'. Mozart's attention to the nuances of effect during this first notational phase of the Confutatis extends to an ostensibly 'minor' matter of the register in which an instrument plays. Thus, the exact expressive content conveyed by an instrument is of prime importance to Mozart, a foundation for the economy of effect praised by Niemetschek and Arnold.

The transition from the second 'Voca me' to 'Oro supplex' has a very different effect from the transition from 'Confutatis' to 'Voca me' (Example 4.19). The entry on an unprepared diminished seventh with tritone skip in the bass at 'Oro' (bar 26) and the subsequent daring modulations are mitigated by elements of continuity. First, the ♫ violin rhythm from 'Voca me' is modestly extended to each beat of bar 24 so that the melody for 'Voca me' smooths over the audible musical seam created by introducing a repeated semiquaver accompaniment figure (bars 25ff.). Second, the instrumental basses enter a bar in advance of the voices – a moment accentuated by their extended eight-bar absence from the preceding 'Voca me' – establishing a pattern of repeated notes on each beat that will prevail in the voices. Finally, the bassethorns and bassoons introduce their sonorous support to coincide with the entry of the basses and before the arrival of the other three voices, thus contributing to a de-emphasized mid-bar entry of soprano, alto and bass, which are already marked *p*. If not necessarily entering unnoticed, the sopranos, altos and tenors emerge gradually from the diminished seventh harmony in the sustained wind and the bass voices, rather than in crisply delineated fashion. The subdued voices, then, are introduced by a staged instrumental transition; the contrite prayer ('Oro supplex') emerges from the plea to be placed among the blessed ('Voca me'), thus in effect supporting that plea.

The transition into 'Oro supplex' is matched by the transition out of it at the end of the movement (Example 4.20). Mozart presumably envisaged the bassethorns and bassoons exiting with the voices on the first beat of bar 39 (assuming the wind contribution to bar 26 – bar 29, beat 1, was intended for replication in bars 30–3, 34–5 and 36–9, as Eybler has it, in the descending sequence of the 'Oro supplex'). But the first violins' semiquaver

Example 4.19   Mozart, Requiem, K. 626, Confutatis, bars 23–30

Example 4.19 (cont.)

Example 4.20 Mozart, Requiem, K. 626, Confutatis, bars 36–40

accompaniment is retained throughout bar 39. Mozart's notation includes the second violin part from bar 38, beat 4, to the end, the A♮s in bar 39 reinforcing the major third in the figured bass (to be played on the organ); and he carefully notated a single crotchet *a* in the viola to complete the dominant seventh chord linking Confutatis to Lacrymosa. He remains meticulously attentive, again, to matters of tiny sonic detail.[41]

Just as the fusing of 'Voca me' and 'Oro supplex' supports textual implications, so too does the famously contorted harmonic progression of 'Oro supplex' (partially given in Examples 4.19 and 4.20), which depicts the desperate supplicant's heart crushed to ashes ('Cor contritum quasi cinis'). Overall, the music does not move far, from A minor (bar 25) to F major (bar 40), with a link via a dominant seventh on A to the D minor of the Lacrymosa. But Mozart's direction of travel is remarkable – cadences on A flat minor (bar 29) and G minor (bar 33) divided by a second bass tritone skip, then a tritone to D♭ predicting a cadence in G flat minor. (Although this cadence does not materialize it is still a possibility in bar 35.) With the third diminished seventh (bar 34) Mozart has used all three of the available versions of this chord. This extraordinary harmonic progression turns the passage between the outer extremes into its own self-contained expressive bubble. Like the secondary development from the slow movement of Mozart's Symphony No. 39 in E flat, K. 543 (bars 91–107), and the majority of the development section from the Andante of his 'Jupiter' Symphony (bars 47–55), for example, the 'Oro supplex' stands both inside its move-ment – the product of a careful transition – and outside it, inhabiting a fundamentally different expressive world from the preceding material. Harmonic associations and interpretative justifications for the chords and keys in this passage, however parsed, can only be a partial explanation, for expressive individuality and disorientation are also at play.[42] Nine years before the composition of the Requiem, Johann Samuel Petri acknowledged the potentially disorientating quality of distant-key modulations.[43] Criticisms of Mozart's harmonic and tonal procedures during his lifetime imply negative experiences of disorientation.[44]

If disorientation is a partial *raison d'être* for the harmonies of 'Oro supplex', it is possible that certain other sounds and effects – including the final note in the Dies irae – were also designed with disorientation in

---

[41] The pencil markings in the autograph separating Mozart's instrumental annotations from Eybler's mistakenly assign the second violin annotation to Eybler rather than Mozart. It can clearly be seen, however, that the second violin is in Mozart's hand.

[42] For more on the Mozart symphonic passages mentioned (plus others) in the context of listener disorientation, see Simon P. Keefe, 'Harmonies and Effects: Haydn and Mozart in Parallel', in Julian Horton (ed.), *The Cambridge Companion to the Symphony* (Cambridge, forthcoming).

[43] Johann Samuel Petri, *Anleitung zur praktischen Musik*, rev. edn (Leipzig, 1782), p. 281, as given in Annette Richards, *The Free Fantasia and the Musical Picturesque* (Cambridge, 2001), p. 41.

[44] For criticism see Deutsch, *Documentary Biography*, pp. 290, 328 and Ernst Ludwig Gerber, *Historisch-biographisches Lexikon der Tonkünstler*, 2 vols. (Leipzig, 1790, 1792), vol. I, col. 979.

mind. 'Ne perenni' in the Recordare, at the reference to the eternal flames, prefigures the harsh contrasts that characterize the alternation of 'Confutatis' and 'Voca me', but, as its own expressive island, foreshadows 'Oro supplex' as well. At any rate, the Confutatis captures in microcosm priorities and strategies associated with Mozart's late music: the aesthetic of blocked contrast that characterizes the late chamber music (and appears from time to time in *Così fan tutte*); the harmonic contortions of the late symphonies and piano concertos; the expressive bubbles of the late symphonies.[45] And, appropriately enough, late Mozart is almost *the late* Mozart, with just eight bars of the Lacrymosa and the incomplete Domine Jesu and Hostias to come.

The Sequence: Lacrymosa

Lacrymosa dies illa,	Ah! that day of tears and mourning!
Qua resurget ex favilla	From the dust of earth returning
Judicandus homo reus:	Man for judgment must prepare him.
Huic ergo parce, Deus.	Spare, O God, in mercy spare him.
Pie Jesu Domine,	Lord all pitying, Jesu blest,
Dona eis requiem.	Grant them thine eternal rest.
Amen.	Amen.

Even though the Lacrymosa is only eight bars long in its incomplete state, its sounds and effects are comparably sensitive as those in earlier, full movements of the work (Example 4.21). The fragile instrumental introduction (bars 1–2) is scored for violins and violas unsupported by bass instruments. The first beat of bar 3 then projects a sonority unique to Mozart's portions of the Requiem, namely the instrumental basses re-entering (after a discernible absence) simultaneously with all four voices. Previous bass re-entries are distinctive[46] – for example, the return to the frenzied 'Confutatis' figuration and the onset of the 'Oro supplex' transition in the previous movement (bars 10 and 25 respectively). In the Lacrymosa the basses help to project warm delicacy, contributing to a full, rounded texture not evident in the previous bars. We must surely assume that Mozart intended to continue the upper strings' accompaniment, including the *suspiratio* violin figures, beyond bars 1–2, in which case both the upper strings and instrumental

---

[45] See Keefe, *Mozart's Viennese Instrumental Music*, pp. 64–85, 105–200.

[46] An exception is the B♭ crotchets appearing in bar 5 of the Tuba mirum after the initial imitation between the trombone and solo bass.

Example 4.21   Mozart, Requiem, K. 626, Lacrymosa, bars 1–8

basses resonate beyond the final vocal quavers of bars 3 and 4 and the detached vocal quavers on each beat of bars 5–6. Roles are reversed in bars 7–8 with the sustained dotted crotchets in the voices potentially enveloping the instruments. Thus, Mozart indicates the beginning of his crescendo on the second beat of bar 7, and foreshadows it on the first beat of bar 7 with the change in the relationship between voices and instruments.

Sounds and their expressive resonances ebb and flow. The fragile delicacy in bars 1–2 becomes warm delicacy in bars 3–6, giving way to force in bar 8, via the crescendo in bar 7. Like several earlier effects in the Requiem – including in the Introit and Dies irae – Mozart's 'homo reus' is unsettling. It is not as if it is unprepared: the sopranos and altos ascend stepwise through an octave and seventh respectively in bars 5–6, continuing their ascents in bars 7–8; the texture thickens on the first beat of bar 7 in anticipation of the climax; and the crescendo occupies three whole beats in bar 7. But as in 'ne perenni', which is preceded and followed by instrumental links and there-fore also elegantly entered and exited, it is the onset of raw power itself, so soon after the establishment of a more subdued mood, that is disquieting.

We repeatedly witness expressive jolts in Mozart's Requiem, between the end of one movement and the beginning of the next (Dies irae – Tuba mirum, Tuba mirum – Rex tremendae, Recordare – Confutatis) and within individual movements (Introit, Rex tremendae, Recordare, Confutatis); it is ultimately impossible to determine whether they represent Mozart's own fears about death and/or his intention to support the seriousness and severity of the text. At any rate they build into the musical equation uncertainties and doubts expressed in the text, through individual sounds and effects and successions of sounds and effects. And the end of Mozart's portion of the Lacrymosa has special significance in this respect. We will never know whether Benedikt Schack's account of the final-day Requiem rehearsal, where Mozart 'at the first bars of the Lacrimosa . . . began to weep bitterly [and] laid the score on one side', is wholly or partially accurate or completely inaccurate.[47] Nor can we be sure that Mozart's reasons for setting aside his Lacrymosa at bar 8 were entirely or mostly musical rather than personal, even accepting the reasonable musical hypothesis that he had reached an important structural juncture in the work, the words 'Dona eis requiem' in the final verse of the Sequence text – which also occur in the Introit and Agnus Dei – encouraging him to ponder issues of inter-movement cohesion.[48] But, come what may, the final sounds of Mozart's

---

[47] Deutsch, *Documentary Biography*, p. 537.   [48] Wolff, *Mozart's Requiem*, p. 30.

Lacrymosa, which could hardly have been better scripted for dramatic effect, grab us by the scruff of the neck demanding attention, explanation and interpretation. Writing only his second (and last) crescendo marking into the score, Mozart has his voices scream *forte* of the 'guilty man' ('homo reus'). The resounding echo of the dominant harmony, like the last note of the Dies irae, is deafening. Does Mozart consider himself, ultimately, the guilty man to be judged? If so, is it perhaps appropriate that he unintentionally left others – first Eybler, then Süssmayr – to make the Sequence's final, definitive appeal to God for clemency ('Huic ergo parce, Deus')? Whether or not we are inclined towards biographical interpretation, the simple fact is that Mozart's contribution to the Sequence comes to an abrupt end at a remarkable juncture in the text. In the discourse on sounds and effects that has comprised Mozart's Requiem thus far, the biggest effect is reserved not for an imposing sound but for the silence that follows it. And, in that silence, even with the Domine Jesu and Hostias to come, Mozart becomes posthumous Mozart reception.

The Offertory: Domine Jesu

Domine Jesu Christe, Rex gloriae,	Lord Jesus Christ, King of glory,
libera animas omnium fidelium	free the souls of all the faithful departed
defunctorum	
de poenis inferni et de profundo lacu:	from the pains of hell and the deep pit:
libera eas de ore leonis,	free them from the mouth of the lion,
ne absorbeat eas tartarus,	do not let Tartarus swallow them up,
ne cadant in obscurum:	nor let them fall into darkness;
sed signifer sanctus Michael	but may the standard-bearer St Michael,
repraesentet eas in lucem sanctam:	lead them into the holy light:
Quam olim Abrahae promisisti et	which you once promised to Abraham and
semini ejus.	his seed.

Like the settings of the Introit and many of the Sequence movements, the musical setting of the Domine Jesu responds to divisions in the text, changes in material and texture co-ordinated with tonal confirmations to demarcate the beginnings and ends of clearly delineated musical blocks: the request to Christ to free the souls of the dead ('Domine Jesu', g – B flat – c, bars 1–14); the request that the dead be freed from the lion's mouth ('libera eas', A flat – b flat and B flat – V/c, bars 15–20); the request that Tartarus not be allowed to swallow them ('ne absorbeat eas', V/c – c – F – d – V/g, bars 21–32); and the prayer that St Michael will lead them to the holy light ('sed signifer', g – c – f – B flat – g, ending V/g, bars 32–43) that was once promised to

Abraham and his descendants ('Quam olim Abrahae', g – B flat – V/g – g, bars 44–78).

Musical surges in the first twenty bars of the movement support strong textual imagery. 'Rex gloriae' (bars 2–3) and 'de ore leonis' (bars 16–17, 19–20) are marked *forte* and receive semiquavers rather than quavers in the instrumental bass (Examples 4.22a and 4.22b). Mini-surges, also *forte*, comprise phrase-links at 'de poenis' ('the pains [of hell]', bars 7, 9, Example 4.22c) and, without text, immediately before 'libera eas' (bar 14, Example 4.22b). The *f* and *p* dynamic contrasts here are meticulously notated by Mozart, the *forte* segments occupying three beats in bars 7 and 9 and three-and-a-half beats in bar 14, but invite as many text-setting questions as they answer. To be sure, the *forte* segments are supported by abrupt leaps in the sopranos (bars 7, 9) after primarily conjunct writing before. But how do we explain the 'pains' being set *forte* by the sopranos and *piano* by the altos, tenors and basses? And how are we to interpret a phrase-link – one that does not set text – marked *forte* against the prevailing *piano* dynamic? We are left to wonder what exactly the *forte*, inter-phrase segments signify, what function they fulfil. The effect, again, is (surely deliberately) disorientating: the 'Rex gloriae' and 'de ore leonis' *forte* segments are straightforward text-painting, but other *forte* interjections are not.

The activation of the 'Quam olim Abrahae' fugue by a jagged, *forte* lead-in (discussed above) is unsettling in a similar way to earlier parallel passages, occurring suddenly and without obvious textual provocation. Mozart has prepared us for the 'Quam olim Abrahae' effect by establishing a precedent

Example 4.22a Mozart, Requiem, K. 626, Domine Jesu, bars 1–3

Example 4.22b   Mozart, Requiem, K. 626, Domine Jesu, bars 13–18

for abrupt, *forte* links between vocal material, but does not thereby diminish its impact. We learn from Arnold that Mozart's economical effects make their biggest impression when heard in combination with, rather than in isolation from, surrounding and supporting musical materials and events. Mozart cultivates his bolt of lightning not only earlier in the Domine Jesu, but also in the Introit and Sequence. As we have seen, instrumental links between vocal statements in the Introit, Recordare and Confutatis repeatedly convey expressive effects; in the transition to 'Quam olim Abrahae', the instrumental link builds on the prominent status achieved by links in earlier movements, now breaking on to the stage dramatically as a raw, forceful, disquieting sound.

Example 4.22c Mozart, Requiem, K. 626, Domine Jesu, bars 6–10

The Offertory: Hostias

Hostias et preces tibi, Domine,	We offer you, O Lord,
laudis offerimus:	sacrifices and prayers of praise;
tu suscipe pro animabus, illis,	receive them on behalf of those souls
quarum hodie memoriam facimus:	whom we remember this day.
fac eas, Domine, de morte transire ad vitam.	Let them, O Lord, pass from death to life,
Quam olim Abrahae promisisti et semini ejus.	as you once promised to Abraham and his seed.

The Hostias offers 'sacrifices and prayers of praise' for the souls of the departed, and is set in homophonic declamation: E flat (bar 1) – c (bar 16) – B flat (bar 21) – b flat (bar 23) – D flat (bar 27) – f (bar 31) – d (bar 39) – E flat (bar 44) – V/g (bars 53–4). Again, instrumental links are prominent in Mozart's score. Coinciding with the return to the tonic E flat, the instrumental introduction from bars 1–2 reappears in bars 44–5 – no instrumental

Example 4.23 Mozart, Requiem, K. 626, Hostias, bars 44–54

contributions aside from the bass line are notated in between – as a transition to 'fac eas, Domine, de morte transire ad vitam', which itself paves the way for the 'Quam olim Abrahae' return (Example 4.23). The first violin from bar 46 onwards grows from the second violin part between vocal phrases in bars 44–5, becoming progressively more angular in the last eight bars with leaps from upper to lower and lower to upper registers culminating in a two-octave jump in bar 52. But the angularity is partially mitigated in bar 53 by Mozart's slur and his eradication of the preceding syncopation. The smoothing-out process activated by the slurred quavers accentuates the abrupt onset of the 'Quam olim Abrahae' da capo by implying resolution to the preceding unevenness rather than the continuation of the unevenness that ultimately characterizes the fugue. The jagged violin transition to 'Quam olim Abrahae' (bars 43–4 of the Domine Jesu) and the violin line that ends the Hostias could not be more different as discrete musical elements, but their functions are similar, namely to dramatize the beginning of the 'Quam olim Abrahae'.

The Domine Jesu link, drawing attention to itself in keeping with *forte* outbursts earlier in the movement, positions the initial dramatic onset ahead of the onset of fugal material; the subdued ending of the Hostias, in contrast, leads to a synchronization of dramatic onset and fugue. The links are equally startling, though, playing with listeners' sonic expectations. Building on earlier procedures – transitional outbursts in the Domine Jesu and one smooth non-modulatory interlude in the Hostias – they retain the element of surprise. As in the Domine Jesu, the expressive jolt in the Hostias is not apparently motivated by the Offertory text: a musically disquieting effect, then, sustains Mozart's note of unsettledness right to the end of his work on the Requiem score.

Requiem sounds and strategies in context

In its incomplete state in Mozart's hand the Requiem autograph offers a particularly sharp perspective on strategies associated with sounds and effects. But Mozart's attention to this area of his sacred music is not limited to the Requiem. The evolution of sounds and effects over extended periods, including the kinds of links and contrasts evident in the Requiem, characterizes his late Salzburg masses, the incomplete C minor Mass, K. 427, and 'Ave verum corpus', K. 618. In May and July 1791 Mozart asked his friend Anton Stoll, a choirmaster and teacher in Baden, to send to Vienna the C major Mass, K. 317 (including all the parts) and the B flat Mass, K. 275, raising the possibility of performances at St Stephen's Cathedral, where Mozart had recently assumed duties as adjunct Kapellmeister.[49] Mozart also owned performance materials (no longer extant) for the C major Mass, K. 337, which could have been heard at the cathedral.[50] These three works, then, alongside K. 427 (his only mass from the Vienna years) and the newly composed 'Ave verum corpus', would probably have loomed large in Mozart's musical consciousness when he turned to the Requiem.[51]

[49] Anderson (ed. and trans.), *Letters*, pp. 950, 965.
[50] Black, 'Mozart and the Practice of Sacred Music', pp. 295–6.
[51] It has often been stated that K. 317 was performed at the coronation celebrations for Leopold II in Prague in 1791; for counter-arguments, and a suggestion that no Mozart mass was performed on this occasion, see Black, 'Mozart and the Practice of Sacred Music', pp. 236–40.

Mozart demonstrates a fascination with sounds and effects in K. 317 (1779) similar to that in the Requiem. Links and contrasts in the Kyrie, for example, are developed, modified and transformed. Contrasting sounds are immediately promoted in the first five bars, in both the oscillations between *f* and *p* and the differing instrumental material (wind sustained notes and strings' austere dotted semiquavers) that serves *inter alia* as links between vocal statements. With the dotted rhythms removed, the semiquavers in both strings and wind – alongside sustained notes in the horns – provide a smooth instrumental transition to the più andante solo portion of the movement (bar 5, beat 4 – bar 7), referencing the opening contrasts in the oscillation between *mf* and *p*. Imitating the solo soprano's più andante theme at a distance of two crotchets, the oboe joins two vocal phrases together (bar 9, with trumpets), subsequently providing links in semiquavers between vocal phrases (bars 11, 13, 15). In the Maestoso reprise, the strings' dotted rhythm is heard *piano* in an antecedent–consequent dialogue with voices and trombones (bars 26–30, Example 4.24), and simultaneously with *piano* oboes (bars 28–9), being fully assimilated now into the prevailing instrumental texture in contrast to its appearance earlier in the movement. In the final two bars (Example 4.24), the returning più andante theme and semiquaver dotted rhythm join forces elegantly to link the vocal exit to the end of the movement. As in the Dies irae, Tuba mirum, Rex tremendae, Confutatis and Domine Jesu from the Requiem, sounds and effects in the Kyrie of K. 317 accrue and develop across the movement, in this case progressively reconciling contrasting sounds.

The quick succession of *forte* and *piano* contrasts in the Kyrie of K. 317 is taken further at 'Et incarnatus est' in the Credo (Example 4.25). The musical *volte face* here is unambiguous and uncompromising: from chorus to soloists, assertive *forte* strings to muted, *piano* chromatic first violins, Allegro molto to Adagio, loud *bassi* to *tasto solo* organ, and diatonic straightforwardness to chromatic, modulatory uncertainty (f – A flat – E flat, bars 60–4). Following Ignaz Arnold, this is a succinct, economical effect (like so many in the Requiem), packing a punch not only for its impact at the moment of delivery, but also for resonating beyond its immediate confines, in this instance back to the Kyrie. And, as in all of Mozart's Requiem movements, a single effect spawns related effects: at 'Crucifixus' (bars 65–71) Mozart introduces trombones and second violins, upping the sonic ante, and moves from *p* to *f* to *pp*, replete with prominent oboe, again invoking dynamic and orchestral effects from the Kyrie; and he returns suddenly to *f* and the *primo tempo* for the main Credo theme at 'Et resurrexit' (bars 72ff.). Like 'ne perenni' (Recordare) and 'Oro supplex'

Example 4.24　Mozart, Mass in C, K. 317 ('Coronation'), Kyrie, bars 26–31

(Confutatis), the 'Et incarnatus est' and 'Crucifixus' exist in their own self-contained expressive bubble that seems both removed from and related to other materials and events in the work.

The Credo from Mozart's next mass, K. 337 in C (1780), also integrates new and old effects. As a whole the Credo combines the bold grandeur of the Gloria with the subtle instrumental participation of the Kyrie; the latter is especially evident at 'Crucifixus'. In between sustained notes and turn-like figures for the oboes and bassoons at 'ex Maria' and 'passus et sepultus est', the winds exchange oscillating figures on a bar-by-bar basis with the voices at 'Crucifixus', while sustained notes are also passed around. At the conclusion of the mass, in the final four bars of the 'Dona nobis pacem'

Example 4.25   Mozart, Mass in C, K. 317 ('Coronation'), Credo, bars 56–62

(Example 4.26), Mozart invokes delicate instrumental effects from the end
of the Kyrie (echo and sustained notes) and from the 'Et incarnatus est' and
'Crucifixus' (sustained notes and tightly intermeshed vocal and instrumental lines) while returning to the interweaving dialogue among solo voice,
oboes, bassoons and organ witnessed earlier in the Agnus Dei. Mozart could
have ended his mass at the big C major cadence five bars from the close, but
chose to append his harmonically static, deftly scored concluding passage
instead, indicating attentiveness to the evolution of, invocation of and
relationship between sounds and effects across the work as a whole.

Mozart is even sensitive to the nuances of instrumental sound and effect
in the small-scale Mass in B flat, K. 275 (presumably 1777; for two violins,
bassi and three *colla parte* trombones) and 'Ave verum corpus', K. 618
(1791; for strings and continuo). The string accompaniment to the Kyrie of
K. 275 begins with repeated quavers, providing a *de facto* link between vocal

Example 4.25 (cont.)

contributions in bars 2 and 3 that evolves into an explicit link at the end of
bar 4; for the first 'Christe eleison', the first violins provide quaver upbeats to
each of the solo vocal entries (bars 8, 10, 12), while the second violins
subsequently embellish the original 'Kyrie eleison' accompaniment with
semiquavers (bars 15–17). The quaver-based accompaniment style at
'Christe' (bars 19–20) includes melodic support for the voices; end-of-bar
echoes greet the next 'Christe' (bars 27, 28), in essence bringing together link
and melodic-support roles. In a final *coup de grâce* (bars 30–3, Example
4.27), Mozart returns to the original thrice-repeated-note accompaniment
not heard since bars 1–6 and applies the violin echo effect for the first time
to 'Kyrie eleison' material. Closely linked to preceding accompaniment
material, the effects are nonetheless accentuated by a sudden *piano* dynamic

Example 4.26   Mozart, Mass in C, K. 337, Dona nobis, bars 113–19

Example 4.27 Mozart, Mass in B flat, K. 275, Kyrie, bars 29–33

(bars 30–1) and an association with new material (bars 32–3). Thus, the K. 275 Kyrie exemplifies (in a relatively early Mozart sacred work) Arnold's inconspicuously evolving accompaniments, each new figure appearing as a natural consequence of a preceding one.

The 'Ave verum corpus', like the Requiem but in a smaller-scale context, promotes instrumental links as generators of melodic content and agents of smooth transition, and individual sounds as *bona fide* effects. The first violins in bars 6 and 7 establish an accompaniment pattern for a single bar – repeated crotchets on the second and third beats, higher-pitched notes on the first and last notes and slurs between the first and second and the third and fourth beats – that subsequently appears in bar 10 in all upper strings as a link to 'Vere passum', assuring smooth passage from one vocal phrase to the next. In bar 29, a link comprising two violins ascending stepwise in thirds for three crotchets generates (in inversion) the stepwise-descending crotchets in thirds in the ensuing sequence (bars 31–4,

Example 4.28   Mozart, 'Ave verum corpus', K. 618, bars 29–39

Example 4.28): vocal material thereby grows from an instrumental link. Individual, unharmonized sounds also create distinctive effects. The d″ and g′ – d″ in the first violin and soprano (bars 15, 37–8) are the only unharmonized pitches in the piece.[52] As pivots between vocal contributions from the altos, tenors and basses, they contrast markedly with the harmonized links, shining pristinely as distinctive individual notes in an otherwise gently harmonized piece. As in the Requiem, Mozart maintains a simultaneously broad and precise perspective on sounds and effects, with an eye (and ear) on both evolving process (the links) and distinctive product (the unharmonized pitches).

Given its status as one of Mozart's biggest, most important sacred works, the C minor Mass, K. 427, will inevitably be compared to the Requiem in terms of sounds and strategies employed. It is different from its counterpart in many respects – the larger wind cohort is clearly more loquacious than would have been the wind cohort in a Requiem completed by Mozart – but is similar in emphasizing, and developing, orchestral effects over time. In the Kyrie, instrumental transitions carry far-reaching sonic implications, as in the Requiem as a whole. In the initial 'Kyrie' section repeated notes in the brass comprise either assertive support or pseudo-ominous preparation for the chorus but subsequently function differently. The transition to the 'Christe', for example, comprises gently repeated *piano* quavers in the oboes, bassoons and horns, sustaining G minor harmony, as well as the dominant of E flat in bar 33. The quietly consoling quality of the repeated quavers in Andante moderato duly surfaces in a repeated-note wind segment in the 'Christe' itself (oboes and bassoons, bars 62–5). The 'Kyrie'–'Christe' transition is in effect re-interpreted right at the end of the movement, where a complete wind and brass sonority (oboes, bassoons, horns, trumpets, trombones, bars 93–4) links the end of the vocal contribution to the end of the movement, the second longest complete sonority in the movement at six beats, and the only one at a quiet dynamic level (*pp*). It resembles the end of the Requiem Introit, then, both in subtly promoting instruments previously used as forceful support (trumpets and timpani in the Introit) and in thereby creating an ostensibly new instrumental effect in the final bars of its movement. It also captures the wind participation from the Kyrie in microcosm, providing a full wind sound, and acts as an agent of transition (both to the end of the movement and, in its fullness, to

---

[52] The *Neue Mozart-Ausgabe* marks the bass part 'senza Vc., B.' in both bars 15 and 37–8, the single-note sounds thus combining first violin, soprano and unharmonized organ. Mozart's autograph does not contain the 'senza Vc., B.', but the *Neue Mozart-Ausgabe*'s marking is surely appropriate. See *Ave verum corpus: Faksimile*.

the Gloria's bold tutti-wind support). Just as the Sequence movements in the Requiem build on the Introit's unsettledness, so the end of K. 427's Gloria builds on the Kyrie's conclusion, the full wind and brass (oboes, bassoons, horns, trumpets) previously employed as emphatic support for the voices now employed, *piano* and *pianissimo*, as a bridge from the vocal exit to the end of the movement (bars 56–60, material derived from bars 27ff.).

Distinctive instrumental effects in transitional contexts at the beginning and end of the K. 427 'Qui tollis' – the first (and only) unaccompanied presentation of the taut dotted rhythm in the strings and the only bar-long iteration of the rhythm in the winds – again highlight evolving instrumental sounds and roles across a complete movement. On this occasion, Mozart contrives a stage-by-stage reconciliation of contrasting materials presented by the strings and the wind and voices. The isolated string accompaniment figure at the opening followed by juxtaposed string accompaniment and the wind and voices (bars 3ff.), draws attention to the different, if mutually reinforcing, musical qualities of the rigid, disjunctive, jagged accompaniment and the flowing, mostly conjunct voice part. The materials are partially reconciled in bars 13–18 and 26–32, the newly conjunct accompaniment tracking the syncopated voices, but the reconciliations are followed by sudden resumptions, *forte*, of the original contrasts in conjunction with reprises of the original 'Qui tollis' vocal material. The corresponding passage from bar 43 onwards finally witnesses a protracted integration of materials: in bars 43–7 the strings follow the contours of the voices (as in the earlier 'miserere' from bars 15–18); in bars 48–50 the winds and voices adopt one accompaniment-related dotted rhythm per bar, so that harmonic intensification (diminished sevenths) is co-ordinated uniformly by vocal and orchestral groups; and in bars 52–5 the repeated-note accompaniment in the strings, following the soprano lines and allowing the winds a modest opportunity to shine, is passed to the winds, *pp*, at the end. As in many Requiem movements, Mozart highlights a distinctive orchestral effect at the opening of the 'Qui tollis' and another at the very end, incorporating in between the kind of intricately developing accompaniment writing praised by Ignaz Arnold.

K. 427 ultimately demonstrates, like the Requiem, sensitivity to the resonance of individual sounds and effects over extended periods. As in the Requiem and Viennese piano concerto autographs,[53] Mozart demonstrates meticulous attention to instrumental detail in the K. 427 autograph

---

[53] See Keefe, 'Mozart the Performer-Composer at Work on the Viennese Piano Concertos'.

even in apparently innocuous contexts: bassoon crotchets on the first beat of bar 24 in the Kyrie are revised to semibreves tied across to bar 25, aligning the bassoons with the oboes and thus *slightly* accentuating the winds' sustained notes in a *forte*, tutti context; and the *bassi* part is lightened in the immediate run-up to the final cadential trill of the Laudamus te, with repeated quaver a″s in the violins also revised to lower pitches (and to a scalar shape paralleling the solo voice, bars 134–5), allowing the solo soprano's stepwise ascent from a low register (beginning on c′) to shine through more pristinely than in the originally conceived version. The trombones, marked on the vocal staves of the autograph, fulfil particularly distinctive roles when departing from *colla parte* participation, such as doubling the trumpets, *piano*, at the end of the initial 'Kyrie eleison' section of the Kyrie (bars 30–2) and falling silent in *piano* segments of the 'Cum sancto' fugue (bars 53–5, 73–5, 156–63, 167–75): in the former they add fractionally (at a *piano* dynamic) to the brass sound; in the latter they allow a little additional prominence for sustained notes in the oboes and bassoons, and reinforce dynamic contrasts between *p* and *f*.[54]

The short Jesu Christe from the Gloria offers a window into Mozart's world where connected effects are concerned. A climactic movement in K. 427 in raw sound, it is initiated in the curtest possible way, by a single note, *forte*, in the full orchestra. As at 'Quam olim Abrahae' in the Requiem's Domine Jesu, a protracted series of instrumental links in K. 427 thus far culminates in a succinct, forceful link, namely a one-note transition from the start of the movement to the entry of the voices (bar 1, beat 2). And, like the violin note that ends the Dies irae, it lends further resonance to Niemetschek's and Arnold's claim for Mozart's 'economy of conjuring up his greatest effect with the least effort, often through the single note of an instrument'.

Conclusion

To contemplate the array of sounds and effects in Mozart's Requiem score is to cherish the glories and the mysteries of the autograph. We actively confront our critical limitations in considering Mozart's notated and un-notated intentions in the Requiem, but (like Salieri in *Amadeus*) can rejoice in our limitations by seizing a rare opportunity to encounter Mozart's

---

[54] For a facsimile of K. 427, see Wolfgang Amadeus Mozart, *Messe c-moll KV427: Faksimile der autographen Partitur* (Kassel, 1983).

creative mind unambiguously *in medias res*. Mysteries unresolved by an incomplete score complement irresolvable mysteries of the Requiem legend, such as the degree of truth in Mozart's premonition of death at the Prater and the account of the final-day rehearsal. Neither in the popular nor in the scholarly imagination have we convincingly separated the music of the Requiem from biographical issues relating to the work, precisely because we cannot – or do not wish to – entirely separate them. Legend and work are mutually reinforcing; implicit and explicit legend-inspired fiction and Mozart-autograph-inspired musical interpretation are kindred spirits, stimulated as much by what is unknown and half known as by what is known. Uncertainty and doubt – in extra-musical and non-musical as well as musical contexts – should be a source of critical inspiration, not a source of critical inadequacy and fear.

But this scholarly *apologia* has its limitations. The legend of the Requiem, where reinforced by the music of the Requiem, has proved a locus of inspiration at least partially through encounters with the work *in toto* rather than with Mozart's portions exclusively. For the practical purposes of completing the work, Eybler (one of very few musicians who will have had an opportunity to contemplate the Sequence autograph manuscript as Mozart left it) and Süssmayr needed to hear, understand and interpret sounds and effects present on the page in front of them. The instrumental links repeatedly brought to the fore by Mozart, while sometimes uncertain in expressive resonance, will have left a lasting impression on the completers. Irrespective of how individually and collectively interpreted in expressive terms, the frequency, and the visual and aural prominence, of links – especially in an incomplete score – will have affected the completers' evaluations of sonic priorities and strategies. The links fulfil a straightforward function, joining one vocal statement to the next, but also create sounds and effects with aesthetic resonance and impact in their own right.

Mozart's instrumental annotations also draw attention to strategies implicit in the shaping of individual movements. As we have seen, sounds and effects acquire momentum and specific directions of travel: the prominent 'Christe' subject in the latter stages of the Kyrie relates to an earlier alteration to the autograph that has implications for the subsequent distribution of 'Kyrie' and 'Christe' entries; instrumental agitation increases over the course of the Dies irae; the opening of the Rex tremendae is re-worked to radically different effect at the end of the movement, a loosely symmetrical middle section appearing in between the related outer sections; instrumental links between phrases develop over the Confutatis; and forceful instrumental segments early in the Domine Jesu evolve into the explosive violin link to the 'Quam olim Abrahae' fugue.

At the time of his death Mozart had (half) completed possibly the first Viennese musical setting of the Requiem Mass in over a decade.[55] As explained in Chapters 1 and 2, many scholars, critics and musicians want to understand and appreciate the Requiem as Mozart's exclusive achievement; we can make sense of his premature demise, after all, if we see it had purpose, namely enabling him to make the ultimate musical pronouncement about death as his own life neared its end. We may choose to believe that biography and music – dual hermeneutic catalysts where understanding Mozart's work on the Requiem is concerned – are in harmony at this most extraordinary moment, perfectly aligned in marking the passing of one of music's great geniuses. But we would be wrong, ultimately, to think in this way. For the Requiem after 5 December 1791 is about life as well as death, about those people (Süssmayr in particular, but Eybler, Constanze and others too) who made sure that Mozart's fragment saw the light of day as a finished, performable work. It is to the continuation and completion of work on the Requiem after Mozart's death that we must now turn our attention.

---

[55]　Black, 'Mozart and the Practice of Sacred Music', p. 357.

5 | After Mozart: the Requiem completion, 1791–1792

Immediately after her husband's death and understandably eager both to retain the advance paid by the Requiem commissioner and to claim the remaining money that had been promised, Constanze set the wheels in motion for completing the work. String and wind parts were added to the Kyrie fugue (doubling vocal lines), in time for a possible performance at the exequies for Mozart at St Michael's in Vienna on 10 December. The hand of the Kyrie contributor, once thought to be that of Mozart's student Franz Jacob Freystädtler, remains unidentified.[1] Eleven days later Joseph Eybler had received both the unfinished score and a contract to complete it by mid-Lent 1792.[2] Writing directly on to the autograph score, Eybler added string parts to the Tuba mirum, Rex tremendae and Recordare, and string, wind, brass and timpani parts to the Dies irae and Confutatis; and he appended two bars to the soprano line in the Lacrymosa. Presumably he intended to write combinations of wind, brass and timpani parts for the movements in which they are not included, but decided first to continue through the score with the strings alone. Giving up his completion task before doing so, he returned the score to Constanze, whereupon Süssmayr's services were engaged.[3]

Why did Eybler not proceed beyond bars 9–10 of the Lacrymosa? It does not seem that he had other pressing compositional commitments in winter 1791 that would have interfered with his completion of the *Requiem*.[4] Moreover his impending appointment as choir director of the Carmelite church in

---

[1] For the Freystädtler identification, see Nowak, 'Instrumentalstimmen in der Kyrie-Fuge des Requiems von W. A. Mozart', pp. 191–201. For rebuttals, see Maunder, *Mozart's Requiem*, pp. 125–9; Moseley, 'Mozart's Requiem', p. 209; Lorenz, 'A Case of Mistaken Identity'. Nowak's claim in the same article that Süssmayr entered the trumpet and timpani parts into the autograph is also unproven. Black has tentatively raised the possibility that the Kyrie instrumentation was carried out by a member of the Theater auf der Wieden company known to Schikaneder. See Black, 'Mozart and the Practice of Sacred Music', pp. 413–14. On the 10 December 1791 performance see Brauneis, 'Exequien für Mozart', to which Black strikes a cautionary note in 'Mozart and the Practice of Sacred Music', pp. 414–15.

[2] For Eybler's statement, see Deutsch, *Documentary Biography*, p. 426.

[3] It is unclear for how long Eybler worked on the completion and when exactly he passed back the score to Constanze; see Hildegard Herrmann, *Thematisches Verzeichnis der Werke von Joseph Eybler* (Munich and Salzburg, 1976), p. 13.

[4] See ibid., *passim*.

Vienna – if, indeed, he was aware of it in December 1791 or early 1792 – would have put a higher, not lesser premium on completing the Requiem, as it surely would have provided a unique type of engagement with the sacred music of a contemporary compositional master and, therefore, invaluable practical experience of church music. Personal problems could have interfered with Eybler's work schedule in winter 1791–2, of course, although nothing has come to light. The most likely explanation, then, is that suggested by Eybler's aborted, two-bar continuation to the Lacrymosa in the first violin of the autograph score, namely that, for whatever reason, he did not consider himself up to the task. Mozart's testimonial for Eybler, dated 30 May 1790, explains that Eybler was 'a painstaking composer, equally skilled in the chamber style as in the church style'.[5] But Eybler's principal achievements in sacred music – masses, a requiem and Te Deum settings – lay in the future; only the *Missa Sancti Hermani* (1781) seems to have preceded his work on the Requiem.[6] Maybe Eybler found the blank canvas of the Lacrymosa and the post-Offertory sections intimidating, given his limited experience of sacred music. If, as seems to be the case, he wanted at all costs to accommodate Mozart's apparent intentions when orchestrating the Sequence, he would have subjugated his own compositional voice entirely to Mozart's and thus not allowed a vision to take shape in his mind for the completion as a whole. Perhaps Eybler was one of the composers who Süssmayr suggested in his letter to Breitkopf & Härtel (discussed below) were fearful of unfavourable comparison with Mozart; this would be unsurprising in one so young. Eybler was certainly in awe of Mozart when composing his own Requiem in C minor in 1803 to commemorate the eleventh anniversary of Emperor Leopold II's death; such awe could also have impeded the formation of a personal vision for the Requiem completion twelve years earlier. In response to Rochlitz's criticism (in the *Allgemeine musikalische Zeitung* of 1826) about musical parallels between Eybler's and Mozart's Domine Jesu movements, Eybler explained: 'As in all of his compositions, thus also here in the Domine, I marvelled at his gigantic spirit; I was carried away unwillingly – the world forgives me this imitation.'[7]

---

[5] My translation. Deutsch, *Dokumente*, p. 322: 'einen gründlichen Komponisten, sowohl im Kammer- als Kirchenstyl gleich geschickten'.

[6] Herrmann, *Thematisches Verzeichnis*, p. 26. On concert performances of Eybler's sacred works for Empress Marie Therese in 1802 and 1803, see John A. Rice, *Empress Marie Therese and Music at the Viennese Court, 1792–1807* (Cambridge, 2003), p. 100.

[7] 'Wie in allen seinen Kompositionen, so auch hier im Domine bewunderte ich seinen Riesengeist; unwillkürlich wurde ich fortgerissen – die Welt vergebe mir diese Nachahmung.' Given in Johanna Senigl, 'Neues zu Joseph Eybler', in Wolfgang Gratzer and Andrea Lindmayr (eds.), *De editione musices: Festschrift Gerhard Croll zum 65. Geburtstag* (Laaber, 1992), pp. 329–37, at 331. For Rochlitz's review, see *Allgemeine musikalische Zeitung*, 28 (1826), cols. 305–9, 321–31.

For reasons she could not recall in 1827, Constanze had been angry with Süssmayr at the time of (or immediately after) Mozart's death and as a result turned to others to complete the work before asking him.[8] Süssmayr duly obliged Constanze, orchestrating the Sequence (freely adapting and adding to Eybler's draft) and the Offertory, and composing the Lacrymosa from bar 9, Sanctus, Benedictus and Agnus Dei. The new score of the Sequence and Offertory (entirely in Süssmayr's hand), together with the autographs of Mozart's Introit and Kyrie, Süssmayr's Sanctus, Benedictus and Agnus Dei and the reprise of Mozart's material from the Introit and Kyrie in the concluding Communio (again in Süssmayr's hand), comprises both the work given to Count Walsegg in February 1792 in order to fulfil his commission and the basis of 'traditional' Mozart Requiem editions performed to this day.[9]

As outlined in Chapter 2, Süssmayr's contributions to the Requiem have always aroused controversy. We are best advised, then, to begin with Süssmayr's own explanation of his involvement in the Requiem completion. It comprises a response dated 8 February 1800 to a letter from Gottfried Christoph Härtel, half of the partnership Breitkopf & Härtel, who published the first edition of the Requiem in 1800 (with Süssmayr's work un-credited) and who were anxious to get to the bottom of a thorny authorship issue potentially damaging to sales of the score. It is translated here in full and the original given in the Appendix.[10]

> Gentlemen!
>
> Your gracious communication of 24 January gave me the greatest pleasure, as I gather from it that you have so much respect for the German public that you do not want to lead them astray by means of works that cannot be attributed in their entirety to my late friend Mozart. I owe so much to the teachings of this great man that I could not tacitly allow a work, the greater part of which is by me, to be passed off as his, as I am firmly convinced that my work is unworthy of his great name. Mozart's compositions are so unique and, I dare say, well

---

[8] The relevant letter to Maximilian Stadler from 31 May 1827 is given in Wolff, *Mozart's Requiem*, pp. 169–70.

[9] For summaries of the Requiem autograph material contained in two codices housed in the Österreichische Nationalbibliothek, see Moseley, 'Mozart's Requiem', p. 203, Wolff, *Mozart's Requiem*, pp. 17–22, and *Neue Mozart-Ausgabe*, II: 5/2/1–2 *Kritische Bericht*, ed. Dietrich Berke, Christoph Wolff and Walburga Litschauer (Kassel, 2007), pp. 15–24.

[10] For the German text see Joseph Eibl, 'Süssmayrs "Requiem"-Brief vom 8. Februar 1800', *Mitteilungen der Internationalen Stiftung Mozarteum*, 24 (1976), pp. 21–3. The translation is my own. For another reproduction of the complete text and a different translation, see Heinz Gärtner, *Mozarts Requiem und die Geschäfte der Constanze Mozart* (Munich, 1986), trans. Reinhard G. Pauly as *Constanze Mozart: After the Requiem* (Portland, OR, 1991), pp. 111–13.

beyond the reach of the majority of living composers that those imitators, especially those who insinuated Mozart's authorship, would fare even worse than the raven who adorned himself with peacock feathers.

That the completion of the Requiem, which led to our correspondence, was entrusted to me came about in the following way. Mozart's widow could no doubt foresee that the posthumous works of her husband would be sought after; death caught him unawares, while he was working on this Requiem. The completion of this work was therefore passed on to several masters; some could not undertake this work on account of numerous commitments, but others did not want their talent compromised by Mozart's talents. Finally this job came to me because it was known that during Mozart's lifetime I had often played through and sung with him the movements already composed, and that he talked to me very often about the working-out of this composition and had communicated to me the ways and means of his instrumentation. I can only wish that I have succeeded well enough at least for connoisseurs to be able to find in it, here and there, some signs of his unforgettable teaching.

Mozart fully completed the four vocal parts and the bass with figuring for the Requiem [aeternam] together with the Kyrie – Dies irae [Sequence] – Domine Jesu Christe [Offertory]; but for the instrumentation he indicated motivic ideas only here and there. In the Dies irae his last line was qua resurget ex favilla and his work was the same as in the first pieces. From the line Judicandus homo reus onwards I completed the Dies irae. The Sanctus, Benedictus and Agnus Dei were composed entirely by me; in order to give more unity to the work I just allowed myself to repeat the Kyrie fugue to the lines cum Sanctis etc.

It will be warmly welcome if through this communication I have been able to perform a small service for you. I would also have carried out with pleasure your other commission 'the directory of the greatest living composers and their relevant works', if I were not prevented from doing so by my daily duties at the theatre and the obligatory jobs they entail.

It is flattering for me that you wish to know which of my works have become familiar to the public.

Moses, oder Der Auszug aus Egypten. A dramatic oratorio in two acts, *L'incanto superato*, and *Il Muselmano in Napoli.* Two Italian operas in two acts.

Der Spiegel von Arkadien, oder Die neuen Arkadier, a German opera in two acts

Die edle Rache. Opera in two acts

Der Vetter in Gefahr, a cantata.

Die freywilligen, an occasional piece in one act

Der Wildfang. Opera in two acts.

> *Der Marktschreier.* Opera in one act.
>
> *Die 3 Sultanninen, oder Soliman der zweyte*, opera in two acts. .
>
> Here you have the complete list; remain favourably inclined to their author and be assured of his deepest respect.
>
> Vienna, 8 February 1800
>
> your   humble servant
Franz Xaver Süssmayr m.p.[mpria]
Imperial Court Kapellmeister

Süssmayr's letter is neither consistent nor correct in every respect, but the nature of the inconsistencies and errors points away from a calculated attempt to deceive. During the so-called *Requiem-Streit* (1825–42) when the authenticity of the Requiem as a work by Mozart was hotly debated, Maximilian Stadler, fair-minded friend and associate of Constanze, affirmed the accuracy of Süssmayr's account to Breitkopf & Härtel.[11] On the basis of what we now know for certain about the involvement of others in the Requiem completion and about Süssmayr carrying out the task after others had been asked, the letter seems in general to stand the test of scrutiny. This applies irrespective of whether we take Süssmayr's phrase 'ganz neu von mir verfertigt' for the Sanctus, Benedictus and Agnus Dei as a statement of sole compositional responsibility or as a statement about preparing or manufacturing these movements from existing materials.[12] We cannot tell whether he *deliberately* claimed authorship of the Lacrymosa from 'Judicandus homo reus' rather than 'Lacrymosa dies illa', thus capturing an additional two bars for himself, but it seems unlikely. It is also likely that he inadvertently grouped the Introit–Kyrie with the later Requiem movements in his memory of the orchestration process, after having carried out such extensive orchestration work on the Requiem a full eight years earlier, rather than that he cunningly thought to get a bit more of the work accepted as his own contribution. Even Süssmayr's most provocative statement in his letter to Breitkopf & Härtel, that 'the greater part [of the Requiem] is by me', is not as overtly dishonest as is sometimes claimed.[13]

---

[11] See Wolff, *Mozart's Requiem*, pp. 149–52, especially 150–1.

[12] The ambiguity underlying Süssmayr's choice of the verb 'verfertigen' was acknowledged as long ago as 1879; see Pole, *Story of Mozart's Requiem*, pp. 74–5; also Moseley, 'Mozart's Requiem', p. 217. It has surfaced in subsequent discussions of the Requiem, for example, Wolff, *Requiem*, p. 42, and Gärtner, *After the Requiem*, p. 114. Süssmayr possibly informed Mozart's biographer Franz Niemetschek as early as 1794 that the Sanctus, Benedictus and Agnus Dei were his own work. The Sanctus, Benedictus and Agnus Dei materials for a performance at Kremsmunster in 1796 were originally gathered separately from the earlier materials in the work, perhaps a statement again from Süssmayr that these movements were by him. See Mozart, *Requiem*, ed. Black.

[13] See Maunder, in Levin et al., 'Colloquy: Finishing Mozart's Requiem', pp. 588–93, at 589.

If Süssmayr's principal criteria were the amount he wrote on the finished score for all instruments in comparison to the amount Mozart wrote on his fragment, and the close engagement he had with all the work's materials in delivering a part-Mozart, part-Süssmayr completion, then it is reasonable to suppose that he could *feel* like the author of most of the Requiem. Those who in effect impugn Süssmayr's moral character in criticizing the veracity of his letter mount a case only on speculative grounds.[14] We cannot assume, moreover, that it would have been in Süssmayr's interests to exaggerate to Breitkopf & Härtel his own participation in the Requiem. To be sure, Mozart's star had risen dramatically between 1791 and 1800, and Süssmayr might have sensed an opportunity to bathe in reflected glory. Equally, though, he could easily have pleased both Constanze and Breitkopf & Härtel by minimizing his own involvement in the Requiem, which he might have perceived as beneficial to his relationship with the latter in particular: Härtel had obviously feigned interest in Süssmayr's compositions in the original letter requesting information (in all likelihood, to keep Süssmayr on-side), by asking for a list of his works, and thus implying possible publication.

As he completed the Requiem in early 1792 Süssmayr may or may not have had Mozart's instructions and advice echoing in his ears, and Mozart's sketches in full view; either way, he will have had to make countless decisions himself, small and large, each with musical and aesthetic ramifications. His statement that the Sanctus, Benedictus and Agnus Dei are 'composed entirely by me' renders this explicit; the subtext of his letter points in this direction too, or at least hints at his confidence in taking on the task at hand. Süssmayr informed Breitkopf & Härtel that other musicians had turned down the opportunity to complete the Requiem on account of existing commitments and for fear of unfavourable comparison with Mozart. He was busy readying his opera *Moses, oder Der Auszug aus Ägypten* in early 1792 for the premiere at the Theater auf der Wieden on 4 May,[15] so certainly did not take on the Requiem in order to fill a hole in his work schedule; thus we can also surmise that he did not have the same fear of damaging comparisons with Mozart (little did he know what the future

---

[14] Maunder explains that Süssmayr 'clearly felt that he had not had adequate recognition for his work', continuing that 'another grievance may have been that Constanze expected him to do [the completion] for nothing'. But no evidence is forthcoming on either point, imagined 'grievances' taking on an unjustified air of fact. (It should be remembered that Süssmayr's letter was solicited, hardly the impetuous act of a frustrated man venting his spleen.) Ibid., p. 590.

[15] Erich Duda, *Das musikalische Werk Franz Xaver Süssmayrs: Thematisches Werkverzeichnis (SmWV)* (Kassel, 2000), pp. 78–9.

would hold). His statement that Mozart's works are inimitable as they are 'so unique and, I dare say, well beyond the reach of the majority of living composers' is also revealing.[16] Superficially he acknowledged that completing the Requiem was a forlorn task but he took it on, and pointedly does not say that Mozart is beyond the reach of *all* contemporary composers. Working with Mozart's intentions closely in mind, he would have realized before, during or after the completion process that his contributions could not simply represent imitations of Mozart. He was complicit, of course, in Constanze's initial attempts to disguise his involvement: the close stylistic resemblance between Mozart's and Süssmayr's handwritings on the Requiem manuscript, the copying-out of the Sequence and Offertory for the submission to Walsegg, the combining of Mozart's material with Süssmayr's own and the forged signature on the first page, 'di me W: A: Mozart mpria 1792' were all designed to promote the uniformity of the work to its recipient (namely as a work exclusively by Mozart).[17] Whether Süssmayr passed off his work as Mozart's out of contractual obligation to Constanze (no contract is extant) and/or out of loyalty to his erstwhile master and friend and in sympathy for Constanze and her financial plight is unclear. But, accepting the musical ramifications of his involvement, he chose to clarify his position in the letter to Breitkopf & Härtel. His statement 'I can only wish that I have succeeded well enough at least for connoisseurs to be able to find in it, here and there, some signs of his unforgettable teaching' is an encouragement less to find his work in Mozart than to find Mozart's *inspiration* in his own work, implying again that he did not feel that he was one of the 'majority' of composers for whom the completion task would have been a task too far; good composition students do not simply replicate the ideas of their teachers but use the ideas to establish their own identities. There is, indeed, a faint aroma of dedicatory rhetoric in Süssmayr's letter – the self-deprecation, the homage to the great and good, the modestly stated desire

---

[16] Imitators of the great masters – Haydn and Mozart in particular – were widely and harshly condemned in the 1790s. For examples, see Simon McVeigh, *Concert Life in London from Mozart to Haydn* (Cambridge, 1993), p. 162; Mary Sue Morrow, *German Music Criticism in the Late Eighteenth Century: Aesthetic Issues in Instrumental Music* (Cambridge, 1997), p. 154; H. C. Robbins Landon, *Haydn: Chronicle and Works. The Years of 'The Creation', 1796–1800* (London, 1977), p. 71; *Allgemeine musikalische Zeitung*, 1 (1798–9), cols. 152–4. See also Johann Karl Friedrich Triest, 'Remarks on the Development of the Art of Music in Germany in the Eighteenth Century' (1801), trans. Susan Gillespie, in Elaine Sisman (ed.), *Haydn and his World* (Princeton, 1997), pp. 321–94, at 366.

[17] For facsimile comparison of Mozart's and Süssmayr's signatures revealing Süssmayr's forgery see Landon, *Mozart's Last Year*, p. 172; see also Wolff, *Mozart's Requiem*, pp. 18–19.

for appreciation[18] – which is not to say, of course, that Süssmayr's admiration for Mozart is in any way insincere. But Süssmayr's letter (like eighteenth-century dedications) implicitly and explicitly asks its recipient to take his contribution seriously.

The two different completion-related tasks dictate the structure and content of this chapter. I look first at the Sequence and Offertory, where Eybler and Süssmayr had to try to respond in their orchestration work to the sounds and implied strategies emanating from Mozart's incomplete autograph (with Süssmayr in compositional mode from bar 9 of the Lacrymosa). I then turn to the Sanctus, Benedictus, Agnus Dei and Communio, for which nothing survives in Mozart's hand, in order to determine how Süssmayr brought the complete Requiem together both by engaging with Mozart's autograph materials and by promoting his own conception of the work. Finally I widen the lens through which the completion is viewed by considering several of Süssmayr's works written in the run-up to December 1791 (and in one important case, the *Missa solemnis*, after it) and by assessing stylistic practices from Mozart's earlier sacred music and operas with which Süssmayr could have been familiar. In Requiem reception history, discussion of Mozart's possible involvement in the final movements usually puts Süssmayr on the back foot *a priori* – good material assumes Mozart's involvement, poor material is Süssmayr's responsibility – and collectively provides widely divergent hypotheses as well (see Chapter 2). I therefore consider it unproductive to add to authorship speculation about the Sanctus, Benedictus and Agnus Dei. By acknowledging Süssmayr as the composer of the Sanctus, Benedictus and Agnus Dei I do not deny the possibility that some Mozart materials were used, but rather postulate that primary authorial responsibility beyond material in Mozart's hand in the autograph ultimately rests with Süssmayr. As a result, my discussion of these movements is not restricted to orchestration-related issues.

The orchestration of the Sequence and the Offertory

Eybler and Süssmayr faced much more than a straightforward and mechanical task in the Sequence and Offertory, judging by the significance attributed just a few years later to individual orchestral sounds, sonorities

---

[18] On eighteenth-century dedicatory rhetoric, focusing on Mozart's own dedication of his six quartets K. 387, 421, 428, 458, 464 and 465 to Haydn in 1785, see Mark Evan Bonds, 'The Sincerest Form of Flattery? Mozart's "Haydn" Quartets and the Question of Influence', *Studi musicali*, 22 (1993), pp. 365–409, at 366–9.

and sound effects, to economical orchestration and to accompanimental writing (see Chapter 4). All we know that they had at their disposal in Mozart's hand was the orchestrated Introit, the Kyrie, and four voices, a bass line and isolated instrumental indications in the Sequence (the Lacrymosa only to bar 8) and Offertory; Süssmayr also had an incomplete draft of the Sequence orchestration written directly on to the autograph by Eybler.[19] Süssmayr probably had relatively fresh memories of other Mozart works from 1791 with which he had been involved (notably *La clemenza di Tito* and *Die Zauberflöte*), but these would naturally have been superseded by any conversations he had had with Mozart about the Requiem, by other experiences of the work up to this point (singing and playing through parts of it, as indicated in his letter to Breitkopf & Härtel, and possibly attending a performance at Mozart's exequies on 10 December 1791) and by the unique challenge of the wind and percussion instrumentation (bassethorns, bassoons, trombones, trumpets and timpani). Following Mozart's lead, Süssmayr used the winds primarily to support the voices, especially in the choral movements (with some doublings of string parts as well); they are quasi-independent agents in the solo movements (Tuba mirum, Recordare), shifting more freely between strings and voices than in the choral movements and including limited obbligato writing. Süssmayr's brief wind links between vocal segments that function independently of string lines throughout the Sequence are also a feature of this support; such links characterize Mozart's Introit, as we have seen.

The Sequence: Dies irae

The Dies irae was one of only two movements for which Eybler provided wind, brass and timpani parts as well as string parts. When the score passed to Süssmayr he made small changes to Eybler's strings, but more significant changes to the wind and brass. Eybler's writing is tauter than Süssmayr's, especially at the opening, where the dotted motif in the trumpets in bar 2 is repeated in bar 4 and evolves into a dotted figure first for bassethorns, bassoons, trumpets and timpani together (bars 5, 6) and then for Mozart's sopranos at 'Teste David' in bar 6, beats 3–4. Sonic drive implied in Mozart's incomplete Dies irae characterizes Eybler's third section of the movement: the winds, absent during the 'Quantus tremor' confrontation (bars 41–8),

---

[19]　The idea that Stadler's orchestration of the Offertory contributed to Süssmayr's completion (see Wolff, *Mozart's Requiem*, pp. 22–6) can be discounted, as Stadler's score was compiled later than 1791. See Mozart, *Requiem*, ed. Black, 'Introduction' and Zaslaw (ed.), *Der neue Köchel*.

are re-introduced at Mozart's moment of unsettling resolution (bars 50–1), which in turn launches the passage conceived by Eybler as the Dies irae's climax (bars 52ff.), with full orchestral accompaniment that includes abundant dotted rhythms in the trumpets and timpani and then with emphatic minim thumps. Süssmayr uses the winds more liberally than Eybler, offering less cleanly and tightly articulated material, and thereby downplays forward propulsion in favour of an enveloping wind sound. Several critics have deemed Eybler's wind orchestration of the Dies irae superior to Süssmayr's.[20] While Eybler's Dies irae is certainly the most significant achievement in his completion, isolated judgments about its superiority over Süssmayr's fail to account for the practical reality facing Süssmayr: his orchestration of the movement needed to accommodate a vision for the Sequence as a whole. The weighty swathe of wind sound in Süssmayr's Dies irae at the beginning of the Sequence, including numerous minims, semibreves, extended tied notes and undifferentiated quavers, ultimately complements the emphatic wind writing in his Lacrymosa at the end.

The Sequence: Tuba mirum

The Tuba mirum demonstrates judicious evolution in orchestration at the hands of both Eybler and Süssmayr (see Example 5.1).[21] Until 'Cum vix justus' (bar 45) Eybler's strings, largely followed by Süssmayr, function only as accompanimental parts, aside from the occasional inter-phrase link. At this point, however, Mozart allows the violins to double the soprano melody and to take the melodic lead in the absence of the voice. Mozart's brief dialogues (the single-note exchanges between strings and voice in bars 45 and 51) are embellished in bar 57 (c'''–e'' quavers in the first violin replacing a single crotchet); the embellishment itself then generates new melodic material (the first-violin quavers in bar 58 growing from the quavers in bar 57). Eybler adds inner string parts from bar 45 onwards that reinforce the first violin and bass lines given by Mozart, but that momentarily assume melodic and thematic independence as well (bars 54–5). Süssmayr duly inserts the bassethorn and

---

[20] See in particular *Neue Mozart Ausgabe*, I:1/2/2, ed. Nowak, p. xii, and Wolff, *Mozart's Requiem*, p. 22.

[21] In Examples 5.1–5.6 Eybler's and Süssmayr's respective contributions are designated by 'E' and 'S' in boxed text under the instrument name. Where Süssmayr revised an instrumental part written by Eybler an 'E/S' is given. An 'M' (Mozart) is added only where Mozart provided a partial – rather than complete – contribution to the line quoted. In Ex. 5.6 Eybler provides material for bassethorns and bassoons from bar 5 to bar 6, beat 1, but Süssmayr's material is discernibly new; an 'S' is therefore given.

Example 5.1 Süssmayr's completion of Mozart's Requiem, Tuba mirum, bars 51–62

bassoon parts, opting for a different sonic allegiance with strings and voices at each of the iterations of 'Cum vix justus': they are absent from the first statement (bar 45), reinforce SATB voices in dialogue with the strings in the second statement (bar 51) and reinforce the strings in dialogue with the SATB voices in the third (bar 57). He has the bassoons double Eybler's second-violin

Example 5.1 (cont.)

and viola parts in bars 55–6, but in bar 58 allows the three-note figure from bar 55 to assume a life of its own in the bassoons and bassethorns, independent of the strings. In bars 57–8, then, Mozart's three-crotchet 'vix justus' in the voices is answered by Süssmayr's three crotchets in the bassethorns and

Example 5.1 (cont.)

bassoons (related motivically to Eybler's inner string parts three bars earlier), occurring at precisely the moment that Mozart's first violins embellish the one-note dialogue with two quavers and then use this embellishment to generate melodic elaboration. Thus, the modest sonic climax of the Tuba mirum (bars 57–60) – the first instrumental tutti marked *forte* – coincides with multi-tiered embellishment, an effect of 'weise Oekonomie' for which Mozart, Eybler and Süssmayr are collectively responsible, and in which melody and accompaniment are (to quote Arnold) 'an inseparable and beautiful whole, so precisely interweaved, that one cannot happily think of one without the other'.[22]

Süssmayr's trombone solo in the middle of the Tuba mirum (bars 24–34, Example 5.2) is less clearly a positive addition. Much derided in the secondary literature, it is accused of ignoring textual implications, 'the trombone [continuing] … even after it has already called all those who have been resurrected before the Throne of God', of constituting a 'crass' manifestation of Süssmayr's schematic approach to instrumentation, of being 'superfluous and paltry to boot, the writing in measures 27–28 … technically poor, and the ending, measures 33–34, abrupt' and of representing an unwelcome by-product of Süssmayr's omission of winds in bars 15–17 'in flat contradiction to [the word] *omnes*'.[23] It has neither the seamless interweaving of the obbligato trombone and bass voice from the beginning of the movement nor the 'necessary' justification in the text, of course, but it is very different in function from the earlier trombone contribution, rendering harsh criticism on either of these grounds potentially misleading. Writing for the voices, strings and winds by a combination of Mozart, Eybler and Süssmayr evolves in different, but interrelated, ways over the course of the Tuba mirum: the voices move from individual solos to collective participation in a four-voice unit, the strings from pure accompaniment at the beginning to melodic equality with the voices at the end (bars 45ff.) via rudimentary, outline doubling of voices (bars 20–8) and inter-phrase links (bars 23, 28, 33),[24] and the winds from ornate obbligato at the beginning to

---

[22] Arnold, *Mozarts Geist*, p. 188.

[23] See Blume, 'Requiem, but no Peace', p. 119; Wolff, *Mozart's Requiem*, p. 90; Mozart, *Requiem*, ed. Beyer, p. viii; and Maunder, *Mozart's Requiem*, pp. 143–44. Doubts are occasionally expressed about Mozart's own solo trombone writing at the opening of the movement, in keeping with a strain of criticism of Mozart's work on the Tuba mirum that continues to surface in the nineteenth and twentieth centuries (see Chapter 2). See, for example, Hutchings, *Mozart: The Man, the Musician*, p. 118: 'After the solemn opening of the Tuba mirum for solo trombone, the same instrument continues with the grotesque *legato* arpeggio accompaniments to the bass solo. The part is written in the tenor clef, which is used for bassoon or cello in its upper compass. Can it be that, trying it on the piano, Süssmayr satisfied Mozart with the sound, so that he did not mention a change of instrument where only one stave and clef was needed? Surely we have good reason to use our own discretion about the instrumentation when we perform this item.'

[24] In bars 23 and 33, Süssmayr reinforces Mozart's bass-line annotations in the upper strings, whereas Eybler does not. Süssmayr also adds offbeat crotchets in the upper strings in the final bar of Mozart's trombone solo (bar 17) in preparation for their participation in the subsequent tenor solo, departing from Eybler, who leaves them blank.

Example 5.2   Süssmayr's completion of Mozart's Requiem, Tuba mirum, bars 24–34

supportive doubling (with glimpses of independence) at the end. In this context, Süssmayr's trombone solo (bars 24–34) represents a middle ground between the winds' roles before and after, externalizing stylistic features beautifully sublimated in Mozart's initial exchange between obbligato

Example 5.2   (cont.)

trombone and bass – inter-phrase joinings and sustained notes, for example – and paving the way for the more explicitly supportive role of the winds later in the movement. Just as the writing for voices and strings evolves in stages, so too does the role of the wind instruments (as exemplified by the solo trombone). To be sure, Süssmayr could have achieved this, in theory, with different (and better) music. But his attention to developments in instrumental participation across the movement at least helps explain why the trombone does not receive more melodically adventurous material in a passage fulfilling a transitional function in participatory terms.

The Sequence: Rex tremendae

Eybler's strings follow Mozart's lead in promoting uniformity of participation in the first section (bars 1–6), contrapuntal participation in the middle section (bars 7–17) and uniformity again in the final section (bars 17–22), albeit with slight solo prominence for the first violins (on account of the dotted rhythm being replaced by smooth quavers in the second violin and viola parts from bars 18ff.). Only the second violins' isolated imitation in the first beat of bar 12 and the string parts in bars 20–1 seem genuinely debatable in relation to what we assume were Mozart's intentions. Süssmayr mostly adopts Eybler's string parts, but also adds winds and timpani to accommodate a wind presence that Mozart's autograph score tells us was intended.[25] A small adjustment to one of Eybler's string lines, in the context of fidelity to Eybler's original parts, underscores Süssmayr's strategic intent. In bar 2 (Example 5.3), Eybler puts the violas on the beat in support of the bass and organ; Süssmayr has them off the beat, with the first and second violins. For Süssmayr, the change in scoring enables his wind sonority of unaccompanied bassethorns, bassoons and three trombones, new to the work in bar 1, to continue to receive unobstructed attention supported only by the basses. The change also reinforces the string responses to the winds' on-beat thuds by adding the violas to the string sound (if only with single notes, low in register and lacking power, rather than the violins' three-note chords). The same wind sonority resurfaces in support of the 'Rex' exclamations in bars 3–5. Süssmayr's first six bars of the Rex tremendae thus gather sonic momentum, bit by bit increasing the

---

[25] Mozart places a bracket around all twelve staves of the first page of the Rex tremendae score. The fourth, fifth, sixth and seventh lines are reserved for wind instruments, although the staves are not labelled. Mozart would have included either two bassethorns and two bassoons, each on their own stave, or (much more likely in this movement) the bassethorns and bassoons on two staves and the trumpets and timpani on the other two staves.

musical drama: the wind chord marked *forte* in bar 1 becomes an antiphonal chord exchange between winds and strings in bar 2 and wind-supported 'Rex' exclamations in bars 3–5; the drama intensifies further in bar 6 with a *ff* dynamic and the extension of wind support to trumpets and timpani.[26] The absence of strings in bar 6 (Eybler and Süssmayr) and the large wind presence (Süssmayr only) solidify the winds' role as support for the voices, a role that continues through the remainder of the Süssmayr-orchestrated movement. Süssmayr has no desire simply to create the loudest possible sound at bar 6 (had he aspired to do so he would surely have included the strings); he rather intends a *specific*, loud sound, one that highlights reinforcement of the voices by full winds and brass and timpani.[27]

Süssmayr's orchestration of the first six bars sheds light on his decision to bring in the bassethorns, bassoons and trombones in bars 1 and 2 (Example 5.3) which has been described as 'premature . . . [and] rather a pity: it destroys the surprise of the choral entrance two measures later'.[28] This is a judgment call, of course: one person's delight at a surprise is another person's delight at a foreshadowing. Süssmayr opts to build on his antiphonal one-note exchanges from the 'Cum vix justus' at the end of the preceding Tuba mirum (described above) in a very different musical context – perhaps with a view to procedural continuity from one movement to the next – simultaneously creating a new wind effect, namely exposed and unsupported bassethorns, bassoons and trombones playing together for the first time in the work.[29]

Thus, Süssmayr follows Mozart's lead in directing attention to precise sounds and effects, but in projecting increased intensity over the first six

---

[26] Richard Maunder claims that the participation of trumpets and timpani in the Rex tremendae was 'obviously an afterthought [for Süssmayr] . . . for there are no staves allocated to them at the start of the movement'. Maunder, 'Süssmayr's Work in Mozart's Requiem: A Study of the Autograph Score', in Manfred Hermann Schmid (ed.), *Mozart-Studien 7* (Tutzing, 1997), pp. 57–80, at 63. But this is not necessarily the case, any more than Mozart's trombones in bars 7–8 of the Introit are an 'afterthought' because they do not have their own staves and are marked on the vocal lines. The trombones do not participate *colla parte* in bars 1–2 of the Rex tremendae, so require their own staves; they cease to require them in bar 6 (Süssmayr writing 'Tromboni colle Parti' on his autograph), whereupon the staves become available for trumpets and timpani. The participation of trumpets and timpani in bars 15–17 does appear to have been a late-stage addition to Süssmayr's score, however, judging by the different (faded) ink colour and the evidence of prior notation of trombones on these staves.

[27] Mozart leaves the first-violin stave blank in bar 6, beats 2–4, rather than marking rests. It is not impossible that eventually he would have included string parts at this juncture, but unlikely given the near omnipresence of first-violin writing in his autograph for this movement.

[28] *Requiem*, ed. Levin, pp. xxii–xxiii. Maunder makes the same point in *Mozart's Requiem*, pp. 151–2.

[29] The only other reference to 'Rex' in the Requiem text – 'Rex gloriae' in bars 2–3 of the Domine Jesu from the Offertory – is greeted by similarly powerful, supportive winds (bassethorns, bassoons and trombones).

Example 5.3   Süssmayr's completion of Mozart's Requiem, Rex tremendae, bars 1–7

Example 5.3   (cont.)

bars does not necessarily match Mozart's intentions, either in detail or in overall trajectory. The absence of the trumpets and timpani at the coming-together of voices in the middle of the second section (bar 11, beat 2– bar 12, beat 1) and the protracted presence of trumpets and timpani at the end of the section (bars 15–17) again supports staged development to a climax. Süssmayr's big sound from bar 15 to bar 17, beat 1 reinforces the effect of Mozart's drop to *piano* for the beginning of the third section (bar 17, beat 2). His doubling of Mozart's 'Salva me' in the bassethorns and bassoons (bars 18–19), followed by his omission of all winds in the final three bars of the movement, enacts a staged withdrawal of wind reinforcement to complement the staged accrual of support in bars 1–6, thus resonating with Mozart's quasi-reverse replay of the first section in his final section (see Chapter 4).[30]

The Sequence: Recordare

Again providing just string parts, Eybler probably intended to return later to the Recordare to add wind parts, following on from Mozart's seven-bar annotation for two bassethorns at the opening. Süssmayr writes material for the bassethorns and the bassoons and modifies Eybler's strings in order to bring them into line with his apparent conception of the movement as a whole.[31] In the transitions in bars 34–6, 68–70, for example, Eybler adds second-violin and viola imitative points to Mozart's imitations from violins to *bassi* to violins, copying Mozart from bar 7; Süssmayr omits Eybler's non-imitative material in the viola and thereby maximizes the impact of the viola's imitative entry. In bar 92, Süssmayr also replaces Eybler's contrary motion string quavers – which would not have fitted particularly well with his own orchestration of the preceding bars, which eliminates Eybler's intricate semi-quaver figures – with an unambiguous iteration of the descending ritornello motif (second violins and violas, bars 92–3) that is immediately imitated by Mozart's bass at bar 93. Thus Süssmayr creates a more fluid link between

---

[30] Süssmayr writes 'senza Tromboni, e Clarini e Timpani' into the autograph, after a page turn to bar 18, to make absolutely clear that their participation in the movement ends on the first beat of bar 17.

[31] Mozart's autograph assigns one stave to each of the bassethorns, rather than one stave for the two together, implying that the two empty staves in his twelve-stave score would have been reserved for the first and the second bassoons. It is possible that Mozart's crotchets for violins and viola at bar 14, beat 1, indicate an intention to double the entering vocal parts with the bassethorns.

verses than Eybler managed, following Mozart's example. He also punctuates within verses, through the winds' cadential figures in verse 4 (bars 75–6, 79–80) and the ascending arpeggios in the first violin (bars 118, 122) that link the closing and opening notes of vocal phrases. In the latter case, Süssmayr reproduces (transposed) the 'ne perenni' figure from a few bars earlier that Mozart had used *piano* to close off the previous verse (bars 105–9).[32] Perhaps the reappearance of the figure at bars 118 and 122 of the Süssmayr-orchestrated score goes against Mozart's putative intentions by stressing the figure's reconciliatory properties. Nevertheless, Süssmayr's redeployment of it indicates a priority for elegant instrumental links that, wherever possible, employ Mozart's own original material.

At 'ne perenni cremer igne' (bars 106–10, Example 5.4), where the reference to eternal damnation foreshadows the textual theme of the Confutatis and also its momentous musical contrasts, Süssmayr builds on Mozart's score in a particularly effective fashion. Mozart introduced one-bar contrasts – in the voices and bass, marking the latter *forte* in bar 105 – and Eybler strengthened the bass part by adding violins and viola an octave above (including an *ff* marking for the first violins in bar 105). Süssmayr, improving Eybler's string parts,[33] heightened contrast by having the basset-horns and bassoons reinforce the vocal parts and by adding *sf* markings, simultaneously strengthening the musical link to the Confutatis (where he again aligned the winds closely with the vocal parts).

Süssmayr's strategies for sounds and effects in the Recordare involve instrument distribution and impact as well as instrumental links and text-setting. His employment of the bassethorns at bars 93–9 (doubling the voices and resting the strings which Eybler used here) follows and is followed by extended absences for them (bars 82–92, bar 99, beat 2–bar 105). A colouristic quality accrues to their contribution here to match their contribution at the beginning of the movement, an appropriate parallel given verse 6's recapitulatory function. Furthermore, the presentation of the main theme first by the bassethorns and then briefly by the strings (at 'Sed tu bonus', bar 99) turns the Süssmayr-orchestrated verse 6 into a kind of compressed reprise not just of verse 1, but of verse 1 *and* the preceding instrumental introduction. Süssmayr's instrumentation thus supports Mozart's articulation of formal shape.

---

[32] Eybler had a different imitative idea at bar 118 and 122, anticipating Mozart's vocal entries.

[33] Süssmayr's violins in bars 106 and 108 follow Mozart's bass by leaping a ninth and a seventh where Eybler has them rise and fall less dramatically by a semitone.

Example 5.4 Süssmayr's completion of Mozart's Requiem, Recordare, bars 103–12

The Sequence: Confutatis

As in the case of the Dies irae, the other movement in the Sequence for which Eybler provides wind and brass parts, Eybler's and Süssmayr's orchestrations of the Confutatis diverge in various respects. They treat the 'Confutatis maledictis' segments differently, for example, Eybler employing bassethorns and bassoons in semibreves, minims and crotchets to enrich the sonority and Süssmayr favouring just two bassoons to reinforce tenors and basses at the unison, thereby producing a barer, more austere texture. Süssmayr reserves the bassethorns (playing alongside the bassoons) for the instrumental links to 'Voca me', the wind sounds in these links prefiguring his swathe of wind sound at 'Oro supplex' and supporting a progression from the bare to the (understatedly) mellifluous across the movement as a whole. Eybler limits wind participation in the 'Oro supplex' to a replication of the pattern laid down by Mozart in the first stage of the musical sequence and does not include winds in the 'Voca me' links.

Whether Süssmayr's wind interpolations in the Tuba mirum and Rex tremendae (described above) directly contravene Mozart's intentions is difficult to say with certainty, but his wind additions clearly do so in the latter stages of the Confutatis (Example 5.5). Mozart introduces his two bassethorns and two bassoons at bar 26 to coincide with the re-entry of the voices for the 'Oro supplex' sequence and signals their exit (again to coincide with the voices) in bar 29 with a crotchet followed by crotchet and minim rests; Eybler follows Mozart's example in subsequent iterations of the sequence by aligning the wind with the voices (bar 30–bar 33, beat 1; bar 34–bar 35, beat 1; and bar 36–bar 39, beat 1), which includes ending their involvement at the first crotchet of bar 39. Süssmayr, however, views things slightly differently, and has his knuckles rapped for '[seeing] fit to correct his master'.[34] Introducing the bassethorns, bassoons and trombones a bar earlier than Mozart (bar 25, rather than 26), Süssmayr then eliminates the rests at the end of the sequential phrases, writing wind semibreves instead (bars 29, 33) and extending wind participation over the final full bar as well. Whether Süssmayr's version is better or worse than the version we (like Eybler) might predict from Mozart – based on extending his wind markings from bars 26–9 through the remainder of the musical sequence – is a matter for debate. Above all, though, Süssmayr's conception of wind involvement in the 'Oro supplex' and, indeed, in the

---

[34] Mozart, *Requiem*, ed. Beyer, p. viii. Nowak is also critical of Süssmayr's adjustment in *Neue Mozart-Ausgabe*, I:1/2/2, pp. xiii–xiv; and according to Maunder, 'Süssmayr has received some well-deserved abuse ... for bringing in the woodwind a bar too early in bar 25. Compared with bar 29, he also continued them a bar too long at the end.' See Maunder, *Mozart's Requiem*, p. 169.

Example 5.5   Süssmayr's completion of Mozart's Requiem, Confutatis, bars 25–30

Example 5.5 (cont.)

Example 5.5 (cont.)

Confutatis as a whole is different from Mozart's and Eybler's. His additional
bar of semibreves (bar 25) and filling-in of rests at the ends of vocal phrases
gives the winds more of a presence than Mozart envisaged for them at this
juncture and takes an edge off the onset of the diminished seventh harmonies,

which in Mozart's version of bar 26 coincides with the entry of the voices *and* the winds after a bar of only string accompanimental writing. Yet Süssmayr's wind interpolations here are coherent with his wind interpolations elsewhere, since they provide support for the voices not only by closely tracking their melodic contour – copying what Eybler wrote with minor adjustments – but also by providing continuity of timbre between vocal statements (namely the semibreves that eradicate Mozart's end-of-phrase rests). The joining of the 'Flammis acribus addictus' and 'Voca me' segments with harmonized bassethorns and bassoons earlier in the Confutatis (bars 6–7, 16–17; see Example 5.6) may again counter Mozart's intentions – he gives only the four-note stepwise descent in the bass, as we have seen, and Eybler adds only violins and violas at pitch and an octave above (although whether Mozart would actually have done this cannot be known). Thus, the austerity of the Mozart–Eybler link in bars 6–7 gives way to the lushness of the Süssmayr link, the bassethorns and bassoons sympathetically foreshadowing the poignancy of the 'Voca me',[35] just as they (and trombones) foreshadow the power of the initial vocal entry in the Rex tremendae. The enveloping wind sound in the Süssmayr-orchestrated concluding stages of the Confutatis also modestly predicts what is to follow at the corresponding juncture of the Lacrymosa, in particular the final sustained wind sounds of the 'Amen'.

The Sequence: Lacrymosa

In the Lacrymosa, Süssmayr – composing as well as orchestrating from bar 9 onwards – underlines a commitment to the continuity of orchestration between movements not necessarily attributable to Mozart by striving for a sonic climax to the Sequence (no easy challenge after the Dies irae, Rex tremendae and Confutatis). Wind instruments are deployed in such ways as to contribute to the sense of climax both for the Lacrymosa in isolation and for the Sequence as a whole.[36] There are no winds in Mozart's bars 1–8, but nor are there rests to indicate they would not be used. Süssmayr brings them in from bar 3, building incrementally from bassethorns and bassoons, then adding trombones with a crescendo to *forte*, which leads to a full wind and

---

[35] The richness (and related beauty) of the bassethorns was often recognized in the late eighteenth century; see Albert A. Rice, *From the Clarinet d'Amour to the Contra Bass: A History of Large-Size Clarinets, 1740–1860* (Oxford and New York, 2009), pp. 105, 107, 109, 180.

[36] The strings retain throughout the Lacrymosa the sigh figures and inner-voice crotchets given to them by Mozart in bars 1–2.

Example 5.6 Süssmayr's completion of Mozart's Requiem, Confutatis, bars 5–8

percussion contingent including *forte* trumpets and timpani. Two bars of silence from the winds (from bar 9) lend power to the re-entry of the bassethorns, bassoons and trombones, *forte*, on Neapolitan harmony at 'Qua resurget', in line with Arnold's observation that the temporary absence

Example 5.6   (cont.)

of instruments lends weight to their subsequent presence.[37] This observation also holds true for the way in which the trumpets and timpani are used in the Lacrymosa in comparison to how they are used earlier in the Sequence. Employed judiciously for occasional emphasis in the Rex tremendae and Confutatis, they feature throughout the climactic 'Dona eis requiem' statement (bars 22–30, partially given in Examples 5.7 and 5.8) – a more protracted involvement than at any stage since the Dies irae – and put the full wind and percussion sonority centre stage up to (and including) the final plagal cadence of the 'Amen'. Indeed, the thunder of the Dies irae, with prominent trumpets and timpani, meets its match (and is perhaps even surpassed) in the last nine bars of the Lacrymosa. Süssmayr creates sonorous wind highpoints at the beginning and the end of the Sequence, building carefully to the latter through his orchestration of the Rex tremendae and Confutatis. Süssmayr's desire to effect a musical climax with the reprise of the main theme of the Lacrymosa at 'Dona eis requiem' is so strong in fact that it overrides implications of the text, beginning mid-sentence.[38]

The sonorous climaxes of the Lacrymosa are matched by an intensification of musical processes stretching back to the beginning of the work, pointing again to the aesthetic of continuity and integration to which Süssmayr remained committed as he discharged his responsibilities. The links for paired bassethorns and bassoons from the Introit (Mozart) and earlier in the Sequence (Süssmayr) flower into a mellifluous two-bar join between the penultimate and concluding choral segments (bars 19–21, Example 5.8). Christoph Wolff has hypothesized quite reasonably that Mozart set aside his score at bar 8 of the Lacrymosa (never to return to it, although he continued on into the Offertory) because he had reached an important structural juncture in his work, whereby the appearance of the words 'Dona eis requiem' – which also occur in the Introit and Agnus Dei – would have encouraged him to ponder issues of inter-movement cohesion.[39] Süssmayr glances back to the orchestration of the Introit in the link between his final choral segments, where he reconstitutes (as it were) Mozart's original introduction of the voices: the obbligato prominence of the bassethorns and bassoons, the three descending *forte* notes in the trombones and the late *forte* arrival of trumpets and timpani all invoke

---

[37] The Neapolitan in bar 11 is praised by Manfred Hermann Schmid for its emphatic realization of the semitone interval that is fundamental to the movement; see Schmid's positive evaluation of Süssmayr's Lacrymosa completion, 'Das "Lacrymosa" in Mozarts Requiem', in Schmid (ed.), *Mozart Studien 7* (Tutzing, 1997), pp. 115–41, at 125.

[38] Richard Maunder takes particular exception to this moment; see *Mozart's Requiem*, p. 35.

[39] Wolff, *Mozart's Requiem*, p. 30.

Example 5.7 Süssmayr's completion of Mozart's Requiem, Lacrymosa, bars 28–30

the introduction of Mozart's Introit, the trombones, trumpets and timpani producing in both cases a forceful return to D minor for the ensuing vocal statement. The 'Dona eis requiem' and preceding link represent an apotheosis of wind support: Süssmayr invokes Mozart's use of winds in an

Example 5.8 Süssmayr's completion of Mozart's Requiem, Lacrymosa, bars 19–23

introductory capacity, also writing his own most elaborate wind episode in the Sequence, and he uses his entire complement of winds principally to double the voices (the strings continue with their own material), rounding off the movement with an emphatically supportive, apex-within-an-apex

Example 5.8 (cont.)

'Amen' (Example 5.7 above). It is wrong to criticize Süssmayr for not working Mozart's 'Amen' sketch into a full-fledged fugue, and not only because there is no certainty that Mozart would have used it had he lived to complete the work.[40] (There is no evidence that Süssmayr actually saw the sketch.) For whether his conception relates to Mozart's or not or does so only in part, the 'Amen' is a coherent climax to Süssmayr's conception of the orchestration of the Sequence, not a weak compromise by a mediocre composer lacking contrapuntal self-confidence.[41] Süssmayr did in fact write lengthy fugues at the end of sections of the mass, notably for the Cum sancto spiritu and Et vitam venturi in his *Missa solemnis* in D, SmWV 106, thus building towards 'Amen' in contrapuntal contexts.[42] The former, sixty bars long, features virtuoso semiquaver writing for the violins and an apposite culmination on 'Amen' replete with arpeggiated flourishes in the horns and trumpets supported rhythmically by the timpani; and the latter, at fifty-six bars, also reaches a textural peak at 'Amen', where bold arpeggiated gestures in the violins, horns and trumpets are again the order of the day.

The Offertory: Domine Jesu and Hostias

Süssmayr's orchestration of the two Offertory movements is consistent with his orchestration of the Sequence, without requiring (or inviting) the Sequence's climactic resonances. In the Domine Jesu, wind and string support for the voices primarily comprises doubling, tracking and elaborating of melodic contour; the strings are given independent material more often than the wind, as in the Rex tremendae, Confutatis and Lacrymosa. The sparing use of winds in the first nineteen bars lends their contributions special prominence, again bringing to mind Arnold's remarks about Mozart employing certain instruments economically to enhance their effect. The words 'Rex gloriae' (see bars 2–3) perhaps encouraged Süssmayr to invoke the opening of the Rex tremendae (the only other reference to 'Rex' in the Requiem text), with its powerful winds; wind support for the bold sequential

---

[40] Bauman, 'Requiem, but no Piece', p. 160.

[41] Wolff, for example, argues that Süssmayr did not complete an 'Amen' fugue because he lacked the confidence to do so; see *Mozart's Requiem*, p. 31.

[42] See Franz Xaver Süssmayr, *Missa solemnis in D*, ed. Walter Wlcek and Erich Duda (Graz, 2010). A secure date for this mass has yet to be established, but it is nearly certain to post-date Süssmayr's work on Mozart's Requiem. Erich Duda gives the probable period of composition as 1795–1802 in *Das musikalische Werk Franz Xaver Süssmayrs*.

tonal shifts at 'de ore leonis' (bars 16–17, 19–20) also parallels passages in the Recordare and Confutatis (the 'Ingemisco' and 'Oro supplex' sequences respectively), reinforcing Mozart's text painting. And the bassethorns in bars 27–8 add a textural strand to the existing dialogue in the voices, as do Süssmayr's interpolations in the 'Cum vix justus' of the Tuba mirum. Wind absences in bars 30–44, partially explained by the vocal solos in this section, and in bars 67–71 lend emphasis to the winds' eventual doubling of the voices in the 'Quam olim Abrahae' fugue and at the onset of the final fugal reprise respectively. In the Hostias, Süssmayr's dotted minims in the bassethorns and bassoons eradicate a two-crotchet gap between the end of a vocal phrase in bar 10, beat 3, and the beginning of the next in bar 11, beat 3, invoking the sustained-note phrase joinings of the 'Oro supplex'. An eleven-bar wind silence (from bar 44, beat 2, to bar 54 inclusive) again draws attention to the subsequent wind participation in the reprised 'Quam olim Abrahae' fugue, while the sustained bassethorn and bassoon notes at the end of the movement (as at the end of the Domine Jesu) strike a chord with the Süssmayr-orchestrated conclusions to the Confutatis and Lacrymosa.

The similarity between the soprano 'et semini ejus' line in bars 67–71 of the Domine Jesu written by Mozart and the bassethorn line in bars 27–8 added by Süssmayr is probably coincidental,[43] but the same cannot be said for the identical semiquavers that comprise Mozart's dramatic violin material in the immediate run-up to the 'Quam olim Abrahae' fugue (bar 43; see Example 4.1 above) and Süssmayr's violin link between 'in obscurum' and 'sed signifier' (bar 32, Example 5.9). There are several reasons for Süssmayr to have included this particular link in bar 32: as in bars 43–4, the *bassi* descend through a fifth in quavers (d–G) confirming G minor; the same instrumental link demarcates the beginning (Süssmayr) and end (Mozart) of the 'sed signifier' passage, capturing both the first return to G minor since the onset of the movement and the re-confirmation of G minor after the modulatory excursions of 'sed signifier'; and Mozart's own material is employed. Süssmayr's link detracts from the novelty of Mozart's – like his wind chords in bars 1–2 of the Rex tremendae in relation to Mozart's vocal chords in bar 3 – but does not lessen the impact of Mozart's as a result, because it is *p* in bar 32 and *f* in bars 43–4. Both Mozart and Süssmayr focus on sound effects and the impact of specific sounds, Mozart on explosiveness, an outgrowth of the mini-explosions earlier in the movement (see Chapter 4), and Süssmayr on quiet innocuousness at the beginning of 'sed signifier' and loud abrasiveness

---

[43] Rising fourths and falling fifths are heard in bars 67–71 at half of their speed in bars 27–8.

Example 5.9 Süssmayr's completion of Mozart's Requiem, Domine Jesu, bars 31–3

at 'Quam olim Abrahae'. Mozart – assuming he would not have incorporated the bar 32 link had he lived to complete the Requiem – prioritizes surprise, whereas Süssmayr, conceiving things slightly differently, prioritizes thematic, but no less dramatic, coherence.[44]

We may conclude from his mainly orchestrational activity so far that for Süssmayr, completing the Requiem seems to have meant engaging actively with his own ideas for the work as well as Mozart's. Pragmatically speaking, Süssmayr's entitlement to an aesthetic vision of his own for the orchestration of the Requiem – highlighting inter-movement continuity and integration, and shaping towards climactic points – can operate only within limits; wholesale, wide-ranging changes to Mozart's fragmentary score in order to realize a personal vision would have been questionable given the task at hand of completing *Mozart's* work. Süssmayr's wind additions, at least those that are independent of vocal and string lines, are small in scale. But viewed in historical, aesthetic and analytical contexts they assume significance, because they concern precisely those individual orchestral sounds,

---

[44] On dramatic process and dramatic coherence in Mozart's instrumental music situated in late eighteenth-century contexts, see, in particular, Keefe, *Mozart's Piano Concertos*, pp. 45–74 and 147–85.

sonorities, sound effects and accompaniments that exemplified Mozart's vaunted economical instrumentation and that were witnessed in Mozart's score in Chapter 4. (Even sustained notes – clear examples of economical usage – were valued as an aesthetic commodity for winds in the late eighteenth century.[45])

Once we, as critics, permit Süssmayr not to follow Mozart's apparent intentions at every single point (accepting that many of these intentions are un-knowable in any case, as with the 'Amen' fugue) the possibility arises of allowing him a positive aesthetic impact on the work and of seeing his putative transgressions as evidence of musical vision rather than musical misjudgment. Süssmayr's interpolated instrumental links and elaborations may act primarily as support for the voices, following similar kinds of support evident in Mozart's Introit and Sequence, but they also direct attention to Süssmayr's broader conception of the orchestration of the Sequence as a whole, encouraging contemplation of individual moments in relation to the larger whole: the Dies irae complements the Lacrymosa; the Tuba mirum and Rex tremendae are shaped towards modest climactic points; the vocal support provided by wind links in the Recordare and Confutatis apparently extends to text expression, reinforcing pleading;[46] and the progression from austere to rich wind scoring in the Confutatis projects towards the climactic conclusion of the Lacrymosa, which is itself shaped in such a way as to maximize the impact of the concluding bars. Whether or not we admire Süssmayr's additions and whether or not we think Mozart would have made them himself had he lived to complete the work, we will recognize that with only a few exceptions they are true to the spirit of both the contemporary aesthetic of orchestration – at least as explicated in the final years of the eighteenth century and first years of the nineteenth for Mozart's works – and of Mozart's precise attention to instrumental detail captured in his autograph score, including in the incomplete Sequence and Offertory.

---

[45] See Jean-Laurent de Béthizy, *Exposition de la théorie et de la pratique de la musique*, 2nd edn (Paris, 1764), p. 306 (on the 'admirable effect' of high sustained notes in the bassoon); Louis Joseph Francoeur, *Diapason général de tous les instrumens à vent avec des observations sur chacun d'eux* (Paris, 1772), p. 22 (on the virtues of sustained notes in the clarinets); and Augustus Frederick Christopher Kollmann, *An Essay on Practical Musical Composition* (London, 1799), p. 18 (on using winds effectively in tutti sections of orchestral works).

[46] The 'Ingemisco' verse in the Recordare (bars 72–83) is a pleading to God to be spared. 'Voca me cum benedictis' (Confutatis, bars 7–10, 17–25) is the supplicant's plea to be grouped with the blessed ones when others are condemned to eternal damnation; 'Oro supplex et acclinis . . .' (Confutatis, bars 25–40) is a contrite prayer for salvation.

The Sanctus, Benedictus, Agnus Dei and Communio

Süssmayr develops his orchestration ideas for the Requiem in the Sanctus and Benedictus, drawing attention to strategies witnessed in the Sequence of climax in the context of sonic reinforcement (Sanctus) and of procedural integration and intensification (Benedictus). His ten-bar Sanctus (Example 5.10) ostentatiously extends orchestration practices from the Sequence, especially in its deployment of winds, brass and timpani. As in the chorus movements from the Sequence, and in keeping with the unequivocal support they offer there, the bassethorns and bassoons almost entirely double the vocal lines, while the strings are given their own distinct figures (as in the Dies irae, Rex tremendae, Confutatis and Lacrymosa). The protracted participation of trumpets and timpani enhances their impact and is favourably evaluated by early commentators (see Chapter 2). Whether or not Süssmayr intended the Sanctus to be perceived as the sublime moment recognized by early commentators, his movement confidently fulfils two of its key criteria: striking like a thunderbolt (especially the hemi-demisemiquavers in the timpani, their most distinctive contribution to the Requiem) and remaining brief.[47] If the late eighteenth-century sublime is indeed best understood as 'part of a sequence of events, even the enactment of a plot',[48] the Sanctus represents an apotheosis in Süssmayr's employment of winds for the purposes of reinforcing vocal lines, irrespective of whether or not trombones are to be included.[49]

Other features of the Sanctus also contribute to its climactic effect. Following the sudden impact of the opening, the three-fold 'Sanctus' statement ascends by a tone each time in the sopranos (bars 1–3), peaking on a g'' in bar 4 that coincides with an increase in the harmonic rhythm from one chord per bar (bars 1–3) to one chord per crotchet (bars 4–5). The big leaps in the upper-string accompaniment (bars 1–3) occur off the beat – from the ninth to the tenth semiquavers of the bar – and do not coincide with the

---

[47] See Elaine Sisman, *Mozart: The 'Jupiter' Symphony* (Cambridge, 1993), pp. 15–20 and 74–9. It is possible that Süssmayr toned down Eybler's rhythmically distinctive timpani (and wind) writing at the beginning of the Dies irae – for which Süssmayr is criticized by Nowak and Wolff among others (*Neue Mozart-Ausgabe*, I:I/2/2, ed. Nowak, p. xii; Wolff, *Mozart's Requiem*, p. 22) – precisely in order to accentuate the distinctive timpani writing of the Sanctus in the context of the Requiem as a whole.

[48] Sisman, *'Jupiter' Symphony*, pp. 19–20.

[49] While Süssmayr's autograph makes no mention of trombones for either the initial Sanctus statement (bars 1–10) or the subsequent 'Osanna' fugue, the *Neue Mozart-Ausgabe* edition of the Requiem (I:1/2/2) includes trombones in the initial Sanctus statement (bars 1–10) and leaves them out of the first 'Osanna'. While the inclusion of the trombones in bars 1–10 is surely right on account of the climactic resonance of this passage, their omission from the first 'Osanna' fugue is less certain.

Example 5.10　Süssmayr's completion of Mozart's Requiem, Sanctus, bars 1–5

vocal articulation on the beat, thus attracting attention. In keeping with
Süssmayr's predilection for anticipating or revisiting Mozart's striking
effects in the Sequence and Offertory, distinctive moments in the second
half of the Sanctus (bars 6–10) are foreshadowed by distinctive moments in

Example 5.10   (cont.)

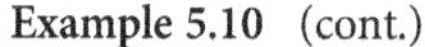

the first half: the C♮s of 'Pleni sunt' by the C♮s in bar 3; and the g″ melodic highpoint from bar 9, sustained in the tenors' g′ shining pristinely through the texture (bars 9–10), by the g″ highpoint in bars 4–5. (The diminished seventh in bar 6, beats 3 and 4, is new, and the harmonic effect is enhanced by appearing immediately after the only unharmonized notes in the Sanctus, that is the C♮s at 'Pleni sunt'.)

The two-pronged critical attack on Süssmayr's 'Osanna' fugue – namely its purported contrapuntal inadequacy and its brevity[50] – reminds me of a Woody Allen joke at the beginning of *Annie Hall* (1977) about two elderly women conversing at a Catskill Mountains resort: one says, 'Boy, the food at this place is really terrible', to which the other responds 'Yes I know, and such small portions.' The brevity of Süssmayr's fugue for the 'Osanna', viewed in relation to Requiem settings by Pasterwitz, Albrechtsberger and Krottendorfer from c.1790–3, is actually 'more characteristic of Viennese practice than the full-scale fugal re-compositions attempted by Duncan Druce and Robert Levin in their editions'; lengthy 'Osanna' fugues are also rare among Mozart's masses.[51] The 'Osanna' fugue of Süssmayr's own *Missa solemnis*, moreover, is short – forty bars in a sixty-nine-bar Sanctus movement – whereas other fugues in the work are significantly longer (Cum sancto spiritu, Et vitam venturi).

Situating the 'Osanna' fugue in the context of the Sanctus as a whole allows us to gauge Süssmayr's strategy. The final five bars of the fugue (Example 5.11) revisit the climactic sounds of the opening five bars of the Sanctus: the voices come together after the counterpoint; the harmonic rhythm quickens in the fourth of the five bars; the melodic peaks in the first violins occur off the beat (d‴, e‴, c♯‴, bar 37), not coinciding with vocal articulation, in analogous fashion to the strings' semiquaver leaps at the opening; the sopranos' melodic kernel in bars 36–7 is the same as that at 'Sabaoth' in bar 5; and the trumpets and timpani make their only protracted contribution to the fugue, resonating with their full contribution to the opening. Alongside these climactic qualities, rapid quaver runs continue in the upper strings, preceded by choppy leaps to a″ in bar 33 that invoke the striking leaps to a″ in the first-violin accompaniment in bars 1–3. In invoking the beginning of his Sanctus at the end of his 'Osanna' fugue, Süssmayr brings to mind Mozart's own careful attention to the sonic

---

[50] See, for example, Maunder, 'Süssmayr's Work in Mozart's Requiem', p. 70 and Mozart, *Requiem*, ed. Levin, p. xxvi.

[51] Black, in Levin et al., 'Colloquy: Finishing Mozart's Requiem', pp. 596–600, at 599.

Example 5.11   Süssmayr's completion of Mozart's Requiem, Sanctus, bars 32–8

implications of beginnings and ends of Requiem movements, including the Dies irae, Rex tremendae, Confutatis and Lacrymosa (see Chapter 4).

If Süssmayr's principal aim in the Sanctus–Osanna as a whole is projecting a climax that builds on sounds and effects achieved in the Sequence, then it stands to reason that he only need write an 'Osanna' fugue of a length sufficient for him to re-establish sounds comparable to those in his initial Sanctus statement (appreciating, of course, that fugues cannot begin climactically). The fugue's brevity becomes a problem only when the magnificent 'Hosanna' double fugue from Mozart's Mass in C minor, K. 427, is a primary point of comparison,[52] overriding Süssmayr's apparent intentions for the Requiem completion, Mozart's own earlier masses and common practices for Viennese requiems in the early 1790s.

---

[52] As it is for Levin, one of the modern-day completers of the Requiem, whose 'newly composed *Hosanna* fugue displays the proportions of a Mozartean church fugue (modeled after the C minor mass)'. See Mozart, *Requiem*, ed. Levin, p. xxvi.

While the Sanctus takes to new heights the strategy of reinforcement and climax from the choral movements of the Sequence, the Benedictus extends independent writing for winds beyond what is encountered in the solo numbers of the Sequence. The variety of wind effects in the Benedictus (when presenting material separately from strings and voices) surpasses that of all previous movements, including Mozart's Introit: the bassoons and bassethorns provide autonomous accompanimental figures and echoes (bars 4–6, 7), and the bassethorns are given sustained notes and a solo (bars 10–12, 21–2); the full winds (including trumpets) offer *ff* chordal segments (bars 18–21, 50–2); and the bassethorns and trombones provide isolated sustained notes (bars 33–4, 38–9).[53] And this is not all: variety of effect is complemented by integration and intensification of orchestration procedures from earlier in the Requiem. Süssmayr may have derived his simple four-note trombone link in bars 3–4, for example, from Mozart's 'et lux perpetua' in the Introit (bars 14–15, 43–4), giving the trombones different material from that of the strings – just as he did for the winds in the instrumental links in the Confutatis – and using the three-quaver rhythm to generate the ensuing independent bassoon accompaniment, akin to subtleties from the end of the Tuba mirum. The next appearances of the trombone rhythmic figure (bars 18–20, 50–2; see Example 5.12) carry further musical significance. In antiphonal exchange with the strings, and performing as a group, the winds now forge a stronger link than in bars 3–4 to the 'et lux perpetua' from the Introit (especially the statement in bars 43–4), and move beyond it too in creating a sound new to the Requiem: for the first time the *entire* wind complement of bassethorns, bassoons, trumpets and trombones is unsupported by strings and/or voices, playing *ff* as well.[54] Thus, Süssmayr's work on the Sanctus and Benedictus reinforces the impression gleaned from the Sequence that he intended to shape orchestration and sound effects in the work to build towards climactic points, while also following a strategy of wind support for the voices that derives ultimately from Mozart's Introit.

Beyond orchestral effects specifically, weaknesses in Süssmayr's Benedictus also seem to highlight his strategies for the Requiem completion as a whole. It is difficult to argue that bars 23–5, for example, are anything other than

---

[53] In addition, the winds share thematic presentation with the strings at the outset, which, although not illustrative of wind independence as such, is indicative of the prominent, quasi-solo role assigned to them.

[54] These wind statements retain the original linking function from bars 3–4 too, providing transitions between vocal statements of the Benedictus in the first instance and between the last vocal statement of the Benedictus and the reprise of the 'Osanna' fugue in the second.

Example 5.12   Süssmayr's completion of Mozart's Requiem, Benedictus, bars 18–20

harmonically uninspired, treading water until an E♭ in bar 25 eventually points to B flat for the reprise in bar 28; the two-and-a-half bars of only F major harmony in an Andante tempo are aurally intrusive to an extent that individual part-writing 'errors' are not. But the sounds of bars 23–5 are strategically comprehensible. This is not to say that the lack of harmonic movement is desirable, but rather to identify a momentary (and unfortunate) disconnection between Süssmayr's instrumental and harmonic priorities. New sounds here build on and point towards earlier and later sounds in the Benedictus: the robust instrumental exchange between the winds and brass and the strings in bars 18–20 extends to the voices, which for the first time divide into a texture of one against three that establishes the basses in the leading role to feature in the reprise a few bars later; the second violins' shimmering semiquaver accompaniment appears in the reprise (bars 33–6); and the bassethorns and bassoons, followed by the two trombones (bars 25–7), re-establish themselves as the core accompaniment configuration where wind and brass participation is concerned, after the tutti wind scoring in bars 18–20 and the solo bassethorns in bars 21–2. On the one hand instruments and voices, melody and accompaniment alike, together present a unified front in bars 23–5 (all performing arpeggiated material) that builds on the uniformity of bars 18–20; on the other hand they point forwards to the accompaniment and instrumentation of the reprise. The function fulfilled by bars 23–5 does not excuse the harmonic stasis – Süssmayr could no doubt have achieved his objectives in a different way – but nonetheless highlights Süssmayr's apparent strategic priority, namely developing and forging relationships between individual sounds and effects.

Süssmayr's decision to bring back the 'Osanna' fugue in B flat at the end of the Benedictus, rather than in D, has also received criticism. Maunder argues that Mozart would probably have chosen C major for the Sanctus,[55] so clearly does not condone B flat for the 'Osanna' reprise. For Wolff, the Sanctus–Benedictus tonal plan is 'problematical' on account of the fugue reprise in B flat: 'If it were in D major, the Sanctus would fit the overall tonal design without strain and would correspond formally to the Offertory, including the move to the submediant (B-flat major in this case) at the start of the Benedictus.'[56] We could add that (allowing for major–minor transferences) a return to D major, rather than a continuation in B flat, would have had the Benedictus as a whole match the Hostias (E flat – g), reverse the tonal progression of the Agnus Dei (d – B flat) and complement the Communio (B flat–d). The Sanctus–Benedictus also would have replicated the tonal closure of all four other major sections of the work (Introit–Kyrie; Sequence; Offertory; Agnus–Communio).

---

[55] Maunder, *Mozart's Requiem*, pp. 38–41. Maunder's argument for a C major Sanctus partly depends on the end of the 'Quam olim' '[sounding] like the dominant of C minor' (p. 39). But it is unclear why we would hear the tonally emphatic conclusion in this way.

[56] Wolff, *Mozart's Requiem*, pp. 98–9.

So why did Süssmayr choose to remain in B flat? The answer again may lie in his strategy for sounds and effects. He makes a number of modifications to the original fugue in the 'Osanna' reprise, shortening it by five bars (giving twenty-three rather than twenty-eight), having the trumpets play for two bars more and the bassethorns participate where they were absent first time. The music of the first fugue was probably deemed too agile for the bassethorns to perform in A major (sounding D), unlike the stately Sanctus; but a key change to F major (sounding B flat) for the reprised fugue made their participation possible.[57] Whatever the verdict for or against trombone participation in the Sanctus 'Osanna', they are marked into the Benedictus 'Osanna', contributing to a slightly bigger overall sound for the latter than for the former.[58] The musical events of the Benedictus – with wind participation taken further than in any other movement of the work – perhaps encouraged Süssmayr to remain in B flat for the Benedictus 'Osanna' in order to facilitate instrumental additions in the fugal reprise. At any rate, strategies of climax and reinforcement and of procedural intensification and integration, initiated by Süssmayr in the Sequence and pursued further in the Sanctus and Benedictus, appear to generate internal developments in the Sanctus–Benedictus complex as well.

In the Agnus Dei, Süssmayr continues to invoke procedures from earlier movements – his own as well as Mozart's – as if preparing the ground carefully for the return to Mozart's Introit and Kyrie material in the Communio. As in most of Mozart's movements, the musical form is dictated by the text: three statements of the complete text thus coincide with three musical statements, each one supporting an iteration of the 'Agnus Dei' and 'dona eis requiem' (d – F; F – C; C – B flat – V/B flat). The first statement (bars 1–17, Example 5.13) also recalls earlier material, the main Introit theme emerging in the *bassi* line, as has often been recognized (bars 1–7). The momentary independence of timpani and trumpet (bars 8–9) resonates with Süssmayr's Sanctus and the choral movements from the Sequence, and goes back ultimately to Mozart's Introit. Likewise, the solo for bassethorns and bassoons (bars 14–16) recreates the sound of Süssmayr's wind solo in the middle of the Lacrymosa – and has a similar effect in linking vocal statements – as well as calling to mind in a more general way the wind echoes of

---

[57] There is no reason, then, to agree with Wolff's assessment (*Mozart's Requiem*, p. 88) that 'Süssmayr's decision to omit the basset horns from the first Hosanna and include them in the second was perverse.'

[58] Admittedly the timpani are present in the Sanctus fugue but not the Benedictus fugue; they rarely participated in a piece in B flat in the late eighteenth century. Their participation in the Sanctus 'Osanna' is limited, in any case, to ten notes.

Example 5.13 Süssmayr's completion of Mozart's Requiem, Agnus Dei, bars 1–17

Example 5.13 (cont.)

Example 5.13　(cont.)

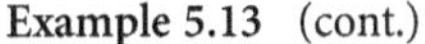

the Benedictus; it also summons up the opening of the Introit, the bassethorn and bassoon pairs giving way to crotchets in the three trombones that 'announce' the ensuing *forte* vocal statement. Indeed, the Agnus Dei ultimately follows the orchestration model of the Sequence choruses in giving the strings independent figures almost throughout while the winds for the most part double the voices. Paving the way respectfully for Mozart's return by drawing on processes Mozart had put in place, then, Süssmayr does not shy away consciously or unconsciously from promoting his own orchestration practices witnessed earlier in the work.

Süssmayr gives careful consideration to string participation in his Agnus Dei as well as to wind and brass effects. The semiquaver accompaniments in the first and second statements contain precisely notated *mf* and *p* markings followed by *ff* markings in bars 8–9 and 23–4. (The juxtaposition of *f* voices and winds and *p* strings – quiet accompaniment sounds that Süssmayr clearly still considers audible against the prevailing *f* – brings to mind Mozart's juxtaposed *p* and (implied) *f* in the links from 'Confutatis maledictis' to 'Voca me'.) The *f* for strings for the entire 'Agnus Dei qui tollis peccata mundi' portion of the third statement (bars 34–41) therefore makes an impact. Bringing together new dotted rhythms for bassethorns and bassoons (*sf* in bar 35), thudding 'Agnus' crotchets in which strings are aligned with voices and winds (bar 34) and a *forte* dynamic for all instruments and voices, the first eight bars of the third statement provide a climax to complement bars 1–9. The absence of winds and brass from the entire 'dona eis requiem' portion of the second statement (bars 24–33) also lends weight to their presence at the beginning of the third statement, again in line with Niemetschek's and Arnold's remarks on apposite orchestral effects.

The Communio, comprising the Lux aeterna and Cum sanctis fugue, brings the Requiem to a close with reprises of the Introit from bar 19 ('Te decet') and the Kyrie fugue.[59] Whether or not the reprise was Mozart's or Süssmayr's idea, there are precedents in eighteenth-century requiems and masses for returns to Kyrie material and (less commonly) to Introit verse materials.[60] Manfred Hermann Schmid is right to highlight liturgical weaknesses in Süssmayr's reprise on the one hand – the inappropriateness of the 'Lux aeterna' repetition in the full chorus and the *tonus peregrinus* set for the Communio antiphon rather than the Communio

---

[59] Small adjustments to the Introit and Kyrie are made by Süssmayr in the Communio to accommodate the different text settings, such as the additional quaver needed for 'Lux aeterna' (bars 8–9) as opposed to 'Exaudi' (Introit, bars 26–7) and the ♩ ♩ ♩ rhythm for the first bar of the 'Cum sanctis' fugue subject rather than the ♩. ♪♩ ♩ rhythm for 'Kyrie e[leison]'.

[60] Schmid, 'Introitus und Communio im Requiem', pp. 33–7.

verse – and Süssmayr's mitigating concerns on the other, such as his desire for 'unity' outlined in the letter to Breitkopf & Härtel ('in order to give more unity to the work I just allowed myself to repeat the Kyrie fugue to the lines cum Sanctis etc.'[61]) which sees artistic considerations and the creation of a complete work prioritized over the liturgical function of specific passages.[62] The immediate progression from Agnus to Communio without a break in the liturgy offers another perspective on the invocations of the Introit in the Agnus, not only at the opening but also at the end. The ♭VI – ♭III6–5 – ♭VI – Aug.6 progression (bars 46–9) emphasizes the flat submediant of B flat, just as B flat itself at the opening of the Lux aeterna is the flat submediant of the eventual tonic, D minor (accepting that the B flat – G flat relationship is chromatic and the D minor – B flat major relationship is not).[63] The recollections of past Requiem events in the Agnus, the prediction of future events and the creation of moments of climax all contribute to the 'unity' that Süssmayr desired for the work.

Süssmayr's completion in context

An aesthetic vision for the Requiem by its principal completer should be considered not a privilege afforded by us when the quality of the work is purportedly high, but rather a right that we expect to be exercised reasonably and pragmatically in trying, time-conscious circumstances. Working at first in a sphere of activity like orchestration where writers were acutely attentive to the aesthetic significance of precise, apposite detail, Süssmayr simultaneously would have had to be true to Mozart's intentions (in so far as he was aware of them) and unafraid to allow his own voice to emerge. With few (if any) materials or instructions from Mozart after the Offertory, Süssmayr would have found Mozart's intentions still more nebulous and his own voice significantly more prominent. Süssmayr's idea of a wind section acting primarily in support of the voices goes back to Mozart's Introit; the derivation of his shaping of effects in ways that maximize orchestral participation at various junctures (the Lacrymosa, Sanctus and Benedictus) and bring the supportive winds to prominence in other capacities (for example links in the Sequence) is less clear. It is not impossible that

---

[61] See Eibl, 'Süssmayrs "Requiem"-Brief', p. 22 (and the letter quoted in full above).

[62] Schmid, 'Introitus und Communio im Requiem', pp. 47–51.

[63] This harmonic progression at 'sempiternam' is similar to the progression at 'mortuorum' in the Credo of Süssmayr's *Missa solemnis* in D, SmWV 106 (bars 152–7); see Walter Wlcek, *Franz Xaver Süssmayr als Kirchenkomponist* (Tutzing, 1978), p. 209.

memories of *La clemenza di Tito* – with which Süssmayr was closely involved in a working capacity in 1791, probably writing a number of the *secco* recitatives – influenced him as he completed the Requiem. Like the Requiem, *Tito* is abstemious in its use of winds (certainly in comparison to Mozart's other mature operas). As climactic moments in the use of winds in supportive and quasi-solo capacities, Süssmayr's consecutive Sanctus and Benedictus are foreshadowed by two consecutive numbers from Act 2 of *Tito*, Vitellia's aria 'Non più di fiori' (No. 23) and the chorus 'Che del ciel' (No. 24). The former takes solo wind writing to new heights (in the context of this opera), featuring ostentatiously virtuosic material for the bassethorn to rival comparable solo clarinet writing in Sesto's aria 'Parto, parto' from Act 1, but going further in promoting other winds as solo participants as well (flute, two oboes, two bassoons, two horns). The latter, deploying, as in the Sequence and Sanctus, a large wind and percussion section to track and outline vocal lines while the strings present independent material, represents a forceful climax to the opera as a whole, and by extension to the winds' reinforcement of vocal lines. Elsewhere in *Tito*, strategies of wind deployment match Süssmayr's in the Requiem: wind effects in the five-section quintet complex in Act 1 (No. 12) reach a climax in the concluding Andante section, matching the attitude to wind effects in, for example, the Lacrymosa; and the progression of wind roles in the Act 2 trio ('Se al volto mai ti senti') from obbligato prominence at the opening to straightforward vocal support at the end, via a middleground of quasi-solo writing, parallels the Tuba mirum.[64] Although memories of Mozart's other opera from late 1791, *Die Zauberflöte*, would probably have proved less useful to Süssmayr, as solo, ornate wind writing assumes a much higher degree of prominence in *Die Zauberflöte* than in the Requiem, Süssmayr might still have derived inspiration from specific passages and sounds: the harmonious tutti wind chords in the Benedictus (unaccompanied by strings) invoke comparable, albeit more dramatic and symbolic, wind chords heard in the overture and the first spoken dialogue in Act 2; and the Queen of the Night's statement in her Act 2 aria that 'death and despair blaze around me' ('Tod und

---

[64] In the Act 2 trio, see the obbligato winds in bars 1–5 and 8–10, the inter-phrase links and other quasi-independent wind writing in bars 14, 22–4, 26–7, 29–31 and 34–5 and the straightforward (if prominent) wind support from 'Mercede al mio dolore' to the end (bars 40–108). The final Andante of the Act 1 quintet includes the following (after an absence of winds in bars 123–7): bassoons, trumpets, horns and timpani in dialogue with the chorus ('oh nero tradimento', marked *p*, bars 128–33); woodwinds (two each of flutes, oboes, clarinets and bassoons) 'floating' above voices and strings ('oh giorno di dolor', bars 138–44); winds and brass reinforcing the solo–chorus dialogue on 'tradimento' (bars 152–4, marked *f*); and a succession of wind effects from bar 155 to the end.

Verzweiflung flammet um mich her') initiates a wind and string link to the ensuing vocal segment similar to bars 6–7 from the Confutatis, both exploiting unison descending strings and harmonized winds in the context of a modulation and occurring immediately after textual references to fire.

Among Süssmayr's own large-scale sacred works, the *Missa solemnis*, SmWV 106, scored for two oboes, two bassoons, two horns, two trumpets, two trombones and timpani plus strings, appears to have most in common with his portions of the Requiem. Süssmayr's own requiems probably date from the mid-1780s, but feature no winds in the case of SmWV 103 and two horns only in SmWV 104. The latter (*Deutsches Requiem*) is a short and light homophonic work, draws on the German Kirchenlied 'Taut Himmel den Gerechten' from the *Landshuter Gesangsbuch* (1777) for the Sanctus and Benedictus, and is a sound-world away from Mozart's Requiem.[65] The *Missa solemnis* cannot cast light on Requiem authorship issues since it almost certainly postdates the Requiem, but it shows that Süssmayr's completion resonates beyond its immediate musical confines for the author himself. The beginnings of the Requiem and *Missa solemnis* Sanctus movements, both in D major, are identical in thematic content (bars 1–3 of the former reappear in bars 1–6 of the latter) and convey a similar sense of climax in their grand, full-orchestral sounds. The openings of the Agnus Dei movements are also alike (Example 5.14): both are in the minor, feature elaborate violin lines and chugging, repeated-quaver accompaniments in the rest of the strings and comprise bold, homophonic statements in the voices, following brief orchestral introductions (four bars in the *Missa solemnis*). The harmonic progression at 'mortuorum' in the Credo of the *Missa solemnis* (bars 152–7) is similar to the progression at 'sempiternam' at the end of the Requiem Agnus mentioned above.[66] The final five bars of the Requiem 'Osanna' are also matched tonally, thematically and harmonically by the final 'dona nobis pacem' statement a few bars before the end of the *Missa solemnis*, both segments fulfilling similar climactic functions in their movements (Example 5.15).

---

[65] On dates for these works, see Duda, *Thematisches Werkverzeichnis (SmWV)*. The Mass in C ('Maria Taferl'), SmWV 102, and Mass in B flat, SmWV 107 feature large wind contingents; according to Duda they could have been written after the Requiem completion rather than before it. Of Süssmayr's multi-movement sacred works scored for more than one wind instrument, only the Mass in C, SmWV 101 (two oboes, two trumpets), seems safely attributable to the years before Mozart's Requiem. (Duda gives 1785–7 as the probable date for SmWV 101.) On the Kirchenlied connection to Süssmayr's *Deutsches Requiem*, see Wlcek, *Franz Xaver Süssmayr als Kirchenkomponist*, p. 132.

[66] See Wlcek, *Franz Xaver Süssmayr als Kirchenkomponist*, p. 209.

Example 5.14   Süssmayr, *Missa solemnis*, SmWV 106, Agnus Dei, bars 1–7

Example 5.15 Süssmayr, *Missa solemnis*, SmWV 106, Agnus Dei, bars 94–9

Süssmayr's use of winds in his pre-1792 compositions – sacred and secular alike – points tentatively towards orchestration strategies subsequently employed in the Requiem. While it is difficult to determine Süssmayr's level of experience at handling a substantial contingent of wind instruments in a multi-movement sacred work before 1792, numerous short sacred works featuring a healthy number of wind participants can be attributed reliably to the years preceding the Requiem.[67] The bass aria 'Alleluia', SmWV 127, composed in Vienna between 1789 and 1791, is probably the last sacred work Süssmayr composed prior to working on the Requiem, and is thus of particular interest in terms of orchestration.[68] Writing for two oboes and two horns, in addition to strings, Süssmayr treats his winds as support for the voice and strings, bringing them in often at the beginnings and ends of phrases only. But wind links – a favoured device for Süssmayr in the Requiem – also hint at the kind of shaping of orchestral effects over an extended period that would come to characterize Süssmayr's participation in the Requiem. An initial link comprises three repeated quavers for two horns with the basses (bars 8–9), subsequently reheard at the reprise of the opening material later in the aria (bars 59–60); a link that immediately follows (bars 65–6), however, is more ornate and the exclusive property of the winds, being scored for two oboes as well as two horns. This glimpse of an exposed wind sonority precipitates the most protracted, quasi-independent participation of winds in the aria as a whole (bars 68–98), with tied minims, and quaver–crotchet rhythms lending a new dimension to wind support. Süssmayr's 'Ave verum corpus', SmWV 121, written in mid-1792 soon after the Requiem completion, is characterized by similar shaping of wind participation. At first he gives modest independence to his two oboes and two horns (bars 1–10); he then has them penetrate the texture more clearly (the horn *sf* indications in bars 22, 32), and finally returns them to modestly independent roles at the end, where he also provides the piece's most striking instrumental effect: in the final instrumental link, from the departure of the voices to the final chord, the oboes soar an octave above the violins (bars 40–3), registrally separate from them for the only time.[69]

---

[67] See Duda, *Thematisches Werkverzeichnis (SmWV)*, pp. 41–64.

[68] My thanks go to David Black for providing me with a copy of Süssmayr's 'Alleluia'. For a brief discussion of the work, and a facsimile of the opening page of the autograph, see Black, 'Mozart and the Practice of Sacred Music', pp. 367–9.

[69] For an edition see W. A. Mozart and F. X. Süssmayr, *Ave verum corpus: Two Motets*, ed. Richard Maunder (Oxford, 1987). See also Maunder's criticism of the piece, focusing on technical 'errors', in *Mozart's Requiem*, pp. 30–2.

The strategic shaping of wind participation in a pre-Requiem context is especially marked in Süssmayr's *Sinfonia turchesa* in C, SmWV 403, even if its level of wind involvement is considerably higher in general than that in the 'Alleluia' or the Requiem.[70] Moving from prominent wind writing that includes solo wind thematic statements and antiphonal exchange with the strings in the first movement through supportive wind doubling and rare independence in the second, and combined doubling and thematic prominence in the minuet and trio, Süssmayr reserves his biggest wind effect for the rondo finale. Thematically prominent throughout the finale, the winds are given a twenty-six-bar solo segment in the latter stages (bars 135–61) scored for the entire wind complement of piccolo, two oboes, two bassoons, two horns and trumpet, and without the janissary percussion instruments that appear with the winds elsewhere – a climactic wind effect in the context not only of this movement but also of the work as a whole.[71]

From discussion in Chapters 4 and 5 it would appear that Süssmayr's progressions of sounds and effects in the completion complement Mozart's in his portions of the Requiem and earlier sacred works. As well as drawing on his own compositional experience and (possibly) experiences of Mozart's 1791 operas, Süssmayr may also have been inspired by Mozart's masses in the Viennese and Baden orbits in 1791 when coming to write the Requiem's Sanctus, Benedictus and Agnus Dei. The Sanctus of K. 317 is forceful and climactic in a similar way to the Requiem Sanctus, both movements replacing the contrasts of earlier movements (the Kyrie and Credo in K. 317; see Chapter 4) with expressive homogeneity. The ending of the K. 337 Agnus Dei, referring back to orchestral effects from earlier parts of the mass (Chapter 4), anticipates Süssmayr's references in the Requiem Agnus to effects earlier in the work. The openings of the Sanctus movements from K. 427 and the Requiem are thematically similar;[72] indeed, Mozart's Sanctus, and the climactic impression it conveys in K. 427 with a big sound that includes a full wind and brass contingent, perhaps acted as a catalyst for

---

[70] Duda states that the *Sinfonia* was probably written between 1784 and 1787 during Süssmayr's time at Kremsmünster; see *Thematisches Werkverzeichnis (SmWV)*, p. 220. The date c.1790 is given in Mary B. B. Inwood's modern edition, in Barry Brook (editor in chief), *The Symphony 1720–1840*, series B, vol. XIV (New York and London, 1985), pp. 211–65, at 211.

[71] For a panoply of wind effects in a Süssmayr instrumental work with a large complement of wind and brass composed shortly after the Requiem, see the sinfonia to his opera *Il turco in Italia* (c.1793–4), which includes two flutes, two oboes, two clarinets, two bassoons, two horns and two trumpets; Franz Xaver Süssmayr, *Sinfonia: 'Il turco in Italia'*, ed. Maria P. Eckhardt (Budapest, 1982).

[72] Mozart's autograph materials for the K. 427 Sanctus comprise only wind, brass and timpani parts; the vocal, string and bass parts are transmitted through contemporary copies. See Mozart, *Messe c-moll KV427: Faksimile* and scholarly editions such as the *Neue Mozart-Ausgabe*, I:1/1/5.

Süssmayr's Requiem Sanctus, encouraging (and/or reinforcing) his desire to enhance the sonority in both the Sanctus and the Benedictus.

Irrespective of Süssmayr's source (or sources) of inspiration for his shaping of orchestral effects in the Requiem, his conception is consistent and coherent, not arbitrarily opportunistic. The places where Mozart's intentions and Süssmayr's conception are demonstrably unaligned are rarely clear-cut, thus revealing the underlying seriousness and respect with which Süssmayr approached his task. Ultimately Süssmayr's modest contravening of Mozart from time to time is indicative of active and creative engagement with the work itself, with the implications of *all* of the materials, procedures and visions contained therein and not only those of Mozart.

Conclusion

While Süssmayr surely would have been disheartened by the tone, implications and criticisms of his words and his work in the *Allgemeine musikalische Zeitung* review of the first edition of the Requiem (see Chapter 2), he would perhaps have come to consider the review a blessing in disguise had he lived beyond 1803. For the uncertainty over authorship encouraged by it, and by other writings from the first twenty-five years of the nineteenth century, at least permitted writers to assess the work from a perspective untainted by presumptions about Süssmayr's inferiority. It would be naive to suppose, of course, that early, exalted opinions of the Requiem in its entirety were not influenced by the assumption that the great Mozart composed it all, just as it would be naive to suppose that these early opinions were not also influenced by the extraordinary, mist-shrouded biographical circumstances surrounding the composition of the work. Even so, the unambiguous early praise for the Lacrymosa, Sanctus, Benedictus and Agnus Dei and for orchestration that Süssmayr was eventually acknowledged universally to have carried out – the devotion, holiness, elevation, unity and sublimity reported in Chapter 2 – must be factored into the evaluative equation in fairness to the man responsible for this work, revealing, as the praise unwittingly does, the perceived aesthetic import of Süssmayr's contribution. Nor must we ignore the fact that the later Requiem movements were among those movements most enjoyed by early audiences (see Chapter 2). It is testimony to Süssmayr's achievement that, before the authorship fights began in earnest in the second quarter of the nineteenth century, his aesthetic contribution to the work was valued so highly, if also unknowingly.

Süssmayr's Requiem completion contains inevitable, unavoidable compromises. The mysteries of Mozart's autograph discussed in Chapter 4 – the enigmatic sounds and effects in the incomplete score – were a theoretical luxury that Süssmayr could not afford. He had to interpret the manifold resonances and implications of the incomplete score as faithfully, creatively and imaginatively as he could, with a view to producing a timely, efficient completion. Mozart's semantically ineffable sonic inferences – the juxtaposition of p and f at bar 6, beat 2, and bar 16, beat 2, of the Confutatis, the 'ne perenni' confrontation and subsequent resolution in bars 105–10 of the Recordare, the first violin's *forte* explosion to initiate the 'Quam olim Abrahae' fugue – accrue sounds, or are foreshadowed or subsequently developed, in Süssmayr's score. Their mystique is therefore a casualty of Süssmayr's conception of the complete work.

In fundamental respects, though, Süssmayr's priorities for the Requiem completion derive from distinctive musical qualities of Mozart's vision. Like Mozart, Süssmayr promotes individual instrumental sounds and effects and also progressions and successions of sounds and effects. His own coterie of memorable ones – the 'Amen' cadence at the end of the Lacrymosa, the onset of the Sanctus, the 'dona eis requiem' segment from the first statement of the Agnus Dei and so on – may have been inspired by contemplating in the autograph the kind of memorable Mozart effects discussed in Chapter 4. Süssmayr highlights instrumental links as aesthetically resonant effects in their own right, following the example that Mozart sets in the Introit, Dies irae, Recordare and Confutatis, as well as treating them as simple functional devices for getting from the end of one vocal statement to the beginning of the next. His apparently 'economical' thematic and motivic mindset in the concluding portions of the Requiem indicates a desire to continue a process that Mozart started: Mozart's manipulations of the main themes of the Introit, Kyrie and Dies irae in his Sequence and Offertory movements are matched by corresponding manipulations in the Sanctus, Benedictus and Agnus Dei;[73] and, as mentioned, Süssmayr's violin link figure in the Domine Jesu (bar 32) pre-echoes an appearance of Mozart's material in the same movement.

The intended 'unity' for the Requiem to which Süssmayr draws our attention in his letter to Breitkopf & Härtel ultimately applies not just to thematic and motivic integration but also to the shaping of the final, completed work. The patterns of intensification and climax that characterize his orchestration

---

[73] For extended discussion on this point, see Wlcek, *Franz Xaver Süssmayr als Kirchenkomponist,* pp. 41–72.

of the Sequence (and his composition of most of the Lacrymosa) project in complementary ways into the Sanctus and Benedictus; the Agnus Dei, aligned with the two previous movements in producing climactic effects, also prepares for the upcoming reprise by invoking effects and material from earlier in the work. Significantly, Süssmayr allows his own early contributions to the Requiem, as well as Mozart's contributions, to inform his work on the Sanctus, Benedictus and Agnus Dei and his overall conception of the Requiem, demonstrating a degree of musical confidence that his predecessor, Eybler, apparently lacked. Willingness to engage with the musical resonances and implications of his own materials, irrespective of inspiration that he ultimately drew from Mozart's portions of the Requiem and earlier works, represented an essential aesthetic, practical and psychological prerequisite to completing the work.

Writing to her loyal friend Maximilian Stadler on 31 May 1827, Constanze reported Mozart 'often' saying to Süssmayr during composition of the Requiem: 'Oy – there you are again at a complete loss [*die Ochsen wieder am Berge*]; you are far from understanding that.'[74] Like so much of the peripheral information that engulfs the Requiem in a mystical cloud and makes its story so appealing, it has an (unverifiable) air of truth to it; after all, Mozart jovially dismissed his hapless assistant in 1791 as an 'idiotic fellow', 'Sauermayr', a 'full-blown ass' and (in scatological mood) a 'Muckshitter', as well as referring to him specifically as an ox.[75] But in reality they were both oxen at a loss, even if they did not know it – Mozart about to contract a fatal illness, Süssmayr straining to keep up with the work required by Mozart, alive then dead – both unaware that the manuscript sitting on the table in front of them would possess extraordinary power to shape their posthumous images.

A positive evaluation of Süssmayr's work on the Requiem should in no way detract from an appreciation of Mozart's work. Reading through Mozart's fragment is an exhilarating, poignant experience, as I tried to

---

[74] 'Ey – da stehen die Ochsen wieder am Berge; das verstehst du noch lange nicht.' See Bauer and Deutsch (eds.), *Mozart: Briefe und Aufzeichnungen, Gesamtausgabe*, vol. IV, p. 491. Extant translations – '(dying) duck in a thunderstorm' (Wolff, *Mozart's Requiem*, trans. Whittall, p. 170; Landon, *Mozart's Last Year*, p. 171) and 'cow at a five-barred gate' (Abert, *Mozart*, p. 1314) – are problematic, as they do not immediately carry the same idiomatic meaning as their German counterpart. The translation given in the preface to Franz Beyer's edition of the Requiem is too literal ('there the oxen are standing in front of the mountain again' in Mozart, *Requiem*, ed. Beyer, p. 32); Reinhard Pauly's translation is better ('Are you really dumbfounded?' in Gärtner, *After the Requiem*, p. 66), but turns the expression unnecessarily into a rhetorical question. I have opted for 'at a complete loss', since (to my mind) it is the English idiom closest to the German.

[75] Anderson (ed. and trans.), *Letters*, pp. 958, 963, 967, 966. For the references to Süssmayr ('Snai') as an ox, see ibid., pp. 958, 961.

convey in Chapter 4. But our collective experiences of the performed Requiem in its 'traditional' completion are surely a different matter; I will certainly not claim that my empathy for the Requiem derives entirely from Mozart's work. Accepting that Süssmayr plays a role in the profoundly moving experience that is Mozart's Requiem need not represent a concession, or a compromise, or a disappointment at wonders lost. For following his master's example, the younger of the two oxen did exceedingly well.

Since 1971, a number of scholars critical (to varying degrees) of Süssmayr's work on the Requiem have produced their own completions, including Franz Beyer (1971), Hans-Josef Irmen (1977), Richard Maunder (1988), H. C. Robbins Landon (1991), Duncan Druce (1993) and Robert Levin (1994).[1] Julian Rushton recently expressed surprise that new completions took until 1971 to appear, arguing that 'there is enough information [from Mozart] to realize most of [the Sequence and Offertory movements] better than Süssmayr did'.[2] In truth, though, there was no real appetite for a revised version before the late twentieth century. As seen in Chapter 2, Saint-Foix (1946) states that the 'often heavy and clumsy' trombones arising from the doubling of voices could be revised, but does not suggest major interferences with the Süssmayr-completed score.[3] Ernst Hess (1959), in contrast, follows his analysis of Süssmayr's faults and deficiencies in the Requiem with a clarion call for a new edition that provides us with 'Mozart's last legacy in a form truly worthy of him, in so far as this is at all possible for a human being who is not Mozart'.[4] Beyer claims that 'in its ever-increasing understanding of Mozart, our day and age has reached the necessary maturity' to produce a revised completion.[5] But critical 'maturity', perhaps determinable for individual works of scholarship on a case-by-case basis, does not bear taxonomical scrutiny for an entire era. It was the spirit of the age, then, that moved scholars to start revising the Requiem.

The modern-day completers approach their task in various ways: Beyer and Landon in the spirit of revising Süssmayr's version – Landon favouring Eybler's contributions over Süssmayr's in the Sequence – while acknowledging its historical importance; Levin and Druce in a similar spirit, but writing their own material as well; and Maunder with a view to excising

---

[1] For detailed consideration of these six completions, see Korten, *Mozarts Requiem KV626*, pp. 59–178.

[2] Rushton, *Mozart*, p. 228.

[3] Saint-Foix, *W.-A. Mozart*, vol. V, p. 281. It is unclear whether Saint-Foix had in mind the late eighteenth-century trombone or the modern trombone, the latter featuring a wider bore and bigger sound than the former.

[4] Given in Mozart, *Requiem*, ed. Beyer, p. v (translation amended).   [5] Ibid., p. ix.

Süssmayr's contribution and providing new material in its place. But they share a common desire to realize Mozart's intentions for the completion of the Requiem 'better than Süssmayr'. I shall examine three (Levin, Beyer and Maunder) that are broadly representative of the different approaches to the task at hand.[6] As acts of modernist minds, modernizing the Requiem with recourse to supposedly rational processes believed to improve the work, the completions occupy a niche position in late twentieth-century musical thought, remaining firmly rooted in *Werktreue* and the primacy of authorial intent, but for a work and a musical text defined by the completers' own differing interpretations of Mozart's documented, partially documented and wholly undocumented thoughts.

Levin, Beyer and Maunder completions

Levin succinctly explains the aims of his completion:

On the one hand the compositional problems of the *Lacrimosa*, the *Amen* fugue, and the movements surviving only in Süssmayr's hand have not been overlooked out of blind piety to their 200-year-old origin. On the other hand, the historical and performance tradition of the Requiem demands respect. A clearly drawn line of separation, in which everything except the contents of Mozart's autograph draft was to be considered spurious per se, was explicitly rejected. Quite the contrary: the goal was to revise not as much, but as little as possible, attempting in the revisions to observe the character, texture, voice leading, continuity and structure of Mozart's music. The traditional version has been retained insofar as it agrees with idiomatic Mozartean practice.[7]

Thus, Levin's faithfulness to the work constitutes faithfulness to Mozart primarily but not exclusively; Süssmayr, as the author of the 'traditional' completion, is also to be accorded respect.

---

[6] Of the remaining modern completions, Druce's is the most audacious; he re-composes the Lacrymosa, the Sanctus and the Benedictus and adds an 'Amen' fugue. The Lacrymosa begins with Eybler's attempted continuation and is lengthened to thirty-eight bars, including a six-bar instrumental interlude (modulating from F to G minor) between the first and second iterations of the complete Lacrymosa text and a six-bar instrumental passage at the end that leads to the new 'Amen' fugue. The Sanctus decorates Süssmayr's accompaniment, lengthens the section by one bar and ends with a pause on the dominant of D; the 'Osanna' fugue on Süssmayr's subject is extended to sixty-nine bars. The Benedictus uses 'the main thematic material of the traditional version' but comprises 'a new movement, following a variety of Mozartean models and hints' and is followed by a shortened fugal reprise (forty-eight bars long) at the end. For the quoted material, see Mozart, *Requiem*, ed. Druce, p. viii.

[7] Mozart, *Requiem*, ed. Levin, pp. xx–xxi.

Levin's vision for the completion of the Sequence differs from Süssmayr's in including an 'Amen' fugue, but is similar in other respects. Arguments about whether Mozart would actually have written a fugue had he lived to complete the work have been well rehearsed;[8] suffice it to say that there can be no certainty that he would have done so. And if there is no certainty, and Mozart's intentions and desires are paramount, we might ask why Levin takes a chance and alters the existing ending (which, for all we know, Mozart could have discussed with Süssmayr, prescribing the plagal cadence). Given the discovery of a Mozart sketch for an 'Amen' fugue in 1962,[9] though, it is not unreasonable for Levin and others to attempt one. Levin's fugue is stylish, with impressive forward propulsion: ultimately it envisages and realizes a climactic end to the Sequence, as does the conclusion to Süssmayr's Lacrymosa. Levin follows Süssmayr's completion quite closely until the end of bar 23 but loses his way somewhat in the final bars (24–7), which need to be altered in order to avoid Süssmayr's plagal cadence and to prepare for the fugue. The last three bars (25–7), which basically oscillate between 6–4 and 5–3 chords on the dominant, lack harmonic direction, treading water while the singers complete the text and while Levin completes his (perhaps superfluous) 'exact citation' of the Introit theme.[10] He also eradicates Süssmayr's bar 21 on the grounds that the 'double function' of bars 19–21, confirming F and transitioning back to D minor, 'seems very questionable for such a short passage' and that bar 21 itself unnecessarily replicates the harmonic progression of the movement's main theme. In so doing, though, Levin gets rid of a bar that forms part of Süssmayr's own invocation of the opening of the Introit, explained in Chapter 5, and turns the onset of the 'dona eis requiem' into an unusual combination of harmonic transition and arrival (F, beat 1, rather than d, followed by Süssmayr's i6, 7–♭5, V7, which replicates Mozart's bar 3).

Elsewhere, Levin's revisions to Süssmayr are on the whole more successful, aligning with Süssmayr's apparent intentions in an effective fashion, or promoting Levin's own conception of the work in a thoughtful way. In the middle section of the Tuba mirum, for example, Levin uses sustained notes and phrase links in the bassoons and bassethorns to colour the music,

---

⁸ See, for example, Simon P. Keefe, '"Die Ochsen am Berge": Franz Xaver Süssmayr and the Orchestration of Mozart's Requiem, K. 626', *Journal of the American Musicological Society*, 61 (2008), pp. 1–65, at 41 and, especially, Bauman, 'Requiem, but no Piece', pp. 158–61.

⁹ Plath, 'Über Skizzen zu Mozarts Requiem'.

¹⁰ Levin describes the end of his Lacrymosa (Mozart, *Requiem*, ed. Levin, p. xxv) as follows: 'Süssmayr's metrically inexact quotation of the INTROITUS theme (mm. 26–27 of his version) has been transformed into an exact citation (mm. 24–25) with an answer on the dominant (tenor, mm. 25–26).' It is unclear why Levin considers an 'exact citation' necessary at this juncture.

skilfully replacing Süssmayr's trombone line but supporting Süssmayr's apparent desire for wind participation that occupies a middle ground between the fully-fledged obbligato writing of the opening and support for the voices in 'Cum vix justus'. Levin's compositional addition to the 'Osanna', the substantially lengthened fugue, also responds to Süssmayr's material. Dissatisfaction with the brevity of Süssmayr's 'Osanna' fugue stretches back to the nineteenth century, as we have seen in Chapter 2. Whatever Mozart's intentions were, Levin's extended fugue adds to the grandeur of Süssmayr's preceding Sanctus in its forceful sound and bold, triumphant ending. Levin's desire for an 'Osanna' reprise in D major, rather than B flat, necessitates re-writing the end of Süssmayr's Benedictus (bars 50–6 in Levin; see Example 6.1). The partial similarity of this passage to the Introit, intended by Levin,[11] evolves organically, not cosmetically, inviting us to draw comparisons between wind instrument effects in both movements; Süssmayr's Benedictus implicitly does the same on account of the climactic role that wind instruments assume in this movement of his completion. It is a shame in this context, then, that Levin does not employ trombones or trumpets in his Benedictus (except for two bars for trumpets at the end), summarily dismissing their involvement in his foreword.[12]

For those who admire Süssmayr's work on the Requiem as well as Mozart's, it is inevitable that some moments in every modern completion will rankle. I find it difficult to understand Levin's inclusion of bassethorns and bassoons simultaneously with the explosive violins in the link to 'Quam olim Abrahae' (bars 43–4), since the powerful clarity of the violins' contribution, dramatically accentuated in Mozart's autograph, is compromised as a result. Similarly, Levin's modifications to the initial Sanctus, above all the additional obbligato violin writing (bars 1–11), detract from the monumentality of Süssmayr's statement, drawing attention to the new melodic and thematic intricacies and away from Süssmayr's full, uniform sound. In general, though, Levin carefully and imaginatively treads the fine line between respect for the Mozart–Süssmayr original and modifications to it, and writes new material with panache.

Levin's alterations at the beginning of the Sanctus raise the issue of modern-day completers' exact intentions in making adjustments rather than large-scale additions to Süssmayr's score. All completers carry out changes even where purported errors are *not* at issue, trying to improve on Süssmayr's orchestration, part-writing and counterpoint where his work is deemed aesthetically rather than technically inappropriate. They thereby

---

[11] Ibid., p. xxvii.   [12] Ibid., p. xxiii.

Example 6.1   Levin's completion of Mozart's Requiem, Benedictus, bars 49–56

compromise the sound-world that Süssmayr apparently wanted to create with or without Mozart's intentions in mind. (As explained in Chapter 4, sounds and textures in Mozart's works are accorded special aesthetic significance in critical literature at the turn of the nineteenth century.) Those with a low opinion of Süssmayr may not consider that much has been lost as a result. Ultimately, though, the judgment call of the Requiem completer altering details of Süssmayr's work in the late twentieth century has to stand comparison with musical priorities and processes that Süssmayr developed for the work as a whole 200 years earlier (see Chapter 5), perhaps with Mozart's instructions ringing in his ears, and at the very least with a practical, ingrained knowledge of contemporary working practices. Of course, I do not wish to suggest that modern completers are deficient in their understanding of these late eighteenth-century practices, but simply recognize, as Levin does, that 'Süssmayr's historical position guarantees him a unique perspective'.[13]

Beyer's edition sheds light on the complex dynamic between late eighteenth-century and late twentieth-century Requiems with particular reference to small-scale adjustments. He is less explicit than Levin in justifying why different types of changes are made, short of explaining that 'it has been the aim of the undersigned to act as a restorer, to cleanse the work from all the impurities of obvious errors and deficiencies, and to try to return as far as is humanly possible to the original concept of Mozart'.[14] But accepting in the preface that much of his orchestration 'overlaps' with Süssmayr and Eybler, Beyer partly revises and partly orchestrates afresh, moving well beyond 'obvious errors and deficiencies'. His adjustments to Süssmayr vary in quantity and in significance. At times he favours a more austere use of winds than Süssmayr, as indicated (for example) in the omission of bassethorns and bassoons from the last two bars of the Tuba mirum and the 'Salva me' statements at the close of the Rex tremendae (bars 18–19). At other times, as in the Recordare, austerity is not necessarily the primary motivating factor, and Beyer's rationale for altering Süssmayr is unclear. *Inter alia*, he adds woodwind inter-phrase links between bars 41–2 and bars 45–6 (bassethorns and bassoons), when Süssmayr reserves them until later in the movement; changes minim–crotchet wind parts to dotted minims in bars 46–9; sets aside the bassethorns' doubling of the voices at the reprise of the Recordare's main theme at 'Preces meae' (bars 93–9), again in favour of dotted minims; and omits almost all of Süssmayr's

---

[13] Levin, in Levin et al., 'Colloquy: Finishing Mozart's Requiem', p. 588. A similar point is made by Druce in Mozart, *Requiem*, ed. Druce, p. viii.

[14] Mozart, *Requiem*, ed. Beyer, p. viii.

woodwind in bars 118–26. When we try to decipher his orchestration strategy for the work as a whole no clear results are forthcoming. To be sure, Beyer favours new sonorities such as dotted minims over wind doubling of voices in the Recordare and elsewhere, perhaps pursuing textural variety to support his view that 'it is incredible how little [Süssmayr] makes use of the unusual combination of instruments'.[15] But on occasion he still brings the winds more closely into line with the voices than Süssmayr, as in the doubling of the voices at 'ne perenni cremer igne' (Recordare, bars 105–9).[16] Nor is it immediately clear why dotted minims in the winds occur at the reprise of the Recordare (bars 93–9), or why the wind participation is so abbreviated in bars 118–26.

From time to time Beyer's changes to Süssmayr's orchestration astutely develop Mozart's and Süssmayr's ideas, notably in bars 5–8 of the Lacrymosa. Mozart includes a crescendo marking at bar 7 of the Lacrymosa; Süssmayr reinforces it by reserving the *forte* entry of the trumpets and timpani until the second half of bar 8. Beyer goes further, with a staged crescendo from bar 5 onwards: the bassethorns and bassoons are given quavers and crotchet rests from bar 5 and Süssmayr's trombones are omitted; bassethorns, bassoons and the entering trombones have dotted crotchets in bar 7; and the trumpets and timpani enter a beat earlier in bar 8 than in Süssmayr's score. Nevertheless, Beyer leaves us with the impression that decisions about revising orchestration are taken from moment to moment with no overarching strategy for the work as a whole and with no concern for what conceivably could be lost as a result of freely altering Süssmayr's contributions.

Maunder draws a clear line of separation, avoided by Levin and Beyer, between Mozart's autograph materials and all subsequent contributions to the completion. It is unsurprising that he did not attempt his own versions of the Sanctus and Benedictus given that he did not intend to present the work for liturgical purposes, and that he is of the view that Mozart made no contribution to these movements. His attempted demolition of Süssmayr, then, understandably comes with an attempt only at partial reconstruction.[17]

Unlike Beyer and Levin, Maunder details on a bar-by-bar basis his re-orchestration of the Dies irae, Tuba mirum, Rex tremendae, Recordare,

---

[15] Ibid.

[16] Other than the a♭″ in the soprano in bar 108 Beyer's doubling is exact; Süssmayr, in contrast, gives minims rather than dotted crotchets in bars 106 and 108.

[17] The recording of Maunder's Requiem completion by Christopher Hogwood (Decca, 1990, 4117122) does not include the Sanctus or the Benedictus; the score gives these movements in an appendix, titled 'Two Movements by F. X. Süssmayr (1766–1803)'; Mozart, *Requiem*, ed. Maunder, pp. 198–222.

Confutatis, Domine Jesu and Hostias, and of the opening of the Lacrymosa. His 'appropriate models'[18] come primarily from Mozart's operas written just before the Requiem, *La clemenza di Tito* and *Die Zauberflöte*. *Werktreue* thus manifests itself here as faithfulness to Mozart through associations with moments and passages from his earlier compositions. To be sure, the cross-pollination of musical ideas, procedures and styles among different genres was a practical reality for Mozart throughout his career; it is also possible that Süssmayr drew some inspiration from *Tito* and *Zauberflöte* when completing the Requiem (see Chapter 5). But Maunder's repeated, protracted use of Mozart's operatic numbers for modelling purposes is problematic on aesthetic grounds. Even if we agree with his questionable claim that the Dies irae and Tuba mirum are 'two movements that might almost have come from *Die Zauberflöte* or *La clemenza di Tito*'[19] we cannot safely predict that Mozart would have considered orchestrating them in similar ways when the contexts of a single movement in a requiem mass and an individual number in a developing operatic plot (in distinct singspiel and opera seria genres as well) are so different.[20] Mozart was concerned to align his Requiem with earlier death music, as we know. For this reason, had he been inclined to look beyond his own work on the Requiem in returning to complete the work, we can speculate that he is at least as likely to have drawn on such death music for general inspiration in the orchestration process as on his own works in different genres.

Maunder's privileging of the technical aspects of Mozartian orchestration over the aesthetic aspects is not unreasonable when his self-appointed task is to re-orchestrate the Requiem Kyrie, Sequence and Offertory in effect from scratch. But it creates musical problems as well, for instance at the opening of the Tuba mirum (see Example 6.2). Maunder explains his editorial decisions:

Bars 1–4. The first two bars should obviously remain unaccompanied, but the bare fifth between bass and trombone in the second half of bar 3 shows that one should beware of jumping to the same conclusion about bars 3–4. Since Mozart wrote rests in the instrumental bass part here, any filling-in must be done by woodwind: but what could be a more fitting accompaniment to Sarastro-in-disguise than sustained chords on (dovetailed) basset-horns and bassoons? It is as well, too, to introduce this characteristic sound as soon as possible, in preparation for what is wanted in bars 10–18 ...

---

[18] Maunder, *Mozart's Requiem*, p. 132.   [19] Ibid., p. 151.

[20] Levin argues similarly that 'the rhetoric and expression of Mozart's sacred music is of a completely different essence' from that of Mozart's operas. For his own completion Levin explains: 'the sound of a church work – and particularly a mass for the dead – could not be taken from a comic German opera (even given its serious sections) or from an *opera seria*'. See Mozart, *Requiem*, ed. Levin, p. xxii.

Example 6.2   Maunder's completion of Mozart's Requiem, Tuba mirum, bars 1–15

Bars 8–10 . . . It is appropriate to bring back the woodwind at the bass entry in bar 9 so as to be ready for bars 11–14.

Bars 11–13 . . . It is clear from the trombone part that the harmony changes in the middle of each bar, and this must be made explicit in the accompaniment, by continuing the Sarastro-like woodwind . . .

Bars 14–15. The word 'omnes' implies a full chord on the first beat of bar 14, and hence (unlike bars 45, 51, and 57) nothing on the second and fourth beats . . .[21]

The addition of woodwinds in bars 3–4 is thus explained on apparently technical grounds and in relation to Mozart's possible intentions, and the setting of 'omnes' by a desire to word-paint; interpolations in between are justified with reference to these events. But decisions in both bars 3–4 and 14–15 are questionable: there is nothing intrinsically wrong with an open fifth in bar 3, and nothing to suggest that Mozart wanted to emphasize 'omnes'. Indeed, had Mozart intended word-painting he might reasonably have been expected to include his solo trombone at 'omnes' on the first two beats of bar 14, when bar 14 is in fact the only complete bar from which the trombone is absent between bars 5 and the end of its solo in bar 18, beat 1. Whether a 'characteristic sound' (in this case, bassethorns and bassoons) is best predicted or left until making the desired impact is a judgment call, as mentioned in Chapter 5 for Süssmayr's orchestration of the opening of the Rex tremendae. Either way, the initial appearance in bars 3–5 is unnecessarily coarse in my view, plodding along with the bass's descending arpeggio in bar 4 (with added strokes for accentuation) and unwittingly masking the simple power of Mozart's opening imitation from trombone to bass. Irrespective of whether Maunder is right to use *Die Zauberflöte* as his model ('Sarastro-in-disguise'), this moment relates to Sarastro's music only superficially: the bassethorns and bassoon comprise part of Sarastro's instrumental sound-world in 'O Isis und Osiris' but not elsewhere; and the note repetition in the operatic number, creating phrase links and snippets of imitation between orchestra and voices, is unimaginatively schematic in Maunder's new context.[22] Maunder's insertion is not incorrect technically, of course. But however well justified it is in relation to subsequent additions

---

[21] Maunder, *Mozart's Requiem*, pp. 142–3.

[22] Maunder recognizes that parallels between 'O Isis und Osiris' and the Tuba mirum 'might seem rather incongruous'. His argument for a link between them is tenuous. It relies on the fact that the text of the opening recitative of Mozart's German cantata *Die ihr des unermesslichen Weltalls Schöpfer ehrt*, K. 619, draws attention to the 'Worte aus der Posaune des Allherschers'. The pacifistic, pantheistic text is not by Mozart, but by Franz Ziegenhagen; Maunder can therefore cite only the 'sincerity' with which Mozart set the words – for voice and keyboard, not voice and orchestra – as support for a connection between 'O Isis und Osiris' and Tuba mirum. See Maunder, *Mozart's Requiem*, p. 141.

or associations with Mozart's earlier music, it strikes me as aesthetically unappealing and unrepresentative of Mozart's orchestration elsewhere in the Requiem.

Maunder's reliance on Mozart's existing music for inspiration at specific moments reaches a logical conclusion in his completion of the Lacrymosa, where he draws on Mozart's earlier material in the Requiem. Rejecting Süssmayr's Lacrymosa completion from bar 9, he re-composes the movement from where Mozart left off. A technically competent completion, it nonetheless sounds exactly as he describes it in his book, namely as a composite of many different (adapted) Mozartian moments, with no overarching vision – Mozartian or otherwise – to support or to transcend the collections of moments, aside from a desire to prepare for the 'Amen' fugue. Internal musical evidence suggests that Mozart may have wanted to tie thematic material together in his Requiem by re-calibrating the main Requiem theme from the Introit in various ways in later movements.[23] But Mozart's approach is subtle rather than blunt and ostentatious: we cannot be sure that the thematic correspondences we detect match his intention in every case. Maunder's bars 10–11 combine the Introit's bars 19–20 and the Lacrymosa's bar 3, his bars 11–12 and 20ff. draw on bars 27–9 and 46–8 from the Introit, and bars 18–20 on bars 38–40 from the Dies irae. His Lacrymosa completion thus comprises a self-conscious collage of Requiem-related sounds that is unconvincing (to me at least) as a result. And there is no reason to suppose that Mozart intended the end of the Lacrymosa to fulfil such a function. In contrast, Maunder, like Levin, handles the 'Amen' fugue well, working towards a rousing climax in the final eleven bars, with the registral peak in the voices (soprano b♭″, bar 70, beat 1), the only protracted use of the trumpets and drums in the fugue with a timpani roll at the end, and pronounced dotted minims for voices and wind, brass and string instruments.[24]

Conclusion

Collectively, modern-day Requiem completions cut a strange figure. They are different in orientation, in content, in the degree to which Süssmayr's

---

[23] For a representative list of such correspondences see Mozart, *Requiem*, ed. Levin, pp. xvii–xix.

[24] Maunder and Levin's opinions differ on a basic feature of the fugue, namely whether it should modulate. As Levin points out (*Requiem*, ed. Levin, p. xx): '[Maunder] has completed the *Amen* fugue, but his version contains modulations. 18th century *Amen* fugues remain in the same key, thereby providing a stable conclusion not just to the movement (*Lacrimosa*), but to the entire section (the SEQUENCE).'

contributions are revised and in the views expressed by their editors about the quality of Süssmayr's work.[25] Purportedly objective and universal assumptions about musical rights and wrongs, favoured by Maunder and Levin (see Chapter 2), are thus illusory and problematic. In pursuing Mozart's intentions to such varied ends, they collectively and unwittingly illustrate just how difficult it is to pin them down.

There is much in our assessment of Requiem completions that resonates with assessments of performance 'authenticity' in the late twentieth century. Maunder certainly foregrounds the link by claiming that 'the aim of "authenticity" is … to recreate the composer's own mental image of his work', thereby aligning goals for authentic performance with his own goals for re-composition and reconstruction.[26] When the completions are evaluated together we can parse their status as modernist constructs positively, as some critics have parsed the musical products of the authenticity movement;[27] they are, after all, important landmarks in the late twentieth-century reception of the Requiem, which encourage us to think afresh about Mozart's achievement and issues of authorial intent.

In demonstrating precisely what their editors intended *not* to demonstrate, namely that Mozart's intentions for the unrealized portions of the Requiem are often unclear, modern completions provide a salutary reminder that the performed Requiem can never be about Mozart alone. The completers may want to revise, or marginalize or excise Süssmayr, but his presence looms large – in the score and our expectations about its practical realization, and in our historical imagination. The recent up-turn in the scholarly fortunes of Süssmayr's completion, in part a reaction to the proliferation of new completions, has been modest, since praise (or appreciation of Süssmayr's work as a historical document) is tempered by criticism, even insult.[28] But Süssmayr's

---

[25] In the recent colloquy, Druce states that Süssmayr 'generally avoids obvious errors' in part-writing, but Maunder and Levin clearly do not concur. See Levin et al., 'Colloquy: Finishing Mozart's Requiem' (quotation at p. 595).

[26] Maunder, *Mozart's Requiem*, p. 198. For a useful, extended summary of twentieth-century perspectives on historically informed performance, see John Butt, *Playing with History* (Cambridge, 2002), pp. 3–50.

[27] See in particular Richard Taruskin, *Text and Act: Essays on Musical Performance* (Oxford, 1995).

[28] See Bin Ebisawa, 'The Requiem: Mirror of Mozart Performance History', *Early Music*, 20 (1991), pp. 279–94, at 289; Wolff, *Mozart's Requiem*, p. 28; Robert Gutman, *Mozart: A Cultural Biography* (New York, 1999), p. 754. Even Bauman's valuable essay – framed more as a response to Richard Maunder's edition and its implications than as a defence of Süssmayr's completion *per se* – does not entirely avoid criticism; see 'Requiem, but no Piece', p. 152. Bauman provides a shorter critique of Maunder's edition in 'On Completing the Requiem'. Piero Melograni speculates with absolutely no justification that Mozart, Constanze and the completers ended up 'confecting a substantially false product … precisely the aim of Walsegg's commission'. He

work on the Requiem has successfully survived the revision process in the scholarly world as well as in the concert hall, with modern completions – though motivated by dissatisfaction with Süssmayr – even inadvertently accentuating his achievement.[29]

We may not have seen the end yet of new completions of, and supplements to, Mozart's Requiem. An event at Canterbury Cathedral conducted by Nicholas Cleobury on 5 December 2006 as part of 'Mozart Now' featured additions to the work by eight contemporary composers including Dominic Muldowney and Philip Wilby; a concert at the 'Dialoge' festival conducted by Ivor Bolton on 4 December 2005 at the Internationale Stiftung Mozarteum in Salzburg included seven 'Klangräume' (sound spaces) by the contemporary composer Georg Friedrich Haas performed after the Dies irae, Tuba mirum, Rex tremendae, Recordare, Lacrymosa, Domine Jesu and Hostias, followed by a rendition of the Sanctus, Benedictus, Agnus Dei and Communio; and a concert in Southampton on 20 November 2011 featured a new version by the composer Michael Finnissy, who imagined Mozart completing the work in the present day. Other unfinished Mozart fragments and incomplete works continue to be finished as well. It will be self-evident that I echo Stanley Sadie's 'preference for a version [of the Requiem] that originates in the Mozart circle in Vienna, and sounds like it, over one that originates in the late twentieth century [Maunder's], and sounds like it'.[30] But in my view it is neither disrespectful nor contentious to suggest that the cottage industry of modern Requiem completions carry the imprint of the era in which they were carried out, bearing eloquent witness not only to modernist aesthetics of improvement and progress, but also to our often complex relationship with achievements of the past. If further completions do in fact materialize, no doubt they too will feed our collective fascination with this extraordinarily compelling work.

---

explains: 'because the composer of the Requiem was supposed to be a dilettante [namely Walsegg], it would have to be written amateurishly lest any listener with a finely tuned ear sense the deception. In other words, Mozart was obliged to hold back, to avoid any strokes of genius, hence to work against his instincts … Mozart's pupils were more suited [to the Requiem task] than their master.' See Melograni, *Wolfgang Amadeus Mozart: A Biography*, trans. Lydia G. Cochrane (Chicago, 2007), pp. 243–4.

[29] See Paul Moseley, agreeing with Erik Smith's comments on Maunder's Lacrymosa completion in comparison to Süssmayr's, in 'Review of Mozart, Wolfgang Amadeus, *Requiem*, K.626, ed. Franz Beyer and *Requiem*, K.626, ed. Richard Maunder', *Music & Letters*, 70 (1989), pp. 588–90, at 589.

[30] Stanley Sadie, 'Communications', *Notes*, 47 (1990), p. 587.

Epilogue: a Requiem for the future

To end, let us return to the beginning of the work (bars 1–8 of the Introit), which, for atmosphere and drama, is surely among the greatest openings in the entire classical repertoire. It is a historical musicologist's dream, self-conscious nods to earlier works and traditions brilliantly re-imagined – and with rhetorical panache – in a new context. Our sense of anticipation for the riches to come is engendered not only by the music we hear but also by the legend of colliding music and biography that we know. To a degree unmatched by almost any other work by any other composer, the Requiem allows us to live actively with its legacy and reception as we listen to it. Mozart stands on the precipice, contemplating his 'leap in the dark', in the supposed last words of the seventeenth-century philosopher Thomas Hobbes,[1] and is propelled to extraordinary artistic heights (or so the legend goes). Just as he, a composer with time ebbing away, seizes a unique compositional opportunity, so we, as scholars with a limited shelf-life, can seize a unique interpretational opportunity, joining Mozart on the precipice.

The Requiem has served us well, offering up a potent cocktail of mystery, mastery, intrigue and beautiful music, but as a community of scholars we have not yet served the Requiem well. Preoccupied with ultimately insoluble concerns about authorship and with refining small matters of historical 'fact', we have been blinded to – perhaps fearful of – the hermeneutic potential unlocked by the work's extraordinary circumstances and compositional history. High-profile critical controversies through the ages – the *Requiem-Streit* of the 1820s and 1830s, Einstein and Blume one hundred or so years later, the lengthy colloquy 'Finishing Mozart's Requiem' in the *Journal of the American Musicological Society* in 2008 – have entrenched existing scholarly views and attitudes more than giving voice to new, imaginative ones. This is perhaps an inevitable result of our collective perception that big biographical, historical, philological, stylistic and aesthetic issues are at stake. But controversies and small-minded concerns have in effect imprisoned the Requiem in an interpretative vortex where scholarship is concerned, stunting hermeneutic growth and deadening our collective critical imagination.

[1] See Eisen, 'Mozart's Leap in the Dark'.

As Requiem scholars inspired by the music, the legend (in its unelaborated or elaborated state) or both, we share important common ground: passion for the work as a whole, or in part; and intense commitment to trying better to understand it. Interpretative passion is abundant in descriptions of nineteenth-century performances, in twentieth-century recordings, in retellings of the legend and in fiction and in films, but conspicuous by its absence as an organic rather than cosmetic component of scholarly discourse. Confronted by a panoply of remarkable sounds and events – the final note of the Dies irae, the breaking-off of the Lacrymosa at bar 8, the violin explosion in the Domine Jesu – we must not recoil from bold interpretation in the face of so much that is unknown, even if semantic uncertainty is a fundamental feature of Mozart's score. Mozart's Requiem provides material for exciting interaction between 'old' and 'new' musicological perspectives. Not only are the well-preserved original sources crucial to the work's ontology – with philology centre stage as a catalyst for interpretation – but so also are the confluence and inseparability of fact and fiction in the work's reception, fiction thus constituting an intellectually legitimate stimulus for scholarly interpretation. We can move seamlessly from one set of scholarly apparatus to another where the Requiem is concerned, varying our viewpoints by remaining as open to inspiration from popular sources as to that from traditional scholarly ones. The Requiem is, and will always remain, controversial. Whether we focus future discussion on (for example) the intensity of reactions to the work, the sounds Mozart and others created, the extraordinary nature of the autograph materials as affecting our understandings of the work or the importance placed on the work by Mozartians, eighteenth-century scholars, musicians and general audiences alike, we will provoke argument and debate. And we will also take the Requiem beyond its traditionally narrow discursive confines, clearing away the finicky authorship-related trees for an unobstructed view of the rich hermeneutic wood.

Mozart's end, then, can be our (new) beginning. With a bleak outlook for our planet, and death always with us, we will continue to need Mozart's Requiem as a source of consolation and hope, whether we are devoutly religious, confusedly agnostic or (like me) firmly atheistic. But we need the Requiem as an inspiration for musicological scholarship too – for Mozart studies, and beyond. As we look to the horizon with the Requiem ringing in our ears, anything seems possible. The redemptive power of the music, and of writing about it, tells us that, just maybe, the best is yet to come.

Appendix: original text of Franz Xaver Süssmayr's letter to Breitkopf & Härtel (1800)

Meine Herren!

Ihre gütige Zuschrift vom 24ᵗ Jenner hat mir das grösste Vergnügen gemacht, da ich aus derselben ersehen habe, dass Ihnen an der Achtung des deutschen Publikums zu viel gelegen ist, als dass Sie dasselbe durch Werke irre führen sollten, die nicht ganz auf die Rechnung meines verstorbenen Freundes Mozart gehören. Ich habe den Lehren dieses grossen Mannes zu viel zu danken, als dass ich stillschweigend erlauben könnte, dass ein Werk, dessen grösster Theil meine Arbeit ist, für das seinige ausgegeben wird, weil ich fest überzeugt bin, dass meine Arbeit dieses grossen Namens ünwürdig ist. Mozarts Composition is so einzig, und ich getraue mir zu behaupten, für den grössten Theil der lebenden Tonsetzer so unreichbar, dass jeder Nachahmer besonders mit untergeschobener Arbeit noch schlimmer wegkommen würde, als jener Rabe, der sich mit Pfauern-Federn schmückte.

Dass die Endigung des Requiem-s, welches unseren Brief-Wechsel veranlasste, mir anvertraut wurde, kam auf folgende Weise. Die Wittwe Mozart konnte wohl voraussehen, dass die hinterlassenen Werke ihres Mannes würden gesucht werden; der Tod überraschte ihn, während er an diesem Requiem arbeitete. Die Endigung dieses Werkes wurde also mehreren Meistern übertragen; einige davon konnten wegen gehäuften Geschäften sich dieser Arbeit nicht unterziehen, andere aber wollten ihr Talent nicht mit dem Talente Mozarts compromittiren. Endlich kam dieses Geschäft an mich, weil man wusste, dass ich noch bey Lebzeiten Mozarts die schon in Musik gesetzten Stücke öfters mit ihm durchgespielt, und gesungen, dass er sich mit mir über die Ausarbeitung dieses Werkes sehr oft besprochen, und mit mir den Gang und die Gründe seiner Instrumentirung mitgetheilt hatte. Ich kann nur wünschen, dass es mir geglückt haben möge, wenigstens so gearbeitet zu haben, dass Kenner noch hin und wieder einige Spuren seiner unvergesslichen Lehren darinn finden können.

Zu dem Requiem samt Kyrie. – Dies irae. – Domine Jesu Christe. – hat Mozart die 4 Singstimmen, und den Grund-Bass samt der Bezifferung ganz vollendet; zu der Unstrumentirung aber nur hin

"

und wieder das Motivum angezeigt. Im Dies irae war sein letzter Vers –
qua resurget ex favilla – und seine Arbeit war die nemliche, wie in den
ersten Stücken. Von dem Verse an – Judicandus homo reus etc: hab ich
das Dies irae ganz geendigt. Das Sanctus – Benedictus – und Agnus
Dei – ist ganz neu von mir verfertigt; nur hab ich mir erlaubt, um dem
Werke mehr Einförmigkeit zu geben, die Fuge des Kyrie, bei dem
Verse – cum Sanctis etc. zu wiederhohlen.

Es soll mir herzlich lieb seyn, wenn ich Ihnen durch diese
Mittheilung einen kleinen Dienst habe leisten können. Ich würde
mich auch mit Vergnügen Ihrer anderen Comission 'das Verzeichnis
der grössten lebenden Tonsetzer und ihrer Werke betreffend' entledi-
gen, wenn mich nicht meine täglichen Theater Geschäfte, und die
damit verbundenen Arbeiten daran verhinderten.

Es ist schmeichelhaft für mich, dass sie zu wissen wünschen, welche
von meinen Arbeiten öffentlich bekannt geworden sind.

Moses, oder Der Auszug aus Egypten. Ein dramatisches Oratorium in
2 Aufzügen, *L'incanto superato*, und *Il Muselmano in Napoli*. Zwei
italiänische Opern in zwey Aufzügen.

Der Spiegel von Arkadien, oder Die neuen Arkadier, eine deutsche
Oper in 2 Aufzügen

Die edle Rache. Oper in 2 Aufzügen

Der Vetter in Gefahr, eine Cantate.

Die freywilligen, ein GelegenheitsStück in einem Aufzuge

Der Wildfang. Oper in 2 Aufzügen.

Der Marktschreier. Oper in einem Aufzuge.

Die 3 Sultanninen, oder Soliman der zweyte, Oper in 2 Aufzügen.

Hier haben Sie das ganze Verzeichnis; schenken Sie dem Verfasser
Ihr ferneres gütiges Andenken, und seyen Sie seiner ganzen
Hochachtung versichert.

Wien den 8 Febr: 1800

Ihr   ergebenster Diener
Franz Xaver Süssmayr m.p.
k: k: Hof-theatral Kapellmeister

Select bibliography

Abert, Hermann. *W. A. Mozart* (1919). Trans. Stewart Spencer, ed. Cliff Eisen. New Haven, CT, 2007

Allgemeine musikalische Zeitung. Ed. Friedrich Rochlitz et al. Leipzig, 1798–1848

Anderson, Emily (ed. and trans.). *The Letters of Mozart and his Family.* 3rd edn, London, 1985

Arnold, Ignaz. *Mozarts Geist: Seine kurze Biographie und ästetische Darstellung seiner Werke.* Erfurt, 1803

Ashley, John. *The Requiem, or, Grand Funeral Anthem Composed by W. A. Mozart . . . as Performed under the Direction of Mr. John Ashley at the Theatre Royal, Covent Garden, during Lent 1801.* London, 1801

Bauer, Wilhelm A., Otto Erich Deutsch and Joseph Heinz Eibl (eds). *Mozart: Briefe und Aufzeichnungen, Gesamtausgabe.* 8 vols. Kassel and New York, 1962–2005

Bauman, Thomas. 'On Completing the Requiem'. *Mozart-Jahrbuch 1991*, pp. 494–8
'Requiem, but no Piece'. *19th Century Music*, 25 (1991), pp. 151–61

Biancolli, Louis (ed.). *The Mozart Handbook.* New York, 1954

Black, David Ian. 'Mozart and the Practice of Sacred Music, 1781–1791'. Ph.D. thesis, Harvard University, 2007

Blom, Eric. *Mozart* (1935). New York, 1966

Blume, Friedrich. 'Requiem, but no Peace'. In Paul Henry Lang (ed.), *The Creative World of Mozart.* New York, 1963, pp. 103–26

Brauneis, Walther, '"Dies Irae, Dies Illa" – "Tag des Zornes, Tag der Klage": Auftrag, Entstehung und Vollendung von Mozarts "Requiem"'. *Jahrbuch des Vereins für Geschichte der Stadt Wien*, 47–8 (1991–2), pp. 33–48
'Exequien für Mozart: Archivfund über das Seelenamt für W. A. Mozart am 10. Dezember 1791 in der Wiener Michaelerkirche'. *Singende Kirche*, 38/1 (1991), pp. 8–11
'". . . wegen schuldigen 1435 f 32 xr": Neuer Archivfund zur Finanzmisere Mozarts im November 1791'. *Mitteilungen der Internationalen Stiftung Mozarteum*, 39 (1991), pp. 159–63

Breuning, Gerhard von. *Memories of Beethoven.* Ed. Maynard Solomon, trans. Solomon and Henry Mins. Cambridge, 1992

Brophy, Brigid. *Mozart the Dramatist.* London and New York, 1964

Brown, Clive. *Classical and Romantic Performing Practice, 1750–1900.* Oxford, 1999

Butt, John. *Playing with History.* Cambridge, 2002

Charlton, David (ed.). *E. T. A. Hoffmann's Musical Writings: 'Kreisleriana', 'The Poet and the Composer', Music Criticism*. Trans. Martyn Clarke. Cambridge, 1989

Churgin, Bathia. 'Beethoven and Mozart's Requiem: A New Connection'. *Journal of Musicology*, 5 (1987), pp. 457–77

Clarke, Bruce Cooper. 'From Little Seeds'. *The Musical Times*, 137 (December 1996), pp. 13–17

Correspondance des amateurs musiciens rédigée par le citoyen Cocatrix suivie de la Correspondance des professeurs et amateurs de musique (1802–5). Reprint Geneva, 1972

Cowgill, Rachel. '"Hence Base Intruder Hence": Rejection and Assimilation in the Early English Reception of Mozart's Requiem'. In Cowgill and Julian Rushton (eds.), *Europe, Empire and Spectacle in Nineteenth-Century British Music*. Aldershot, 2006, pp. 9–27

'Redeeming the Requiem: Themes in the Early English Reception of Mozart's Last Work'. Unpublished paper given at the Institute of Musical Research, London, 17 May 2007

Davenport, Marcia. *Mozart*. New York, 1932

Davison, Alan. 'Painting for a Requiem: Mihály Munkácsy's *The Last Moments of Mozart* (1885)'. *Early Music*, 39 (2011), pp. 79–92

Deutsch, Otto Erich. *Mozart: Die Dokumente seines Lebens*. Kassel, 1961. Trans. Eric Blom, Peter Branscombe and Jeremy Noble as *Mozart: A Documentary Biography*. 3rd edn, London, 1990

Duda, Erich. *Das musikalische Werk Franz Xaver Süssmayrs: Thematisches Werkverzeichnis (SmWV)*. Kassel, 2000

Ebisawa, Bin. 'The Requiem: Mirror of Mozart Performance History'. *Early Music*, 20 (1991), pp. 279–94

Eibl, Joseph. 'Süssmayrs "Requiem"-Brief vom 8. Februar 1800'. *Mitteilungen der Internationalen Stiftung Mozarteum*, 24/1–2 (1976), pp. 21–3

Einstein, Alfred. *Mozart: His Character, his Work*. Trans. Arthur Mendel and Nathan Broder. Oxford, 1945

Eisen, Cliff. 'Mozart's Leap in the Dark'. In Simon P. Keefe (ed.), *Mozart Studies*. Cambridge, 2006, pp. 1–24

New Mozart Documents: A Supplement to O. E. Deutsch's Documentary Biography. London and Stanford, 1991

Fétis, François-Joseph. 'Sur l'authenticité du Requiem de Mozart'. *Revue musicale*, 1 (February 1827), pp. 25–30

Gärtner, Heinz. *Mozarts Requiem und die Geschäfte der Constanze Mozart*. Munich, 1986. Trans. Reinhard G. Pauly as *Constanze Mozart: After the Requiem*. Portland, OR, 1991

Geiringer, Karl. 'The Church Music'. In H. C. Robbins Landon and Donald Mitchell (eds.), *The Mozart Companion*. London, 1956, pp. 361–76

Gerber, Ernst Ludwig, *Historisch-biographisches Lexicon der Tonkünstler*. 2 vols. Leipzig, 1790, 1792

Neues historisch-biographisches Lexicon der Tonkünstler. 4 vols. Leipzig, 1812–14

Ghéon, Henri. *In Search of Mozart* (1932). Trans. Alexander Pru. London, 1934

Gruber, Gernot. *Mozart and Posterity.* Trans. R. S. Furness. London, 1991

Hahn, Albert. *Mozart's Requiem. Zum besseren Verständniss bei Aufführungen mit einer neuen Uebersetzung nebst einem Nachtrage und den Resultaten eines Vergleiches der Breitkopf und Härtelschen Partitur mit den Original-Manuscripten der K. K. Hofbibliothek zu Wien.* Bielefeld, 1867

Halliwell, Ruth. *The Mozart Family: Four Lives in a Social Context.* Oxford, 1998

Handke, Robert. 'Zur Lösung der Benedictusfrage in Mozarts Requiem'. *Zeitschrift für Musikwissenschaft*, 1 (1918), pp. 108–30

Hausner, Henry. *Franz Xaver Süssmayr.* Vienna, 1964

Hazard, Dorothy (ed.). *The Poetical Works of Mrs Felicia Hemans, Complete in One Volume.* Philadelphia, 1836

Heartz, Daniel. *Mozart, Haydn and Early Beethoven, 1781–1802.* New York and London, 2009

Herrmann, Hildegard. *Thematisches Verzeichnis der Werke von Joseph Eybler.* Munich and Salzburg, 1976

Holmes, Edward. *The Life of Mozart, Including his Correspondence* (1845). Ed. Christopher Hogwood. London, 1991

  A Ramble among the Musicians of Germany. London, 1828

Hutchings, Arthur. *Mozart: The Man, the Musician.* London, 1976

Jahn, Otto. *Life of Mozart* (1856). Trans. Pauline Townsend. 3 vols. London, 1891

Keefe, Simon P. 'Beyond Fact and Fiction, Scholarly and Popular: Peter Shaffer and Milos Forman's *Amadeus* at 25'. *The Musical Times*, 150 (Spring 2009), pp. 45–53

  '"Die Ochsen am Berge": Franz Xaver Süssmayr and the Orchestration of Mozart's Requiem, K. 626'. *Journal of the American Musicological Society*, 61 (2008), pp. 1–65

  '"Greatest Effects with the Least Effort": Strategies of Wind Writing in Mozart's Viennese Piano Concertos'. In Keefe (ed.), *Mozart Studies.* Cambridge, 2006, pp. 25–46

  'Harmonies and Effects: Haydn and Mozart in Parallel'. In Julian Horton (ed.), *The Cambridge Companion to the Symphony.* Cambridge, forthcoming

  Mozart's Piano Concertos: Dramatic Dialogue in the Age of Enlightenment. Woodbridge and Rochester, NY, 2001

  Mozart's Viennese Instrumental Music: A Study of Stylistic Re-Invention. Woodbridge and Rochester, NY, 2007

  '"We hardly knew what we should pay attention to first": Mozart the Performer-Composer at Work on the Viennese Piano Concertos'. *Journal of the Royal Musical Association*, 134 (2009), pp. 185–242

Kirkendale, Warren. 'Ciceronians versus Aristotelians on the Ricercar as Exordium, from Bembo to Bach'. *Journal of the American Musicological Society*, 32 (1979), pp. 1–44

Kolb, Annette. *Mozart* (1937). Trans. Phyllis and Trevor Hewitt. London, 1939

Konrad, Ulrich. 'The Historical Idiom in the Music of Wolfgang Amadé Mozart'. Trans. Thomas Irvine. In Sean Gallagher and Thomas Forrest Kelly (eds.), *The Century of Bach and Mozart: Perspectives on Historiography, Composition, Theory and Performance*. Cambridge, MA, 2008, pp. 253–78

'Sigismund von Neukomm: *Libera me, Domine* D-moll NV 186: Ein Beitrag zur Liturgischen Komplettierung von Wolfgang Amadé Mozarts *Requiem* D-moll KV626'. In Paul Mai (ed.), *Im Dienst der Quellen zur Musik: Festschrift Getraut Haberkamp zum 65. Geburtstag*. Tutzing, 2002, pp. 425–34

Korten, Mattias. *Mozarts Requiem KV626: Ein Fragment wird ergänzt*. Frankfurt, 2000

Kramer, Elizabeth. 'The Idea of Transfiguration in the Early German Reception of Mozart's Requiem'. *Current Musicology*, 81 (2006), pp. 73–107

Küster, Konrad. *Mozart: A Musical Biography*. Trans. Mary Whittall. Oxford, 1996

Landon, H. C. Robbins. *1791: Mozart's Last Year*. London, 1988

Levey, Michael. *The Life and Death of Mozart*. London, 1973

Levin, Robert, Richard Maunder, Duncan Druce, David Black, Christoph Wolff and Simon P. Keefe. 'Colloquy: Finishing Mozart's Requiem. On "'Die Ochsen am Berge': Franz Xaver Süssmayr and the Orchestration of Mozart's Requiem, K. 626" by Simon P. Keefe, Spring 2008'. *Journal of the American Musicological Society*, 61 (2008), pp. 583–608

Liszt, Franz. *Zwei Transcriptionen über Themen aus Mozart's Requiem für Piano*. Leipzig, 1865

Lorenz, Michael. 'Franz Jacob Freystädtler: Neue Forschungsergebnisse zu seinen Spuren im Werk Mozarts'. *Acta mozartiana*, 44 (1997), pp. 85–108

'Freystädtler's Supposed Copying in the Autograph of K. 626: A Case of Mistaken Identity'. Paper presented at the conference 'Mozart's Choral Music: Composition, Contexts, Performance', Bloomington, IN, 12 February 2006

Macfarren, G. A. *Requiem; Service for the Dead, the Music Composed in the Year 1791, by Wolfgang Amadeus Mozart, with an Analysis of the Work Written Expressly for the Sacred Harmonic Society*. London, 1857

Marx, Adolph Bernhard. 'Ueber Mozarts Requiem'. *Berliner Allgemeine musikalische Zeitung*, 2 (1825), pp. 378–82

Maunder, Richard. *Mozart's Requiem: On Preparing a New Edition*. Oxford, 1988

'Süssmayr's Work in Mozart's Requiem: A Study of the Autograph Score'. In Manfred Hermann Schmid (ed.), *Mozart-Studien 7* (Tutzing, 1997), pp. 57–80

McVeigh, Simon. *Concert Life in London from Mozart to Haydn*. Cambridge, 1993

Mitchell, Donald. 'The Consciousness of Mortality'. CD liner notes to Mozart, Requiem: Benjamin Britten, Aldeburgh Festival Chorus and English Chamber Orchestra. BBC Legends, 2003, BBCL 4119–2, pp. 6–7

Morrow, Mary Sue. *German Music Criticism in the Late Eighteenth Century: Aesthetic Issues in Instrumental Music*. Cambridge, 1997

Mosel, Ignaz von. *Über die Original-Partitur des Requiem von W. A. Mozart* (Vienna, 1839). Trans. in *The Musical World*, 34 (1856), pp. 292, 309–10, 324–5, 339–40, 356, 389–90

Moseley, Paul. 'Mozart's Requiem: A Re-Evaluation of the Evidence'. *Journal of the Royal Musical Association*, 114 (1989), pp. 203–37

Mozart, Wolfgang Amadeus. *Ave verum corpus: Faksimile nach dem in der Österreichischen Nationalbibliothek in Wien aufbewahrten Autograph*. Vienna, 1956

　　Messe c-moll KV427: Faksimile der autographen Partitur. Kassel, 1983

　　Messe de Requiem par Mozart, executée pour la premiere fois à Paris par le Conservatoire de Musique. Paris, 1805

　　Missa pro Defunctis Requiem. W. A. Mozarts Seelenmesse im Klavierauszuge, mit lateinisch und deutschem Texte. Ed. Johann André. Offenbach, 1801

　　Neue Ausgabe sämtlicher Werke (Neue Mozart-Ausgabe). Kassel, 1955–2007

　　Requiem d-moll/D minor KV 626. Ed. and completed Robert D. Levin (1994). Stuttgart, 2004 (study score)

　　Requiem, for Soprano, Alto, Tenor and Bass Soli, SATB and Orchestra K. 626. Ed. and Completed Duncan Druce. London, 1993

　　Requiem für Soli, Chor, Orchester und Orgel d-moll KV 626. Ed. and completed H. C. Robbins Landon. Wiesbaden, 1991

　　Requiem, K. 626. Ed. and completed Richard Maunder. Oxford, 1988

　　Requiem KV 626, Instrumentation Franz Beyer. Zürich, 1971

　　Requiem KV626. Ed. David Ian Black. Frankfurt, forthcoming

　　Requiem, KV626: Vollständige Faksimile-Ausgabe im Originalformat der Originalhandschrift in zwei Teilen nach Mus. Hs. 17.561 der Musiksammlung der Österreichischen Nationalbibliothek. Ed. Günter Brosche. Kassel, 1990

Neukomm, Sigismund. *Libera me, Domine* (1821). Ed. Luciane Beduschi and Vincent Boyer. Lyons, 2006

Niemetschek, Franz Xaver. *Leben des K. K. Kapellmeisters Wolfgang Amadeus Mozart*. Prague, 1798. Trans. Helen Mautner as *The Life of Mozart*. London, 1956

Nissen, Georg Nikolaus von. *Biographie W. A. Mozarts* (1828). Hildesheim, 1991

Nowak, Leopold. 'Wer hat die Instrumentalstimmen in der Kyrie-Fuge des Requiems von W. A. Mozart geschrieben?' *Mozart-Jahrbuch 1973–4*, pp. 191–201

Oulibicheff, Alexandre. *Nouvelle biographie de Mozart*. 3 vols. Moscow, 1843

Plath, Wolfgang. 'Über Skizzen zu Mozarts Requiem'. In Georg Reichert and Martin Just (eds.), *Bericht über den internationalen musikwissenschaftlichen Kongress Kassel 1962*. Kassel, 1963, pp. 184–7

Pole, William. *The Story of Mozart's Requiem*. London, 1879

Pushkin, Alexander. *Mozart and Salieri* (1830). Trans. James E. Falen. In Svetlana Evdokimova (ed.), *Alexander Pushkin's Little Tragedies: The Poetics of Brevity*. Madison, WI, 2005, pp. 321–9

Rau, Heribert. *Mozart: A Biographical Romance* (1858). Trans. E. R. Still. Boston, 1870

Rice, Albert A. *From the Clarinet d'Amour to the Contra Bass: A History of Large-Size Clarinets, 1740–1860*. Oxford and New York, 2009

Rice, John A. *Empress Marie Therese and Music at the Viennese Court, 1792–1807*. Cambridge, 2003

Rosselli, John. *The Life of Mozart*. Cambridge, 1998

Rushton, Julian. *Mozart*. Oxford and New York, 2006

Saint-Foix, Georges de. *W.-A. Mozart: Sa vie musicale et son oeuvre*, vol. V: *Les dernières années (1789–1791)*. Paris, 1946

Schaden, Adolph von. *Mozarts Tod: Ein Original-Trauerspiel in drei Akten*. Augsburg and Leipzig, 1825

Schlichtegroll, Friedrich. *Johannes Chrysostomus Wolfgang Gottlieb Mozart* (1793). Ed. Erich Hermann Müller von Asow. Leipzig, 1942

Schmid, Manfred Hermann. 'Introitus und Communio im Requiem: Zum Formkonzept von Mozart und Süssmayr'. In Schmid (ed.), *Mozart Studien 7*. Tutzing, 1997, pp. 11–55

'Das "Lacrymosa" in Mozarts Requiem'. In Schmid (ed.), *Mozart Studien 7*. Tutzing, 1997, pp. 115–41

Schubert, Ingrid. 'Eine frühe Abschrift von Mozarts "Requiem" aus dem Besitz des Aloys Weiß – Umfeld und Folgerungen'. In Joachim Brügge (ed.), *Musikgeschichte als Verstehensgeschichte: Festschrift für Gernot Gruber zum 65. Geburtstag*. Tutzing, 2004, pp. 331–46

Schuler, Manfred. 'Mozarts Requiem in der Tradition Gattungsgeschichtlicher Topoi'. In Annegrit Laubenthal (ed.), *Studien zur Musikgeschichte: Eine Festschrift für Ludwig Finscher*. Kassel, 1995, pp. 317–27

Senigl, Johanna. 'Neues zu Joseph Eybler'. In Wolfgang Gratzer and Andrea Lindmayr (eds.), *De editione musices: Festschrift Gerhard Croll zum 65. Geburtstag*. Laaber, 1992, pp. 329–37

Sievers, Georg. *Mozart und Süssmayr*. Mainz, 1829

Sisman, Elaine. *Mozart: The 'Jupiter' Symphony*. Cambridge, 1993

Sitwell, Sacheverell. *Mozart*. Edinburgh, 1932

Solomon, Maynard. 'The Rochlitz Anecdotes: Issues of Authenticity in Early Mozart Biography'. In Cliff Eisen (ed.), *Mozart Studies*. Oxford, 1991, pp. 1–59

Spitzer, John and Neal Zaslaw. *The Birth of the Orchestra: History of an Institution, 1650–1815*. New York, 2004

Stadler, Maximilian. *Nachtrag zur Vertheidigung der Echtheit des Mozart'schen Requiem*. Vienna, 1827

Zweyter und letzter Nachtrag zur Vertheidigung der Echtheit des Mozart'schen Requiem. Vienna, 1827

Stafford, William. *The Mozart Myths: A Critical Reassessment*. Stanford, CA, 1991

'The Story of "The Requiem"'. In E. Litell (compiler), *Littell's Living Age*, 25 (Boston, 1850), pp. 37–44

Süssmayr, Franz Xaver. *Missa solemnis in D*. Ed. Walter Wlcek and Erich Duda. Graz, 2010

Sinfonia: 'Il turco in Italia'. Ed. Maria P. Eckhardt. Budapest, 1982

Sinfonia turchesa in C. Ed. Mary B. B. Inwood. In Barry Brook (editor in chief), *The Symphony 1720–1840*, series B, vol. XIV. New York and London, 1985

Taruskin, Richard. *Text and Act: Essays on Musical Performance*. Oxford, 1995

Triest, Johann Karl Friedrich. 'Remarks on the Development of the Art of Music in Germany in the Eighteenth Century' (1801). Trans. Susan Gillespie. In Elaine Sisman (ed.), *Haydn and his World*. Princeton, 1997, pp. 321–94

Weber, Jacob Gottfried. 'Über die Echtheit des Mozartschen Requiem'. *Cäcilia*, 3 (1825), pp. 205–29

  'Weitere Nachrichten über die Echtheit des Mozartschen Requiem'. *Cäcilia*, 4 (1826), pp. 257–352

Winterberger, Johann. *Franz Xaver Süssmayr: Leben, Umwelt und Gestalt.* Frankfurt, 1999

Wlcek, Walter. *Franz Xaver Süssmayr als Kirchenkomponist.* Tutzing, 1978

Wolanski, Andrzej. 'Mozarts "Lacrimosa" in der Geschichtsperspektive'. *Mozart-Jahrbuch 1991*, pp. 468–74

Wolff, Christoph. *Mozart's Requiem: Historical and Analytical Studies, Documents, Score.* Trans. Mary Whittall. Berkeley, CA, 1994

Zaslaw, Neal (ed.). *Der neue Köchel.* Wiesbaden, forthcoming

Abert, Hermann 47–8, 69–70
Adlgasser, Anton Cajetan 4, 5
Albrechtsberger, Johann Georg 4, 213
Allen, Woody 213
Allgemeine musikalische Zeitung 7, 12, 15, 17,
    44, 47, 48, 230
Amadeus 38–40, 72, 81, 169
André, Johann Anton 56, 57, 64
    editions of Mozart's Requiem 52–3, 54–5, 64,
    83–5
Arnold, Ignaz 49, 112–15, 120, 142, 147, 156,
    160, 165, 168, 169, 185, 200, 206, 222
Ashley, John 48, 84
Ayrton, William 53

Bach, Johann Sebastian 78
    Mass in B minor 67
Barenboim, Daniel
    recording of Mozart's Requiem 93–4
Bartók, Béla 6
Bauman, Thomas 77, 109
Becker, Carl Ferdinand 55
Beethoven, Ludwig van 5, 31, 37, 38
    Missa solemnis 67
    Mozart Requiem performance at his
    memorial 86, 87, 90
Bellini, Vincenzo 61
Berger, Ludwig 86
Berlioz, Hector 5, 86, 92
    Grande messe des morts 5
Bernstein, Leonard
    recording of Mozart's Requiem 97, 102, 103,
    104, 105
Beyer, Franz
    completion of Mozart's Requiem 96, 101,
    102, 103, 104, 234, 235, 239–40
    on Süssmayr's work on Mozart's Requiem
    75–6
Black, David 172
Blasis, Virginia 86
Blom, Eric 69, 70, 71, 72, 75
Blume, Friedrich 75, 79, 247
Bolton, Ivor 246

Bonno, Giuseppe 4, 5
Boughton, Rutland 68
Brahms, Johannes 83, 84
Brauneis, Walther 1
Breitkopf & Härtel 3, 12, 18, 23, 45, 46, 79, 82,
    83, 84, 113, 173, 174, 176, 177, 178,
    180, 249
Breuning, Gerhard von 87
Brissler, Friedrich Ferdinand 85
Britten, Benjamin 6
    performance and recording of Mozart's
    Requiem at Aldeburgh 81, 94, 99,
    101, 103
    War Requiem 6
Brophy, Brigid 72–3
Burgos, Rafael Frühbeck de 94
Busby, Thomas 19

Cebotari, Maria 93
Cherubini, Luigi 12, 46
Christie, John 93
Chopin, Fryderyk
    Mozart Requiem performance at his funeral
    86, 90
Choron, Alexandre-Étienne 86
Clarke, Bruce Cooper 15
Cleobury, Nicholas 246
Closset, Dr Thomas 32
Cole, Hugo 99
Comelin, Jean-Paul 41
Correspondance des amateurs musiciens 46–7
Czerny, Carl 85

Davenport, Marcia 35–6, 66
Dawes, Rufus
    'Mozart's Requiem' (poem) 24, 25
Delfs, Andreas 105
Der Baierische Landbot 14
De Sabata, Victor
    recording of Mozart's Requiem 96, 97, 98
Donizetti, Gaetano 61
Druce, Duncan
    completion of Mozart's Requiem 213, 234, 235

Duhan, Hans
    Mozart (opera) 36
Dupont, Alexis 90
Dussek, Jan Ladislav 86

Eberlin, Johann Ernst 4, 5
Edge, Dexter 2
Einstein, Alfred 69, 70–1, 72, 79, 247
Eschenbach, Christoph 94
Eybler, Joseph 56, 57
    contributions to Mozart Requiem
        completion 2, 3, 10, 73, 81, 107, 109,
        110, 147, 154, 170, 171, 172–3, 174,
        179–80, 232, 234, 239
        orchestration of Confutatis 195–9
        orchestration of Dies irae 180–1, 195
        orchestration of Recordare 192–3,
        239–40
        orchestration of Rex tremendae 188–9
        orchestration of Tuba mirum 181–5
    Missa Sancti Hermani 173
    Requiem in C minor 173

Fasch, Carl 86
Fellini, Federico 93
Fétis, François-Joseph 54, 57, 64
Feuillade, Louis
    La mort de Mozart 36–7, 38
Fischer, Johann Martin 1
Forman, Milos 38–40, 81
Freystädler, Franz Jacob 107–8, 172
Fux, Johann Joseph 5

Gardiner, John Eliot
    recording of Mozart's Requiem 94, 101, 102,
        103, 105
Garnett, Catherine Grace
    'On the Sister of Körner, the German Poet'
        (poem) 25
Gassmann, Florian
    Requiem in C minor 4, 5, 118–20
Gat, Emanuel 41
Genet, Jean 41
Gerber, Ernst Ludwig 64
    *Neues historisch-biographisches Lexicon der
        Tonkünstler* 50
Gerl, Franz Xaver 27
Ghéon, Henri 66, 69
Giulini, Carlo Maria
    recording of Mozart's Requiem 99–100, 101
Godard, Jean-Luc 41
Goethe, Johann Wolfgang von 54, 86
Gossec, François-Joseph 4, 5, 46

Greenfield, Edward 93
Guest, George 105

Habeneck, François 88, 89
Hahn, Albert 59, 61, 63
Haibel, Sophie (*née* Weber) 8, 25, 37, 55
Hallé, Charles 86
Handel, George Frideric 4, 61, 73,
        115–16
    Anthem for the Funeral of Queen Caroline
        (HWV 264) 4, 118, 120–2, 123
    'Dettingen' Anthem (HWV 265) 4, 128
    Joseph and his Brethren (HWV 59)
        4, 128
Handke, Robert 69, 70
Härtel, Gottfried Christoph 174, 177
Hartl, Karl
    Wen die Götter lieben (film) 37–8, 39, 73
Hass, Georg Friedrich 246
Hasse, Johann Adolf 4, 5
Haydn, Franz Joseph 9, 31, 48, 61, 86
Haydn, Michael
    Requiem in C minor 4, 5
Heartz, Daniel 72
Hemans, Felicia
    'Mozart's Requiem' (poem) 24–5
Henrici, Johann 1
Herzog, Anton 75
Hess, Ernst 234
Hiller, Johann Adam 3
Hobbes, Thomas 247
Hofer, Franz de Paula 27
Hoffmann, E. T. A. 12, 45
Hofmann, Leopold 4, 8
Hogarth, George 57
Hogwood, Christopher
    recording of Mozart's Requiem 101–2, 103,
        104, 105
Holmes, Edward 58
Hussey, Dyneley 66–7, 68, 75
Hutchings, Arthur 185

Innes, Henry 25
Irmen, Hans-Josef 234

Jahn, Otto 24, 32, 47–8, 62–3, 64, 72
Janáček, Leoš 6
Jochum, Eugen
    recording of Mozart's Requiem 96, 97–8, 99,
        101, 105
Joffrey, Robert 41
Jommelli, Niccolò 4, 5
Joseph II, Emperor 118

Kennedy, President John F. 93
Kertész, István
    recording of Mozart's Requiem 98–9, 101,
        103, 105
Kittel, Bruno
    recording of Mozart's Requiem 96–7, 98
Klindworth, Karl 85
Knigge, Adolf Baron 113
Kolb, Annette 35, 36, 66
Körner, Theodor 87
Kraus, Karl 92
Krottendorfer, Joseph 213

Lablache, Luigi 86
    performances of Mozart's Requiem 87, 88,
        90–1
Landon, H. C. Robbins 2, 234
Lange, Aloysia (*née* Weber) 37
'Last Moments of Mozart' (fiction, c.1840) 29,
        31, 33
Leitgeb, Franz Anton 1
Leopold II, Emperor 1, 173
Levey, Michael 73, 75
Levin, Robert D.
    completion of Mozart's Requiem 96, 102,
        104, 105, 213, 234, 235–7, 238, 239, 240,
        244
    on Süssmayr's work on Mozart's Requiem
        77–8, 239, 245
Lichnowsky, Prince Karl 2
Lichtenthal, Peter 49
Ligeti, György 6
Liszt, Franz 5–6, 90
    Totentanz, Paraphrase über 'Dies irae' 86
    transcription of Confutatis and Lacrymosa
        from Mozart's Requiem 85

Macfarren, George Alexander 58, 59, 60–1
Mackerras, Charles
    recording of Mozart's Requiem 101, 103, 104
Mahler, Gustav 6
Mainzer, Joseph 55, 57, 86
Maria Theresia, Empress 118
Marx, Adolph Bernhard 54
Maunder, Richard
    completion of Mozart's Requiem 96, 101, 102,
        104, 234, 235, 240–4, 245, 246
    on Süssmayr's work on Mozart's Requiem
        76–7, 79–80, 177, 189, 195,
        217, 245
Méhul, Étienne-Nicolas 46
Melograni, Piero 245–6
Mendelssohn, Felix 61

Mitchell, Donald 94, 99
Mitchell, Nicholas 25
Montholon, General Count 89
Mosel, Ignaz von 24, 56–7, 60
'Mozart and Schach: An Imaginary Dialogue'
        (fiction, c.1851) 30, 31
Mozart, Constanze (*née* Weber) 2–3, 7, 8, 9, 14,
        15–16, 17, 20, 22–3, 24, 33, 39, 51, 56,
        57, 60, 64, 74, 171, 172, 174, 176, 177,
        178, 232
    in nineteenth-century fiction 32
    in twentieth-century films 37, 38
Mozart, Leopold 9, 72, 73
Mozart, Maria Anna ('Nannerl') 9, 111
Mozart, Wolfgang Amadeus
    Acis and Galatea (orchestration of Handel)
        (K. 566) 4, 115–16
    Alexander's Feast (orchestration of Handel)
        (K. 591) 4, 115
    'Ave verum corpus' (K. 618) 1, 159, 162,
        165–7
    Clarinet Concerto in A (K. 622) 1
    Clemenza di Tito, La 1, 2, 66, 113, 180,
        224, 241
    Così fan tutte 1, 27, 151
    Don Giovanni 1, 37, 72, 112, 113, 114
    Entführung aus dem Serail, Die 1, 113, 114
    Idomeneo 113
    Laut verkünde unsre Freude (K. 623) 1, 2
    Mass in B flat (K. 275) 162–5
    Mass in C (K. 317) 159, 160–3, 229
    Mass in C (K. 337) 159, 162, 164, 229
    Mass in C minor (K. 427) 137, 159, 167–9,
        214, 229–30
    Messiah (orchestration of Handel) (K. 572) 4,
        115
    Nozze di Figaro, Le 1, 137
    Ode for St Cecilia's Day (orchestration of
        Handel) (K. 592) 4, 115, 116
    Piano Concerto in A (K. 488) 39
    Piano Concerto in C (K. 467) 38
    Piano Concerto in D minor (K. 466) 38
    piano concertos 104, 111, 151, 168
    Requiem in D minor (K. 626)
        autograph materials 10, 56–7, 74, 83,
            107–11, 122, 124–5, 128–9, 137, 146–7,
            155, 169–70, 172, 178, 179, 206, 231,
            232, 237
        commissioning, composition, completion
            (1791–2) 1–3
        Communio 71, 174, 218, 222–3
        completion (said to be by Mozart) 11, 12,
            17, 23

completions (modern-day) 10, 44, 234–46
Confutatis 5, 37–9, 45, 46–7, 48, 50, 51, 53,
     63, 69, 71, 76, 83, 109–11, 143, 145–51,
     153, 156, 160, 161, 170, 172, 214,
     222, 231
in dance 40–1
Dies irae 36, 39, 46, 51, 66, 67, 70, 76, 83,
     87, 91, 107, 112, 129–35, 137, 139,
     140–1, 150, 153, 154, 160, 169, 170, 172,
     214, 231, 244, 248
Domine Jesu 5, 35, 39, 45, 46, 51, 56, 71,
     76, 83, 107, 108–9, 111, 151, 154–6, 157,
     158, 159, 160, 169, 171, 173, 231, 248
editions in nineteenth century 79, 82–6
first edition (Breitkopf & Härtel 1800) 3,
     80, 82–3
Hostias 39, 45, 50, 51, 56, 83, 107, 151, 154,
     157–9, 217
Introit 4, 6, 44, 45, 48, 59, 69, 71, 76, 91,
     107, 108, 112, 113, 117–27, 128, 137,
     142, 145, 153, 154, 156, 167, 168, 174,
     180, 202–3, 209, 215, 218, 222, 223, 231,
     236, 237, 244, 247
Kyrie 4, 5, 39, 50, 59, 69, 70, 76, 85,
     107, 108, 128–9, 170, 172, 174, 180,
     218, 231
Lacrymosa 5, 36, 39–40, 45, 47, 53,
     56, 58, 59, 60, 62, 69, 70, 83, 107, 108,
     146, 150, 151–4, 172, 173, 202, 214, 240,
     244, 248
legend 8, 9–10, 11–43, 44, 65–7, 72–3, 81,
     92–4, 105–6, 170, 247, 248
liturgy 3
in nineteenth-century criticism 44–65
in nineteenth-century fiction 27–33
in nineteenth-century plays 26–7
in nineteenth-century poetry 24–6
performances and recordings from 1900
     onwards 92–106
performances in 1790s 3
performances in nineteenth century
     86–92, 105–6
Recordare 5, 37, 38, 39, 44, 48, 51, 53, 62,
     69, 70, 71, 73, 142–5, 153, 156, 160,
     172, 231
Rex tremendae 5, 39, 44, 46, 49, 51, 58, 59,
     62, 69, 70, 71, 83, 107, 139–42, 153, 160,
     170, 172, 214
Tuba mirum 5, 39, 44, 50, 52, 62, 67, 69, 70,
     71, 72, 76, 82–3, 90, 92, 135–9, 153, 160,
     172
in twentieth-century plays and films
     36–40, 41

in 20th- and 21st-century criticism and
     scholarship 65–81
   see also under Süssmayr, Franz Xaver
String Quintet in C (K. 515) 38
String Quintet in G minor
     (K. 516) 38
symphonies 104, 151
Symphony No. 39 in E flat (K. 543) 150
Symphony No. 40 in G minor
     (K. 550) 38
Symphony No. 41 in C ('Jupiter') (K. 551)
     38, 150
Zauberflöte, Die 1, 2, 8, 28, 30, 37, 38, 67, 112,
     180, 224–5, 241, 243
'Mozart's Requiem: A Sketch by Ortleff'
     (fiction, c.1849) 30, 31
Muldowney, Dominic 246
Müller, Karl Wilhelm 86, 87
Munkáscy, Miláhy 5

Napoleon
   Mozart Requiem performance at his
     memorial service at Les Invalides 86,
     88–90, 92
Neukomm, Sigismund 91
   'Libera me' completion of Mozart's
     Requiem 91
Nichols, Peter 41
Niemetschek, Franz 7, 9, 15–16, 17, 18, 19, 23,
     33, 48, 84, 111–12, 113, 120, 142, 147,
     169, 176, 222
Nippold, Friedrich 13
Nissen, Georg Nikolaus 23, 51, 55, 64
Novello, Vincent 21, 53
Nowak, Leopold 107, 172

Oliver, Stephen 75
Oulibicheff, Alexandre 32, 59, 61

Paisiello, Giovanni 86, 90, 91
Panofka, Henri 89
Parker, John R. 51
Parsons, H. M. 33
Pasolini, Pier Paolo 41
Pasterwitz, Georg Robert von 213
Pearlman, Martin
   recording of Mozart's Requiem 101, 102, 103,
     104, 105
Petri, Johann Samuel 150
Plath, Wolfgang 74
Pole, William 62
   Story of Mozart's Requiem, The 63–5
Puchberg, Michael 2

Punto, Giovanni 86
Pushkin, Alexander
    'Mozart and Salieri' 26, 28, 33

Raphael 17
Rau, Heribert
    Mozart: A Biographical Romance 31–3
'Requiem de Mozart, Le' (fiction, c.1833)
    28–9, 31
Requiem-Streit 9, 22, 49–57, 58, 60, 64, 79,
    176, 247
Reutter, Georg (Reutter der Junge) 4, 5
Rilling, Helmuth
    recordings of Mozart's Requiem 99, 101, 105
Rimsky-Korsakov, Nicolay 6
    Mozart and Salieri 6, 33–4
Rochlitz, Johann Friedrich
    anecdotes about Mozart's Requiem 7–8, 9,
        15, 16–18, 33, 38, 42, 50
    criticism of Eybler's Requiem 173
    review of first edition of Mozart's Requiem
        (Breitkopf & Härtel) 44–6, 47, 48, 50–1,
        53, 56, 82, 113, 230
    source for nineteenth-century accounts of
        Requiem legend 18–19, 22, 33
Romberg, Andreas 86
Rosselli, John 72
Rossini, Gioachino 5, 61, 86
Rubinstein, Anton 6
Runciman, John F. 69
Rushton, Julian 234

Sadie, Stanley 246
Saez, Vicente 41
Saint-Foix, Georges de 69, 71, 72, 75, 234
Salieri, Antonio 27
    in *Amadeus* 38–40, 169
    in nineteenth-century fiction 26, 33–4
Salzburger Intelligenzblatt 14
Savage, John 11
Schack, Benedikt 8, 27, 30, 153
Schaden, Adolph von
    Mozarts Tod (play) 26–7
Scharl, Placidus 48
Scherzer, Birgit 41
Schicht, Johann Gottfried 86
Schikaneder, Emanuel 27, 172
    in nineteenth-century fiction 27–8
    in twentieth-century film 37
Schiller, Friedrich 86
Schlichtegroll, Friedrich 9
Schmid, Manfred Hermann 202, 222
Schrattenbach, Prince-Archbishop 4

Schreier, Peter
    recording of Mozart's Requiem 99,
        100–1
Schubert, Franz 5, 61, 86
Seyfried, Ignaz Ritter von 47, 64
Shaffer, Peter 38–40, 81
Sievers, Georg 57, 64
    Mozart und Süssmayr 55
Silverstolpe, Frederick Samuel 23, 75
Sitwell, Sacheverell 66
Smetana, Bedřich 6
Sortschan, Dr Johann Nepomuk 1, 23, 107
Spering, Christophe 105
Stadler, Anton 1
Stadler, Maximilian 23, 54, 55, 56, 57, 58, 176,
        180, 232
    in nineteenth-century fiction 27, 28
    'Vertheidigung der Echtheit des
        Mozart'schen Requiem' 51, 52
Staël-Holstein, Anne Louise Germain (Madame
        de Staël) 20
Stafford, William 8
Stanford, Charles Villiers 6
Stasov, Vladimir Vasil'evich 34
Stierle, Edward 41
Stoll, Anton 159
'Story of "The Requiem", The' (fiction, c.1850)
        27–8
Strauss, Richard 6
Suard, Jean-Baptiste-Antoine 48
sublime, the 210
Süssmayr, Franz Xaver 174–233, 234–46
    'Alleluia' (SmWV 127) 228, 229
    'Ave verum corpus' (SmWV 121) 228
    completion of Mozart's Requiem 2–3, 8, 10,
        24, 39, 40, 42, 44, 45, 46, 47–8, 50, 52, 54,
        55, 56–7, 60–2, 64, 68–9, 70, 71, 72,
        73–80, 81, 83, 96, 98, 99, 102, 103, 104,
        107, 111, 154, 170, 171, 172
        Agnus Dei 45, 46, 47, 53, 54, 56, 60, 61, 62,
            64, 66, 68, 70, 74, 78, 79, 83, 153, 174,
            176, 177, 179, 217, 218–22, 223, 225,
            229, 230, 231, 232
        Benedictus 45, 47, 49, 53, 54, 55, 56, 57, 60,
            61–2, 64, 68, 69, 70, 71, 74, 77, 78, 79, 83,
            85, 174, 176, 177, 179, 210, 215–18, 222,
            223, 224, 230, 231, 232, 237
        Lacrymosa completion 174, 179, 181,
            199–206, 207, 209, 210, 218, 223, 224,
            230, 231, 232, 235, 236, 240, 244
        letter to Breitkopf & Härtel on his
            involvement 45, 48, 50, 51, 52, 54, 56,
            60, 64, 174–9, 223, 231, 249–50

orchestration of Confutatis 195–200, 202,
    206, 207, 209, 210, 215, 225
orchestration of Dies irae 180–1, 199, 202,
    209, 210
orchestration of Domine Jesu 206–8, 231
orchestration of Hostias 207
orchestration of Recordare 192–3, 194,
    207, 209
orchestration of Rex tremendae 188–92,
    195, 199, 202, 206, 207, 209, 210, 243
orchestration of Tuba mirum 181–8, 189,
    195, 207, 209, 215, 224, 237
Sanctus 45, 47, 49, 53, 56–7, 60, 61–2, 64,
    68, 69, 70, 71, 74, 77, 78, 79, 174, 176,
    177, 179, 210–15, 217–18, 223, 224, 225,
    229–30, 231, 232, 237
in nineteenth-century fiction 32
Sinfonia turchesa (SmWV 403) 229
Der Spiegel von Arkadien 55, 175
Il Muselmano in Napoli (*Il turco in Italia*)
    175, 229
Missa solemnis in D (SmWV 106) 179, 206,
    213, 223, 225–7
Moses 175, 177
Requiem (SmWV 103) 225
Requiem (SmWV 104) (*Deutsches Requiem*)
    225
in twentieth-century films 37
see also Mozart, Wolfgang Amadeus,
    Requiem in D minor, autograph
    materials
Swieten, Baron van 3, 4, 115, 120, 122
Szymanowski, Karol 6

Talmage, Rev. Thomas De Witt 33
Tchaikovsky, Pyotr Il'yich 6
Tharp, Twyla 40
Trotter, Stewart 41

Vanhal, Johann Baptist 4
Van Tiegham, David 40
Viardot, Pauline 90
Vienna
    Hofkapelle 4, 118
    St Stephen's Cathedral 4, 8, 97, 117, 118

Wagner, Richard 6, 62, 65–6
    Tristan und Isolde 65
Walsegg, Franz, Count von 1–2, 3, 23, 24, 35,
    56, 57, 64, 107, 174, 178
Walsh, Stephen 75
Walter, Bruno
    recording of Mozart's Requiem 96, 98, 99,
        101–2, 103, 105
Walton, William 6
Warren, Joseph 53
Watzmann, Rudolph Friedrich 13, 59
Weber, Carl Maria von
    Mozart Requiem performance at his funeral
        86–7
Weber, Jacob Gottfried 5, 24, 53, 56, 57,
    61, 79
    'Über die Echtheit des Mozartschen
        Requiem' 49–51, 52, 54–5, 57
Wesley, Samuel 47
Wilby, Philip 246
Wilder, Thornton
    Mozart and the Gray Steward 36
Winter, Peter 4, 5
Wolff, Christoph 74, 202, 206, 217

Yastrebtsev, V. V. 34
Young, Filson 58–9, 60

Zeitung für Damen und andere
    Frauenzimmer 14
Zelter, Carl Friedrich 54, 57, 62

For EU product safety concerns, contact us at Calle de José Abascal, 56–1°,
28003 Madrid, Spain or eugpsr@cambridge.org.